The Drapers in America

Being a History and Genealogy, of Those of That Name and Connection

By Thomas Waln-Morgan Draper

"'What craftsman art thou,' said the King,
'I pray thee telle me trowe?
'I am a Draper, Sir, by my trade.
Now telle me, what art thou?'"

Published by Pantianos Classics

ISBN-13: 978-1-78987-651-2

First published in 1892

Contents

Dedication

This History is dedicated to those brave men who left Home and Fireside, for Conscience sake, and who planted the seeds of the greatest of Republics. To those who answered the Lexington Alarm, and helped to conquer our land's Independence. To those who, later, were ever to the front in defence of the Unity of our Nation and one Flag. To them — one and all. May their descendants ever hold the name as synonymous with love of Country, Home and Liberty, emulate their deeds, and keep their memory green.

Preface

"O ye who proudly boast,
In your free veins, the blood of sires like these,
Look to their lineaments. Dread lest ye lose
Their likeness in your sons. * * * * *
Turn ye to Plymouth Rock, and where they knelt.
Kneel, and renew the vow they breathed to God."

SIGOURNEY

The verse that heads this page seems particularly appropriate to peruse before entering upon the task of reading the History of a Puritan family. I have carefully scanned the lives of all the descendants, and can truthfully say that they have been an ancestry of sound bodied, clear minded. Christian men and women; which is hardly to be over-valued, certainly not to be despised, by our posterity; and in spite of the verse attributed to Tom Moore —

"Seek not too far, my honest friend,
Perchance you will find a rope at the other end."

to which a friend called my attention when I began this history, those who follow us may search in vain for a fulfilment of such a prophecy.

The Draper men have ever been to the front in all emergencies of private and public life. They have held offices of all kinds in the village, town, city, county or country, at home and abroad. They have been soldiers, sailors, statesmen, lawyers, doctors, engineers, authors, merchants, farmers, manufacturers, in the church and school, and have brought to each and every one of these occupations an earnestness and steadfastness of purpose and success of the highest order.

The women, their wives and daughters, have not often had a role to play in public, but to whatever position they have been called, they have always fulfilled the duties assigned to them, not alone as helpmates and equal partners in life's struggles, but with credit to themselves and the name, and have ever, in the truest sense, been women.

The author's thanks are especially due to — General William F. Draper, of Hopedale, who has lent him not alone the kindly assistance of his mind, but has freely given of his means, to make this undertaking a success; to Mr. Charles Draper, of W. Dedham, for his cordial hospitality; to Mr. Warren F. Draper, of Andover, for his efficient researches; to James L. Draper, of Canton, to whom we are indebted for all the information on the Canton branch of the family; to Miss Adelaid H. Draper, of S. Boston, for the notes on the descendants of the sea captain, Samuel Draper; to Mrs. Samuel D. Mason and Dr. Frank E. Draper, of N. Attleboro, for their researches, kindly aid and generous hospitality; ably seconded by the Misses Antoinette and Anna Draper, of Providence; to Mr. Thomas Draper, of New York, and Mrs. Dr. Eunice Draper Kinney, of Roxbury, for the information on the Irish branches of the family. Also to the secretaries and officers of the Mass. Genealogical Historical Society, the Boston Public Library, and the Dedham Historical Society; and to many more, whose help has been of exceeding value to the author, are his sincerest thanks and grateful acknowledgments due. When they, one and all, see their handiwork in these pages, they will feel, with the author, that this book is the work, not alone of him who has collated it, but of all the family.

In the hundreds of replies received by the author, from all over the country, there has been but one discourteous one, which should prove to the satisfaction of all the gentleness and natural good manners of those who bear our name or are connected with that name.

THOMAS WALN-MORGAN DRAPER.

March 1, 1892.
St. George's, Staten Island, N. Y.

Abbreviations

s. son. dau. daughter, b. born. d. died. m. married, o. s. old style.

The Latin numerals denote the number of the child in any given family in rotation. Example: IV. Mary — she is the fourth child, in rotation of birth, of her father.

The regular numerals denote the number of any one person, the same number never being used twice in the same branch of the Drapers. Example: James 17 — a descendant of James the Puritan — James, a descendant of Captain Samuel Draper, which is an entirely different branch, would have a number of his own. Each branch begins with the number one (1).

Authorities Consulted

An Account of the Silver Wedding of Mr. and Mrs. F. P. Draper at Westford. N. Y. Genealogical Tables of the "Griffitts Family," by Frank P. Griffitts.

Ye Ancestors of Beulah Bradford Draper, by Geo. B. Draper.

Sketch of the History of Attleborough, by John Daggett.

Memoir of Dr. John William Draper, by George F. Barker.

Memoir of Dr. Henry Draper, by George F. Barker.

Ancestry of Calvin Guild and others, by Howard Redwood Guild.

Biography of Dr. Lyman C. Draper, by Reuben G. Thwaites.

Biographical Sketch of James Draper, of Canton.

The Whitney Family History.

The Chandler Family History.

Unrealized Ideals. In Commemoration of Robert Draper, of Canton, by Rev. Henry F. Jenks.

History of Washington, N. H.

History of Antrim, N. H., by W. R. Cockrane.

Sabine's "Loyalists."

Trumbull's "McFingal."

History of Roxbury, by Francis S. Drake.

History of Milford, Mass., by Adin Ballou.

Historical Annals of Dedham, by Herrman Mann.

Oldham Records, by Don Gleason Hill. Vol. I., Church and Cemetery. Vol. II., Births, Marriages and Deaths.

History of Spencer, Mass., by James Draper.

History of North Brookfield, Mass., by Temple.

Boston, Mass., Church Records.

Roxbury, Mass., Church Records.

Sketches of the Town of Lancaster, Mass., by J. Willard.

History of Printing in America, by Isaiah Thomas, LL.D.

Drake's History of Boston.

Holton's Lists of Emigrants to the American Colonies.

Hudson's History of Lexington, Mass.

Savage's Genealogical Dictionary.

History of Francestown, Mass.

Wight Genealogy.

Wyman's Charlestown, Mass.

History of Concord, Bedford, Acton, Lincoln and Carlisle, by Lemuel Shattuck.

List of Farm Owners in the States of Maine and Massachusetts.

Genealogies and Estates of Charlestown, by Thomas B. Wyman.

History of Medfield, Mass., by Wm. S. Tilden.

Records of the Town of Dover, Mass.

Suffolk County, Mass., Records.

Records of the City of Boston, Mass.

Vital Statistics of the Cities of Boston, New York, Philadelphia and many others.

English Authorities

Heptonstall Parish Church Records.

Genealogical Guide, by Marshall.

The Genealogist.

History of the Parish of St. Leonards, by Henry Ellis.

The Antiquities of Gainford, by J. R. Walbran.

Jewitt's Reliquary.

Collectanea Topographica et Genealogica.

Nichols' History of the County of Leicester.

Transactions of the London and Middlesex Archaeological Society.

Surtees' Durham.

Thornton's Nottinghamshire.

Miscelanea Genealogica et Heraldica.

History of the County of York.

History of Halifax.

Burke's Extinct Baronetcies.

Burke's General Armory.

Nichols' Account of the Company of Ironmongers.

"Junius' Letters."

History of the Family of Stansfeld, of Stansfeld, by John Stansfeld, 1885.

Family Crest Book.

Genesis of the United States.

Drapers

The Original Lists of Persons of Quality, Emigrants, Religious Exiles, Political Rebels, Serving-men sold. Apprentices, Children stolen. Maidens pressed, and others who went from Great Britain to the American Plantations, 1600-1700.

— By John Camden Hatton.

Per ship "Faulcon" de London. Thos. Irish, Master. April 14, 1635: — Joseph Drap (Draper), 21. To be transported to the Barbadoes.

Per ship "Ann and Elizabeth." Jo. Brookhaven, Master. Bartholomew Draper, 20. Shipped to St. Christophers, Barbadoes.

July 6, 1635. Per ship "Paul" of London. Leonard Betts, Master, bound to Virginia. Thomas Draper, 26.

Robert Draper. A servant in the "Jacob." 1624, aged 16.

(In the list of inhabitants in and about the towne of St. Michaels, Barbadoes, 1680, Robert Draper, the above, has two hired servants and five slaves.)

In the census of the living and dead in Virginia, Feb. 16, 1623, we find as residing at Elizabeth Citie, Henry Draper,

Henrie Draper, aged 14, was a servant sent out in the "George," in 1621.

Cleare Drap (Draper), ag. 30, went out in the "Francis," of Ipswich, Master, John Cutting, the last of April, 1634.

From Genealogies and Estates of Charlestown and Concord

Roger Draper, m. Mary Hadlock. Children: — Lydia, b. Nov. 11, 1641. m. John Luce, 1660. Adam, m. Rebecca Brabrook, 1666, and had Samuel, Joseph, Elisha, Adam. They moved to Marlborough about 1680.

Roger Draper was a freeman in Concord, March 16, 1639. He d. before his wife, Mary. She d. Sep. 27, 1683. Goodman Draper's estate taxed in 1658, his widow, administratrix of N. Hadlock, sold to W. Ford house on south side of Hill, Concord, to Sconce point towards river — N.E. street, 74; S.W. part of Mary Draper's garden, 78. S.E. M. Long and J. Coggan, 47; N.W. lane to marsh, 37. 1649, rec. 1667-8., rep. G. Newman. Same to Crispen Wadlen, lot, on street from the common street to Salt Creek — N.W. Street, 52; N.E. W. Ford, 76; S.W. J. Drinker, 89; S.E. M. Long, 62. 1668, rec. 1671.

Derivation of the Name Draper and Various Ways of Spelling the Same

Drap.	Drapur.	Drapper.	Draper.
Le Drapour.	Dreaper.	Drappert.	
Drapour.	Drapar.	Drapert.	

Drape — To cover, or ornament with cloth or drapery.
Drape — To make cloth.
Draper — One who deals in cloth.
Draperised — Furnished with drapery.

Drape-y — 1. Cloth, woolen stuffs.
2. Cloth-work, to trade of making cloth.
3. Curtains, hangings, tapestry.
4. The representation of the dress or clothing of the human figure.

Draper — Cloth. Coverlet.

Places Named After the Drapers

Draperstown

Is located near Belfast, Co. Downe, Ireland, and is supposed to have been named after two English officers of the name of Draper, who went to Ireland in 1676 to the relief of Derry. It has 500 inhabitants.

Drapersville

Mecklenburg County, Virginia. About 15 miles north of Boydton, the county seat. A small place and post-office; was named after the family of the celebrated Dr. John William Draper, who were settled here before removing to New York City.

Draper's Valley

A small town and post-office on the North Carolina Extension of the Norfolk & Western R.R. in Pulaski Co., Va. There is here also a high eminence called "Draper's Mountain." and the railroad station is called "Drapers." All are named after the family of John Draper, the first white man who settled in that section of the country about 1765-6.

Draper

A small hamlet and post-office in Jackson County, Ind., named after Silas Draper, who went there from Indiana. He had been a Quaker, but opened a store and sold liquor to the miners, took to drinking himself, and finally shot himself, March 8, 1866. He had been a school teacher at one time.

Draper

A post village in Salt Lake County, Utah, on the Utah Southern R.R., near the River Jordan, and 17 miles south of Salt Lake City. It has a Mormon church, and the place is named after the Mormon Drapers.

Draper's Springs

At Bloomington, Putnam County, Tenn. Fine mineral springs, hotel and church.

Draper

A post-office in Jasper County, Iowa.

Draper

A post-office in Miami County, Ind.

Draper

A post-office in Tioga County, Penn.

Drapers

A post-office in Halifax County, N. C.

Introductory

HEPTONSTALL

The Drapers, way back in the dim recesses of the past, were natives of Yorkshire, England, and of or near Heptonstall, and undoubtedly all of that name are descended from William, John and Henry le Drapour. The Roxbury, Mass., branch is most easily traced, but all others are equally of the same English ancestry, hailing from other English counties in later years before emigrating to America, but descendants alike from the common parent Yorkshire stem.

The native place of the Drapers and Stansfields is a village and Parochial Chapelry in Halifax Parish, West Riding, Yorkshire, England.

The village stands on a bleak eminence, adjacent to the river Hebden, one and a half miles N.W. of Hebden-Bridge and Station, and eight miles W. by N. of Halifax, and has a Post-office under Manchester, and a cattle-fair on Easter Tuesday. The Chapelry includes also the hamlets of Erringden, Langfield, Stanfield and Wadsworth. Acres, 5,320. Real property, 10,687 pounds. Population, some 4,000. Houses, 790. A decrease in population has been caused by depression in hand-loom weaving. The property is much sub-divided. The manor belongs to the trustees of the Saville estates Much of the land is moor and common. There are silk, cotton and cotton-spinning manufactories. The living is a Perpetual Curacy in the Diocese of Ripon. Value, 300 pounds; with habitable Glebe-house. Patron, the Vicar of Halifax. The church was built in

1854, near a previous church which became dilapidated; is in the later English style, and consists of nave, aisles and chancel, with square tower. There are Chapels for Baptists and Wesleyans, a grammar school and several small chanties.

Such is the description of the old village as it now exists. In the days when James and Miriam left there for the New World, it was a market town of some importance. Now it is a sleepy village; its location on a high hill, preventing its participation in the busy hum of the surrounding valleys.

There are many descendants of the two families. Draper and Stansfield, living in and near there, and it is curious to note that the old christian names are still retained for their children, and that many of them are still dissenters, as were the old Puritans To this day, in the village of Heptonstall, there is a "Drapers Lane," and formerly all the land on either side of it was the property of our ancestors.

Where the Mechanics' Institute stands was the site of an old Draper dwelling. Many more such data undoubtedly remain for the future historian of the English Drapers to discover; as our predecessors were unquestionably large land-holders in Heptonstall and its dependencies — Wadsworth, Erringden, Sowerby, Stanfield, and other smaller villages within one or two miles of Heptonstall.

The tracing of an American family, back through the hazy past, to first its origin in the United States, and then following it through the dim and uncertain labyrinth of English records, is one of great difficulty. Some headway has been made in the case of the Drapers, but not what the author would have wished or desired; and it is well here to. state that no pains or expense has been spared to thoroughly search all known records in this country and England that have been attainable. It may further be stated that, up to the reign of Queen Elizabeth (1558-1603), no records of a reliable nature were kept in the English Parishes, of births, deaths and marriages; but, about 1580, the Queen decreed that thereafter all such records should be kept in an orderly manner. In these pages are the exact copies of the Heptonstall Parish Records of the Drapers, beginning with the first year (1590) in which they were kept. But the founder of our family of that Parish, Thomas Draper, must either not have been baptized, or he was baptized prior to the year 1590, for no record exists of his birth, or of his marriage, the name of his wife, or many other details which would have been of great and vital interest to the readers of this volume.

Thomas Draper was a clothier and fuller, or one who manufactured cloth and fulled it ready to be fashioned into clothes; in other words, he was a weaver of cloths, by means of looms, and used water-power. In addition to the weaving, he also fulled other people's cloth. They raised their own wool or flax, carded, spun and weaved it into cloth in their own families, and then sent it to the clothier's mill to be fulled, colored, shorn and finished, ready on its return to them to be made into clothes. Webster's Dictionary gives the following definitions. Fuller: "One whose occupation is to full cloth"; Fullers' Earth: "A variety of clay, compact, but friable, unctuous to the touch, and of various colors, usually with a shade of green. It is useful in scouring and cleansing cloth, as it imbibes the grease and oil used in preparing wool"; Fulling Mill: "A mill for fulling cloth by means of pestles or stampers, which alternately fall into and rise from troughs, where the cloth is put with the fullers' earth or other cleansing material." Thomas Draper's ancestors had followed this calling before him; and his American descendants have frequently done likewise in New England.

We have the names of his children and the order in which they were born, and some little additional history relative to them. But one date — that of the birth of his son James — has been accurately ascertained; and, as he was the founder of the Drapers who have spread over America most numerously, it is much to be grateful for; because this volume does not claim to be a history of the Drapers all the world over, but as accurate a compilation of facts as it has been possible to obtain of the Drapers in America.

It is here to be especially dwelt upon, that the errors and blanks occurring in this work are largely due to indifference on the part of individuals to oft-repeated enquiries, and that the dates of occurrences are frequently by a brother and sister — say of the death of a parent — given as occurring at different times.

Heptonstall Parish Records

Baptisms. From 1599 to 1750.

John, of Michael Draper Hep., 22 Feb 1617
Grace, of Nathan Draper Hep., 16 Dec 1619
Miriam, of Gideon Stansfield Hep., 27 Nov 1625
Susan, of Thomas Draper Hep., 14 Sep 1628
Mary, of Thomas Draper Hep., 19 Dec 1630
Thomas, of Thomas Draper Hep., 15 Mar 1634
Sara, of Thomas Draper Hep., 31 May 1636
Mary, of Nathan Draper Hep., 19 July 1636
Henry, of Nathan Draper Hep., 11 Feb 1637
Mary, of Thomas Draper Hep., 22 July 1638
Grace, of Thomas Draper Hep., 4 Feb 1643
Susanna, of (Robert?) Draper Hep., 25 Aug 1644
Miriam, of James Draper Hep., 7 Feb 1646
Grace, of John Draper Hep., 30 Jan 1647
Jane, of Thomas Draper Hep., 25 Aug 1644
Mary, of Henry Draper Hep., 15 Aug 1646
Thomas, of William Draper Err., 24 Apr 1659
Mary, of Henry Draper born Hep., 8 Aug 1658
Thomas, of William Draper born Err., 13 Apr 1659
Henry, of Henry Draper born Hep., 11 Aug 1660
Martha, of William Draper Err., 4 Nov 1660
Grace, of Henry Draper Hep., 11 May 1662
John, of William Draper Hep., 12 Apr 1663
Hester, of Henry Draper Hep., 2 Apr 1665
William, of William Draper Hep., 28 Apr 1667
Mary, of Henry Draper Hep., 27 Apr 1673
Henry, of Henry Draper Hep., 30 Sep 1677
William, of Thomas Draper Hep., 27 Feb 1680
Susan, of Henry Draper Hep., 13 Nov 1681
John, of Thomas Draper Hep., 24 Feb 1683
John, of Thomas Draper Hep., 18 Oct 1685
Thomas, of Thomas Drapper Hep., 31 May 1691
Thomas, of Thomas Drapper Stans., 25 June 1695
James, of Thomas Drapper Stans.; 4 Oct 1696
Elizabeth, of Thomas Drapper Stans. 24 Apr 1699

Thomas, of Thomas Drapper Stans. 22 Mar 1601
Henry, of Thomas Drapper Stans., 21 Sep 1605
John, of John Drapper Stans., 14 Nov 1714
John, of John Drapper Stans., 25 Dec 1715
William, of John Drapper Stans., 26 May 1717
Thomas, of John Drapper Stans., 1 Feb 1718
Mary, of Martha Wilksos and Thomas Draper (base born). .Stans., 20 Mar 1720
Mary, of John Drapper Stans., 22 Apr 1722
Mary, of Sim. Drapper Stans., 17 June 1722
Susan, of Henry Drapper (Yeoman) Hep., 1 Oct 1722
George, of John Drapper Stans., 29 Feb 1723
Thomas, of John Drapper Stans., 3 Jan 1730
Mary, of John Drapper Stans., 11 Mar 1738
Joseph and Mary, of William Drapper Stans., 18 Apr 1739
Sarah, of John Drapper Stans., 28 Nov 1740
Ann, of John Drapper Stans., 5 Dec 1742
George, of John Drapper (Weaver) Hep., 19 Oct 1749
William, of John Drapper (Weaver) Hep., 21 July 1751

Burials. From 1593 to 1750.

Thomas Draper, of Hep 6 July, 1603
. . . . Draper, of Sowerby 11 Dec, 1616
Agnes Draper, of Hep 23 Feb., 1617
Henry Draper, of Hep 12 Apr., 1621
John Draper, of Hep 7 Dec, 1621
Michael Draper, of Sowerby 12 Jan., 1634
Infant of Thomas Draper, of Hep 2 Aug., 1635
William Draper, of Hep 3 Oct., 1635
Infant of Gideon Stansfield, of Wads 23 Nov., 1635
Wife of Henry Draper, of Sowerby 29 Apr., 1636
William Draper, of Hep 26 Dec, 1636
Infant of Thomas Draper, of Hep 30 Oct., 1640
Infant of Thomas Draper, of Hep 10 May, 1644
Mercy Draper, of Hep 31 May, 1645
Infant of John Draper, of Hep...16 Apr., 1648
Nathan Draper, of Hep 13 Apr., 1654
Gideon Stansfield, of Hep 9 Majs 1658
Henry, of Henry Draper, of Hep 17 Aug., 1660
Infant of Henry Draper, of Hep 7 June, 1661
Widow of Nathan Draper, of Hep 26 Dec, 1666
Infant of Henry Draper, of Hep 3 Aug., 1667
Wife of William Draper, of Hep 10 Jan., 1669 o. s.
Infant of Henry Draper, of Hep: 7 Oct., 1670
Infant of Henry Draper, of Hep 21 Sep., 1671
Infant of Henry Draper, of Hep 14 May, 1676
Grace, of Henry Draper, of Hep 7 Sep., 1679
Infant of Henry Draper, of Hep 7 Dec, 1680
Wife of Henry Draper, of Hep 7 Jan., 1683
Susan, of Henry Draper, of Hep 15 Apr., 1684
John, of Thomas Draper, of Hep 27 Sep., 1684
John, of Thomas Draper, of Hep 15 Nov., 1688
Infant of Thomas Draper, of Hep 16 Dec, 1689
Wife of Thomas Drapper, of Stans 18 Feb., 1693
Thomas Drapper, of Hep 7 Feb., 1694
Thomas, of Thomas Drapper, of Stans 13 Oct., 1695
James, of Thomas Drapper, of Stans 27 Feb., 1697
Child of Thomas Drapper, of Stans 25 Aug., 1702
Infant of Thomas Drapper, of Stans 7 Nov., 1703
Infant of Thomas Drapper, of Stans 30 Dec, 1703
John, of John Drapper, of Stans 5 Apr., 1715
Henry Drapper, of Hep 19 Sep., 1720
Child of John Draper, of Stans 8 Feb., 1720 o. S.
Thomas, of Thomas Drapper, of Stans 19 May, 1721
Wife of Thomas Drapper, of Stans 3 Aug., 1723
Wife of Henry Draper, of Hep 31 Mar., 1727
Wife of John Draper, of Stans 3 Oct., 1728
Thomas Drapper, of Stans. (Poor) 28 Dec, 1734
Wife of Job Drapper, of Stans 21 Sep., 1738
Child of William Drapper, of Stans 1 May, 1739
Wife of William Drapper, of Stans 22 May, 1739

William Drapper, of Stans. (Poor) 10 Feb., 1744 o. s.
Child of John Drapper, of Hep 16 Dec, 1746
George Drapper, of Wads. (Weaver, Poor) 10 May 1749
Henry Draper, of Hep. (Yeoman) 5 Oct., 1750

Marriages. From 1593 to 1750.

Adam Wedopp & Isabell Draper 2 Jan., 1593
William Coke & Brigit Draper 10 July, 1596
William Taylyar & Joyce Draper 24 Dec, 1598
John Crabtry & Grace Draper 21 Sep., 1603
Richard Bouth & Elizabeth Draper 28 Apr., 1618
Richard Ratclife & Susanna Draper 8 Dec, 1620
Jonas Robtshaw & Debora Draper 13 Nov., 1627
Thomas Draper & Susan Horsfall 10 Dec, 1627
Christopher Shackleton & Mary Draper 21 Dec, 1630
William Draper & Hellen Wood 24 Sep., 1633
John Thomas & Bridget Draper 21 Apr., 1634
John Mitchell & Grace Draper 23 June, 1645
James Draper & Miriam Stansfield 21 Apr., 1646
William Draper & Sara Greenwood 25 May, 1658
Richard Sutclifife & Mary Draper 24 Mar., 1659
Gideon Stansfield & Grace Eastwood 21 Feb., .1624
Henry Draper, of Hep., & Susanna Sutcliffe, of Golden (Hep.) 8 July, 1657
William Draper, of Err., & Sarah Greenwood, of Stans May, 1658
Richard Eastwood & Sara Draper 25 Feb., 1660
William Draper & Grace Sutcliffe 2 May, 1672
Thomas Draper & Mary Carker 14 Nov., 1680
Paul Hoyle & Martha Draper 10 Feb., 1688
John Shackleton & Sarah Draper 12 Nov., 1694
John Drapper & Jane Haworth, of Stans 25 Apr., 1714
Henry Drapper, of Hep., & Martha Greenwood, of Err 5 Feb., 1721
John Drapper, of Stans. Web., & Sarah Wadsworth, of Hep. Sp. . . . 4 Apr., 1738
John Drapper, of Hep. Web., & Grace Wadsworth, of Wads. Sp. . . .21 Sep., 1738
George Drapper, of Stans. Web., & Abagaill Heartley, of Wads. Sp.21 Sep., 1747
John Drapper, of Stans. Web., & Sarah Robertshaw, of Hep. Sp., 15 June, 1749

Drapers of Heptonstall

Argent on a fesse engraved between three Annulets gules, as many covered Cups or.

CREST

A Stag's head gules, attired gold, charged on the neck with a fesse between three Annulets or.

MOTTO

Vicit perpecit. He conquered, he spared.

On this subject, the author has given

Coat of Arms of English Drapers

careful thought, as to the advisability of introducing the subject of Heraldry into the History of an American family. But after careful consideration, he believes it to be as much a part of the History of the Drapers, as any other data; especially as through Heraldry and its symbols can be traced family lineage when all other sources have failed. Therefore, the Arms, and as far as possible, sketches of the individuals to whom they were granted and who bore them, follow, with the distinct understanding, however, that this is an American Genealogy and History, and not an English one, and that every possible way, from this side of the Ocean, has been followed, to make it as correct as possible.

The Arms finally settled on, after due research, as being those which the English Drapers bear, most closely connected by ties of blood to the American Drapers; and these Arms, with the Stansfield Quarterings, which the children of James Draper and Miriam Stansfield, are entitled to bear; and also the Stansfield Arms proper, are given in colors in the pages herewith. The authorities consulted on this subject have been the "College of Arms & Heraldry" in London; Burke's "General Armory;" Burke's "Extinct Baronetcies," "Family Crest Book," and numerous others; all of which are considered the highest authority in England.

Draper, John. Bishop of Neapolis. Suffragen of Winchester, 1539.

Draper, Sir Christopher. Lord Mayor of London, 1567. Knighted 1568. Sheriff 1560. Arms, Ar. on a fess betw. three annulets gu. a mullet of the field, betw. two covered cups or. Another coat quartered by the same, in the second quarter ar. on two cheverons betw. three escalopes sa. six martlets or. Quartering also Ancher and Erswick.

Draper. (Flintham, Co. Nottinghamshire and London. Thomas Draper, of the former, and his kinsman, Vincent Draper, of the latter, descended from John Draper, of FHntham, temp. Henry IV. Visit. Notts. 1614.) Arms: Ar. on a fesse betw. three annulets gu. as many covered cups or. Crest: A cubit arm erect, habited vert, slashed and cufifed ar. holding in the hand p.p.r. a covered cup or. on each three fleur-de-lis vert.

Draper. Ar. on a fesse betw. two roses gu. an annulet of the first betw. as many cups or.

Draper. (Colebrook, Co. Middlesex.) Confirmed Oct. 14, 1571. Or. on a fesse betw. three annulets gu. as many covered cups of the field.

Draper. (Newcastle, Northumberland.) Az. a chev. erminois betw. three mullets of six points or. Crest: a cubit arm erect, vested erm. holding in the hand p.p.r. a mullet as in the Arms.

Draper. (London.) Ar. on a fesse gu. betw. three torteaus, a mullet betw. two covered cups of the field.

Draper. (Granted by Camden Clarenceaux, 161 3, to Draper of Stroud-Green, Co. Middlesex.) Arms: Gu. four bendlets or. on a chief per fesse ar. and erm. three fleurdc-lis sa. Crest: a Buck's head couped gu. gorged with a fess ar. thereon three fleurde-lis sa.

Draper. (London. Granted 1618.) Same Arms as preceding. Crest: a Stag's head gu. gorged with a fesse betw. two gemelles ar. charged with a fleur-de-lis sa.

Draper. (Brownlow and Walton, Co. Salop.) Bendy of eight gu. and vert, three fleur-de-lis or.

Draper. (Melton Mowbray, Cos. Leicester and Nottingham.) Ar. on a fess, betw. three annulets gu. a mullet of the field betw. two covered cups or. Crest: a cubit arm erect, vested vert, cufifed and pufifed ar. holding in the hand p.p.r. a covered cup ar.

Draper. (Cos. of Bedford, Middlesex and Oxford.) Ar. on a fesse engraved, betw. three annulets gu. as many covered cups or. Crest: a Tiger's head vert, tufted or. pierced through the neck with an arrow of the last.

Draper. (Great Marlowe, Co. of Bucks.) Gu. three bends or. a chief per fesse erm. and ar. in chief, three fleur-de-lis sa. Crest: a Camel's head erm. bridled or. waved sa.

Draper, of Sunninghill. Created June 9, 1660. Extinct Dec, 1703. Sir Thomas Draper, of Sunninghill Park, Co. of Berks, who was created a Baronet in 1660. m. an heiress of the family of Carey, of Sunninghill, but having no son, the title expired with him in 1703. His grandson, Thomas Draper Barber, Esq., eventually inherited Sunninghill and sold it in 1769 to Jeremiah Crutchley, Esq.

Draper. (Major-General Sir William Draper, installed K. B. June 15, 1772.) Ar. on a fesse engr. betw. three annulets gu. as many covered cups or. Crest: a Stag's head gu. attired or. charged on the neck with a fesse betw. three annulets or. Motto: Vicit Perpecit. "He conquered, he spared."

Lieut. -General Sir William Draper. (Ingleby, William, Thomas, Thomas.?) b. Bristol, Eng., in 1721. d. Bath, Eng., 1787. His father, Ingleby Draper, was an officer of Customs at Bristol. According to Granger, his grandfather was William Draper, of Beswick, near Beverly, and was a famous Yorkshire fox-hunting Squire. He had also an uncle, Charles Draper, who was a Captain of Dragoons, and a cousin. Col. Edward Alured Draper, b. at Merton, Oxfordshire, Oct. 22, 1776. This generally proves the relationship of the Yorkshire and Oxfordshire Drapers, as descending from the same stock in Yorkshire, and there seems to be no doubt but the Middlesex and other Drapers in the various Counties all owed their origin to the same source. Sir William Draper was educated at Eton and at King's College, Cambridge, for the Church, but preferring the military profession, went to the East Indies in the Company's service, where, in 1760, he received the privilege of ranking as a Colonel in the Army with Lawrence and Clive, and returned home that year. In 1761 he was promoted to the rank of Brigadier in the expedition to Bellisle. In 1763 he, with Admiral Cornish, conducted the expedition against Manilla. They sailed from Madras, Aug. 1st, and anchored Sep. 27 in Manilla Bay, where the inhabitants had no expectation of their coming. The fort surrendered Oct. 6, and was preserved from plunder by a ransom of four millions of dollars, half to be paid immediately, and the other half in a time agreed upon. The Spanish Governor drew on his Court for the first half, but payment was never made. The arguments of the Spanish Court were clearly refuted by Colonel Draper in a letter to the Earl of Halifax, then Premier. Succeeding administrations declined the prosecution of this claim from reasons of State which were never divulged; and the Commander-in-Chief lost, for his share of the ransom, 2,500 pounds. The colors taken at this conquest were presented to King's College, Cambridge, and hung up in their beautiful chapel, and the conqueror was rewarded with a Red Ribbon. Upon the reduction of the 79th Regiment, which had served so gloriously in the East Indies, His Majesty, unsolicited by him, gave him the 16th Regiment of Foot as an equivalent. This he resigned to Col. Gisborne for his half-pay, 200 pounds Irish annuity. In 1769 the Colonel appeared, and with much credit, in a literary character, drawing his pen against that of "Junius," in defence of his friend the Marquis of Granby, which drew a retort on himself, answered by him in a second letter to "Junius" on the refutation of the former charge against him. On a republication of "Junius" first letter. Sir William renewed his vindication of himself, and was answered with great keenness by his famous antagonist. Here the controversy dropped for the present, but he is supposed to have entered the lists once more under the signature of "Modestus," with that extraordinary and still concealed writer, in defence of General Gansel, who had been arrested for debt, and was rescued by a party of soldiers. On Oct. 11, 1769, he retired to South Carolina, arriving in Charlestown in January, 1770, sailing on the ship "Brice," of Bristol, Capt. Muire, for the recovery of his health, and took the opportunity to make the tour of North America. That year (Oct. 13, 1770) he married Miss Susan de Lancy, dau. of Brigadier-General Oliver de Lancy, of the British Army, and his wife, Phila Franks, and niece of Chief Justice de Lancy, of New York. She d. July, 1778. By her he had a dau, b. Aug. 18, 1773. Previously he had married a dau. of the second son of the Duke of St. Albans. She d. without issue Sep. 1, 1769. On May 29, 1779, Sir William, being then in rank a Lieut.-General, was appointed Lieut.-Governor of Minorca, on the unfortunate surrender of which important place, he exhibited 29 charges against the late Governor, General Murray, Nov. 11, 1782. Of these, 27 were deemed frivolous and groundless, and for the other two the Governor was reprimanded. Sir William was then ordered to make an apology to General Murray for having instituted the trial against him, in which he acquiesced. From this time he appears to have lived in retirement at Bath till his decease, which happened Jan. 8, 1787. Many particulars respecting his controversy with "Junius," as well as the controversy itself, may be seen in the splendid edition of "Junius' Letters," pub. by Mr. Woodfall in 1812.

The Stansfelds, or Stansfields, have been so closely connected with the Drapers in England for centuries, finally culminating by a daughter of that house becoming the wife of James the Puritan, and the mother of the whole American race of that branch, that the author has deemed it wise to insert here, also, a sketch of that family with numerous links between it and the

Drapers, down to the time when that old, grey, slatestone slab which, to this day, still marks the final resting place in Roxbury Cemetery, was placed over all that remained of James the Puritan and Miriam Stansfeld, his wife.

Stansfeld or Stansfield

Coat of Arms of the English Stansfields

ARMS.

Sable, Three Goats trippant Argent.

MOTTOES

Nosce Teipsum — Know Thyself.

"Know thou thyself, presume not God to scan. The proper study of mankind, is man."

(Pope.)

Virtus post funera vivit — Virtue lives after the Tomb.

"Still bloom the deeds of those who cannot die.

Crowned with eternal fame they sit sublime,

And laugh at all the little strife of time."

(Crabbe.)

STANSFIELD LINEAGE

The Family of Stansfleld, or Stansfeld of Stansfeld, as anciently written, trace their descent from Wyon Maryon, the descendant of a noble line in Brittany and a companion-in-arms of William the Conqueror, who obtained from his Royal Master a grant of the extensive Township of Stansfeld in the County of York, England, and assuming therefrom his surname, was founder of this Family. His descendants have remained in this county ever since, enjoying high respectability. The ancient residence, Stansfleld Hall, is still to be seen in the once beautiful valley of the Todmore. Like the Drapers, branches have scattered over the British Isles and America.

Extracts From the Records of Yorkshire Concerning the Stansfields and Drapers

"William le Drapour, Chaplain, granted to Thomas Drapour, his brother, certain lands, etc., which he has of the feoffment of John Drapour, his brother.

WITNESSES:

Rad'us de Stansfeld, Henry Savell de Cuppeley, Thomas del Schagh, Henry del Brigg, Richard de Wadsworth."

(The above would prove the Drapers to have been of French or Brittany ancestry, like the Stansfields; and it also conclusively proves their arrival or origin in Yorkshire prior to 1415.)

1429-30. John Rawlyn Drapur quitclaimed to Thomas Drapur his inheritance in Brodebotham Burlees in Wadesworth.

WITNESSES:

Hugh de Kyghley, Rudolphus de Stansfelde, John de Stansfelde and others.

(The above would show that the Drapers were large landholders in Yorkshire as early as 1400, as the above speaks of an inheritance.)

Thomas Stansfeld was Head Greave of Sowerby, 18th Henry VII. (1502-3), and in the 22d year of the following reign (1530-1), the wife of Thomas Drapar was Greave for lands in Marshehay and had help from Christopher Filde, John Drapar and others.

On the 29th May, 6th Henry VIII. (1515), Jacobus Stansfeld, nup' de Stansfeld, in the Parish of Heptonstall, in com. Ebor generosus, was bound to Henry Draper in 40 pounds to keep covenant.

(Here, for the first time, is the family name evolved from le Drapour, Drapur, Drapar, spelt as it is at the present day.)

James Stansfield, son of Ralph Stancefeld, deceased, surrendered a parcell of land within the course of the water of Calder, and a certain attachment of a mill pool for a fulling mill, lying between Redycar and Hawkschough, to the use of Henry Draper, of Wadsworth.

Aug. 21, 1515. Court Roll.

(Here is the earliest evidence of the Drapers being engaged in the making and fulling of cloth; which some of their descendants to this day are still engaged in — notably the firm of Draper Bros., in Canton, Mass.)

1517. This Indent, made the 28th day of March, 8th yr. of the reign of our Sovereign Lord, Kyng Henry VIII., betwix James Stansfeld, cosyn & heyr to Geoflfray Stansfeld, of that one p'tie, & Henry Draper, of Wadsworth, of that other p'tie, etc., James Stansfeld grants a parcel of ground 16 yards by 8, in Wadsworth, in a close calle Longsike, whereon to build one, or two, walk milus, and to attach a mill dam, etc.; Also liberty to carry away, all stone and timber necessary, from the closes of said James, caled, Hilhouse Closes & Tillyclyflfs in Wadsworth.

(The Drapers here increase their milling facilities, quite extensively for those days.)

James Stansfeld & Isabell, his wife, are declared debtors for 26*s.* 8*d.* in the will of John Draper, of Heptonstall. May 21, 1561.

(This Draper is the grandfather of Thomas Draper I.)

WILL

Vol. XVIJ. f. 413. a. Dated 11th October, 1564. Proved March 26, 1565.

Thomas Stancefeld, of Hyginchamber in Sourbie, yoman, recites that he stands seazed in fee simple, in a messuage and certain cottages, called Netherswyneshead, with lands, etc., appertaining, in Langfield, purchased of Thomas Draper of Brodbottom, in occupation of testator & James Crabtree.

Edward Stansfeld was named as tenant of Burley Carr in Wadsworth, the property of Testator Thomas Draper of Broadbottome. June 28, 1572.

Henry Draper received a small legacy from Agnes Sutclif of Howhoole in Earingden, a widow. Dec. 24, 1597.

(The above entries are all taken from authentic sources, and are believed to be all that exist, showing transactions between the Families of Draper & Stansfield.)

Entries in the Heptonstall Parish Registers of the Stansfields Who Were Connected with the Drapers

MARRIAGES

1624-5. February. Gideon Stansfield et Grace Eastwod, 21 day.

1646. Aprilis. James Draper et Miriam Stansfeild, nupt. fuer. 21 die.

BAPTISMS

1625. November. Mirriam Giddon Stansfeld, H. 27.

1627-8. January. Marie Gedeon Stansfield, Wad. 20 die.

1631-2. March. Abraham, fil Gideon Sta'sfeild de Wadsworth, bapt. 11 day.

1634. Julye. Debora, fil Gideon Stansfeild de Wad., 27 die.

1636-7. Mensis ffebruarie. John fil Gideon Stansfeild de Wad., bapt. 5 daie. 1638. Mensis Novembris. Abigail fil Gideon Stansfeild, bapt. 25 day. 1641. Mensis Maiji. Sara fili Gideon Stansfeild de Wad., bap, 30 day.

BURIALS

1635. Novembr. Infans Gideon Stansfeild, Wad. sepul 22 day.

1637. December. Infans Gibson (Gideon.) Stansfeild de Wad., sepult. 31 day.

1656. November. Gedeon Stansfeild younger of Heptonstall, was buried the 29.

1658. May. Gedeon Stansfeild of Heptonstall was buried the 9.

1682. August. Grace Stansfeild, Stan — 14.

(The above are the parents and brothers and sisters of Miriam Stansfield Draper.)

Of the other Draper families in America all has been done to trace their ancestry that it is possible to do; but they are much more recent arrivals, most of them in the present century, so that they have had but a short period in which to identify themselves with the country; but it is creditable to the name that the author is able to say they are worthy members of the family.

It is not the object of this History to trace back the propinquity of all the branches of the Drapers in England. That is a task that may be done at some other time, and by some other person. But enough is known of them to say positively that they had, about the year A. D. 1400, a common Ancestor, coming to England from the Netherlands, Normandy or Brittany.

The reasons for the migration of the earlier Drapers to America were principally religious ones. Those who have come later have done so in the hope that in this freer land of ours, their chances in life were better, which has proven to be the case.

The earlier religious and political exiles have in some instances left their mark and a posterity; others have dropped entirely from sight; all have been accounted for as far as possible. But one especially rises up through the misty tangle of over two centuries to be a lesson and a beacon for the guidance, not alone of his own posterity, but of all who bear the name he did — James Draper — called variously, the "First," the "Emigrant," and best, truest of all, "The Puritan," for that he was persecuted for "Righteousness' Sake" in the old home.

It was during the reign of King James I. that the excitement under the laws relating to uniformity of religion arose. The Puritans, to avoid the persecutions which these laws would inflict upon them and to enjoy in peace that mode of worship they deemed most consonant to the Scriptures, emigrated in large numbers to Holland and the New World, settling in Plymouth and Massachusetts Bay, in 1620.

The spirit of individual independence and the love of personal liberty and freedom of conscience which was aroused by the great religious excitement, had a deep influence on James as it had upon his father, Thomas Draper, and his brothers. What we learn of him hereafter very largely goes to prove this; be this as it may, he caught the feeling which was carrying so many to the rugged shores of the Western World, and with others from the same neighborhood, who cherished sentiments adverse to the claims of the Established Church and the Prerogatives of Royalty concerning it, he, with his wife, Miriam, emigrated to this country but a few years after the landing of the Pilgrims at Plymouth Rock. The exact date cannot be ascertained, but from careful research and calculation, the author believes it to have been in the year 1647-8.

The first public Record of James is in 1654, as one of the proprietors of the newly laid out Town of Lancaster. But he had not lived there, but in Roxbury where, shortly after his arrival, he built what, for those early days, was considered a very substantial house. A picture of this building is inserted in this History, and the house stood until destroyed by fire some 20 years ago. Near its site stands a slightly more modern one, which was built by his son and is, to this day, occupied by one of his descendants. James gave largely of his means and time to build the Church and sustain it; and he was foremost in its councils and those of the Town. In the old cemetery at Roxbury he and his wife lie buried together, and one slab marks their common grave.

The authenticity of connection between the Drapers of Heptonstall, England, and of James Draper and his descendants of Roxbury, Mass., is very clear. Not alone by the English Records, but by the following affidavits made many years ago, and amply proven, to the entire satisfaction of Dr. Abijah

Draper, his son. Dr. Abijah Weld Draper, and the celebrated Historian, Dr. Lyman Copeland Draper:

"John Draper, of Dedham, aged eighty-two years or thereabouts, under oath declares, that he hath often heard his father and mother say, that the deponent's grandfather's name was Thomas Draper, who lived in Hepstontall Brige or Bridge, in Yorkshire, and was a clothier by trade, and had sons, Thomas, John, William and James — the deponent's father. The three former died in England, never came into this country, and two sisters, Mary and Martha, who also died there. The deponent's mother's surname was Stansfield, dau. of Gideon Stansfield, alias Standfast, of the same place in Yorkshire, near the said Bridge, blacksmith by trade, who only had one son, that had not the use of speech, and the deponent's said mother, Meriam, and Abigail, who came together into this country, and who left their said father, Gideon, in Yorkshire, and who had estate there, but the deponent knows not what became thereof."

New England, Province of Massachusetts Bay, Suffolk, SS.
Roxbury, Mass., 25th April, 1742.

"Then John Draper made solemn oath to the truth of the above declaration by him subscribed, before Wm. Dudley, Justice of the Peace for said Province."

(The above is a copy of a paper in the possession of William Draper, Roxbury, May, 1808, copied by Dr. Abijah Draper, and the copy in possession of Dr. Abijah Weld Draper — 1854 — and already transcribed from the original by Dr. Lyman Copeland Draper. The time of his (James Draper's) coming to this country is not ascertained, but that he was married here, as it would seem from the above deposition that Meriam and Abigail "came together to this country." The earliest record yet found of his name is in Roxbury records of Births, etc., "1668, Patience, daughter of James Draper (born or baptized), Aug. 17th.")

"I, Thomas Baker, of Roxbury, Suffolk Co., Province of Mass. Bay, in New England, yeoman, in the 78th year of my age, do testify and declare, that about 70 years ago, I well knew one James Draper, who then followed the business of a weaver, but I have heard he was a cordwainer; and he was then an old man, I believe between 60 and 70 years of age, and then lived in the said town of Roxbury. I also well knew said James Draper's wife, and they often declared, and I always understood, that they came from Yorkshire, in Old England; and I also knew the sons of the said James Draper, which he had by his 2d wife, who I always understood came from England after he, the said James, came to this country; and the names of their sons were James, John, Moses, Daniel and Jonathan; and I was well acquainted with them, and I knew that the same James was the eldest son of the first mentioned James Draper, who is long since dead. And I do further declare, that the last mentioned James (by his wife, whose maiden name was Abigail Whiting), had five sons, to wit: Nathl., William, James, Gideon and Ebenezer; but William died young, and I was not well acquainted with him, but I was well acquainted with the others— and that the same Nathanl. lived and died in said Roxbury, and was the same James's oldest (son) and goes on to substantiate to the 2d Nathl."

(signed) Thos. Baker.

The above was sworn to, the 12th of February, 1754, before Saml. Watts and Ebenezer Pierpont.

Justices of the Peace & Quorum.

The author of this book, however, had had the advantage not only of the English records but of some American ones not reached by the three doctors, and is able to furnish the proofs in these pages that James the Puritan had but one wife — Miriam. Also that Miriam and her sister, Abigail, did come together from England; but the former was already the wife of James Draper, as the Heptonstall Parish Records amply denote. Her sister, Abigail, however, married in this country, Samuel May, of Boston, May 7, 1654. She was then sixteen years old and must have been a child when she came to America with her sister.

Descendants of James the "Puritan."

2. James Draper, (1. Thomas.) 4th s. and child of Thomas Draper of the Priory of Heptonstall, Vicarage of Halifax, Yorkshire County, England, b. Heptonstall, 1618. d. Roxbury, Mass., July, 1694. m. Heptonstall, Apr. 21, 1646. 3. Miriam, dau. of Gideon Stansfield and Grace Eastwood of Wadsworth, Yorkshire, (m. Feb. 21, 1624-5. Gideon d. May 9, 1658. Grace d. Aug. 12, 1682.) She was b. Heptonstall, Nov. 27, 1625. d. Roxbury, Mass., Jan., 1697.

Coat of arms of the American descendants of James Draper and Miriam Stansfield

Although James Draper is found in history as one of the original proprietors of the Town of Lancaster, there is no evidence that he ever lived there. His first residence was in Roxbury, and there Sarah, Susanna and James, his first American children, were born. He then moved into the next Town of Dedham, for we find that his sons John, Moses and Daniel were born there, and the following official data from the records of that town confirms this view. He probably then returned to his first home in Roxbury where his youngest children. Patience and Jonathan, were born, and where he and his wife died and are buried. He was made a Freeman of Roxbury in 1690. All of Roxbury is now contained within the corporate limits" of the City of Boston, yet it is still the country, and not built up to any extent, leaving the old landmarks untouched. James was also for a short time in Charlestown, Mass., for we find him notified in 1676, and that he sold to Jonathan Carey part of an orchard there in 1672. Deed recorded 1684.

The following official records, bearing upon James Draper's career and the final settlement and division of his estate, are of great interest to his descendants, and it is pleasant to know that these original records are still extant and carefully preserved. In fact, no praise is too great for the wise laws instituted in the earliest days of the settlement of New England for the making and preservation of evidence of the early settlers.

Petition of Widow Miriam to Judge of Probate Court, Suffolk Co., Mass. No. 2387.

"As the Honorable Wm. Houghton Esq. Judge of Probate is informed that I am leaft a widow throu God's providence therefore I do desire that my youngest son Jonathan Draper with my Eldest son James Draper may have adminestraytion granted unto them one the Estate of my deseased Husbands Estate I being agad and Crosey and not able forto undertack a invuny.

August 19, 1697. Mariam Draper. M.

John Alldis. her mark.
Jonathan Whiting.

Administration Bond of James Draper. Aug. 19, 1697.

Know all men by these presents That We, James Draper, Jonathan Draper, John Davis, Yeoman, and Joseph Warren, Carpenter, all of Roxbury within the County of Suffolk — within his Majesty's Province of the Massachusetts Bay in New England are holden and stand firmly bound and obliged unto William Houghton Esq. Judge of the Probate of Wills and Granting administrations within the said County of Suffolk, in the full sum of Four hundred pounds currant -money in New England. To be paid unto the same William Houghton his successors in the said Office or Assignes. To the true payment whereof, we do bind ourselves, our heirs. Executors and Administrations jointly and severally firmly by these presents. Sealed with our Seals. Dated the nineteenth day of August Anno Domini 1697.

Armog R. Rs. Gulieane Fertu Anglio di nono.

The condition of this present obligation is such that the above bounden James & Jonathan Draper appointed administrators of all and singular the Goods chattels Rights and Credits (lying and being in the County of Suffolk aforesaid, and elsewhere within the Province) of their Father James Draper late of Roxbury aforesd Weaver, deceased intestate, do make a true & perfect inventory of all and singular the Goods Chattels Rights & Credits of the said deceased at the time of his death which at any time after shall come to the hands or possession of the said James & Jonathan Draper or any other person or persons for them do well and truly administer according to law. And further do make or cause to be made a just & true account of the said administration upon oath at or before the Nineteenth day of August which will be in the year of our Lord One thousand six hundred ninety eight, and all the rest & residue of the said Goods Chattels Rights & Credits which shall be found remaining upon the said Administrators Account (the same being first examined and allowed of by the Judge or Judges for the time being of Probate of Wills and Granting Administrations within the said County of Suffolk) shall deliver & pay unto such person or persons respectively as the said Judge or Judges by his or their Decree or sentence pursuant to law shall limit or appoint. And if it shall hereafter appear that any last Will or testament was made by the Deceased and the Executor or Executors therein named do Exhibit the same into the said Court of Probate making request to have it allowed and approved accordingly. If the said James & Jonathan Draper, within bounden, being thereunto required do render & deliver the said letters of Administration (Approbation of such Testament being first had and made) into the Registers Office of the County of Suffolk aforesaid. Then the within written obligation to be void and of none effect, or else to abide and remain in full force and virtue.

Sealed & Delivered James Draper (seal)
in presence of Jonathan Draper (seal)
Beny 2 Eliott John Davis (seal)
Edward Humfrey. Joseph Warren (seal)

An Inventory of the Estate of James Draper, late of Roxbury, Weaver deceased. Approved by us the Subscribers.

	£	s.	d.
To house & shop and halfe barne & home lands	25	00	00
To one acre & roode of meadow in Deadham	1	00	00
To rights of lands in Deadham bounds	2	00	00
To 1 mare & 2 cows	7	00	00
To one swine	0	15	00
To corn and apples and to bakon	3	15	00
To mirror and brass	5	00	00
To iron tongues fireshovel handirons & other things	1	10	00
Chairs, tables, pails, dishes	1	00	00
To agur and other small things	2	10	00
To beds & bedding	9	00	00
Wooling and lining clothes	2	00	00
to books	1	00	00
Chests, boxes, cubord	1	00	0
to yarn lining & wooling	1	00	0
Wheels and lumber	1	10	0
looms and tacklin	5	00	0
Cart and a cidar mill	1	10	0
	72	00	0

John Alldis
Thomas Lion

Tombstone of James Draper, the "Puritan," and Miriam Stansfield his Wife, at West Roxbury, Mass.

Suffolk. By the Honorable Wm. Houghton Esq. Judge of Probate, etc., Jonathan Draper, surviving Administrator of the Estate of his Father James Draper late of Roxbury, Weaver, deceased, Exhibeted the above written And made oath that it contains a just and true Inventory of the Estate of the said Deceased. So far as hath come to his knowledge And that if more hereafter appears he will cause it to be added.

Boston. May 12, 1698. Wm. Houghton.

Suffolk, *The Account of Jonathan Draper Admt. of all &c. singular the Goods Chattels Rights and Credits of his father James Draper late of Roxbury Weaver Deceased.*

The said Accountant Chargeth himself with all and singular the Goods Chattels etc. of the Deceased specified in an Inventory Exhibited into the Registry of the Court of Probate on the day of Amounting in the whole to ye sum of £73 10 0.

Payments.

Letter of Administration	£00	7	6
Recording the Inventory	00	2	6
Funeral charges for my Father	6	7	10
Do. for my Mother	6	6	00
Rates paid to the Constable	0	12	6
Paid John Puffer	1	10	6
Paid a debt of keeping my Mother 3 years & six months	50	0	0
For allowing Drawing & Recording this Account	0	9	0
	£65	17	10

Suffolk. By the Honorable Samuel Sewell
Esq. Judge of Probate, etc.

Jonathan Draper, surviving Administrator presented the above written and made oath that it contained a just and true account of his administration on the Estate of his Father James Draper late of Roxbury Deceased And Produced Receipts and Vouchers for several payments therein mentioned. Which I do accordingly allow and approve of.

Lib. S. Folio 173. Samuel Sewall. June 9, 1718.

Children.

4. I. Miriam, b. Heptonstall, England, Feb. 7, 1646-7. d. England, in infancy.

5. II. Susanna, b. Roxbury, Mass., about 1650. m. Charlestown, Mass., John Bacon, 1668.

6. III. Sarah, b. Roxbury, Mass., 1652. m. May 19, 1669, James Hadlock. Child: — I. Sarah (12½). b. Roxbury, Dec. 16, 1670. Bap. as an adult, Oct. 24, 1686. m. about 1686, John Marcy. They had 8 sons and 3 daughters.

7. IV. James, b. Roxbury, Mass., 1654. d. Roxbury, Apr. 30, 1698.

8. V. John, b. Dedham 24th day of 4th month, 1656. d. Dedham, Apr. 5, 1749.

9. VI. Moses, b. Dedham, Sep. 26, 1663. d. Boston, Aug. 14, 1693.

10. VII. Daniel, b. Dedham, May 30, 1665. d. Dedham.

11. VIII. Patience, b. Roxbury, Mass., Aug. 17, 1668. m. Mar. 13, 1689, Ebenezer Cass of Boston. (No issue found or further data.)

12. IX. Jonathan, b. Roxbury, Mass., Mar. 10, 1670. d. Roxbury Feb. 28, 1746-7.

7. James. (2. James, 1. Thomas.) 4th child, eldest s. of (2) James Draper and (3) Miriam Stansfield, of Roxbury, Mass. m. by Rev. Mr. Walter, Feb. 18, 1681, to Abigail, dau. of Nathanial Whiting and Hannah Dwight, of Dedham. She was b. Roxbury, June 7, 1663, and d. there Oct. 25, 1721. She was a granddau. of John Dwight, from whom President Timothy Dwight of Yale and other prominent men are descended.

He was a soldier in the King Philip War during the year 1675. James had received from his father part of his farm at Roxbury. This he subsequently sold to John Aldis. He then bought the estate below Baker Street, where he, and after his death, his widow, kept an ordinary. The location of this ordinary is fixed, beyond a peradventure, by James' granddau., Jemima (1474) Turner. Her father Ebenezer (19), when she was quite a girl, took her behind him on a pillion, and carried her down to visit the old house where he was born. (She related this and other subjects to Dr. A. W. Draper, who made careful note of them.) It was from here that the sons James (17) and Ebenezer (19) went to Green Lodge, Dedham.

A. D. 1683. Leave is granted by the Town of Dedham to Nathanial Whiting and (his son-in-law) (7) James Draper, to erect a Fulling Mill, below the Corn mills on the stream, called Mother-brook, and facilities are allowed them by the Town for that object, (p. 20, Historical Annals of Dedham, by Herman Mann.)

In folio 18, p. 24, Suffolk Co., Mass., Deeds, is recorded the sale of (8) John Draper's ¼ interest in the above Mill, to Samuel and Timothy Whiting, of Dedham, and (7) James Draper, of Roxbury. Dated Nov. 17, 1697. The mill was also a saw-mill.

This property did not remain many years in the hands of the Drapers, they gradually parting with their interests to the Whitings; for (see p. 27, Hist. Annals of Dedham, by Herman Mann), under date of May 11, 1789, a committee was chosen to ascertain the Town's claim to the Mother-brook stream and land adjoining, formerly granted to Nathanial Whiting and (7) James Draper, which committee reported that Messrs. Joseph Whiting, Paul, Moses and Aaron Whiting, have consented to give the Town six pounds for an acquittance of the Town's claim to said stream, and advise a compliance with these terms. This report was accepted, and the Town Treasurer directed to give a quitclaim in behalf of the Town, on receipt of the money.

The Nathanial Whiting above was one of the original proprietors of Dedham, as entered in the records of the Town, under date of 6th of 12th month, 1642.

James Draper (7) d. when in the prime of life, and a most interesting anecdote is related of him by his granddau., Mrs. Jemima (1474 Draper) Turner, dau. of (19) Ebenezer Draper — she was very old (b. 1756, d. 1856) but retained all her faculties till the last) — of how her grandfather met his death. She said that he lost his life from an injury sustained in wrestling on a Mayday. This day was, after the English custom, kept as a festival; a Maypole was set up, about which wrestling, pitching quoits and other games were kept up. On such a day a person appeared, claiming to be champion of the ring, challenging any who might choose to enter the ring with him. A number accepted, but he threw them all with so much ease that there was no one left to compete with him. Pretty soon enquiries were made for James (7) Draper, and remarks to the effect that he would be a match for the champion were heard. In a moment he was seen coming on horseback, with his wife. Mistress Abigail, behind him. The crowd urged him to dismount and try a bout with the stranger. At first he declined, but he was almost taken from his saddle. Mistress Abigail holding on to his coat as long as she could. He met his antagonist in the ring, and at the word, laid him on his back. The cry of "unfair" was set up, and he tried him again, and at the word, the stranger was once more laid on his back by the stalwart James. But in doing this a second time he broke a sinew in his leg, from which he never recovered. He was carried back to his house, but was never able to go out again.

James and Abigail are buried in the First Parish Cemetery at Dedham, Mass., and the following is inscribed on the stone that marks their grave:

2 Sam. I. 23. They were lovely & pleasant in their lives, and in their death they were not divided.

"The stroke of death, hath laid my head
Down in this dark & silent bed.

The Trump shall sound, I hope to rise,
And meet my Saviour in the Skies."

Suffolk Records. Lib. 3. Folio 257. May 30, 1698.

An Inventory of the Estate of James Draper: late of Roxbury, deceased, taken by us the subscribers.

	£		
Housing & Homestead	90		
A small piece of salt marsh & fresh meadow	21		
In bedding & furniture	7	2	6
In brass, iron, pewter & earthen ware	4		
In wooden ware & lumber	2	3	
In carpentry & husbandry tools	2		
In cart tackling and logg chaise	2	1	
In meat kine, horse, & swine	20		
In Shingles	3		
In cloathing &c, &c, a	18		
	£172	6	6
In Deeds interest in 2 mills at Dedham	40		

John Colburn, John Grigs, Isaac Morris.

Suff. SS.

Abigail Draper, relict, widow & administrator, &c. &c. a true inventory of estate of sd. deceased:

Approved, June 9, 1698.

Letters of administration granted unto Abigail Draper, widow, on estate of her husband, James Draper, late of Rox., carpenter, deceased.

Granted 9th day of June, 1698.

Lib. 16, Folio 258.

The acct. of Abigail Draper, administrator of James Draper, late of Rox. &c. husbandman. "Nathanial Draper, eldest son of said deceased, being present at the allowance of this account."

March 20, 1706-7.

There is this item mentioned in the account: —

"Paid to Samuel Gore for his wife's portion; £25,"

CHILDREN:

13. I. Abigail, b. Roxbury, Mass., Dec. 29, 1681. m, James Griggs.

14. II. Nathanial, b. Roxbury, Mass., Apr. 2, 1684. d. Dec. 30, 1721.

15. III. William, b. Roxbury, Mass., May 15, 1686. d. young.

16. IV. Eunice, b. Roxbury, Mass., June 5, 1689. m. Nathanial Aldis, June 24, 1708. She d. June 13, 1714.

17. V. James, b. 1691. d. Apr. 24, 1768.

18. VI. Gideon, b. Roxbury, Mass., 1694.

19. VII. Ebenezer, b. Roxbury, Mass., Apr. 27, 1698. d. Attleboro, June 3, 1784.

14. Nathanial. (7. James, 2. James, 1. Thomas.) Eldest s., 2d child of James Draper and Abigail Whiting, m. Abigail Lyon, of Roxbury, Jan. 22, 1706.

The First House Built by the Roxbury Drapers

(Destroyed by about 1870.)

CHILDREN:

I. Nathanial, b. Roxbury, Oct. 10, 1706. d. Roxbury, Mar. 28, 1767.

II. William, b. Plainfield, Feb. 20, 1707.

III. Benjamin, b. Plainfield, July 13, 1710. d. Roxbury, Sep. 15, 1711

IV. Abigail, b. Plainfield, Sep. 13, 1712.

V. Eunice, b. Roxbury, Apr. 24, 1715.

VI. Jonathan, b. Roxbury, Jan. 20, 1717. d. Feb. 28, 1746. VII. Jemima, b. Roxbury, Mar. 30, 1720.

The following are official records relative to the settlement of Nathanial Draper's estate, etc.

Lib. 27, Fol. 159.

I, Eunice Draper (24) a minor, aged about 15 years, dau. of Nathl. late of Rox. husbandman, etc. do nominate and appoint &c. Ebenezer Draper (19) of Stoughton,

County of Suffolk, husbandman, to be my guardian.

E. D. her mark.

Witness:

Mary Clarke.

Approved, Oct. 6, 1729.

Lib. 27, Fol. 270. Settlement of Nathl Draper's (14) estate (real) appraized by John Cobburn, John Weld, Ben. Smith.

House and all land on west side of road leading to Dedham, £387.

Other buildings, with all the orchard, meadow and land on the east side of sd. road at, £540

Meadow land lying in Dedham, £50

4¾ acres of salt marsh lying in Roxbury, £33

Upland and meadow land lying at Green Lodge, commonly so called, in Stoughton, £400.

Pasture lands lying at Woodstock, 75 acres, both high and low land, £100.

Nathanial Draper (20), eldest son of sd. deceased, takes the "estate, paying to his brothers & sisters or their heirs, &c. viz: to the heirs of William Draper (21), deceased, Eunice Draper (24), Benjamin Draper (22), Jemima Draper (26), each the sum of £251 13 4

20. Nathanial. (14. Nathanial, 7. James, 2. James, 1. Thomas.) Eldest s. and child of Nathanial Draper and Abigail Lyon. m. Mehetable Weld,. May 25, 1732. She was b. Roxbury, 171 5. d. Roxbury, Mar. 28, 1757.

CHILDREN, ALL B. ROXBURY:

27. I. William, b. July 28, 1734.

28. II. Mehetable, b. Feb, 5, 1737.

29. III. Abigail, b. May 28, 1738. m. Feb. 23, 1762, John, s. of John and Abigail Baker, of Roxbury. He was an Ensign and Captain of Artillery, b. Feb. 8, 1736. d. Aug. 10, 1781. They were m. by Rev. Nathan Walter.

30. IV. John, b. Aug. 18, 1740. d. Roxbury, Dec. 27, 1772. m. Ann Child.

They had: Nancy (63), b. W. Roxbury, Mar. 8, 1761.

31. V, Paul, b. Nov. 1, 1743. d. Jan. 29, 1788.

27. William. (20. Nathanial, 14. Nathanial, 7. James, 2. James, 1. Thomas.) Eldest s. and child of Nathanial Draper and Mehetable Weld. m. Elizabeth, dau. of Caleb Ellis, Sep, 24, 1757. She d. Oct. 28, 1771, aged 36.

At the beginning of the Revolutionary War, Roxbury Mass., had three companies of minute men, commanded respectively by, 1st: Moses Whiting; 2d: by (27) William Draper; 3d: by Lemuel Child. The Lieutenants were, 1st: Jacob Davis and John Davis; 2d: Lemuel May and Moses Draper; 3d: Thomas Mayo and Isaac Williams. They all, with full ranks, responded to their country's call on the 19th April and did good service on that occasion. It is related of Captain William Draper and his son, William, that they were ploughing with a pair of horses on the afternoon of the 19th April, 1775, when they heard the news of the battle of Lexington. Leaving the plough in the furrow they went to the house, when the younger William was ordered by his father to beat the long roll, and together they proceeded to Roxbury Neck where the troops were mustering. The son, very much to his disappointment, was not allowed to join the army at that time. Capt. William d. of disease whilst on the Ticonderoga expedition.

The Muster Roll of the 2d Roxbury Co., dated Dec. 7, 1775, states: "Being a true and just Roll of the 2d Co. of Roxbury, commanded by Capt. William Draper, in Col. Heath's Regiment, the 19th day of April, when called, to the 3d day of May, and then dismissed. Captain William Draper.

1st Lieut. Thomas Mayo.

2d Lieut. John Davis."

In addition the Co. had 40 non-commissioned officers and privates, amongst whom are found 2d Sergt. Paul Draper and privates Jonathan and Nathanial Draper.

In the 3d Roxbury Co. are found the names of Aaron and Ichabod Draper as privates. The original rolls of these companies are on file at the State House in Boston.

From Hudson's History of Lexington and the History of Antrim, it appears that Capt. William Draper went from Roxbury to Lexington in 1782, and the same year, he being a widower, his 1st wife, Elizabeth, having d. in 1771, he m. Sarah Barnes, of Lexington. They left there soon after. It is related of Sarah Barnes that she watched the Red Coats when they first fired upon the American Volunteers and saw their disastrous retreat later in the day. Capt. William Draper and wife moved from Lexington to Francistown.

In the depositions taken by order of the Provincial Congress, as to whether the regular troops or the citizens began the firing at the battle of Lexington, William Draper, who happened to be present at the time, says: "The regular troops fired before any of Captain Parker's Company fired."

CHILDREN, BY ELIZABETH ELLIS, ALL B. AT ROXBURY:

32. I. William, b. Apr. 27, 1760. d. Oct. 18, 1834.

33. II. Nathan, b. Sep. 18, 1761. d. May 31, 1828.

34. III. Aaron, b. Nov. 28, 1762. m. Keziah.

35. IV. Elizabeth, b. Sep. 16, 1767, m. Nathanial Tileston of Dorchester, Nov. 9, 1790.

36. V. Egbert, b. Aug. 6, 1771. d. unmarried. Deaf and dumb.

CHILDREN, BY SARAH BARNES:

37. VI. Jonas, bap. Oct. 5, 1783.

38. VII. Timothy W., b. Francestown. d. Antrim, N. H., Apr. 10, 1874.

32. William. (27. William, 20. Nathanial, 14. Nathanial, 7. James, 2. James, 1. Thomas.) Eldest s. and child of Captain William Draper and Elizabeth Ellis, m. Aug. 13, 1782, Rebecca, dau. of (Saddler) Nathanial Richards and Mary Colburn. She was b. Roxbury. d. Nov. 17, 1833.

He was the drummer of his father's company, the 2d Roxbury, but was not allowed to go to the war at the beginning, though he took part in subsequent hostilities as a private in Capt. Lemuel May's Co., Roxbury Lines, in Feb., 1779.

CHILDREN B. IN ROXBURY:

39. I. William, b. Feb. 28, 1783. d. Feb. 14, 1810. m. Nancy, dau. of Deacon Murdock, of Roxbury. After his death she m. Capt. Randolph Goodwin, of Boston, Oct. 6, 1818.

40. II. Mary, b. Feb. 13, 1785. d. Dorchester, Jan. 24, 1880. m. May 16, 1832, Zenas White, of Dorchester.

41. III. Paul, b. July 30, 1788. d. Apr. 14, 1859.

42. IV. Betsy, b. Apr. 23, 1791. d. Mar. 29, 1884. (Unmarried.)

Betsy Draper was engaged to Nathanial Fisher, of Boston, at one time. The Ints. of Marriage had been procured Sep. 20, 1838, but she broke off the marriage. It is related of her that at the time of her death she was the oldest inhabitant of the village in which she resided (West Roxbury), being 92 years, 11 months and 6 days. She kept a store for many years and was much respected. A constant attendant at the Unitarian Church — the old First Parish — gathered in 171-, and for 84 years occupied the same seat in the same pew. She and her brother, Paul (41), were b. in the same house in which they d., now occupied by her nephew, William Willard Draper (45).

41. Paul. (32. William, 27. William, 20. Nathanial, 14. Nathanial, 7. James, 2. James, 1. Thomas.) 3d child, 2d s. of William Draper and Rebecca Richards, m. June 13, 1816, Nancy, dau. of Col. Moses Mann, of Roxbury. She was b. Mar. 19, 1792. d. June 2, 1839.

Paul Draper soon after his marriage established himself in business in West Brookfield, Mass., where he remained a number of years, when, yielding to the importunities of his sister Betsy, he returned to his native town to assist in the care of his father and mother who had become quite feeble. Soon after his return he was appointed the first postmaster of West Roxbury. He was one of the first to move in the establishment of an orthodox church in the village, and spent liberally of his time and means for the promotion of that object.

CHILDREN:

43. I. Mary Ann, b. W. Roxbury, Mar. 21, 1817. d. Nov. 13, 1839. m. July 2, 1837, Joseph Priest.

44. II. Lucy Rebecca, b. W. Roxbury, Mar. 30, 1819. d. Dec. 15, 1820.

45. III. William Willard, b. W. Brookfield, Feb. 13, 1821. m. Elizabeth R. Wiswall, of Boston, Oct. 7, 1845.

He is a farmer and occupies the house his great-grandfather (27) William Draper built in W. Roxbury. (?)

CHILDREN:

46. IV. Emma Lizzie, b. W. Roxbury, Apr. 1, 1847. m. George C. Tate, Jr., of Boston, Jan. 1, 1879. Children: — 50. Hattie Richards, b. July 6, 1879. 51. James Love, b. Feb. 10, 1881. 52. Maria Louisa, b. Oct. 13, 1883. 53. Charles William, b. May 17, 1890.

47. V. William Edward, b. W. Roxbury, July 29, 1848. d. Oct., 1848.

VI. William Edward 2d, b. W. Roxbury, Oct. 21, 1853. m. Feb. 2r, 1878, Ida VV. Gooding. She was b. June 5, 1859. 1. Emma L., b. W. Roxbury, Mar. 7, 1860, d. Sep. 29, 1860.

Timothy W. (27. William, 20. Nathanial, 14. Nathanial, 7. James, 2. James.) 2d s. and 2d child of Captain William Draper, by his 2d wife, Sarah Barnes. b. April 2, 1824, Mary Flanders, of Lancaster.

They went to Antrim, N. H., in 1849. He rented first Reuben Boutwell's farm, and then William Tuttle's. But in 1851 bought of John E. Parmenter the place opposite [he Centre Church, in Antrim, where he lived until he died. He was a very lame man, but had no sickness, and d. in his chair one morning whilst waiting for his breakfast.

CHILDREN:

54. I. George A., b. 1825. d. 1847.

55. II. Charles G., b. m. 1855, Elizabeth S. Jones, of Milford, Child: — 61. George C. b. Bemington, March 5, 1864.

For some reason unknown he dropped the name of Draper, and taking his 2d name of Gibson, he called himself Charles Gibson.

56. III. Maria M., b. 1828. d. 1856.

57. IV. Austin R., b. 1830. d. 1837, at Francestown.

58. V. Lucy A., b. June 8, 1833. m. Dec. 14, 1852, Alvin G. Charters, of Lowell, Mass. He d. May 11, 1859. Child: — Aloia A. 62. b. Antrim, May 4, 1859.

59. VI. Richards, b. July 24, 1837, Antrim. Left there in 1857. Last heard of in Kansas.

60. VII. William H., b. 1840. d. March 20, 1860.

31. Paul. (20. Nathanial, 14. Nathanial, 7. James, 2. James, 1. Thomas.) 3d s., youngest child of Nathanial Draper and Mehetable Weld. m. Sarah.

He was a farmer, and served as 2d Sergeant in his brother's company of minute men, the 2d Roxbury, Capt. William Draper (27). Was 2d Lieut, of Capt. Lemuel May's Co., Roxbury Lines.

CHILDREN:

64. I. Paul, bap. Aug. 15, 1773. d. Sep. 28, 1778.

65. II. Otis, bap. July 21, 1776. d. Sep. 20, 1777.

66. III. John, b. Sep. 2, 1778.

67. IV. Polly, bap. Oct. 22, 1780. d. in infancy.

68. V. Polly 2d, b. July 22, 1783.

69. VI. Sarah, bap. Jan. 1, 1786.

33. Nathan. (27. William, 20. Nathanial, 14. Nathanial, 7. James, 2. James, 1. Thomas.) 2d s., 2d child of Captain "William Draper and Elizabeth Ellis, m. Dec. 25, 1788, Hannah, dau. of William Whiting and Hannah Ellis. She was his cousin, and was b. Apr. 10, 1768. d. Aug. 12, 1843. William Whiting, her father, was the eldest s. of Jonathan Whiting, the brother of Abigail, who m. (7) James Draper. Nathan was a private in Capt. Lemuel May's Co., Roxbury Lines, in Feb., 1779.

CHILDREN:

70. I. Elizabeth, b. Apr. 16, 1790. d. Sep. 14, 1870.

71. II. Hannah, b. Aug. 23, 1792. d. Nov. 24, 1868. m. Oct. 11, 1821, James White, of Northfield, Mass., s. of Asaph White. He was b. Heath, Mass., Mar. 9, 1781. Child: — Julia Draper, b. May 18, 1823.

72. III. William Whiting, b. Aug. 18, 1794. d. June 26, 1881.

73. IV. Charlotte, b. Sep. 6, 1796. d. Aug. 18, 1866.

74. V. Julia E., b. Nov. 13, 1798, d. Aug. 18, 1866.

75. VI. Mary, b. Nov. 25, 1800. d. Dec. 9, 1800.

76. VII. George, b. Nov. 30, 1801. d. Aug. 8, 1866.

77. VIII. Emily, b. Dec. 6, 1803. d. July 20, 1865. m. Mar. 22, 1841, John P. Haven, s. of John Aldis Haven and Julitta Richards, b. Charlton, Mass., Apr. 22, 1800. Child: — 81. Emily Hannah, b. Apr. 8, 1844.

78. IX. Caleb Ellis, b. June 9, 1806. d. July 24, 1855, New York.

79. X. Catherine, b. May 1, 1808. d. Feb. 2, 1878.

80. XI. John, b. June 4, 1811. d. Oct. 25, 1812.

Miss (74) Julia Draper was associated with her sisters (77) Emily and (79) Catherine as Principal of the Misses Draper Seminary, established at Hartford, Conn., in 1830, and for more than 30 years well and favorably known throughout this country and abroad. (73) Charlotte Draper, who had been an invalid for some years, d. Aug. 18, 1866, and ere the morning of another day, Julia Draper had also passed away. An obituary, written by one of her pupils, thus speaks:

"The mention of the name of Miss Julia Draper will stir memories in many hearts which will grieve to hear she is gone; memories of bright girlhood, promise of fair womanhood, trained by her counsels under her kind guidance. From all parts of our own land, from South America, from Cuba, the young have come to her to receive instruction. Trained from early youth in the principles of our beloved Church, and embodying in her life their purity, she instilled them into the youthful minds under her care. While winning and demanding respect and reverence, she gained their love by her unvarying kindness and sense of justice. Admirably qualified for her work, and aided by her gifted sisters, she has left her impress on many lives. She has gone to her reward, leaving behind the record of a life fall of responsibility and care, ably met in the fear of God."

72. William Whiting. (33. Nathan, 27. William, 20. Nathanial, 14. Nathanial, 7. James, 2. James, 1. Thomas.) Eldest s., 4th child of Nathan Draper and Hannah Whiting, m. Mar. 8, 1821, Eliza Greene, dau. of Major Clark Chandler and his wife Nancy Lyon, dau. of David Lyon, who m., Feb. 9, 1764, Abigail Draper, of Roxbury. Eliza Greene Chandler was b. Coleraine, Mass., July 6, 1800. d. Greenfield, Mass., Oct. 12, 1880. Major Clark Chandler was the grandson of Hon. John Chandler, of Worcester, Mass., the maternal grandfather of George Bancroft, the historian.

(72) William Whiting Draper, whilst quite young, removed with his parents to Greenfield, Mass. He early evinced a talent for mechanics, and was the inventor of the scythe snath, a patent tool handle, and other useful devices. He was also interested in scientific pursuits, and claimed to have been the first to discover the fossil footprints of extinct birds in the Connecticut River valley, which claim was conceded by Professor Hitchcock, of Amherst College. He was a vigorous man, possessing a sound mind and a sound body.

CHILDREN, ALL B. IN GREENFIELD, MASS.:

82. I. Ellen, b. Feb. 11, 1822. m. Mar. 1, 1858, Jonathan, s. of Jonathan Ellis, of Boston, Mass., and cousin of the Rev. George E. Ellis, author and historian.

83. II. Jane, b. Mar. 8, 1823. d. Sep. 14, 1824.

84. III. Mary, b. July 25, 1824. d. Dec. 8, 1845.

85. IV. Charlotte, b. Apr. 3, 1826. d. New York, June 3, 1866. m. Henry, s. of James Brewster and Mary Hequembourg, of New Haven, Conn., a lineal descendant of Elder William Brewster. Children: — 91. Henry Draper, b. Aug. 4, 1862. 92. William, b. June 2, 1866.

86. V. Harriet, b. Jan. 10, 1829. m. June 9, 1853, Dr. Joseph Sidney, s. of Sidney Crane and Catherine Hequembourg, sister of Mary, who m. James Brewster. He was b. June 10, 1821. His father, who came from Columbia, S. C, was a descendant of Jasper Crane, of New Haven, Conn., 1639. Children: — 121. Catherine, b. June 21, 1856. 122. Amelia Brewster, b. Nov. 22, 1862. 123. Charles Sidney, b. Oct. 27, 1866. 124. Charlton Wells, b. June 15, 1872.

87. VI. Jane 2d, b. Nov. 13, 1830. d. Sep. 21, 1831.

88. VII. Elizabeth, b. Jan. 28, 1832. d. May 8, 1881.

89. VIII. Catherine, b. Jan. 13, 1834. m. Oct. 27, 1857, Thomas Vern Hall, s. of Nehemiah T. Hall and Dorcas Howes, b. Nov. 22, 1823. She d. May 2, 1864. Children:— Ellen Ellis, b. Oct. 24, 1860. William Thomas, b. Apr. 15, 1864.

90. IX. George Ellis, b. May 13, 1835. A veteran of the 7th Regiment N. G. S. N. Y., and served with his command in the Draft Riots in New York. Resides in Brooklyn, N. Y. (Unmarried.)

76. George. (33. Nathan, 27. William, 20. Nathanial, 14. Nathanial, 7. James, 2. James, 1. Thomas.) 8th child, 2d s. of Nathan Draper and Hannah Whiting, m. Feb. 6, 1826, Lucy R. Barnard, dau. of Levi Barnard and Lucy Page. She was b. Lunenburg, Vt., Jan. 4, 1806. d. Apr. 9, 1883.

CHILDREN:

93. I. George Barnard, b. Brattleboro, Vt., Jan. 20, 1827. d. New York City, Nov. 24, 1876.

94. II. Charles Edward, b. July 22, 1828. d. Jan. 3, 1831.

95. III. William Henry, b. Oct. 14, 1830.

96. IV. Royal Joyslin, b. Sep. 8, 1832. d. Feb. 14, 1835.

97. V. Frank Ellis, b. Oct. 10, 1835. m. Sep. 17, 1863, Mary Goodhue, dau. Of Mary Ann and William Pitt Cune, of Brattleboro, Vt. She was b. Oct. II, 1842. d. May 11, 1879. One adopted child: — Julia, b. Apr. 12, 1871.

98. VI. Lucy, b. Oct. 2, 1838. d. Mar. 14, 1841.

99. VII. James Frederick, b. Nov. 28, 1841. d. Feb. 19, 1849.

100. VIII. Julia Allen, b. Oct. 18, 1845. m. June 2, 1868, Charles Nelson, s. of Richard Peabody Kent and Emily Mann Oakes. He was b. May 14, 1843. Children: — 101. Helen Barnard, b. July 12, 1869. d. Oct. 20, 1874. 102. George Rowell. b. Dec. 27, 1871. d. Dec. 30, 1872. 103. Richard Peabody. b. Nov. 11, 1873. 104. Charles Nelson, b. Nov. 24, 1875. 105. Julia, b. June 14, 1879. Mary. b. Dec. 8, 1881. 106. Ruth. b. Nov. 24, 1883. 107. William Draper, b. Mar. 27, 1886. d. Apr. 18. 1886. 108. Lucy. b. July 3, 1888.

78. Caleb Ellis. (33. Nathan, 27. William, 20. Nathanial, 14. Nathanial, 7. James, 2. James, 1. Thomas.) 11th child, 3d s. of Nathan Draper and Hannah Whiting, m. Aug. 20, 1850, Jeanne Josephine Elizabeth, only dau. of Claude François Ferdinand de Brossard and Rosalie Pestel, and the granddaughter of Nicolas de Brossard, a nobleman who held several important offices at the Court of Louis XVI. "Ecuyer, Conseiller, Secrétaire du Roi, Maison Couronné de France et de ses finances, Greffier en chef en la Chambre des Comptes de Dauphiné." Her father was awarded, in 1814, the decoration of the "Fleur de Lys," for services rendered to Louis XVIII. She was b. St. Etienne, France, June 23, 1828. She was very beautiful and in her youth two duels were fought for the possession of her hand.

CHILDREN:

109. I. Jeanne de Brossard, b. Jan. 5, 1852. m. July 18, 1877, Seth Enas, s. of Seth Smith, of Cherry Valley, N. Y. He was b. July 11, 1849. Children: — 112. Erminia Draper, b. Racine, Wis., May 14, 1878. d. young. 113. Jennie Isabel, b. Detroit, Mich., Nov. 3, 1879, d. young. 114. Florence Frisbie. b. Detroit, Mich., Nov. 9, 1882.

110. II. Francis Simpson, b. New York, Mar. 16, 1853. d. Hartford, Conn., July 6, 1860.

111. III. Ellis Ferdinand, b. New York, Dec. 18, 1854. m. Feb. 24, 1881, Eliza Weed, dau. of Joseph Platt Tobias and Amanda Malvina Weed. She was b.

Stamford, Conn., Nov. 11, 1855. Child: — Erminia Josephine, 135. b. New York, May 31, 1882.

93. George Barnard. (76. George, 33. Nathan, 27. William, 20. Nathanial, 14. Nathanial, 7. James, 2 James, 1. Thomas.) Eldest s. and child of George Draper and Lucy R. Barnard, m. Lucy Blake Goodhue, b. Brattleboro, May 30, 1830.

He came with his parents early in life to New York. His academic studies were begun at Trinity School and completed at Columbia College, graduating at the age of nineteen. He then entered the general Theological Seminary and graduated June 28, 1849, and in July following was called to the office of Deacon; ordained Priest Mar. 16, 1851, and then became Rector of St. Andrews P. E. Church, Harlem. This was his only cure. He came to it Sunday the 23d June, 1850, and he laid down his office and closed his labors on earth on Sunday, Nov. 24, 1876. He received the degree of S. T. D. from Columbia College in 1868.

CHILDREN, ALL B. NEW YORK CITY:

115. 1, George Wells, b. Aug. 23, 1851. d. Emporia, Kansas, Dec. 6, 1888.

116. II. Frederick Goodhue, b. Aug. 23, 1854.

117. III. Walter & 118. IV. Arnold (Twins), b. June 27, 1857. Arnold d. New York City, Aug. 23, 1858. Walter m. Oct. 26, 1887, Emma C. Stallman, of Baraboo, Wis. Child:— 123. Gladys, b. St. Paul, Aug. 26, 1888.

119. V. Frank B., b. Nov. 10, 1859. m. Sep. 23, 1889, Isabel Mercine, dau. of John Hyde Coley and Mary Mercine Everit. She was b. Sep. 17, 1859. He is now Rector of All Saints Church, New Milford, Conn. Child: — Marion Coley, 120. b. Dec. 4, 1890, at New Milford.

120. VI. Laura Barnard, b. Jan. 1, 1862. m. Feb. 24, 1881, William Corlies, of St. Paul, Minn.

121. VII. Lizzie Eldridge, b. Aug. 30, 1864. m. Feb. 16, 1887, John Wilder Merriam, of St. Paul, Minn. Child:— 124. John L. b. St. Paul, Oct. 30, 1887. d. St. Paul, Mar. 27, 1891.

122. VIII. Lucy Goodhue, b. July 1, 1866. d. New York, July 23, 1867.

95. William Henry, (76. George, 33. Nathan, 27. William, 20. Nathanial, 14. Nathanial, 7. James, 2. James, 1. Thomas.) 3d s., 3d child of George Draper and Lucy R. Barnard, m. Oct. 15, 1861, 1st: Elizabeth Waldo Kinnicutt, descendant from the Kinnicutt family, of Worcester, Mass. She d. Dec. 19, 1869. He then m. 2dly: Dec. 5, 1877, Ruth, dau. of Hon. Charles A. Dana, of the New York "Sun," and Eunice McDuniel. She was b. Dosoros, L. I.

William Henry Draper graduated at Columbia College in 1851, and at the College of Physicians and Surgeons in 1855. He then went abroad and continued his studies in London and Paris. He was Clinical Professor of Diseases of the Skin in the College of Physicians and Surgeons from 1869 to 1880, when he was appointed Professor of Clinical Medicine, Vice-President of New York Academy of Medicine, 1886, and later a Trustee of Columbia College. He is now (1891) Consulting Physician at St. Luke's P. E. Hospital, the Presbyterian and New York Hospitals, and Attending Physician of Roosevelt Hospital.

CHILDREN, BY 1ST WIFE:

125. I. William Kinnicutt, b. Feb. 2, 1863. Graduated at Harvard University, 1885. College of Physicians and Surgeons, New York, 1888.

E. 126. II. Martha Lincoln, b. Aug. 21, 1864.

E. 127. III. Robert Watts, b. Dec, 1867. d. Aug., 1868.

CHILDREN, BY 2D WIFE:

E. 128. IV. Charles Dana, b. Jan. 11, 1879.

E. 129. V. George, b. May 21, 1880.

E. 130. VI. Dorothea, b. Sep. 20, 1881.

E. 131. VII. Alice Olin, b. Mar. 22, 1883.

E. 132. VIII. Ruth, b. Dec. 2, 1884.

E. 133. IX. Paul, b. Nov. 29, 1886.

116. Frederick Goodhue. (93. George Barnard, 76. George, 33. Nathan, 27. William, 20. Nathanial, 14. Nathanial, 7. James, 2. James, 1. Thomas.) 2d s., 2d child of Rev. George Barnard Draper and Lucy Blake Goodhue, m. Nellie Price, Oct. 5, 1881. She was b. Dec, 1857.

CHILDREN:

E. 136. I. Helen Hersey, b. St. Paul, June 23, 1882. d. Aug. 26, 1883.

E. 137. II. Rachel Lilian, b. St. Paul, Nov. 23, 1886.

[Note] The Nos. 126 to 137 inclusive, were by mistake duplicated. The letter E. has therefore been placed against the children of 95. William Henry Draper, and 116. Frederick Goodhue Draper, as a distinguishing mark.

17. James. (7. James, 2. James, 1. Thomas.) 5th child, 3d s. of James Draper and Abigail Whiting, m. 1st: May 2, 1716, Rachel, dau. of John and Mary Aldis. She was b. Mar, 15, 1690. d. May 16, 1717. He m. 2dly: Nov. 12, 1719, Abigail, dau. of Joshua Child and Elizabeth Morris, of Brookline, Mass. She was b. 1698. d. Nov. 23, 1767. She was a sister of Dorothy, who m. (19) Ebenezer Draper.

"Nov. 14, 1734, Church West Roxbury voted the dismission of Eb. Draper, James Draper, and Abigail, his wife, to ye church in Dedham."

The reason James (17) and Ebenezer (19) left the house and ordinary at Baker Street, Roxbury, for Dedham, was want of room; the granite rocks on the one side, and the wet lands of Charles River on the other, limited their farming operations. They found in Green Lodge more room. Here they, with their cousin Jeremiah Whiting, who was a carpenter, removed and built each a house in style and character fully up to the time. They soon had their farms under way; in accordance, carrying on all branches of manufacture within themselves, each lending the other assistance, and, with their children, forming quite a flourishing village. Although some 13 miles from Boston, they sent to its market wood and charcoal and, in the summer, vegetables. The brothers kept four or five horses apiece, and carried the vegetables on horseback in panniers. The marketing was done by females, who often let themselves for the season. String and shell beans were an important article; it was not uncommon for them each to plant four or five acres. There were generally two persons at each place going on alternate days, it being considered too much for either person or animal to go on successive days without rest. Potatoes were considered too bulk)'to carry, except a few that were produced very early. Wood and charcoal were carried in ox carts, there being no wagons; they generally preferred to go in winter, and use sleds for coal and wood.

The records of Dedham show that on Dec. 19, 1733, a highway was authorized to be laid out from the country road, beginning at the former line between Dedham and Dorchester, and running by the house of Jeremiah Whiting, at Green Lodge, and the houses of (17) James and (19) Ebenezer Draper, towards Dedham Meeting House. Green Lodge was an outlying settlement, about 2 miles E. from Dedham, on the present Green Lodge Road, on the Neponset River. It was much nearer to Dedham than to Dorchester; and, consequently, in the annals of Dedham, under date of Nov. 29, 1732, (17) James Draper, Henry Crane, Robert Swan, (19) Ebenezer Draper, Jeremiah Whiting and Thomas Witherby, of Stoughton (in Dorchester), petitioned the General Court, setting forth the great difficulties in attending upon the public worship of God, as well as civil and military duties, by reason of the great distance to Dorchester, and prayed that they might be, with their families and estates, set off from Stoughton and annexed to Dedham,

This petition was granted, although Stoughton fought against it strongly.

Captain (17) James Draper had a negro servant, named Sharper Gulder, who was m. July 31, 1760, by the Rev. M. Tyler to Rozella Allen, a negro servant of Esther Fisher.

(17) James Draper was a Captain of the Trained Bands; was elected a Selectman in 1746, to serve one year, and again in 1756, to serve two years. He was a prosperous man, a large land owner, prominent in the affairs of the town of Dedham, and highly respected.

CHILD, BY 1ST WIFE:

126. I. John, b. Jan. 29, 1716. Bap. Mar. 10, 1717. d. Mar. 10, 1717.

CHILDREN, BY 2D WIFE:

127. II. James, b. Stoughton, Sep. 22, 1720. d. Spencer, Mar. 2, 1781.

128. III. Abigail, b. Stoughton, Dec. 12, 1721. d. Spencer, Nov. 3, 1817.

129. IV. John 2d, b. Stoughton, June 16, 1723. d. Dedham, Nov. 8, 1745. He went to Spencer in 1744, but his health was so bad that he returned to Dedham, where he died. (Unmarried.)

130. V. Joshua, b. Stoughton, Dec. 25, 1724. d. Spencer, Oct. 27, 1792.

131. VI. Josiah, b. Stoughton, Apr. 3, 1726. d. Aug. 18, 1726.

132. VII. Josiah 2d, b. Stoughton, Sep. 12, 1727,

133. VIII. Rebecca, b. Stoughton, June 30, 1729. d. Spencer, Jan. 30, 1820.

134. IX. Mary, b. Stoughton, Sep. 24, 1731,

135. X. Abijah, b. Dedham, July 13, 1734. d. Nov. 18, 1734,

136. XI. Abijah 2d, b. Dedham, July 11, 1735. d. Feb. 13, 1737.

137. XII. Abijah 3d, b. Dedham, May 10, 1737. d. Dedham, May 1, 1780.

138. XIII. Samuel, b. Dedham, Dec. 5, 1740. d. Nov. 29, 1750.

VZ^. James. (17. James, 7. James, 2. James, 1. Thomas.) 2d s., 2d child of James Draper and his 2d wife Abigail Child, m. 1st: by Rev. Samuel Dexter, Mehetable Whiting, Nov. 1, 1743. She was b. 1719. d. July 18, 1763. He m. 2dly: Mrs. Martha (Burnett) Ward, widow of William Ward, of Southboro. She d. Mar., 1791, leaving no issue.

He went from his father's place at Green Lodge, Dedham, shortly after his first marriage in 1743, to Spencer. He owned there the east parts of lots 33 and 34, now owned by Amos Kitteridge. He was elected to the office of Captain of the Trained Band of Spencer, which, however, he declined to accept. Selectman in 1757-63-70-71-73. Assessor, 1756-61-62-63-67.

CHILDREN, BY MEHETABLE, ALL B. IN SPENCER:

139. I. Rebecca, b. May 2, 1743. m. Nov. 1, 1768, Benjamin, s. of Samuel Bemis and Rebecca Newhall, of Spencer. Col. Bemis was a patriot of the Revolution; a member of the Committee of Correspondence and Safety for the year 1780; Assessor, 1785; Town Clerk, 1781, 1782, 1786; Selectman, 1784, 1785, 1786. He and his wife both d. at Worcester, Mass. Children: — I. Mary, 144. b. Jan. 24, 1770. m. her cousin, Simeon Draper (339), of Spencer. II. Mehetable, 145. b. Nov. 12, 1772. m. Dr. Hamilton, of Dublin, N. H., and was killed by being thrown out of a carriage. III. Rebecca, 146. b. Aug. 17, 1774. m. Joshua Patch, of Worcester. IV. Martha, 147. b. Apr. 13, 1777. m. Mr. Ward, of Canandaigua, N. Y. V. Reuben, 148. b. Aug. 25, 1779. d. W. Springfield (had two wives). VI. Benjamin, 149. b. July 5, 1781. m. a Miss Hitchcock. Was a physician, and d. in Brookfield, Mass. VII. James Draper, 150. b. July 1, 1783. Was m., and went to Canandaigua, N. Y. He was a bookseller and editor of a paper; accumulated considerable property, became insane, and d. in the insane asylum at Utica, N. Y.

140. II. John, b. Nov. 6, 1745. d. Dec. 20, 1822.

141. III. James, b. July 24, 1747. d. Aug. 29, 1825.

142. IV. Ira, b. Feb. 14, 1753. d. young; scalded to death by a kettle of boiling water falling on him.

143. V. Mehetable, b. Aug. 29, 1756. m. Noah Forbush, of Brookfield. He d. in 1824, leaving no children. She was blind several years before her death.

140. John. (127. James, 17. James, 7. James, 2. James, 1. Thomas.) 2d s., 2d child of James Draper and his first wife, Mehetable Whiting, m. Rebecca, dau. of Deacon John Muzzy, Dec. 24, 1770. She was b. Spencer, June 24, 1750. d. Apr. 29, 1818. He was a Captain in the Militia and a celebrated auctioneer. Was 1st Sergt. of Capt. David Prouty's Co., Maj. Asa Baldwin's Div. of Militia of Worcester Co., Mass., that marched to reinforce the Northern Army by order of Council, Sept. 22, 1777.

CHILDREN:

151. I. Zenas, b. May 31, 1772. d. Jan. 9, 1853.

152. II. Olive, b. Jan. 30, 1774. d. Mar. 23, 1858. m. Nov. 10, 1791, Elias, s. of Stephen and Ruth Hatch. He was b. Hanover, Mass., Aug. 29, 1769, and was a Captain in the Cavalry, d. Albany, N. Y. Olive went to the Shakers, at Shirley. Children: — I. Lucy, 162. b. Oct. 24, 1792. d. Mar. 31, 1806. II. Cheeney, 163. b. Apr. 3, 1795. III. Dwight, 164. b. Aug. 2, 1797. IV. Nancy, 165. b. Jan. 11, 1802. V. Sophia, 166. b. Mar. 29, 1804. VI. William, 167. b. Apr. 11, 1805. VII. Olive, 168. b. Sep. 5, 1806. VIII. John, 169. b. Jan. 21, 1816.

153. III. Ethan, b. Feb. 4, 1776. d. Aug. 24, 1778.

154. IV. Reuel, b. Dec. 28, 1777. d. Aug. 27, 1778.

155. V. Sarah, b. Aug. 8, 1779. d. May 27, 1855. m. 1798, Jacob, s. of John Biscoe and Deborah Prouty. He was b. June 12, 1772. d. Apr. 7, 1837. Children: — I. Dwight, 170. b. Apr. 27, 1799. Has been a representative to the General Court for the Town of Leicester several times. II. Chloe, 171. b. Aug. 30, 1800. m. Spencer Prouty, Aug., 1818. III. Adeline, 172. b. Nov. 16, 1801. m. Abiathar Johnson, 1826. IV. Forster, 173. b. July 16, 1803. m. Eunice W. Rice, 1830. V. Emily, 174. b. Sep. 10, 1804. m. Liberty Pound, Apr. 12, 1837. VI. Alden, 175. b. Oct. 25, 1806. VII. John, 176. b. Oct. 9, 1808. VIII. Hull, 177. b. Nov. 10, 1810. IX. Roswell, 178. b. Apr. 16, 1813. m. Abigail Whittemore, Aug. 4, 1838. X. Lavinia, 179. b. Aug. 16, 1815. m. Reuben B. Hill, May 10, 1839. XI. Jacob, 180. b. Oct. 8, 1817.

156. VI. Chloe, b. Nov. 18, 1781. d. June 20, 1864. m. Thomas, s. of Nathanial T. and Sarah Watson Loring, Sep. 27, 1803. He was b. Apr. 5, 1779. d. May 10, 1805. She was his 2d wife, and, after his death, went to the Shakers in Shirley. Child: — I. Lucious, 181, who d. in Oakham.

157. VII. Nancy, b. Oct. 28, 1783. d. Sept. 6, 1874. m. Samuel Gleason, Feb. 3, 1811. (No issue.)

158. VIII. Becca, b. Apr. 10, 1786. d. July 6, 1860, m. Jan. 18, 1807, Willard, s. of Isaac Prouty and Anna Bunnell. He was born May 4, 1786. d. by suicide, Jan. 5, 1834. His widow went to the Shakers at Shirley. Children: — I. Isaac Warner, 182. b. Oct. 6, 1800. II. Harriet Amelia, 183. b. Dec. 12, 1809. She went with her mother to the Shakers.

159. IX. John, b. July 22, 1788. d. May, 1877. "iDec. 4, 1817, Lovinia, dau. of Eli Prouty and Rebecca Bemis. She was b. Aug. 11, 1796. He went to the town of Spencer, Ohio.

160. X. Rhoda, b. July 10, 1791. d. Nov. 9, 1859. m. Apr. 3, 1817, Ebenezer Cogswell, and went to live in Leicester. Children: — I. Sophia, b. Aug. 14, 1818. II. John Draper, b. May 21, 1820. m. Sept. 22, 1845, Fanny Harriet Leonard, of Windhall, Vt. She was b. Aug. 30, 1822. (Children:— I. Louisa Maria, b. July 15, 1846. m. June 10, 1869, Edwin Lucius Watson. He was b. Jan. 22, 1841. Child: — Walter Cogswell, b. May 21, 1870. II. John Walter, b. Dec. 1, 1848. d. Aug. 27, 1849. III. Fanny Sophia, b. May 22, 1851. d. Oct, 5, 1851.)

III. Nancy, b. Mar. 19. 1822. d. Mar. 2, 1872. IV. Harriet Amelia, b. Nov. 10, 1827. d. Feb. 19, 1856. V. Cheney Hatch, b. Nov. 5, 1831. d. Aug. 19, 1837.

161. XI. Eleazar Bradshaw, b. Aug. 26, 1795. d. Feb. 21, 1849.

151. Zenas. (140. John, 127. James, 17. James, 7. James, 2. James, 1. Thomas.) Eldest s. and child of John Draper and Rebecca Muzzy, m. Jemima, dau. of Israel and Thankful Allen. She was b. Shrewsbury, April 22, 1773. d. Jan. 19, 1846.

CHILDREN:

184. I. Alpha, b. Dec. 13, 1797d. June 23, 1846.

185. II. Julia, b. Nov. 12, 1800. d. Aug. 7, 1865. m. Spencer Prouty. Child:— I. Chloe, 193. b. Spencer, Oct. 24, 1826. m. May 21, 1844, Henry H. Sparks, of N. Brookfield. She d. Nov. 8, 1860.

186. III. Lura, b. Nov. 19, 1802. d. Apr. 2, 1831.

187. IV. Roxana, b. Dec. 28, 1804. m. Silas Groat, Apr. 24, 1823. She d. Apr. 17, 1846, and he m. her younger sister Eliza, 190.

188. V. William Allen, b. Dec. 28, 1806. d. May 25, 1855.

189. VI. Edwin, b. Jan. 20, 1809. d. Worcester, Mar. 29, 1866.

190. VII. Eliza, b. Apr. 5, 1811. m. her sister Roxana's widower, d. Oct. 18, 1869.

191. VIII. Nancy, b. May 5, 1813. d. Aug. 10, 1854. m. Oct. 30, 1834, Sumner, s. of Martin and Maria Bridges. He was b. Jan. 4, 1813. d. Nov. 19, 1887. Children (b. in Greenville, Mass.):— I. Lyman, 194. b. Jan. 15, 1836. m. Anna Osgood. II. Francis, 195. b. Apr. 7, 1838. m. 1868, Chicago, Ill., Mary S., dau. of Dr. Timothy Eastman, of Eastmanville, Mich. (Children -.—I. Robert Sumner, 197. b. July 22,1870. d. Aug. 5, 1871. II. Francis Eastman, 198. b. Jan. 15, 1872. III. Lyman Albert, 199. b. May 27, 1881.) Mr. Francis Bridges served in the Rebellion honorably for 4 years and 9 months. In Sept., 1861, he enlisted in the 25th Mass. Regt. under Col. Upton, and was in the "Burnside Expedition." Was subsequently 1st Lieut. in the 20th U. S. Colored Infantry, and was stationed at New Orleans until the close of the war. After the war he located in Chicago, In 1879 removed to California. III. Ann Eliza, 196. b. Mar. 17, 1840. m. Albert Anderson Gordon, Jan. 6, 1861.

192. IX. Rebecca, b. May 6, 1815. m. May 3, 1836, Timothy P., s. of Deacon Nathan Rockwood and Elizabeth Newton, d. Dec. 4, 1878. Children (b. Leicester, Mass.):— I. Cornelia Elizabeth, 200. b. Apr. 12, 1838. m. Worcester, Mass., July 16, 1861, John G. Brady. He was b. Norwich, Conn., Oct. 28, 1833. (Child:— I. Winifred Barton, 204. b. Worcester, Mass., Dec. 31, 1862. d. Aug. 6, 1863.) II. Edward Payson, 201. b. Oct. 28, 1840. d. Dec. 26, 1868 (unmarried). III. Mary Eliza, 202. b. Dec. 26, 1846. d. Dec. 26, 1868 (unmarried). IV. Louisa Maria, 203. b. Mar. 16, 1850. d. Dec. 9, 1884. m. Worcester, Mass., Jan. 8, 1878, Mirick H., s. of John Cowden and Dorinda D. Hubbard. He was a lawyer and b. Aug. 7. 1845, Rutland, Mass.

184. Alpha. (151. Zenas, 140. John, 127. James, 17. James, 7. James, 2. James, 1. Thomas.) Eldest s. and child of Zenas Draper and Jemima Allen, m.

Dec. 14. 1822, Lucia, dau. of J. Parker and Eunice Rice, of Brookfield. She d. Jan. 26, 1842.

CHILDREN, ALL B. N. BROOKFIELD, MASS.:

205. I. John Alonzo, b. July 27, 1824.

206. II. William Edwin, b. Feb. 24, 1827. d. Mar. 10, 1851.

207. III. Lucia Maria, b. June 7, 1829. d. Feb. 12, 1856. m. Ezra D. Batcheller, N. Brookfield, Apr. 2, 1851. Child:— I. Emma Lucia, b. Mar. 14, 1852. d. Worcester, May 5, 1857.

208. IV. Laura Alzena, b. Dec. 15, 1830. m. Henry, s. of Benjamin Belcher and Temperance Wilbur, of Spencer, Sep. 17, 1869.

209. V. Mary Eliza, b. Mar. 1, 1833. d. N. Brookfield, July 10, 1868. m. Nathanial H., s. of James Forster and Nancy Henry Jan. 17, 1855. Children: — I. Mary Lucia, 212. b. N. Brookfield, Oct. 23, 1855. d. N. Brookfield, Sep. 5, 1882. II. Addie Lione, 213. b. Nov. 22, 1859. m. June 12, 1888, Albert Wood Poland, d. Jan. 5, 1891.

210. VI. George Oscar, b. June 3, 1835. d. May 7, 1855.

211. VII. Henry Parker, b. July 5, 1838. m. Mary Ann, dau. of Joel Wilson and Annie Howe, May 24, 1865. Children: — I. Warren Alpha, 214. b. Jan. 13, 1869. II. Anna Lucia, 215. b. Mar. 9, 1870.

205. John Alonzo. (184. Alpha, 151. Zenas, 140. John, 127. James, 17. James, 7. James, 2. James, 1. Thomas.) Eldest s. and child of Alpha Draper and Lucia Parker, m. Nov. 12, 1860, Charlestown, Mass., Elsie, dau. of John Wilbur and Mary Sumner of Akron, O. She was b. Sep. 4, 1841.

CHILDREN:

216. I. Alice Maria, b. Feb. 25, 1864.

217. II. Gertrude Louise, b. July 18, 1865. m. July 4, 1891, Henry P., s. of Edwin Hamburg, of Spencer.

218. III. William Henry, b. Apr. 1, 1867. m. Nov. 26, 1890, Fannie M. Hinkley, of Barre, Mass.

219. IV, Mary Elsie, b. Oct. 3, 1872.

220. V. Walter Elmar, b. July 1, 1874.

188. William Allen. (151. Zenas, 140. John, 127. James, 17. James, 7. James, 2. James, 1. Thomas.) 5th child, 2d s. of Zenas Draper and Jemima Allen, m. Nov. 26, 1833, Calista A. Watson, of Leicester.

Mr. Draper was engaged in the manufacture of boots and shoes in Spencer, Mass., until the year 1838, when he removed his business to Worcester and continued there until 1853. He was active in public affairs and was a member of the first Board of Aldermen of Worcester when it was incorporated as a city. He had a strong taste for horticulture, and aided much in advancing the interests of the Worcester Horticultural Society. He was one of the founders of the Union Congregational Society, and remained a member of it until his death. He was also an officer of various financial institutions in that city.

CHILDREN:

221. I. William, b. Jan. 16, 1835.

222. II. Ann Eliza, b. Feb. 20, 1837, d. Jan. 5, 1869. m. May 5, 1859, George Hunger, of Bridgeport, Conn.

223. III. Sophia Amelia, b. Jan. 18, 1840. d. Worcester, Mass., Sep. 2, 1875.

224. IV. James, b. Aug. 31, 1842.

225. V. Maria Calista, b. Feb. 12, 1846. m. Sep. 26, 1871, George Munger, of Bridgeport, Conn. d. Dec, 22, 1880, Bridgeport, Conn.

226. VI. Sophia Caroline, b. Oct. 21, 1847. m. Oct. 26, 1865, John T. Richardson, of Delphi, Ind. He d. Oct. 7, 1880.

227. VII. Lizzie Jane, b. Aug. 17, 1851. d. Jan. 25, 1877.

221. William. (188. William Allen, 151. Zenas, 140. John, 127. James, 17. James, 7. James, 2. James, 1. Thomas.) Eldest child and s. of William Allen Draper and Calista A. Watson, m. Dec. 6, 1858, Helen Mary, dau. of Aquila Jones and Mary Ann Sweet, of Fleming Co., Ky.

CHILDREN, B. DELPHI, IND.:

228. I. William Aquila, b. Oct. 22, 1859. Killed accidentally out hunting Mar. 30, 1874.

229. II. Mary Amelia, b. July 12, 1861. m. Jan. 25, 1882, William Bradford, s. of William Barton Price and Susanna Merwin Clark. Child:— I. Helen Merwin, 235. b. Sep. 22, 1884.

230. III. Sara Sylvia, b. Feb. 9, 1864. d. Nov. 28, 1864.

231. IV. Jessie Helen, b. Oct. 23, 1865. m. Sep. 23, 1887, Edward E., s. of Andrew Jackson Yeoman and Lydia A. Shull. Child:— I. Bessie, 236. b. Aug. 21, 1888.

232. V. Anna Blanchard Caroline, b. June 25, 1868. (She is a school teacher.)

233. VI. Winifred Josephine, b. Apr. 5, 1871.

234. VII. George Ernest, b. Remington, Ind., Nov. 5, 1874. d. there Nov. 29, 1874.

224. James. (188. William Allen, 151. Zenas, 140. John, 127. James, 17. James, 7. James, 2. James, 1. Thomas.) 4th child, 2d s. of William Allen Draper and Calista A. Watson, m. Sep. 20, 1866, Josie C. Deane, of Fall River, R. I.

He was educated in the Worcester schools, and when 12 years old his father died. His inclinations led him early to look to the soil for his maintenance, and when but 18 he began business as a market gardener, supplying customers in the city with vegetables and milk. He had at his command a farm of about 15 acres, and his trade increasing, he devoted 5 or 6 of them to the raising of vegetables. Through the large profit derived from a small bed of strawberries his attention was turned to the raising of berries of various kinds for the market, and he was so successful in this that people came to him for plants from great distances. This opened a way of enlarging his business, and in 1867, he issued his first catalogue, advertising to sell plants, and from this has grown the Bloomingdale Nurseries which have more than local fame. In 1874, he established his drain pipe works, and in 1889, he added a department for the manufacture of artificial stone vases. He has served as a member of the Worcester Parks Commission for 4 years, and during this time has done valuable work. Lake Park and East Park have been his special province, and his practical knowledge has been a most important feature in their development. Mr. Draper accepted the office of Parks Commissioner because he saw in it an opportunity to serve the city in a better way than he might have done in other capacities, although he has been a member of the School Board from 1872 to 1875. He also served three terms as a member of the Board of Overseers of the Poor. In 1872, the Worcester Grange of the Patrons of Husbandry was organized, the second in the country. Mr. Draper became its Master. He held that office for 3 years, and later rose from Secretary to be Master of the State Grange, holding the position 8 years. While Master of the State Grange he was elected an Overseer of the National Grange, and, owing to the death of its Master, Mr. Draper became during the year 1880 the head of this powerful farmers' organization. He has been very prominently connected with the Worcester Horticultural Society, and is a Trustee of the Worcester Agricultural Society, the Massachusetts Agricultural College and a member of the Board of Management of the Hatch Experiment Station. Mr. Draper is a member of Morning Star Lodge, F. & A. M., which he joined in 1862, and is also identified with Worcester County Commandery, Knights Templar and Eureka Chapter, Royal Arch. He was one of the pioneers of narrow gauge railroad building in this country, the Worcester & Shrewsbury R. R. being the second narrow gauge road built. He was the first Superintendent of the road. When Plymouth Church was formed, he was one of the original members and has remained with it ever since. He was also one of the promoters of the Y. M. C. A.

CHILDREN, ALL B. WORCESTER:

237. I. Alice Gertrude, b. Dec. 29, 1868.
238. 11. Effie Blanche, b. July 1, 1870.
239. III. Lizette Marie, b. June 26, 1872.
240. IV. Sophie Anna, b. Nov. 13, 1878.
241. V. Sylvia Louise, b. Sep. 28, 1881.
242. VI. James Edwin, b. Aug. 24, 1886.

189. Edwin. (151. Zenas, 140. John, 127. James, 17. James, 7. James, 2. James, 1. Thomas.) 6th child, 3d s. of Zenas Draper and Jemima Allen, m. 1st: Johnstown, N.Y., Mar. 15, 1838, Abigail, dau. of Benjamin Richardson and Juditii Mason. She d. Aug. 1, 1844. He m. 2dly: Sep. 16, 1845, Harriet Porter, dau. of Jeremiah Healy and Elizabeth Porter, of Worcester. She was b. July 16, 1819. d. Harvard, Mass., Nov. 21, 1883.

Mr. Draper's business was that of a wholesale dealer in flour and grain. He was prominently identified in city as well as State affairs, having served in all the branches of the City Government, and been a member of the House of Representatives. He was a pronounced and aggressive Prohibitionist. He was an enthusiastic horticulturist and a member of the Horticultural Society. He was all his life a member of the Salem Street Congregational Society.

CHILDREN BY 1ST MARRIAGE, ALL B. WORCESTER:

243. I. Julia Ann, b. July 19, 1841. d. Feb. 19, 1842.

244. II. Edwin R., b. June 2, 1844. d. Aug. 2, 1844.

CHILDREN BY 2D MARRIAGE:

245. III. Abby Eliza, b. Jan. 16, 1847. d. July 2, 1848.

246. IV. Albert J., b. June 30, 1849. d. Oct. 23, 1854.

247. V. Eliza, b. Nov. 7, 1850, Worcester, m. June 7, 1882, Dr. Joseph H., s. of Joseph Robinson and Emmarilla Hewitt, of Harvard, Mass. He was b. Stonington, Conn., Jan. 28, 1840. Child: — I. Edwin Draper, 249. b. Worcester, July 7, 1887.

248. VI. Henry A., b. Sep. 26, 1853. d. Nov. 23, 1855.

161. Eleazar Bradshaw. (140. John, 127. James, 17. James, 7. James, 2. James, 1. Thomas.) Youngest child and s. of John Draper and Rebecca Muzzy, m. May 15, 1 82 1, Louisa, dau. of Reuben Prouty and Sally Bartlet, of Spencer. She was b. Apr. 7, 1802.

Mr. Draper was postmaster of Spencer, and kept the famous Jenks Tavern. He was Town Clerk in 1842, 1843, 1844, 1845. Selectman, 1839, 1840, 1841. Representative to the General Court, 1839, 1840, 1841, 1845.

CHILDREN, B. SPENCER:

250. 1, Albert Manly, b. July 3, 1822. d. Dec. 9, 1846. m. Clarinda, dau. of Otis Watson and Harriet Snow. She was b. Jan. 1, 1819.

251. II. Mary Lucinia, b. June, 1825. m. William L. Powers.

252. III. Dwight D., b. June 22, 1828. m. Lydia Ann, dau. of Wilbur Howland and Augusta Marsh, of Spencer, 1849. She was b. Apr., 1828.

253. IV. Chloe L., b. Sep. 9, 1829. m. Benjamin F. Cheever, 1849.

254. V. John, b. Aug. 31, 1831. d. Feb. 27, 1853.

255. VI. George S., b. Aug. 4, 1833. d. Apr. 18, 1854.

256. VII. Harriet J., b. July 10, 1834. d. Oct. 10, 1837.

257, VIII. Lorenzo, b, Nov. 21, 1838.

258. IX. Sophia E., b. Aug. 6, 1840. d. Aug. 28, 1841.

141. James. (127. James, 17. James, 7. James, 2. James, 1. Thomas.) 3d child, 2d s, of James Draper and Mehetable Whiting, m. May 31, 1769, Mary, dau. of David Prouty and Elizabeth Smith. She was b. May 21, 1745. d. Dec. 22, 1819. He was drummer of Capt. David Prouty's Co., Maj. Asa Baldwin's Div. of Militia, Col. Saml. Deming's Regmt., of Worcester Co., Mass., that marched to reinforce the Northern Army, by order of Council, Sept. 22, 1777.

CHILDREN, ALL B. IN SPENCER:

259. I. David, b. July 3, 1770. d. Apr. 30, 1845. m. July 7, 1799, Matilda Moore. She d. Leicester, Aug. 24, 1854, aged 76. He was, for two years, a student at Williams College. Assessor in 1814, 1815, 1818, 1819. Town Clerk,

1820, 1821, and Deputy Sheriff. Children (b. in Spencer): — I. John M., 270. b. Sep. 26, 1800. II, Harriet, 271. b. June 5, 1802. III. Charlotte, 272. b. Dec. 28, 1805. IV. Angelina, 273, b. Sep. 14, 1814.

260. II, Betsey, b. Feb. 19, 1772. d. Dec. 29, 1846. m. Joseph, s. of Isaac Prouty and Priscilla Ramsdell. He was b. Mar. 26, 1767. d. June 19, 1829. Children: — I. Philinda, 274. b. Sep. 29, 1792. m. Jabez Bigelow. d. Apr. 29, 1854. II. Calvin, 275. b. Nov. 5, 1793. d. Mar. 7, 1808. III. Emelia, 276. b. Jan. 7, 1796. m. Edmund Newton, Dec. 5, 1827. IV. Horace, 277. b. Apr. 5, 1798. d. by drowning, July 8, 1815. V. Charles, b. May 7, 1800. VI. Cyrus, 278. b. Sep. 14, 1802. m. Mary Ann Bride, May 12, 1827. d. by suicide. May 11, 1851. VII. Elmira, 279. b. Aug. 2, 1804. m. Joshua E. Goodell, Aug. 25, 1825. VIII. Luther, 280. b. July 18, 1806. d. Dec. 12, 1807. IX. Calvin Luther, 281. b. Mar. 16, 1808. Alden. b. Nov. 10, 1810. d. by drowning, Aug. 17, 1811. X. Mary Draper, 282. b. Feb. 2, 1813. XI. Betsy, 283. b. Aug. 19, 1816. m. Winthrop Prouty. XII. Joseph Horace, 284. b. Aug. 13, 1818.

261. III. Martha, b. Nov. 17, 1773. d. Sep. 14, 1778.

262. IV. Mary, b. Dec. 12, 1775. d. Sep. 15, 1778,

263. V. James, b. Feb. 25, 1776. d. Oct. 28, 1868.

264. VI. Ira, b. Jan. 15, 1780. d. May 1, 1780.

265. VII. Ira 2d, b. Apr. 1, 1781. d. Feb. 9, 186r.

266. VIII. Martha 2d, b. Mar. 10, 1783. m. Dec. 27, 1801, Joseph Wilson.

Children (b. Spencer): — I. Laura, 285. b. Oct. 11, 1802. II. Sewall, 286. b. June 15, 1805. III. Joel, 287. b. Oct. 11, 1811. IV. Lavinia, 288. b. Feb. 11, 1815. V. Martha Draper, 289. b. Feb. 7, 1818. VI. Mary Jane, 290. b. Sep. 30, 1821. VII. Samuel Austin, 291. b. Mar. 11, 1826.

267. IX. Mary 2d & 268. X. Sarah (Twins) b. June 7, 1785Mary 2d d. Apr. 14, 1854.

Mary 2d, 267. m. Oct. n, 1807. Pliny, s. of John Muzzy and Mary Ball. Captain Muzzy was a captain in the militia. He removed to Pennsylvania, where he was a Justice of the Peace, Nov 18 1846. Children (b. in Spencer):— I. Edwin Augustus, 292. b. Apr. 7, 1808. II. Mary Ann. b. Nov. 26, 1809. III. Lorenzo, 293. b Oct 25, 1811, d. Wisconsin. IV. Lucinda, 294. b. August 18, 1813 V. Emmeline, 295. b. Sep. 27, 1815. d. Oct. 7. 1815. VI. lames Draper, 296. b. Mar. 1, 1817. VII. Mehetable, 297. b. Feb. 22, 1819. VIII. Pliny Dwight, 298. b. July 8, 1821. IX. John Bradshaw, 299. b. June 18, 1824.

Sarah, 268. m. Mar. 14, 1813, Stephen, s. of Sylvanus Gates and Elizabeth Graham. Children:— I. Harrison, 300. b. Aug. 25, 1813. II James Draper, 301. b. Mar. 15, 1815HI. Sarah. 302. b. Oct. 16 1816 IV. Sylvanus Howe, 303b. May 27, 1818. V. David Draper 304. b. June 4, 1820. VI. Charles Addison, 305. b. Oct. 30 1823 VII. Joel Prouty, 306. b. May 27, 1825. VIII. Mary Elizabeth, 307. b. May 21, 1829. IX. Lucy Ann, 308. b. Feb. 23, 1831.

269. XI. Mehetable, b. 1788. m. 1st: Charles Lyon, May 1, 1808. Children: I. Mary Prouty, 309. b. Oct. 10. 1808. II. Angeline, 310. b. July 19. 1810. She m. 2dly: James S., s. of John Bigelow and Persis Wright Feb 28, 1819. Lived in

Leicester. Children:— III. Julia Ann"3i'i. b. June 13, 1821. IV. Samuel Barker, 312. b. Aug. 18, 1824.' V. James E., 313. b. May 12. 1826. VI. Alfred, 314. b. June 21. 1828. VIL John H., 315. b. July 12, 1829. VIII. Albert, 316. b. Jan. 7, 1832.

263. JAMES. (141. James, 127. James, 17. James, 7. James, 2. James, 1. Thomas) 5th child, 2d s. of lames Draper and Mary Prouty. m. Lucy dau of Captain Samuel Watson, of Leicester. June 6, 1805. She was b. Jan. 28, 1788. d. July 7, 1848.

Mr. Draper received a farm from his father, and cultivated it as his principal means of subsistence until he was thirty. Having been born in the stirring times of the American Revolution, when the ravages of war had so impoverished the whole country that the great mass of the people were obliged to toil and struggle hard to obtain the bare necessities of life, the means of obtaining even a common school education w re exceedingly limited. He possessed a strong and unconquerable desire for the acquisition of knowledge, and. during the years of his early manhood, by diligently improving his leisure moments, he finally qualified himself for the position of a teacher, and, in the Winter of 1797, began to teach, cultivating his farm in the Summer; which he continued for II years. Possessing a taste for music, he occupied his Winter evenings during this time in teaching the young people of the vicinity music. In 1808, finding that farming was little to his taste and not profitable, he engaged in mercantile pursuits, and also kept a tavern in Spencer. These two callings he followed for 14 years. In 1810 he received from Governor Gore a commission as Justice of the Peace, which office he held for 50 years. During that time he sat and presided on trials in 1,032 civil and criminal cases. He has joined many couples in marriage, written many wills, innumerable deeds, leases, etc. Between the years 1813 and 1837 he was a member of the Massachusetts Legislature 12 times, and was a Senator in 1831 and 1832. In 1820 he was a member of the Constitutional Convention. In 1832 he was appointed, by Governor Lincoln, County Commissioner for Worcester Co., which office he held for 3½ years. In 1837 Governor Everett appointed him chairman of the commission to visit and advise as to the disposition to be made of the unincorporated lands of the State. He served his native town of Spencer in the capacities of Town Clerk, Selectman, Assessor, Treasurer, Overseer of the Poor, and Town Agent. He was also a surveyor of land for a number of years. As executor, administrator, etc., he investigated and finally settled 66 estates of deceased or insolvent persons. He has also investigated the claims of many U.S. pensioners, and obtained pensions and lands to which the claimants were entitled. In 1856 he was Assistant Marshal in taking the census. In 1841 he wrote and published the History of Spencer, and 20 years later rewrote and revised the same. It is but justice to him to say that, in all the important positions he has been placed in during a long and active life, he discharged his duties faithfully and with singular ability, and won for himself the entire confidence and respect of his fellow men to the day of his death.

[The author of this History is indebted to the notes and publications left by the Hon. James Draper for many valuable points and suggestions made use of in this work.

CHILDREN, B. IN SPENCER:

317. I. Emmeline, b. Apr. 6, 1806. m. June 21, 1830, William, s. of Peter Rice. d. Gloucester, Mass., Sep. 4, 1854.

318. II. Julia Ann, b. June 22, 1808. m. July 12, 1832, J. Ellis Lazell. On his death, she m. 2dly: May 12, 1840, Chandler Mason Pratt, of Grafton. She d. Grafton, Mar. 25, 1841.

319. III. Sophia Amelia, b. May 4, 1811, m. Sep. 24, 1838, Moores Mirick White.

320. IV. Lucy Watson, b. Dec. 17, 1813. m. Dec. 25, 1837, Emory Rider.

265. Ira. (141. James, 127. James, 17. James, 7. James, 2. James, 1. Thomas.) 7th child, 4th s. of James Draper and Mary Prouty. m. Dec. 27, 1801, Sarah Hammond, of Oakham.

CHILDREN:

321. I. Fidelia, b. Sep. 9, 1802 (.?). m. Boston, Aug. 25, 1833, Joseph D. Phillips.

322. II. Elijah Hammond, b. July 10, 1803.

323. III. Octavia, b. Oct. 8, 1807 (?). m. Boston, Sep., 1830, Sylvester Stover, of York, Me.

324. IV. Sarah C, b. Apr. 12, 1812.

325. V. James P., b. Aug. 21, 1814.

326. VI. Aurelia H., b. Aug. 14, 1818 (?). m. Boston, Nov., 1841, Francis Herrington.

128, Abigail. (17. James, 7. James, 2. James, 1. Thomas.) Eldest dau. 2d child of James Draper and his 2d wife Abigail Child, m. 1st, Sep. 30, 1741, by Rev. Samuel Dexter, at Dedham, Henry White. They removed to Spencer soon after their marriage, where he d. in 1748. He owned the northern part of Lot 79 in the latter town. She m., 2dly, Major Asa, s. of David Baldwin, of Spencer, Mar. 7, 1750. Major Baldwin was a member of the Committee of Correspondence and Safety, an officer in the War of the Revolution and a Major in the Militia; Selectman, 1754, 57-59-63-64-65-67-68-69-71; Assessor, 1754, 56-62-66.

CHILDREN BY 1ST MARRIAGE:

327. I. Rebecca, b. Dec. 11, 1741, m. Apr. 28, 1763, John Worcester.

328. II. William, b. May 27, 1744, m. May 12, 1768, Esther Lynde. Was a Deacon, and a Major in the Militia.

329. III. Abigail, b. Apr. 4, 1747. m. May 21, 1767, Johnson Lynde.

CHILDREN BY 2D MARRIAGE:

330. IV. Ruth, b. Apr. 8, 1751. m. Jan. 28, 1773, Samuel Watson, of Leicester.

331. V. Chloe, b. Oct. 12, 1755. m. May 4, 1779, James Sprague.

332. VI. Olive, b. May 15, 1758. m. Nov. 12, 1778, Peter Rice.

333. VII. Lucy, b. July 10, 1760. m. Oct. 19, 1786, Phineas Jones.

130. Joshua. (17. James, 7. James, 2. James, 1. Thomas.) 4th child and 3d s. of James Draper, 3d, and his 2d wife Abigail Child, b. Dorchester, Mass., Dec. 25, 1724. d. Spencer, Mass., Oct. 27, 1792. m. 1st, by Rev. Samuel Dexter, at Dedham, Mass., Apr. 14, 1748, Abigail Fairbanks, who d. Feb. 17, 1762. He m. 2d, the widow, Sarah Wright, of Brookfield, Mass., who d. Apr. 12, 1820. Joshua was one of four children of James, 17, who went from Dedham to Spencer. He was a member of the Revolutionary Committee of Correspondence for the year 1777; Assessor from 1765 to 1771; and was considered, for those times, to be a rich man.

CHILDREN BY 1ST WIFE:

334. I. Joshua, b. May 25, 1749. d. May 12, 1839, Westford, N. Y.

335. II. Sarah, b. Mar. 19, 1751.

336. III. Samuel, b. May 8, 1752. m. his cousin, Millie, 711, dau. of Josiah Draper, 132, of Attleboro. (See Attleboro branch.)

337. IV. Abigail, b. May 2, 1756. (Unmarried.)

CHILDREN BY 2D WIFE:

338. V. Asa, b. Mar. 11, 1763.

339. VI. Simeon, b. Mar. 27, 1765.

340. VII. Ira, b. Feb. 18, 1767. Went to sea and was never heard of after.

341. VIII. Joel, b. June 18, 1769. d. unmarried, in Otsego, N. Y.

342. IX. William, b. Dec. 9, 1771. d. Dec. 30, 1845.

334. Joshua. (130. Joshua, 17. James, 7. James, 2. James, 1. Thomas.) Eldest s. and child of Joshua Draper and Abigail Fairbanks, m. Mary Pratt, Aug. 5, 1773. She was b. Hanover, Mass., Jan. 28, 1750, and d. of consumption Sep. 1, 1823. Joshua lived for many years in Chester, Mass. He was one of the Revolutionary patriots who helped to achieve his country's independence. The magnetic thrill which was sent through the land by the news of the battles of Concord and Lexington, aroused him, and leaving family and all he had, he was soon in the ranks at almost the beginning of the struggle. He was a private in Capt. Benj. Richardson's Co. from Spencer, Col. Nicholas Dikes' Regiment. He was at the Battle of Bunker Hill, at the Relief of Dorchester, Sep., 1776, and the family still possess the ancient musket which he carried on that occasion. His services were rewarded for many years prior to his death by a Government pension. A few years after the war he migrated with his family from Massachusetts to New York, and settled in Westford, Otsego Co. That section, then called Cherry Valley, was an unsettled wilderness, but with his ax and the help of his sons, he cleared a quantity of land and built a comfortable home in the wild forest. That location was at the foot of a hill in the town of Westford, which still bears his name. The tales of hardship, distress and suffering which the early settlers were doomed to encounter in the wilderness from toil, cold, famine, wild beasts and savages, are recalled on many pages of the history of the county. Only one instance can be mentioned here of the hardships through which he was forced to go. At the time of his settlement in this wild region there was no grist mill nearer than the village of Cherry Valley, twelve miles distant, and it was upon this mill alone that his family depended for flour and meal. He had to go the entire distance on foot, with a bag of corn or wheat on his back, returning with the bag of meal or flour. He was obliged to take the journey on foot, because at that time the country was a dense forest, through which it was impossible for a horse to pass. His family was broken up, in 1823, by the death of his wife, after which he lived with his son Sylvester in the old homestead.

CHILDREN:

343. I. Bethuel, b. Aug. 27, 1774. d. Mar. 25, 1814.

344. II. Lucy, b. Jan. 22, 1776. m. Asa Bidlake, and d. Nov. 9, 1811. Children: — I. Eunice, 355. II. James, 356. III. Lucy, 357.

345. III. Hazor Enon, b. Sep. 6, 1777.

346. IV. Rufus, b. Jan. 28, 1779. m. Hannah Ingles. A log rolled on him in the woods and broke his leg. He took cold before he was found, lived a week, and d. Jan. 19, 1822.

347. V. Mary, b. Sep. 14, 1780. d. Oct. 1, 1780.

348. VI. Abijah, b. Sep. 3, 1781.

349. VII. Sylvester, b. May 14, 1783. d. May 8, 1852.

350. VIII. Joshua, b. Jan. 23, 1785. m. Betsey Vaughn.

351. IX. Dexter, b. Dec. 8, 1786.

352. X. Abigail, b. April 14, 1790. d. April 21, 1827. m. Reuben Wilder.

353. XI. Achsah, b. Feb. 16, 1792. d. June 22, 1823. Unmarried.

343. Bethuel. (334. Joshua, 130. Joshua, 17. James, 7. James, 2. James, 1. Thomas.) Eldest s. and child of Joshua Draper and Mary Pratt, m. Polly Vaughn.

CHILDREN:

358. I. Amos, b. April 5, 1804.

359. II. Joel N., b. Nov. 28, 1805.

360. III. Harriet S., b. Jan. 5, 1809. m. Dr. Calvin C. Covil.

361. IV. Emily W.

362. V. Mary.

363. VI. Hannah.

345. Hazor Enon. (334. Joshua, 130. Joshua, 17. James, 7. James, 2. James, 1. Thomas.) 3d child and 2d s. of Joshua Draper and Mary Pratt, m. 1st: Hannah Pratt, Sep. 6, 1803. She was b. Spencer, Mass., May 6, 1771. d. there May 12, 1810. m. 2dly: the widow Ruth (Pratt) Lane, sister of his 1st wife, Dec. 2, 1810. She was b. Oct. 23, 1775, at Spencer.

CHILDREN, BY RUTH, ALL B. AT LEEDS, ME.

364. I. Hannah, b. June 16, 1811. m. Oct. 24, 1832, Rufus Ramsdale. He was b. Hanson, Mass., Jan. 21, 1800. Children: — I. Dexter D., 369. b. Sep. 25, 1834. d. Apr. 13, 1835. II. Alice B., 370. b. Apr. 2, 1836. m. Mar. 30, 1859, Orin C. Bryant. III. Ruth Ann, 371. b. Sep. 5, 1841.

365. II. Stephen H., b. Apr. 1, 1813.

366. III. Deborah P., b. Apr. 25, 1815.

367. IV. Rufus D., b. Apr. 2, 1818.

368. V. Joshua L., b. Dec. 3, 1821. m. Martha Van Nute, and had: I. Alonzo H., 386. b. Lowell, Mass., May 14, 1848.

365. Stephen H. (345. Hazor Enon, 334. Joshua, 130. Joshua, 17. James, 7. James, 2. James, 1. Thomas.) 2d child of Hazor Enon and Ruth Lane. m. Mar. 31, 1836, Huldah Bemis.

CHILDREN:

373. I. Jerome B., b. Sep. 18, 1836, at Livermore, Me. m. Rhoda Anne Patton, July 25, 1858.

374. II. John B., b. Oct. 7, 1839, at Livermore, Me.

375. III. Joshua D., b. Sep. 30, 1842, at Leeds, Me.

376. IV. Isaac D., b. July 22, 1844, at Leeds, Me.

377. V. Frederick H., b. Jan. 22, 1854, at Leeds, Me.

366. Deborah P. (345. Hazor Enon, 334. Joshua, 130. Joshua, 17. James, 7. James, 2. James, 1. Thomas.) 3d child, 2d dau. of Hazor Enon Draper and Ruth Lane. m. June 9, 1839, Sumner Taylor.

CHILDREN, ALL B. AT LIVERMORE, ME.

378. I. Lucinda M., b. Feb. 25, 1841.

379. II. Charlotte B., b. Mar. 22, 1843. d. Sep. 1, 1845.

380. III. Calista, b. July 15, 1845. d. Sep. 21, 1850.

381. IV. Willard A. S., b. July 9, 1848.

382. V. Lucretia D., b. July 10, 1852.

567. Rufus D. (345. Hazor Enon, 334. Joshua, 130. Joshua, 17 James, 7. James, 2, James, 1. Thomas.) 4th child, 2d s. of Hazor Enon Draper and Ruth Lane. m. Mar. 12, 1843, Almira Libby.

CHILDREN:

383. I. Anne Sophia, b. Oct. 11, 1843.

384. II. Sarah A., b. Jan. 20, 1850.

385. III. Abba G., b. Oct. 29, 1853.

348. Abijah. (334. Joshua, 130. Joshua, 17. James, 7. James, 2. James, 1. Thomas.) Was the 6th child and 4th s. of Joshua Draper and Mary Pratt, m. Jan. 30, 1812, Isabelle Van Tuyl.

CHILDREN, ALL B. AT COBBLESKILL, N. Y.

387. I. Achsah A., b. Jan. ii, 1814. m. Jan. 14, 1832, John G, Hilts.

388. II. Mary, b. Dec. 8, 1815. d. Feb. 27, 1859. m. Mar. 29, 1834, John E. Moore.

389. III. Hiram, b. May 20, 1818. m. April 7, 1842, Mehitable Crane.

390. IV. Ira, b. Feb. 8, 1820. d. Sep. 7, 1857. m. Sep. 14, 1842, Cynthia P. Spaulding.

391. V. Joshua, b. Apr. 18, 1822. m. Apr. 20, 1847, Mary E. Stephens, a physician.

392. VI. John, b. Dec. 31, 1823. d. Feb. 16, 1824.

393. VII. Isaac, b. Apr. 10, 1825. (Married.)

394. VIII. Eliza, b. Jan. 22, 1828. d. Apr. 18, 1828.

395. IX. Abraham, b. Mar. 27, 1832.

396. X. Henry, b. Feb. 26, 1835.

349. Sylvester. (334. Joshua, 130. Joshua, 17. James, 7. James, 2. James, 1. Thomas.) 7th child and 5th s. of Joshua Draper and Mary Pratt, m. Worcester, N. Y., Dec. 22, 1808, Sukey, dau. of Dr. Uriah Bigelow, widely known as a successful physician and public spirited citizen. She was b. Aug. 21, 1789, at Boylston, Mass. d. Worcester, N. Y., June 12, 1863. Sylvester Draper was b. Chester, Mass., and when but a mere youth, went with his parents to Worcester, N. Y. He returned to the old homestead in Westford in 1812. Here all of his children were born except the two eldest. He lived much respected and honored as a worthy member of society.

CHILDREN:

397. I. Sylvester Bigelow, b. Feb. 19, 1810. d. Albany, N. Y., Apr. 21, 1890.

398. II. Susan Gregory, b. May 22, 1811.

399. III. Josiah Harrington, b. Feb. 6, 1813.

400. IV. Caroline Maria, b. June 19, 1815.

401. V. Adelia Sophia, b. Oct. 11, 1817.

402. VI. Fernando Pratt, b. Aug. 9, 1819.

403. VII. Lysander, b. Oct. 2, 1821. m. Rachel Anne Gurney, Oct. 11, 1855. (No children.) For a number of years after his marriage he carried on the old homestead farm, but sold it in 1867 and moved to Maryland.

404. VIII. Marinda, b. Oct. 10, 1823. m. Luther M. Robinson, of Seward, Oct. 5, 1853. Mr. Robinson by his 1st wife had 3 children, viz.: — I. Libbie, who m. Josiah Kilts. 11. Anne, and III. Luther. Marinda had one son, Willard M., 416. b. in Seward, July 18, 1859. Now lives in Cobbleskill.

405. IX. Lucy b. Aug. 12, 1826. d. Aug. 14, 1827.

406. X. Milton, b. June 24, 1829. d. Goodland, Ind., Nov. 24, 1877.

407. XI. Maria, b. Sep. 12, 1832. m. John E. Moore, of Richmondville, Jan. 29, 1865. They have no children, but he had by his 1st wife 3, viz.: — Oliver, Celia B. and Libbie.

397. Sylvester B. (349. Sylvester, 334. Joshua, 130. Joshua, 17. James, 7. James, 2. James, 1. Thomas.) Eldest s. and child of Sylvester Draper and Sukey Bigelow. m. 1st: Amy Westcott, of Milford, May 4, 1836. She d. Feb. 19, 1845. m. 2dly: Jane Sloan, of Worcester, June 14, 1846. In 1847, whilst proprietor of a flax mill near Westford, he had his arm broken in thirteen places by having it caught in a flax brake: necessitating amputation at the shoulder next day. He removed to Albany in 1855, where he resided until his death.

CHILDREN, BY 1st WIFE, ALL B. IN WESTFORD:

408. I. Olive, b. May 25, 1837. d. Schenevus, N. Y., July 22, 1891.

409. II. Anne Elizabeth, b. June 28, 1839. d. Albany, Dec. 19, 1885.

410. III. Perlia Marinda, b. July 11, 1842.

411. IV. Orlo Westcot, b. Dec. 29, 1844. d. Jan, 9, 1845.

408. Olive, m. Silas H. Walker, of Albany, July 2, 1863.

CHILDREN:

420. I. Francis E., b. June 4, 1864. d. Sep. 3, 1865.

421. II. Willie L., b. Oct. 6, 1867.

422. III. Sylvester D., b. March 28, 1869.

423. IV. Frederick A., b. June 13, 1871.

424. V. Andrew S., b. April 19, 1874, at Schenevus, N. Y. d. Aug. 26, 1874.

409. Anne Elizabeth, the 2d child, m. John M. Brightmyer, of Albany, Dec. 13, 1858. He served during the war of the Rebellion in the 43d N. Y. Volunteers.

CHILDREN:

425. I. Charles M., b. July 26, 1860, d. April 25, 1861.

426. II. Charles S., b. June 18, 1865.

427. III. Jenny D., b. Jan. 8, 1868. d. Nov. 20, 1874.

428. IV. Perlia, b. July 8, 1870.

CHILDREN OF SYLVESTER B. DRAPER, BY HIS 2D WIFE:

412. I. Andrew Sloan, b. June 21, 1848, at Westford.

413. II. Harlen Page, b. June 19, 1851, at Westford. m. Anna Belle Bryce, of Albany, N. Y., May 14, 1874.

414. III. Julia Isabella, b. July 12, 1852, at Westford. d. there March 9, 1855.

415. IV. Jenny, b. Aug, 30, 1864, at Albany, d. there July 16, 1865.

412. Andrew Sloan. (397. Sylvester B., 349. Sylvester, 334. Joshua, 130. Joshua, 17. James, 7. James, 2. James, 1. Thomas.) Eldest child and s. of Sylvester B. Draper and his 2d wife, Jane Sloan. She was born April 14, 1821. Andrew, m. May 8, 1872, Abbie Louise Lyon, of New Britain, Conn.

Andrew Sloan Draper was b. on a farm in the town of Westford, N. Y. His mother, Jane Sloan, was the daughter of Samuel and Rachel Sloan, of Worcester, N. Y., who were of Scotch-Irish "covenanter" stock, came from the north of Ireland to this country in 1812, and settled in the town of Salem, Washington County, N. Y. He attended the public schools of Albany from 1855 to 1863, when he was fortunate enough to win at a competitive examination a prize scholarship at the Albany Academy, from which institution he graduated in 1866. During his entire academic course he supported himself by work in the office of the "Albany Evening Journal." Through the four succeeding years he was employed in the office of a leading house in the Albany lumber district in the Summers, and taught school Winters. One Winter he taught at the "Westford Literary Institute," at Westford, N. Y., another in the "Albany Academy," and a third, he was principal of a graded school at East Worcester,

N. Y. In 1870, he pursued the course of study at the Albany Law School, and was admitted to the bar at the General Term of the Supreme Court in May, 1871. Immediately forming a partnership with his cousin, Mr. Alden Chester, under the firm name of Draper & Chester, he entered upon and continued the practice of his profession until 1885, when his practice was interrupted, and in 1887 his firm was formally dissolved.

In January, 1885, Andrew S. Draper was nominated by President Arthur, whose warm personal and political friend and admirer he had long been, to be one of the judges of the United States Court of Alabama Claims, and was promptly confirmed by the Senate. The business of this tribunal, constituted for the determination of claims against the Geneva award, was most laborious. In the year 1885 it heard and determined more than two thousand cases.

Mr. Draper has always been active in politics and much interested in the success of the Republican party. He made many addresses in the presidential campaign of 1868, although he was not old enough to vote for General Grant on election day, and he has been heard in every State and National campaign since. In 1880, 1881 and 1882 he was chairman of the Republican County Committee of Albany County.

In 1881 he was elected to the Legislature. Was a member of the standing committees on Ways and Means, Judiciary, Public Education and Printing. He was also a member of the special committee which investigated the affairs of the Elmira Reformatory, as well as of the committee which investigated the charges of bribery against Senator Loren B. Sessions, growing out of the celebrated contest over the selection of United States Senators to succeed Messrs. Roscoe Conkling and Thomas C. Platt. In that contest Mr. Draper supported Mr. Conkling and Mr. Platt.

In 1883 and 1884 he represented the XIX. Congressional District upon the Republican State Committee. He was a delegate to the National Convention in 1884, and zealously supported the candidacy of General Arthur for renomination to the presidency. Immediately following the convention he was chosen Chairman of the Executive Committee of the Republican State Committee, and as such had the immediate charge of the business of the committee in the ensuing campaign. Upon invitation he visited Mr. Blaine at his home in Augusta, and attended to all the general arrangements for and accompanied Mr. Blaine upon his two famous journeys through the State of New York. Although the campaign was a losing one, it gained for Mr. Draper the warmest thanks and the lasting friendship of the distinguished candidate.

Mr. Draper has from boyhood been actively identified with educational work. In 1878 he was elected a member of the Board of Education in the city of Albany. In 1882 he was nominated by the State Superintendent and confirmed by the State Board of Regents as a member of the Executive Committee of the State Normal School at Albany. Largely through his instrumentality the character of this institution was so changed in 1890 as to admit only students of academic grade and qualify them for teaching in the secondary schools, and its name was changed to that of "The State Normal College." In 1886 Mr. Draper was elected by the Legislature, upon joint ballot, to the position of State Superintendent of Public Instruction. He was re-elected without opposition in 1889 and still holds the position. Of his administration of this department, Mr. C. W. Bardeen, editor and publisher of the "School Bulletin," of Syracuse, New York, which paper had strongly opposed his election in the first place, spoke as follows at the great meeting of welcome extended to the National Educational Association at St. Paul, Minnesota, in 1890:

"Mr. President, I bear good tidings. Speaking particularly for New York, but of a movement extending beyond its borders, I report a recent progress almost incredible. If any of you were asked to name the greatest awakening in American educational history, you would point to the work of Horace Mann half a century ago. Knowing that work, and weighing my words, I believe that more than Horace Mann did for Massachusetts in twelve years, Andrew S. Draper has done for New York in five. Here are facts:

Hon. Andrew S. Draper of Albany N.Y.

"Five years ago the annual expenditure for schools was fifteen millions. To-day it is twenty millions.

"Five years ago schools engaged their teachers 'during the pleasure of the Board.' One ingenious trustee hired his teacher every evening for the ensuing day. To-day no contract can be made for less than ten weeks.

"Five years ago the contract was usually verbal and disputes were frequent. To-day a blank for written contract is printed in the school register and must be filled.

"Five years ago trustees used to hire their teachers for so much 'and board around;'. or, still worse, 'and board with him.' To-day a teacher's wages can be paid only in money.

"Five years ago the time of payment was indefinite, and thrifty trustees got five per cent, for advancing money. To-day all salaries must be paid monthly.

"Five years ago trustees had ways of keeping their teachers from institutes. To-day the school can draw no money for the weeks the institute is in session unless the school has been closed, the teacher has been at the institute, and full wages have been paid the teacher for the time in attendance.

"Five years ago teachers were licensed by a hundred and forty different men on examinations each of those one hundred and forty men prepared for himself. To-day certificates are granted only on uniform questions prepared for the Department of Public Instruction, sent under seal to all parts of the State, and opened at the same hour in every county.

"Five years ago, on the morning after the annual election of trustee, the fields were black with men and women hurrying across lots to his house to be first on hand and secure the appointment. To-day the trustee searches in vain for certificated teachers at the former starvation wages, and when he has doubled the pay, he often has to look far to find a candidate.

"What is better than all, we have now the spirit of progress. Five years ago we shrugged our shoulders and said, 'The politicians won't let us.' To-day the politicians are with us.

"Five years ago the colleges pulled one way, the normal schools another, the academies another, while the common schools looked on and didn't pull at all. To-day it is a long pull, a strong pull, and a pull all together, and we are learning what the united teachers of a State can accomplish under competent leadership."

Mr. Draper has made addresses at nearly or quite all of the educational conventions of his State and of the National Educational Association during his official term. His addresses upon the following subjects have been published, viz.: "What Ought the Common Schools to Do?" "How can It be Done?" "How to Improve the Country Schools"; "The Powers and Obligations of Teachers"; "School Administration in Large Cities"; "The Indian Problem in the State of New York"; "Origin and Development of the New York Common School System"; "The Responsibility and Authority of Trustees"; "The Normal and Training School System of New York"; "A Teaching Profession"; "The Authority of the State in the Education of Her Children," and "The Legal Status of the Public Schools."

Of his address on "The Authority of the State in the Education of her Children," at Peoria, Illinois, the "Illinois School Journal" said:

"The address of State Superintendent Draper, of New York, at this meeting in Peoria, was in every way worthy of the cause he advocated, and of the intelligent audience of teachers and citizens that filled the Opera House at 11 o'clock in the morning to listen to him. Judge Draper was bred a lawyer, but he was evidently born to be an educator. His training as a jurist has especially fitted him to analyze the educational problems of the day, and his clear, strong style of putting things makes him an effective advocate. He won golden opinions from the Illinois people during his recent visit."

Of his address before the Massachusetts State Association on "A Teaching Profession," the "Academy" magazine said: "Of all the men who appeared before the association, we think none left so good an impression on so many of those present as Superintendent Draper"; and the "Educational Review" said:

"One of the strongest features of the Worcester meeting was the address delivered by State Superintendent Draper, of New York, upon 'A Teaching Profession.' Its strength depended, in about equal measure, on the rugged good sense of the views enunciated and the marked personality of the speaker. Such efforts upon educational topics as come from Mr. Draper's pen or voice are characterized by a certain 'taking' quality, one which is generally conspicuous by its absence from educational utterances. Unless I mistake, this quality is the outcome of Mr. Draper's preparation for, and experience at, the bar, emphasized undoubtedly by his contact with successive legislative bodies at Albany. The subject of his address upon this occasion had nothing of novelty to command attention. Under one caption or another, it has been repeatedly discussed at meetings of the Massachusetts Association, but, so *far as I know, never with the clearness, precision and force which characterized Mr. Draper's treatment of it. The address has been printed, and a careful perusal of it is recommended to all readers of the 'Educational Review.'"

In 1889 Mr. Draper was chosen President of the Department of Superintendence of the National Educational Association, and re-elected in 1890.

In 1889 Colgate University conferred upon him the honorary degree of LL.D.

In religion he is a Presbyterian, and is an Elder in the First Presbyterian Church of Albany.

CHILDREN:

429. I. Lottie Leland, b. Nov. 21, 1875, at Albany, N. Y.

430. II. Edwin Lyon, b. Aug, 19, 1882, at Albany, N. Y.

398. Susan Gregory. (349. Sylvester, 334. Joshua, 130. Joshua, 17. James, 7. James, 2. James, 1. Thomas.) 2d child and eldest dau. of Sylvester Draper and his wife Sukey Bigelow. m. Alden Chester, of Maryland, Sep. 5, 1838. He was b. May 26, 1803, at Groton, Conn., and d. Mar. 4, 1857. At the time of her marriage with Mr. Chester he had one son, Dwight, by his 1st wife Mary H. Chappel. This son was born in Maryland, Mar. 2, 1835, and married Mary J. Storrs, of Worcester, Sep. 7, 1862, and is the father of two daughters — Mary E., b. in that city Apr. 14, 1866, and Lizzie, b. Mar. 8, 1868. The latter d. in infancy.

CHILDREN:

431. I. Horace, b. Oct. 29, 1842. m. Anastasia E. Hill, Sep. 8, 1867. They have: I. Carey R., 434. b. June 17, 1868. m. Alice M. Hebard, of Schenevus, N. Y., Dec. 11, 1889. II. L. Francelia, 435. b. Schenevus, N. Y., Feb. 6, 1874. III. Horace Coryell, 436. b. June 25, 1876. IV. Alden Hill, 437. b. Mar. 9, 1878. d. Nov. 16, 1881. V. Lola Ethel, b. Apr. 18, 1880.

432. 11. Arthur, b. Feb. 22, 1847. He was a clergyman, d. Brooklyn, N. Y., Nov. 12, 1889.

433. III. Alden, b. Sep. 4, 1848. m. Lena Thurber, of East Worcester, N. Y., Oct. 5, 1871. Lives in Albany. One child, Amy, 438. b. July 19, 1877.

399. Josiah H. (349. Sylvester, 334. Joshua, 130. Joshua, 17. James, 7. James, 2. James, 1. Thomas.) 3d child and 2d s. of Sylvester Draper and Sukey Bigelow. m. 1st: Adelia W. Babcock, of Westford, Feb. 22, 1837. She was b. Oct. 19, 1819. He received a divorce from his wife in 1858, and m. Mrs. Helen Avery, of Albany, Oct. 15, 1861. She d. Sep. 19, 1877. He m. 3dly: Fanny Rathbone, of Albany, N. Y., Nov. 31, 1878.

CHILDREN, BY 1st WIFE:

439. I. James R., b. Dec. 1, 1837, at Westford, N. Y. m. and had one s. and a dau., both of whom d. in infancy.

440. II. Mary J., b. Davenport, N. Y., July 5, 1841,

441. III. Melville, b. Albany, N. Y., Nov. 16, 1848. d. Apr. 3. 1850.

442. IV. Maria Elizabeth, b. Albany, N. Y., Nov. 9, 1852. d. Mar. 20, 1889. m. Harvey Goodrich, of Albany, N. Y., in 1885. Had one child, Mary Adelia, 443. b. at Albany, in 1885, and d. in infancy.

400. Caroline M. (349. Sylvester, 334. Joshua, 130. Joshua, 17. James, 7. James, 2. James, 1. Thomas.) 4th child and 2d dau. of Sylvester Draper and Sukey Bigelow. m. Benjamin Westcott, of Milford, Jan. 22, 1846, who was b. July 14, 1815. She had one dau., Luretta M., 444. b. Dec. 20, 1847, at Milford. d. May 10, 1875. m. Madison Hilts, of Richmondville, July 4, 1867. Their children are: I. Hattie, 445. b. Mar. 8, 1868; and II. George Benjamin, 446. b. Jan. 20, 1872. Benjamin Westcott d. Dec. 17, 1864. She m. 2d: Asa H. Cleveland, of Richmondville, N. Y., July 31, 1878.

401. Adelia S. (349. Sylvester, 334. Joshua, 130. Joshua, 17. James, 7. James, 2. James, 1. Thomas.) 5th child, 3d dau. of Sylvester Draper and Sukey Bigelow. m. Henry W. Wilson, of Whitestown, Apr. 13, 1842, who was b. May 22, 1809, and d. Mar. 12, 1884. At the time of her marriage with Mr. Wilson he had, by his 1st wife, one son, Milo.

CHILDREN, ALL B. IN WHITESTOWN:

447. I. Helen J., b. May 24, 1844.

448. II. Sarah S., b. July 10, 1846. m. Burt Seymour, Mar. 27, 1878. Have: I. Adelia Cyrenia, 450. b. Mar. 27, 1881. H. Laura Belle, 451. b. Sep. 26, 1885.

449. III. William H., b. Feb. 5, 1849. m. Emma Lewis, Sep. 12, 1883.

402. Fernando P. (349. Sylvester, 334. Joshua, 130. Joshua, 17. James, 7. James, 2. James, 1. Thomas.) 6th child and 3d s. of Sylvester Draper and Sukey Bigelow. m. Lucy A. Preston, of Westford, June 16, 1846. She was b. Westford, N. Y., Feb. 20, 1822.

CHILDREN:

452. I. Ella A., b. Aug. 7, 1849. m. John M. Chase, Aug. 28, 1873. They have: I. Irma Wickham, 455. b. Mar. 2, 1877. d. Nov. 27, 1887. II. lima Currie, 456. b. Oct. 23, 1878. III. Henry Lord, 457. b. Mar. 25, 1880.

453. II. C. Amanda, b. June 8, 1853.

454. III. Emma R., b. Mar. 8, 1858. m. Murray J. Faulkner, Feb. 18, 1885. They have: I. Earl Draper, 458. b. Nov. 18, 1885. d. Nov. 27, 1887. II. Charles Bryan, 459. b. Mar. 11, 1890, at San Francisco, Cal.

406. Milton. (349. Sylvester, 334. Joshua, 130. Joshua, 17. James, 7. James, 2. James, 1. Thomas.) 10th child and 5th s. of Sylvester Draper and Sukey Bigelow. m. Jerusha C. Talcott, of Willeston, Vt., Oct. 19, 1858. She was b. Dec. 31, 1827, at Willeston, N. Y. He removed to Illinois in 1865, and from thence to Goodland, in Indiana.

CHILDREN, ALL B, IN WESTFORD, N. Y.:

460. I. Jenny M., b. Aug. 3, 1859. m. Elmer E. Crane, Apr. 19, 1883. Have one child, Rayner Draper, 463. b. March 3, 1888.

461. II. Mary E., b. Feb. 23, 1861. d. Apr. 10, 1864. III. Carry L., 462. b. Feb. 6, 1863. d. Apr. 2, 1864.

351. Dexter. (334. Joshua, 130. Joshua, 17. James, 7. James, 2. James, i Thomas.) 9th child and 7th s. of Joshua Draper and Mary Pratt, m. Oriel Babcock, Aug. 1, 1816. She was b. Feb. 7, 1778, at Partridgeville, Mass. He d. of numb palsy, Oct. 21, 186-.

CHILDREN, ALL B. AT WESTFORD, N. Y.:

464. I. Alvira, b. July 9, 1817.

465. II. Hazor E., b. June 27, 1820. m. Malinda Tipple, May 5, 1857. Had one child, Fanny, 369. b. July 21, 1859, at Westford.

466. III. Betsey, b. Apr. 1, 1824. d. Apr. 28, 1833.

467. IV. Abigail, b. Apr. 10, 1827. d. Apr. 11, 1833.

468. V. Fanny, b. Aug. 17, 1829. d. Apr. 25, 1833.

335. Sarah. (130. Joshua, 17. James, 7. James, 2. James, 1. Thomas.) 2d child and eldest dau. of Joshua Draper and Abigail Fairbanks, m. Jonas, s. of John Muzzy and Abigail Reed, May 2, 1771. He was b. Jan. 2, 1748. She d. about 1777, and Jonas then m. Abigail Lamb, June 9, 1778. Jonas Muzzy was a captain in the Militia, a Representative to the General Court, Selectman of Spencer, Mass., and held various other local offices.

CHILDREN, BY JONAS MUZZY:

470. I. Sarah, b. Jan. 1, 1773.

471. II. Jonas, b. Apr. 2, 1775. Removed to the State of New York.

472. III. Sardine, b. Mar. 30, 1777. m. Catherine, dau. of Jonas Beamis, 1806, and had: I. Laura, 473. b. Nov. 27, 1806. II. Catharine, 474. b. June 6, 1810. III. Judith, 475. b. July 6, 1814.

476. IV. Nancy & 477. V. Eliza, (Twins, b. Dec. 11, 1815.

Sardine Muzzy, 472, was a captain of the Militia in Spencer. He lived in Rutland.

338. Asa. (130. Joshua, 17. James, 7. James, 2. James, 1. Thomas.) Eldest s. and child of Joshua Draper by his 2d wife, Sarah Wright, of Brookfield. m. Ruth Whittemore, niece of Pliny Earl of Leicester, July 19, 1785. She was b. 1766. d. June 12, 1836. He d. at Claremont, N. H.

CHILDREN:

478. I. Clarissa, b. July 8, 1786, at Spencer, m. Dr. Leonard Jarvis, of Claremont.

479. II. Sallie, b. Oct. 23, 1787, at Spencer, d. July 11, 1828. m. Uriel Andrews.

480. III. Ralph, b. July 6, 1788. d. Sep. 27, 1788.

481. IV. Henry, b. Sep. 23, 1790, at Spencer, m. Miss Green, of Mount Holly, Vt.

482. V. Asa, b. Aug. 19, 1792, at Spencer, d. Mar. 19, 1813.

483. VI. Eli, b. Oct. 7, 1793. m. 1st: Sarah, m. 2dly: Abigail, both daus. of Ephraim Tyler. Child: I. Lorenzo, 492. m. 1st: Sep. 14, 1837, Nancy Jane Newman, of Acworth, N. H. m. 2dly: Aug. 20, 1845, Matilda Fay, of Wethersfield, Vt. Children, by 1st wife:— I. Sarah Jane, 493. m. 1st: Frank Brad (one son), m. 2dly: Jonathan Farwell, of Boston, Mass. II. Ruth, 494, d. in infancy. III. Hattie E., 495. m. Amos C. Chase, of Kingston, N. H. (two daus.). One m. John Sanborn (had a dau.), the other m. Charles Curier, of Haverhill, Mass. (had a dau.). Children, by 2d wife: — IV. Mary, 496. Unmarried. V. Lorenzo, Jr., 497. b. Surrey Co., N. H., June 9, 1849. m. by Rev. Wm. Rogers, at Wareham, Mass., Jan. 1, 1873, Angelina Clifton, dau. of Joseph H. Williams and Berthia L. Holmes. Children: — I. Clifton Fay, 498. b. Wareham, Mass., July 14, 1874. II. Herbert Lathrop, 499. b. Brookline, Mass., Nov. 16, 1875. d. Jan. 12, 1876. III. Alfred Gordon, 500. b. Ravenswood, L. I., Oct. 31, 1880.

484. VII. Ira, b. Nov. n, 1795, at Springfield, Vt. d. Dec. 12, 1821.

485. VIII. Elizabeth E., b. Aug. 16, 1797, at Springfield, Vt. m. Chester Spencer, of Castleton.

486. IX. Thomas Whittemore, b. Aug. 28, 1799, at Spencer, m. 1st: Clarissa Ives of Mt. Holly, Vt. m. 2dly: 1855, Mrs. Sarah West Godfrey. Children by 1st wife: — Horace, 501. d. aged 12 years. Eli, 502. d. 1891. m. Amanda Ferguson, of Dryden, N. Y. She d. 1876. Child: — Leroy A., 507. d. 1871. Mary A., 503. m. Nathan Rowell, of Fulton, N. Y. Children:— I. Burr. II. Rowell, 508. III. Sophronia A., 504. d. 1882. m. Isaac Ford. Children: — Edith A. and Harry. Latter b. Dryden, N. Y. d. 1886. Clarissa, 505. A teacher, lives Dryden, N. Y. Simeon d. in infancy. Child by 2d wife: — James Hervey, 506. m. Etta Fred, of Ithaca, N. Y. Had two children, 509 and 510.

487. X. Esther, b. Oct. 7, 1801, at Springfield, Vt. d. Feb. 2, 1802.

488. XI. John, b. Jan. 1, 1803, at Springfield, Vt.

489. XII. Simeon, b. June 24, 1805, at Springfield, Vt.

490. XIII. Mary, b. Oct 1, 1808, at Springfield, Vt. m. Mr. Sabin. Lives at Wallingford, Vt.

491. XIV. George Gardiner, b. Brookfield, N. H., Oct. 7, 1813. d. Montclair, N. J., Apr. 18, 1876. m. Dec. 5, 1846, Miss Anne C. Ballard, of New York. Children:— I. Georgia Annie, 511. II. Charles Ballard, 512. m. Norwalk, Conn., Sep. 24, 1888, Marion Carter Olmstead, of Norwalk. Children: — I. George Gardiner, 516. II. Isabel Carter, 517. III. Rebecca Ballard, 513. IV. Ruth Clara, 514. V. Frank Ballard, 515. Mrs. Draper, Sr., still resides with her family at the old homestead, "Willowdale," Montclair, which is a large estate.

"Mr. Draper, formerly well known in dry goods circles in New York City, was in his day one of the most popular and energetic of New York merchants. He entered mercantile life in New York some forty years ago as a clerk of the once prominent firm of L. & V. Kirby. His large acquaintance with Vermont and New Hampshire business men, together with his peculiar abilities as a salesman made for him a recognized position in the trade and soon enabled him to begin business on his own account. About the year 1840, he formed the house of Welling, Root & Draper, and subsequently was a member of the firms of Draper, Aldrich & Frink, Draper, Aldrich & Co., Draper, Knox & Ingersoll. and Draper, Knox & Co., importers and commission merchants. In these several connections he was uniformly successful, until in the financial cyclone of 1857, the last named firm succumbed. Since that time Mr. Draper has been comparatively inactive in business, although busily and conscientiously occupied in an honorable closing up of his old affairs. During the past 18 years of his life he resided with his family at Montclair, N. J., where he enjoyed universal respect and the esteem of hosts of friends. His death was a shock to a very large circle, not only in Montclair and in New York, but in Vermont, New Hampshire and other States to whom he had proved his title to be considered an honest man, a faithful friend, and an exponent of the kindest sympathies."

(The above is from the "New York Herald" of April 20, 1876.)

339. Simeon. (130. Joshua, 17. James, 7. James, 2. James, 1. Thomas.) 2d s. of Joshua Draper and his 2d wife, Sarah Wright. He was b. at Spencer, and m. 1st: Mary, 144, dau. of Col. Benjamin Bemis, of Spencer and his wife Rebecca Draper, 139, the latter being a dau. of James Draper, 127. Consequently, Mary Bemis was his own first cousin. They were m. Aug. 24, 1786. She was b. Spencer, Jan. 29, 1770, and d. in Cambridgeport, Aug. 4, 1828. After his wife's death, Simeon Draper m. 2d: the widow Catherine C. Lewis. She was b. in Boston, Dec. 5, 1788, and was the dau. of John and Rebecca Cannell. She was first m. to Asa Packard Lewis on Nov. 8, 1807. He was b. July 27, 1786, and was lost at sea some time in Feb., 1812, aged 26. It is interesting to note here that Asa Packard Lewis was the elder brother of Henry Lewis, who m. Sophia Draper, 525, dau. of the above Simeon and Mary, Therefore, the 2d Mrs. Simeon Draper's stepdaughter was by her marriage to Henry Lewis also her stepmother's sister-in-law. The 2d Mrs. Simeon Draper had only one son by her first marriage. His name was Winslow Lewis, b. April 23, 1809. d. Sep. 26, 1814. She m. Simeon Draper Sep. 10, 1832, and d. in Brookfield, Mass., March 13, 1866. Her maiden name was Catherine Cubin Cannell. The Simeon Drapers lived in Spencer until April 1, 1795, where their six eldest children were born. On that date they moved to Brookfield (S. Parish), and remained there until March 26, 1801, when they moved to W. Brookfield. Here they stayed until April 1, 1804, three children being born to them during their residence there. They then returned to the S. Parish (Brookfield) and lived in the house where Col. Reed formerly resided, but on July 1, 1813, Simeon Draper moved his family into the house which he had bought of Mr. Oliver Cushman. Again, on April 1, 1814, he moved into what was known as the Holbrook house in which he thereafter resided. Simeon Draper enlisted in the Revolutionary army when only sixteen years of age. The accompanying certificates of his services in the ranks of the Continental army attest to his patriotic fervor when still a youth. He was always interested in public matters, and a very well known character throughout the old Bay State. In the history of Worcester Co., Mass., Vol. 1, page 340, we learn that Simeon Draper owned and kept the old Brookfield tavern at W. Brookfield, which was the stopping place of all travelers between the East and West. Distinguished men in making their progress through the country tarried there. It was the halfway house of the judges of the Supreme Court, passing between Worcester and Springfield. In addition to this he owned and operated the stage line from Brookfield west to Springfield, and east to Worcester. He was elected a representative to the General Court from Brookfield for the years 1809, 1812, 1815, 1816, 1817, 1818, 1819, 1829 and 1830, and was a member of the Constitutional Convention of 1820. He also held many minor town offices, both in West and South Brookfield, such as Justice of the Peace and Selectman. Having entered the army as a private, he was, for gallant services, after the peace was declared, commissioned a captain by Governor Hancock in the militia of Massachusetts. In the year 1800 he was appointed captain in the U. S. Army by President John Adams, serving principally in Oxford, Mass., until the standing army was abolished. When General Lafayette re-visited the United States, he was a guest of Simeon Draper at his house in Brookfield. It is related that he arrived there after dark, and his way from the carriage to the house door was lighted by torches, every one of which was held in the hands of Simeon Draper's numerous sons.

Captain Simeon Draper of Brookfield, Mass.

Commonwealth of Massachusetts, Secretary's Department, Boston.

Revolutionary Record of Simeon Draper, *of Spencer, taken from the Revolutionary Rolls among the Massachusetts Archives.*

V. 33:332, *Misc. Rolls.*

"Descriptive Lists of Enlisted Men."

"Simeon Draper, of Spencer, Worcester Co. Age, 16, height, 5 ft. 6 in. Complexion, Light, Occupation, Farmer — Time of Inlisting, Jan. 12 — Term for. During 3 years — Colonel's name, Washburn — Captain's name, Bemis."

(Year not given — undoubtedly 1781.)

V. 50: File 8. *Misc. Rolls.*

"Muster Roll of Capt. Libbens Drews Company 4th Massachusetts Regiment of foot in Service of the United States of America. Commanded by Wm. Shepard Esqr Colonel for the month of June 1781."

"Simeon Draper — Private — Enlisted, Jan. 12th 1781 — Term — 3 years."

Roll dated "Phillipsburg July 16th 1781."

V. 50: File 8. *Misc. Rolls.*

"Muster Roll of Capt Libbens Drews Company in the 4th Masst. Regiment of Foot in Service of the United States of America. Commanded by William Shepard Esqr. Colo, for the Month of July 1781."

"Simeon Draper — Private."

Roll dated "Phillipsburg August 4 1781."

V. 50: File 8. *Misc. Rolls.*

"Muster Roll of Capt. Lebbens Drews Company in the 4th Massachusetts Regiment of foot in Service of the United States of America Commanded William Shepard Esqr. Colonel for the Month of August 1781."

"Simeon Draper — Private."

Roll dated Sept. r, 1781."

V. 50: File 8. *Misc. Rolls.*

"Muster Roll of Capt Lebbens Drews Company in the 4th Massachusetts Regt. of foot in the Service of the United States of America Commanded by Wm. Shepard Esqr. Coll. for the Month of September 1781."

"Simeon Draper— Private— Remarks, On command Jersey Continental Village October 1st 1781."

V. 50: File 8. *Misc. Rolls.*

"Muster Roll of Capt. Lebbens Drews Company in the 4th Massachusetts Regt. of foot in Service of the United States of America Commanded by Wm. Shepard Esqr. Coll. for the month of Oct. & Nov. 1781."

"Simeon Draper — Private."

Roll dated "York Heitts Deer, 17th 1781."

V. 50: File 8. *Misc. Rolls.*

"Muster Roll of Capt Lebbens Drews Company in the 4th Regiment of foot in Service of the United States of America Commanded by William Shepard Esqr. Colo. for the month of Deer. 1781."

"Simeon Draper — Private."

Roll dated "York Heitts Jany 17th 1782."

Commonwealth of Massachusetts,

Office of the Secretary, Boston, June 5, 1891.

The foregoing abstracts are true copies from the Revolutionary Rolls among the Massachusetts Archives.

Witness the seal of the Commonwealth.
(Signed) Wm. M. Olin,
(SEAL.) *Secretary of the Commonwealth.*

Commonwealth of Massachusetts,
Adj. Gen's Office,
Boston, Jan. 9, 1892.

"It appears on record on the military rosters in this Office that Simeon Draper, of Spencer, Mass., was commissioned Ensign, First Regiment, First Brigade, Seventh Division, M, V. M, (Worcester County), Sep. 1, 1789. Promoted Captain, July 25, 1790. Discharged. Succeeded by William Watson, of Spencer, as Captain, Sep, 14, 1795."

(Signed) Samuel Dalton, *Adjutant General.*

War Department. Adjutant General's Office.
Washington, D. C, Jan. 11, 1892.

"Simeon Draper was a Captain in the 14th U. S. Infantry from Jan. 8, 1799, to June 15, 1800."

(Signed) J. Kilume, *Assist. Adjutant General.*

CHILDREN OF SIMEON DRAPER AND HIS 1ST WIFE, MARY BEMIS:

(No issue by 2d marriage.)

518. I. Abigail, b. March 12, 1787, at Spencer, d. July 24, 1788.

EPITAPH

"Babe thither caught
From womb and breast,
Claims right to sing
Above the rest."

519. II. Betsy, b. Sep. 6, 1788, at Spencer, d. Aug. 2, 1828.

520. III. Henry, b. June 10, 1790, at Spencer, d. at Rochester, July 3, 1841.

521. IV. Lorenzo, b. Mar. 27, 1792, at Spencer, d. at New York, Jan. 25, 1868.

522. V. Horace, b. Jan. 30, 1794, at Spencer, d. at Springfield, June 21, 1846.

523. VI. A son, b. 1795.

524. VII. Mary, b. Dec. 5, 1796, at W. Brookfield. d. at Brookfield, June 16, 1800.

EPITAPH

"Sleep on my child, and take thy rest,
God called thee Home, He thought it best."

525. VIII. Sophia, b. Feb. 14, 1799, at W. Brookfield. d. at Brookfield, Sep. 17, 1870.

526. IX. William Frederick, b. April 2, 1801, at W. Brookfield. d. at W. Brookfield, June 20, 1801.

527. X. Francis, b. Dec. 26, 1802, at Brookfield. d. at W. Brookfield, Dec. 30, 1802.

528. XI. William Bemis, b. W. Brookfield, Feb. 15, 1804. d. at Flushing, L. I., April 17, 1885.

529. XII. Simeon, b. Jan. 19, 1806, at Brookfield. d. at Whitestone, Nov. 6, 1866.

530. XIII. Mary Adeline, b. Brookfield, Aug. 21, 1807. d. there Aug. 19, 1837, m. June 30, 1830, Silas C. Herring, of Albany, N. Y. Children: — I. William Draper, 535. b. Aug. 12, 1832. d. Mar. 12, 1876 (was married). II. Silas Frederick, 536. b. Nov. 21, 1834. Killed at the battle of Stone River, near Murfeesborough, Dec. 29, 1862. m. Marion, dau. of Philip Wolferburger and Margaret Gilliard, of Harrisburg, Pa. She was b. June 3, 1834. (Child: — Frederick Clark, 537. b. Aug. 22, 1856.)

531. XIV. Benjamin Harrison, b. May 9, 1810, at Brookfield. d. at Brookfield, June 29, 1836.

532. XV. Sarah Anne, b. Feb. 27, 1812, at Brookfield. d. at Brookfield, Sep. 23, 1833. m. Emmons, s. of Martin Twitchell (b. 1779, d. Aug. 31, 1834) and Eleanor Lamb (b. 1784, d. Aug. 28, 1872). Emmons, b. 1808. d. Jan. 13, 1891. They had one child: Sarah Ann, 538. b. Sep. 23, 1833. d. Oct. 16, 1833.

533. XVI. Joshua, b. Sep. 3, 1814, at Brookfieldi d. at Worcester, Mar. 29, 1874.

534. XVII. Theodore Sedgwick, b. June 15, 1816, at Brookfield. d. at New York, Apr. 3, 1878.

520. Henry. (339. Simeon, 130. Joshua, 17. James, 7. James, 2. James, 1. Thomas.) 3d child and eldest s. of Captain Simeon Draper and Polly Bemis. m. at Pittsfield, Mass., June 7, 1813, Harriet (b. Chesterfield, Mass., Nov. 28, 1793; d. Janesville, Wisconsin, Oct., 1871), dau. of John Stone of Chesterfield, Hampshire Co., Mass. He met his wife whilst stationed with his regiment at Pittsfield, Mass., during the war of 1812. According to the records on file in the office of the Treasury Department, Washington, D. C, he was an ensign in Col. S. Larned's 9th Regt. of U. S. Infantry, his commission dating Mar. 18, 1812. He served until the regiment was mustered out on Nov. 30 of the same year. The records show that he was also stationed with part of his regiment at Brookfield, Mass. Henry Draper removed with his family from Brookfield to Rochester, N, Y., in June, 1817, and lived there until his death.

CHILDREN:

539. I. Adelia Stebbins, b. May 24, 1814, at Brookfield. d. there Dec. 2, 1814.

540. II. Lorenzo Cornelius, b. Nov. 26, 1815, at Brookfield. d. Rochester, Jan. 3, 1855.

541. III. Anne Maria, b. Dec. 26, 1817, at Rochester, m. Dr. George Swinburne, of Rochester, N. Y.

542. IV. Henry Stone, b. Feb. 8, 1821, at Rochester, d. Apr. 10, 1886.

543. V. John Stone, b. Nov. 18, 1823, at Rochester.

544. VI. Harriet Elizabeth, b. Dec. 9, 1825, at Rochester, d. there Mar. 28, 1827.

545. VII. Simeon Bemis. b. Dec. 15, 1827, at Rochester, d. at Detroit, June 7, 1848.

546. VIII. William Bemis, b. July 11, 1830, at Rochester, d. at Washington, D. C, Apr. 2, 1857. He was the chief telegrapher in Commander Perry's Japan Expedition, and was the first to operate the magnetic telegraph in that country. (Unmarried.)

547. IX. George Horace, b. June 15, 1832, at Rochester, d. there Feb. 7, 1833.

548. X. Harriet Aurelia, b. Mar. 22, 1834, at Rochester, d. Apr. 26, 1834.

549. XI. Harriet Elizabeth, b. Nov. 29, 1837. d. Sep. 20, 1840.

542. Henry Stone. (520. Henry, 339. Simeon, 130. Joshua, 17. James, 7. James, 2. James, 1. Thomas.) 4th child and 2d s. of Henry Draper and Harriet Stone, m. Apr. 20, 1853, Emily Aurelia, dau. of Timothy and Mary C. Barnes, of Rochester. She was b. Garse, Monroe Co., N. Y., Mar. 6, 1830. (Living in Dec, 1891.)

CHILDREN:

550. I. Henry Barnes, b. Feb. 4, 1854, at Rochester, m. Jan. 14, 1875, Anna Maud Whiting, of Weedsport, N. Y. One child: Harold Whiting,

554. b. Rochester, N. Y., Dec. 26, 1875.

551. II. Florence, b. Rochester, July 6, 1856. d. Jan. 15, 1886. m. July 6, 1882, Rev. L. C. Davis.

552. III. George Swinburne, b. May 5, 1863. d. Aug. 21, 1865.

553. IV. Herbert Stone, b. Mar. 21, 1865.

543. John Stone. (520. Henry, 339. Simeon, 130. Joshua, 17. James, 7. James, 2. James, 1. Thomas.) 5th child, 3d s. of Henry Draper and Harriet Stone, m. July 5, 1855, Susan Bower, dau. of Isaac Lewis and Eliza Bower, of Scottsville, Monroe Co., N. Y.

Mr. Draper left Rochester, N. Y., in 1850, went to Milwaukee, and engaged in the telegraph business. He built a line from Milwaukee to Chicago in 1850, and one to Madison, Wis., and had the Milwaukee office and superintendence of the Milwaukee State Line, and was a stockholder. He quit the business in 1857; removed to Janesville, Wis., in 1858 (where he has since resided), and engaged in the grain business.

CHILDREN, ALL B. AT JANESVILLE, WIS.:

555. I. Grace, b. Aug. 4, 1860.

556. II. Susan, b. Oct. 19, 1862. m. Frank B., s. of Carlos White and Ann McAllister, Janesville, Sep. 11, 1888. Child:— Hubert Draper White, 560. b. Dec. 24, 1889.

557. III. Fanny, b. Dec. 14, 1864. m. Frederick A., s. of Lucius P. Sperry and Emily Chatfield, of New Haven, Conn., Janesville, Aug. 4, 1891.

558. IV. John Lewis, b. Oct. 28, 1866.

559. V. Bryant, b. Jan. 16, 1869.

521. Lorenzo. (339. Simeon, 130. Joshua, 17. James, 7. James, 2. James, 1. Thomas.) 4th child, 2d s. of Simeon Draper and Polly Bemis. m. 1st: Rosamund Cook, of Boston, Apr. 20, 1816. She was b. Boston, Sep. 24, 1798. d. Boston, May 31, 1825. m. 2dly: Sarah Elizabeth Dolliver, of Dorchester, Mass., Mar. 27, 1826, at Philadelphia. She was b. Dec. 14, 1799. d. Paris,

France, May 11, 1840. He m. 3dly: Ann Alicia, widow of Dr. Hamilton Hawkins, U.S.A., of Baltimore, in Paris, Oct. 1, 1851. She d. in Baltimore.

Lorenzo Draper was a merchant in Boston, New York and Paris. He was appointed U. S. Consul at Paris by President Harrison, Mar. 15, 1841, succeeding Consul Brent. He held the office until Aug., 1844. Subsequently he was appointed U. S. Consul at Havre by President Tyler, May 29, 1849, and held this office until June 1, 1853.

CHILDREN, BY 1ST WIFE:

561. I. Rosamund, b. Jan. 11, 1817, at Boston, d. Aug. 23, 1824.

562. II. A child, b. Apr. 28, 1818, at Boston, d. Apr. 30, 1818.

563. III. Lorenzo, b. May 2, 1820, at Boston, d. at New York, Apr. 12, 1858.

564. IV. George Henry, b. May 10, 1823, at Boston, m. in Paris, France, June 17, 1869, Charlotte Maria Dash, dau. of Jacob and Harriet Bininger, of New York. She was b. in New York, Nov. 20, 1829. d. in Havre, France, Sep. 18, 1881. (No issue.)

565. V. Rosamund Cook, b. Boston, Apr. 30, 1825. d. there Feb. 4, 1826.

CHILDREN, BY 2D WIFE:

566. VI. Infant, b. Apr. 11, 1827. d. in New York.

567. VII. Elizabeth Smith, b. June 23, 1828, in Boston.

568. VIII. Frances Amelia, b. Nov. 5, 1830, at Dorchester, Mass. m. John Lamson, Jr., at New York, Dec. 20, 1852. He d. in Paris, France, Mar. 10, 1868. (No issue.)

569. IX. Charles Augustus, b. Oct. 6, 1834, at Paris, France, d. Whitestone, L. I., July 12, 1855.

567. Elizabeth Smith. (521. Lorenzo, 339. Simeon, 130. Joshua, 17. James, 7. James, 2. James, 1. Thomas.) 2d child of Lorenzo Draper and his 2d wife. Sarah Elizabeth Dolliver. m. in New York, Apr. 30, 1846, Abraham Bininger. He was b. in New York, Apr. 3, 1816. She was lost at sea on the S.S, "Ville du Havre," off the French Coast, on Nov. 22, 1873.

CHILDREN:

570. I. Elizabeth Draper, b. Feb. 26, 1847, in New York.

571. II. Harriet, b. Dec. 2, 1849, in New York. m. Frank Alfred Post, in New York, Feb. 25, 1873. They had: I. Frederick, 574. b. in Paris, Dec. 16, 1873. II. Wright, 575. b. in Paris, Dec. 10, 1874. III. Elizabeth Charlotte, 576. b. in Paris, Jan. 2, 1875. IV. Donnell Shepperd, 577. b. in Paris, Feb. 12, 1876. V. George Henry Draper, 578. b. at Fontainebleau, France, June 27, 1881.

572. III. William Buyer, b. June 11, 1852, in New York.

573. IV. Frances Agnes, b. Oct. 24, 1853. m. New York, Aug. 25, 1887, Francis Robert Rives, Jr. He d. at Freehold, N. J., June 7, 1890.

522. Horace. (339. Simeon, 130. Joshua, 17. James, 7. James, 2. James, 1. Thomas.) 5th child, 3d s. of Captain Simeon Draper and Polly Bemis. He m.

Aug. 2, 1821, Eliza Andrews Tufts, of Boston, Mass. He was a merchant in Boston several years and then moved to Brooklyn, and from thence to Springfield, where he d. June 21, 1846. She d. May 12, 1867, aged 67.

CHILDREN:

579. I. Caroline E., b. Nov. 18, 1823, at Boston, m. Mar. 18, 1847, Edward Trask, of Springfield, Mass.

580. II. Horace T., b. July 4, 1825, at Brookfield.

581. III. William Henry, b. June 23, 1827, at Boston, d. at Brooklyn, N. Y., July 14, 1855. (Unmarried.)

582. IV. Simeon Francis, b. Nov. 9, 1830, at Brookfield. d. San Francisco, Oct. 21, 1891.

580. Horace T. (522. Horace, 339. Simeon, 130. Joshua, 17. James, 7. James, 2. James, 1. Thomas.) 2d child of Horace Draper and Eliza A. Tufts, m. Elizabeth, dau. of Michael Kern Erben and Miss Ortley. The Erbens were a well known Knickerbocker family. One of them, Henry Erben, was a celebrated organ builder. Horace T. Draper went to sea when 17 years of age, from Springfield, Mass., his first voyage being from New York to China. He continued in his profession for 23 years, during which time he went through all the grades up to Captain of one of the finest ocean steamers. He served as an officer on the flagship "Hartford" under Admiral Farragut during the Civil War. Appointed Acting Master U. S. Navy, Jan. 25, 1862. Resigned Aug. 9, 1862. Commissioned Acting Ensign Oct. 1, 1862. Appointment revoked, on account of sickness, Jan. 14, 1865. His wife was b. on May 6, 1827. d. July 16, 1884.

CHILDREN:

583. I. Horace, b. July 17, 1860, at Philadelphia, Pa. m. Dec. 10, 1885, Florence Davenport Hurr, of Philadelphia. One child, Louis Erben, 587. b. Oct. 21, 1886.

584. II. William Francis, b. Aug. 5, 1862. m. in Philadelphia, Oct. 12, 1887, Maude D., dau. of Frederick Turner and Mary Dinmore. She was b. May 30, 1862, in Philadelphia. One child, Maude E., 588. b. in Philadelphia, Apr. 11, 1889.

585. III. Charles Henry, b. Aug. 18, 1864.

586. IV. Louis Erben, b. Nov. 4, 1866. d. July 15, 1867.

525. Sophia. (339. Simeon, 130. Joshua, 17. James, 7. James, 2. James, 1. Thomas.) 8th child and 4th dau. of Simeon Draper and Polly Bemis. m. Oct. 13, 1817, at Brookfield, Henry Lewis. He was b. July 22, 1792, in Marlboro, d. in Brookfield, Sep. 9, 1860.

CHILDREN:

589. I. Henry Augustus, b. June 28, 1818, in Brookfield. d. Nov., 1819.

590. II. A son, d. on date of birth.

591. III. A dau., d. on date of birth.

592. IV. Sophia Augusta, b. June 27, 1821. d. Sep., 1822.

593. V. Joseph Warren, b. June 7, 1823, in Boston.

594. VI. Henry, b. Dec. 21, 1824, in Boston, d. Oct. 20, 1886, in Philadelphia.

595. VII. Mary Draper, b. Feb. 28, 1827, in Roxbury. m. Charles O. Brewster, of Boston, Dec. 27, 1854, in Philadelphia, d. Apr. 10, 1873. He was b. Oct. 10, 1827. d. Aug. 27, 1888. Buried in Brookfield. Children:— I. Charles Osmyn, 600. b. Philadelphia, Oct. 4, 1856. II. Sophia Lewis, 601. b. Philadelphia, Apr. 11, 1858. III. Lewis, 602. b. Philadelphia, Oct. 10, 1860, d. Brooklyn, June 7, 1890. IV. Mary Jones, 603. b. Brookfield, March 20, 1862. V. William Lewis, 604. b. Germantown, Aug. 2, 1866. VI. Walter Stoughton, 605. b. Brookfield, Feb. 26, 1868.

596. VIII. Walter Herron, b. Nov. 5, 1829, at Roxbury.

597. IX. Sophia, b. July 16, 1832, in Brooklyn, N. Y. d. Dec, 1833, in Brooklyn, where she is buried.

598. X. Sarah Ann, b. Sep. 10, 1834, in Brooklyn, N. Y. m. in Brookfield, July 24, 1862, Christian K. Ross, of Philadelphia. He was b. at Middletown, Pa., Nov. 6, 1823. Children:— I. William Lewis, 606. b. Apr. 24, 1863. d. Apr. 25, 1863. II. Augustus Stoughton, 607. b. Philadelphia, April 10, 1864. d. Orange, N. J., Dec. 3, 1890. III. Henry Augustus, 608. b. Philadelphia, Nov. 1, 1865. IV. Sophia Lewis, 609. b. July 14, 1867, Germantown, Pa. V, Walter Lewis, 610. b. Oct. 12, 1868, at Germantown, Pa. VI. Charles Brewster, 611. b. Germantown, Pa., May 4, 1870. Stolen in Germantown, July 1, 1874. Never recovered. VII. Marian Kimball, 612. b. June 8, 1872, in Germantown, Pa. VIII. Ann Christian, 613. b. Nov. 16, 1873, in Germantown. IX. Winslow Lewis, 614. b. Jan. 1, 1880, at Germantown. d. Cape May, N. J., July 7, 1880.

599. XI. William Draper, b. Apr. 6, 1840, in Philadelphia, d. June 14, 1866, in Brookfield, where he is buried.

593. Joseph Warren. (525. Sophia, 339. Simeon, 130. Joshua, 17. James, 7. James, 2. James, 1. Thomas.) m. Ann Homer, Nov. 9, 1848, dau. of Joseph and Nancy Kidder, of Boston. She was b. in Boston, July 27, 1825.

CHILDREN:

615, I. Francis Draper, b. Boston, Aug. 29, 1849. m. in Philadelphia, Apr. 28, 1887, Mary H. Chandler. She was b. at Zanesville, O., May 5, 1864. Their children are: — I. Mary Chandler, 619. b. in Philadelphia, Aug. 10, 1888. II. Joseph Warren, 620. b. in Philadelphia, Aug, 20, 1889. III. Julia Peabody, 621. b. in Philadelphia, Sep. 24, 1890.

616. II. Katherine Kidder, b. in Philadelphia, Mar. 5, 1851.

617. III. Joseph Kidder, b. in Philadelphia, Apr. 9, 1859. m. at Philadelphia, June 21, 1887, Sally Benedict Potter, of Philadelphia. She was b. Dec, 1864. Children: — I. George Draper, 622. b. Evanston, Ill., May 25, 1888. II. Raymond Potter, 623. b. Evanston, Ill., Mar. 20, 1891.

618. IV. George Draper, b. Jan. 11, 1861, in Philadelphia.

594. Henry. (525. Sophia, 339. Simeon, 130. Joshua, 17. James, 7. James, 2. James, 1. Thomas.) 6th child, 4th s. of Sophia Draper and Henry Lewis, m. Sep., 1849, Fanny Hannah Wilson, of Philadelphia. He was a prominent merchant of Philadelphia; head of the firm of Lewis Bros. & Co., of Philadelphia, New York, Boston, Chicago and Baltimore, in each of which cities they had branch houses. He was a director and officer in several railroads, steamship lines and banks. A highly respected, genial and much beloved man in Philadelphia, the place of his residence, and wherever he went. His brothers, Joseph, 593, and Walter, 596, were partners in business with him.

CHILDREN, ALL B. IN PHILADELPHIA:

624. I. Simeon Draper, b. July 1, 1850. d. Florence, Italy, Apr. 14, 1870.

625. 11. Henry, b. Nov. 18, 1855. m. Apr. 30, 1879, Sarah Jane, dau. of John F. Orne, of Philadelphia. Have Ethel Lewis, 627, b. Philadelphia, Feb. 12, 1880.

626. III. William Draper, b. Apr., 1867.

596. Walter Herron. (525. Sophia, 339. Simeon, 130. Joshua, 17. James, 7. James, 2. James, 1. Thomas.) 8th child, 5th s. of Sophia Draper and Henry Lewis, m. Feb. 14, 1856, in New York, Arabella Brazier Dash. She was b. New York, Dec. 15, 1829.

CHILDREN:

628. I. Fannie Draper, b. Dec. 3, 1856, in Paris, France, d. Dec. 13, 1863, in Philadelphia.

629. II. Arabella Catherine, b. Jan. 14, 1858, in Philadelphia, d, Oct. 27, 1869, in New York.

630. Ill, Walter Herron, b. Oct. 17, 1859, in Philadelphia,

631. IV. William Dash, b. July 5, 1861, at Germantown, Pa. d. Jan. 12, 1866, in New York.

632. V. Alice Madeline, b. Sep. 3, 1872, in Newport, R. I.

633. VI. Mabel Anzonella, b. Dec. 23, 1875, in New York.

528. William Bemis. (339. Simeon, 130. Joshua, 17. James, 7. James, 2. James, 1. Thomas.) 11th child, 7th s. of Simeon Draper and Polly Bemis. m. Mar. 18, 1841, Elizabeth, dau. of John Haggerty, of New York, and Maria Allaire of Nova Scotia, and granddau. of the Due de Bouillon. She was b. in New York, Jan. 17, 1819, and was the sister of Frances S., who married Simeon Draper, 529, a younger brother of William Bemis.

Mr. Draper enjoyed a good school education, and then entered business. When about 24 years old he went to Paris, France, and started a wholesale dry goods store. He remained abroad about ten years, returning to America with a considerable fortune. He then began the same business in New Orleans, largely increasing his wealth, and retired about 1840 from all business. From that time until the War of the Rebellion, Mr. Draper devoted his time between this country and Europe, where his travels were long and extensive. He became connected with a number of mercantile enterprises in New York, as a silent partner, and was, in 1855, Treasurer of the New York & Harlem R.R. Company. In company with Morris Franklin, formerly the well known President of the New York Life Insurance Company, and Samuel B. Parsons, he organized the Flushing and Queens County Bank, of which he was for many years the President. Mr. Draper was an earnest and active Republican, and gave large sums for the prosecution of the war, and was actively employed by President Lincoln in several financial emergencies. Both Mr. Lincoln and General Grant tendered Federal office to Mr. Draper, but he preferred to remain in private life. Old age weakened his interest in politics, but when James G. Blaine was nominated for the Presidency, Mr. Draper supported him warmly, and was taken from his sick bed to the polls to vote by his nephew, Col. T. W.-M. Draper, 651, and his son-in-law, Robert S. Bowne. He was always much interested in the history and genealogy of the family, and accumulated some of the data which has been used in this history. He took great pride in the old homestead at Brookfield, and was a liberal contributor to its charities and public institutions. He secured, while in New Orleans, a writing desk which had been part of the furniture of the private library of King Louis XVI. at Versailles, and donated it to the Public Library at Brookfield. Of his many unostentatious deeds of charity much might be said in the way of praise. He never let his right hand know the many deeds of charity done by his left. In an editorial speaking of his death, the Flushing "Times," of April 18, 1885. said, amongst other things: "Few men could have left us whose memory will be so widely cherished. For there dwelt in his heart no unkind thought, no uncharitable disposition. This genial nature had room for every friend, and they were so many that they occupied it to the entire exclusion of an ungracious sentiment."

CHILDREN:

634. I. Francis, b. Jan. 31, 1842, in New York. Drowned at Whitestone, L. I., Aug. 8, 1850.

635. II. Jessie, b. Jan. 7, 1846, in New York. m. at Flushing, June 1, 1864,

Robert Southgate, s. of Walter Bowne, of Flushing, and Eliza Rappalye, of East New York. He was b. at Flushing, Sep. 18, 1842.

CHILDREN, ALL B. AT FLUSHING.

636. I. Elizabeth Haggerty, b. Dec. 4, 1866.

637. II. Francis Draper, b. July 21, 1868.

638. III. Walter, b. Apr. 2, 1870. m. at Flushing, Jan. 27, 1892, Catharine, dau. of Frederic A. Guild.

639. IV. Marion Southgate, b. Oct. 3, 1872.

529. Simeon. (339. Simeon, 130. Joshua, 17. James, 7. James, 2. James, 1. Thomas.) 12th child, 8th s. of Simeon Draper and Polly Bemis. m. at New York, Oct. 30, 1834, Frances S., dau. of John Haggerty and sister of Elizabeth, who m. Simeon Draper's older brother, William Bemis, 528.

Mr. Draper was a celebrated figure in New York, one of those who sat at Philip Hone's "Round Table" where Henry Clay, Daniel Webster and John Jacob Astor used to meet. He was a prominent merchant in New York and Boston, but was unfortunate in business and became an auctioneer for the Government. He was an active Whig, and was among the personal friends of William Seward, but soon after the formation of the Republican party he opposed Gov. Seward's policy. He was several times a member of the New York Whig State Central Committee, and in 1864 was chairman of the Republican party. He was Provost Marshal for New York City in 1862, and was appointed Collector for the Port of New York, Sep. 7, 1864, by President Lincoln, but resigned in 1865. At the time of his death he was Government Cotton Agent, having charge of all the cotton received at New York. For many years before the Civil War Mr. Draper was one of the Board of Governors in charge of the City Charities which controlled Blackwell's Island, etc., and after the law creating this Board was repealed he was Commissioner of Public Charities and Correction until his resignation of that office in 1864. His sudden death prevented the carrying out of a well developed plan for his nomination for Governor on the Republican ticket.

CHILDREN:

640. I. Marie, b. 1835.
641. II. Fanny, b. 1837.
642. III. John Haggerty, b. Apr. 4, 1839. d. Aug. 1, 1890.
643. IV. Julian, b. 1841. d. in infancy.
644. V. Henry, b. 1843.

642. John M. (529. Simeon, 339. Simeon, 130. Joshua, 17. James, 7. James, 2. James, 1. Thomas.) 3d child, eldest s. of Simeon Draper and Frances Haggerty. m. in New York, Oct. 22, 1862, Victorine Upshur, dau. of Col. Robert C. Wetmore and Adelia Geer. She was b. in New York, Jan. 25, 1843.

Few men in New York were better known than John H. Draper. This was due not alone to his calling which brought him in contact with hosts of people, but also to his genial temperament, his ready wit, and his great good fellowship. A man of commanding physique, 6 ft. 4 in height, he was always conspicuous in a crowd, and was not unfrequently an object of raillery among his innumerable acquaintances; but he always returned their sallies with interest and was rarely worsted in such encounters. His social connections were such that he was on terms of intimacy and familiarity with numbers of club men, and this fact gave him an inestimable advantage in his business. For instance, in making a sale he would often single out some well known face from those before him and bombard the unfortunate victim with witticisms and jests upon incidents of their social relationship. Such an expedient invariably put the crowd of buyers in good humor, and proportionately augmented the success of the sale. But his jests were always without sting, and his sallies without venom. He was a loved and admired husband and father, and thousands will remember his wife and himself as the most distinguished couple of their time on Fifth avenue. He was educated at the public schools of New York and Columbia College, and was an enthusiastic member of the famous 7th Regiment, being a Quartermaster Sergeant when he went with his regiment to the front in the Civil War. He at one time had his brother Henry and George T. Kellog associated with him in business after the death of his father. The firm was subsequently dissolved on account of financial embarrassments, and he became associated with his brother-in-law, C. F. Wetmore, in the Fifth Ave. Auction Rooms. When Joel B. Erhardt became Collector of the Port of New York, he appointed Mr. Draper Auctioneer of the Custom House, as also did U. S. Marshal Jacobus. He was a member of the Union Club from 1868; also of the Metropolitan Club of Washington and of the Coney Island Jockey Club. He was a member of the Holland Lodge F. & A. M., and had taken the 32d degree.

CHILDREN:

645. I. Amy, b. Sep. 10, 1864, in New York. m. Dr. William, s. of Dr. William May, of Washington, D. C, in New York, Nov. 14, 1888.

646. II. Edith, b. Oct. 10, 1866, in New York.

644. Henry. (524. Simeon, 339. Simeon, 130. Joshua, 17. James, 7. James, 2. James, 1. Thomas.) 5th child and 3d s. of Simeon Draper and Frances Haggerty. m. in New York, Sep. 6, 1864, Gertrude, dau. of Joseph Burroughs Vandervoort, of New York, and Laetitia Van Wyck, of Fishkill, N. Y. She was b. Apr. 14, 1843.

CHILDREN:

647. I. Henry Julian, b. Jan. 17, 1867, in New York. d. Aug. 6, 1867.

648. II. William Vandervoort, b. Feb. 25, 1869, in New York.

649. III. Francis Simeon, b. Mar. 20, 1871, in New York. d. Feb. 1, 1872.

534. Theodore Sedgwick. (339. Simeon, 130. Joshua, 17. James, 7. James, 2. James, 1. Thomas.) 17th child, 13th s. of Simeon Draper and Polly Bemis. m. in Philadelphia, Pa., Dec. 9, 1851, Elizabeth, dau. of Thomas Wain-Morgan and Hannah Griffiths. She was b, at Philadelphia, Aug. 9, 1819. d. at Dresden, Saxony, Dec. 7, 1874.

Mr. Draper was a well known figure in New York social and business life, a merchant of prominence in Paris and New York, associated at one time with his brother Simeon in business. But on the dissolving of that firm he went into the brokerage business in Wall street, which he gave up in 1866 to take his family abroad to educate his children. Prior to the Civil War he was Lieut. Col. and then Colonel of the 2d Regiment, Washington Greys, New York State Militia, which subsequently became the 11th Regiment, N. G. S. N. Y. He was frequently offered appointments under the general Government. The only one he accepted was near the close of his life, when he was appointed Deputy Collector of the Port of New York when President Chester A. Arthur was Collector. He was a great admirer and a warm personal friend of the President as he was of General Grant, who offered him at various times during his residence in Europe the Consulship of Dresden, Munich and Brussels, all of which he declined except the Munich Consulship, which he consented to hold for a short time pending the selection of a competent person. He was like all the family almost without an exception, a strong Republican in politics, an earnest upright man, and one generally respected and beloved, not only by his family, but by all his acquaintances.

CHILDREN:

650. I. Florence Morgan, b. in Philadelphia, May 24, 1853. m. in Dresden, Saxony, Mar. 1, 1870, Henri Antoine de Meli. They have: I. Henri Gabriel Diophebe, 653. b. at Vevey, Switzerland, Nov. 29, 1870. II. Marie Antoinette, 654. b. in Dresden, Saxony, June 20, 1875.

651. II. Thomas Waln-Morgan. (534. Theodore Sedgwick, 339. Simeon, 130. Joshua, 17. James, 7. James, 2. James, 1. Thomas.) 2d child, eldest s. of Theodore Sedgwick Draper and Elizabeth Morgan, b. in New York, Mar. 12, 1855. m. by Rev. Dr. Nelson, at Grace Church, New York, June 4, 1884, Jeanne Louise Graham, dau. of Dr. Alexander Kelsey and Elizabeth Boyd Gould, of Rochester, N. Y. She was b. June 6, 1862.

Mr. Draper went to private schools in New York until he was 12 years old, and then with his parents, sister and brother, went abroad to complete his education. There he attended school, first in Germany, then for a short time in England, and completed his schooling in Paris and Switzerland. He was now prepared, and entered the Royal Polytechnicum at Munich, Bavaria, graduating therefrom as a Civil Engineer in the Class of 1873. He then entered the Royal School of Mines at Friberg, Saxony, graduating as a Mining Engineer in 1875. During the Franco-German War of 1870, he participated as a volunteer with the regiment to which he was attached, the 2d Saxon Lancers, forming part of the 12th Army Corps, and saw much service with them— the siege of Metz, the battle and capitulation of Sedan, the siege of Paris, and the first and second battles of Orleans. His regiment also participated with General von Werder's army in the pursuit of General Bourbaki's army, which they finally drove over the frontier into Switzerland. During his long residence in Europe Col. Draper visited almost every part of the Continent, and the British Isles, taking these trips during the Summer vacations between the school or college terms. At Munich he belonged to the Corps Vitruvia, and at Friberg to the Corps Montania. He had the usual number of affairs of honor thought necessary at a German University, being once severely wounded in a sabre duel. In the Summer of 1874 Col. Draper was insulted by a local banker of Friberg, whom he thereupon challenged. The banker declared that he would give satisfaction and would not apologize, but immediately informed the authorities of the fact of his having been challenged, the result being, that although the legal code in Germany frowns upon duelling, as a matter of fact none of the local authorities care to prosecute such cases, having participated in them themselves; but being forced to take action in the matter, Mr. Draper and his second were sentenced respectively to two months' and one month's imprisonment, as State prisoners in the celebrated fortress of Konigstein. Mr. Draper, however, served only one month, as His Majesty King John of Saxony, granted him a pardon as soon as the case had been laid before him. The result of the trial was that principal and second (he was a Mr. Barandian Eyredy) passed a delightful month at the Virgin Fortress, which overlooks the river Elbe — virgin because it has never been captured by an enemy— and they then returned to Friberg to become the lions of the hour. Col. Draper returned to the United States in the early Spring of 1876, and was immediately put in charge, through the friendship of President Grant for his father, as principal assistant of Professor Baird, of the collection made to illustrate the mineralogical and geological resources of the United States, at the Centennial Exposition in Philadelphia. This collection occupied the entire northwest corner of the Government Building in the Exposition grounds, and comprised over fifty thousand specimens, which had been all classed and arranged by the close of the month of August. The President, Genl. Grant, visited this collection on two occasions. Don Carlos of Spain was also a visitor. But the visitor who spent the most time and took the greatest interest in the collection was Dom Pedro, ex-Emperor of Brazil, who spent four days under Col. Draper's guidance, examining the entire collection.

In the Fall of 1876, Mr. Draper went to Colorado and the Western States and territories, and remained there in the practice of his profession, superintending mines and reduction works, etc. During this period, and in subsequent years, Col. Draper visited all the Western States and territories, Mexico, and parts of Central America, both in the prosecution of his professional duties, as well as for the investigation of the ancient remains of the former inhabitants of this hemisphere. His interest had been early awakened in the ancient history of America, by visits to the Pueblos in New Mexico, and Arizona of the Moqui and Zuni Indians. He was one of the earliest expounders of the faith that these village Indians were the descendants of the frontier inhabitants of the great Aztec Empire, conquered by Cortez. And in his search to prove this belief, he, in charge of expeditions fitted out by himself, or under the auspices of the Government, made many incursions into Mexico and Guatemala, in search of a mysterious city. Col. Draper has written a great deal on this subject in pamphlets, essays and stories. In 1878, Governor Frederick W. Pitkin of Colorado, commissioned Mr. Draper as Assistant Inspector General of the Colorado National Guard, with the rank of Captain, and subsequently, in Governor Pitkin's second term of office, he was promoted to the rank of Inspector General, with the rank of Colonel. During this period, the celebrated Ute Indian outbreak took place, in which the National Guard of Southern Colorado, to which Col. Draper was attached, was compelled to hold the frontier against the Indians for some weeks, until the Federal troops could come up and relieve them. It was a Winter of great and heavy snows, and many hardships were experienced by the troops, and many skirmishes took place. At the celebrated Chicago Republican Convention, at which James A. Garfield was nominated for the Presidency, Col. Draper was one of Colorado's six alternate delegates. It will be remembered that the State representatives voted from first to last for General Ulysses S. Grant for a third term of the Presidency. In 1882, Mr. Draper returned to the East and established himself in his native City of New York as Consulting Engineer. During this time he married, and resided at Flushing, L. I. In the Winter of 1888, he received the offer of the position of Assistant Genl. Mgr. and Chief Engineer, to build the Atlantic & Danville Railway. This he accepted, and went South to Norfolk, Va., to live, where he has since resided. After building the Atlantic & Danville Railway, which is a standard gauge road, running from Norfolk, Va., to Danville, Va., a distance of 206 miles, having numerous branches, be resigned to accept the position of Vice Presdt. and Genl. Mgr. of the Danville & East Tennessee R. R., which is the western extension of the Atlantic & Danville, from Danville, Va., to Bristol, Tenn., a distance of 180 miles. This road he is now engaged in constructing. During Col. Draper's residence in New York as Consulting Engineer, Col. Edward A. McAlpine requested him to take command of one of the companies of the 71st Regiment, National Guard, State of New York, to help to reorganize the regiment. This he accordingly did, commanding Company B of that famous organization. When the reorganization was completed, he resigned. Col. Draper has been a member of the Episcopal Church all his life. He was Senior Warden of St. James the Less, Lake City, Col., of which parish he was one of the founders. He is a member of the American Society of Mechanical Engineers, the Virginia Association of Engineers and Architects, the New York Society of the Sons of the Revolution, the Dedham Historical Society and numerous other clubs and organizations. He is the author of the "History of the Drapers in America," and has written on many other subjects. He has been a consistent National Republican in politics.

CHILDREN:

655. I. Louis Wain-Morgan, b. at Flushing, N. Y., Mar. 21, 1885. d. at Flushing, July 14, 1885.

656. II. Elizabeth Kelsey, b. at Flushing, May 3, 1886.

657. III. Dorothy Morgan, b. at Flushing, Dec. 4, 1887.

658. IV. Thomas Waln-Morgan, Jr., b. at St. George's, Staten Island, N. Y., Jan. 1, 1892.

652. III. Theodore Sedgwick. (534. Theodore Sedgwick, 339. Simeon, 130. Joshua, 17. James, 7. James, 2. James, 1. Thomas.) 3d child, 2d s. of Theodore Sedgwick Draper and Elizabeth Morgan, b. Apr. 12, 1857. m. in New York, Oct. 15, 1884, Matilda B. Downes. She was b. at Kilkee, Ireland, May 15, 1867. d. at Saratoga, N. Y., Sep. 15, 1886. He m. 2dly: in New York, Oct. 26, 1891, by Rev. A. J. Derbyshire, S. T. B., Nellie Areson, dau. of William H. Webb.

Mr. Theodore Draper is a member of the 7th Regiment, and Contractor on Public Works. He was educated in German)'and Switzerland.

342. William. (130. Joshua, 17. James, 7. James, 2. James, 1. Thomas.) 5th child and s. of Captain Joshua Draper and Mrs. Sarah Wright, m. Aug. 27, 1796, Betsy, dau. of Judge Niles, of Otsego, N. Y. She was b. at Pownal, Vt., Jan. 8, 1779. d. Otsego, N. Y., Mar. 17, 1813. He m. 2dly: Oct. 23, 1817, Clarissa, dau. of Squire Sprague. She was b. June 2, 1784. d. Jan. 5, 1855.

Mr. Draper moved from Spencer to Springfield, Mass., and from there to Granby, Otsego Co., N. Y. He was a member of high standing in the Episcopal

Church, and confirmed as such by the Right Rev. Bishop de Lancey. He was Senior Warden of St. Luke's Protestant Episcopal Church, at Granby. He held several important town and county offices, and was much esteemed.

CHILDREN, BY 1ST WIFE, ALL B. AT OTSEGO, N. Y.:

659. I. Sarah, b. July 29, 1797. d. July 11, 1843.

660. II. Simeon, b. Aug. 2, 1799.

661. III. Mary, b. Nov. 5, 1801. d. Dec. 14, 1828. m. Dr. Henry Harper, May 18, 1828.

662. IV. John M., b. Sep. 28, 1803. d. Jan. 3, 1853.

663. V. Eliza B., b. May 2, 1807. d. Nov. 9, 1840. m. 1st: Dr. Mason Tilden, of Warren, Herkimer Co., N. Y., July 21, 1822. Child: — William M., 669. b. Warren, N. Y., Nov. 18, 1823. m. 2dly: Dr. Dennis Kennedy, at Fulton, Oswego Co., N. Y., Jan. 1, 1838. He was b. in Connecticut, 1789. Child: — Dennis, 670. b. Lysander, Onondaga Co., N. Y., Feb. 26, 1839.

664. VI. Asa M., b. Apr. 7, 1809. d. Aug. 18, 1846.

665. VII. William S., b. Jan. 5, 1811. d. Mar. 1, 1849.

CHILDREN, BY 2D WIFE, ALL B. AT GRANBY:

666. VIII. Lavinia, b. Sep. 29, 1819.

667. IX. Alexander, b. Feb. 23, 1823. d. Nov. 21, 1823.

668. X. Clarissa, b. Dec. 26, 1824. d. Jan. 12, 1838.

659. Sarah. (342. William, 130. Joshua, 17. James, 7. James, 2. James, 1. Thomas.) Eldest child and dau. of William Draper and Betsy Niles. m. Otsego, N. Y., June 12, 1817, Jesse W. Baker. He was b. Oswego, Sep. 28, 1796.

CHILDREN:

671. I. Albert I., b. Richfield, June 29, 1818. m. Syracuse, N. Y., Jan. 1, 1841, Lucy Bicknell.

672. II. Elizabeth J., b. Richfield, Aug. 30, 1820. m. Granby, Dec. 1, 1842, Aaron Rice.

673. III. William 1., b. Richfield, Jan. 6, 1823. m. Steuben Co., N. Y., Sep. 1, 1843, Nancy Crysler.

674. IV. De Witt C, b. Richfield, Aug. 1, 1825. m. Granby, Jan. 8, 1848, Eliza J. Wilkey.

675. V. Asa Draper, b. Richfield, Jan. 16, 1827.

676. VI. James M., b. Richfield, Mar. 8, 1832. m. Feb. 6. 1853, Lydia Crysler.

677. VII. Mason E., b. Granby, Aug. 6, 1835. m. July 4, 1857, Mahalda Hannum.

660. Simeon. (342. William, 130. Joshua, 17. James, 7. James, 2. James, 1. Thomas.) Eldest s., 2d child of William Draper and Betsy Niles. m. June 17, 1828, Abigail Wright. She was b. Norwich, Hampshire Co., Mass., Dec. 28, 1808.

CHILDREN, ALL B. AT WATERLOO, N. Y.:

678. I. Mary E., b. July 8, 1829. m. Waterloo, N. Y., Oct. 18, 1857, Dr. Theron Bradford.

679. II. William R., b. May 17. 1831. d. Dec. 2, 1855.
680. III. Simeon D., b. Jan. 6, 1834. d. Dec. 26, 1837.
681. IV. Orin E., b. Oct. 29, 1836.
682. V. Theusa J., b. Feb. 4, 1839.
683. VI. Sarah E., b. July 1, 1841.
684. VII. Henry C, b. Apr. 3, 1845.
685. VIII. Charles, b. Jan. 9, 1848.

662. John M. (342. William, 130. Joshua, 17. James, 7. James, 2. James, 1. Thomas.) 4th child, 2d s. of William Draper and Betsy Niles. m. Warren, Herkimer Co., N. Y., Mar. 2, 1826, Fanny Wright. She was b. Norwich, Hampshire Co., N. Y., Apr. 16, 1803.

CHILDREN, ALL B. AT GRANBY, OTSEGO CO., N. Y.:

686. I. Mary E., b. Jan. 18, 1829. m. Granby, Jan. 18, 1848, B. F. Wilson.
687. II. Laura A., b. Nov. 9, 1838. m. Granby, June 14, 1853, D. Bosworth. d. Oct. 26, 1853.
688. III. Imogene, b. Nov. 19, 1836.
689. IV. Josephine J., b. May 25, 1839.
690. V. John, b. Oct. 27, 1843.
691. VI. Clinton W., b. May 24, 1847.

664. Asa M. (342. William, 130. Joshua, 17. James, 7. James, 2. James, 1. Thomas.) 6th child, 3d s. of William Draper and Betsy Niles. m. Utica, N. Y., July 29, 1830, Achsah Warne. She was b. in Cayuga Co., N. Y., Dec. 4, 1812.

CHILDREN:

692. I. Roderick M., b. Cayuga Co., N. Y., June 25, 1831.
693. II. Charles W., b. Cayuga Co., N. Y., May 23, 1833.
694. III. Catherine A., b. Cayuga Co., N. Y., July 2, 1834. m. Waterloo, N. Y., Sep. 6, 1854, Walter Quimby.
695. IV. Asa, b. Waterloo, N. Y., Oct. 13, 1837.
696. V. Achsah, b. Waterloo, N. Y., Nov. 17, 1839.
697. VI. Aaron C, b. Waterloo, N. Y., Aug. 11, 1842.
698. VII. De Lancy, b. Waterloo, N. Y., Nov. 2, 1844.

665. William S. (342. William, 130. Joshua, 17. James, 7. James, 2. James, 1. Thomas.) 7th child, 4th s. of William Draper and Betsy Niles. m. Granby, N. Y., Jan. 6, 1831, Mary Bowen. She was b. Granby, N. V., in 1816. d. Jan. 6, 1848.

CHILDREN, ALL B. AT GRANBY, N. Y.:

699. I. Elizabeth, b. Apr. 22, 1832. m. Nov. 2, 1850, Anson Haffron.
700. II. Ordelia, b. Mar. 9, 1835. m. Granby, N. Y., Feb. 17, 1855, Dr. Edward Haffron.
701. III. Clorissa, b. July 20, 1837. m. Granby, N. Y., Oct. 2, 1856, Perry Haffron.
702. IV. Mary b. Oct. 24, 1842.

666. Lavinia. (342. William, 130. Joshua, 17. James, 7. James, 2. James, 1. Thomas.) Eldest child and dau. of William Draper and Clarissa Spraguc. m.

Granby, N. Y., Dec. 26, 1843, Edward Somerville. He was b. Granby, N. Y., May 14, 1814.

CHILDREN, ALL B. AT GRANBY, OSWEGO CO., N. Y.:

703. I. William, b. Nov. 1, 1843.

704. II. Edward, 705. III. John (Twins), b. Aug. 4, 1845.

706. IV. Eugene, b. July 28, 1848.

707. V. Clarrissa, b. June 1, 1858.

132. Josiah. (17. James, 7. James, 2. James, 1. Thomas.) 5th s. and 6th child (2d of same name, the 1st dying in infancy,) of James Draper and his 2d wife, Abigail Child, m. at Dedham by Rev. Samuel Dexter, to Sarah, dau. of Aaron Ellis and Zipporah Lewis of Dedham, Jan. 31, 1751. She was b. May 22, 1733. d. Feb. 5, 1817. Josiah enlisted as a drummer in Capt. Ezekiel Plympton's Co., of Medfield, Mass., Sep. 25, 1778.

CHILDREN:

708. I. Sarah, b. Nov. 24, 1751. d. Sep. 16, 1794. m. Browne, of Wrentham.

709. II. Josiah, b. Oct. 14, 1753. d. May 17, 1819.

710. III. John, b. Sep. 25, 1755. d. June 23, 1823.

711. IV. Mille, b. Jan. 25, 1758. d. Apr, 21, 1824. m. Samuel Draper, 336, of Brookfield, her cousin.

712. V. Abigail, b. June 19, 1760. m. Mar. 28, 1782, Noah Robinson. He d. June 30, 1788. They had: I. Nabbie R., 720. b. June 10, 1783. m. James Thurber, of Providence, Jan. 26, 1806. He d. and she m. 2dly: Aaron Ellis, of Dedham, Sep. 1, 1809. She d. Mar. 14, 1836. II. Noah, 721. b. Sep. 18, 1785. d. 1786. Abigail m. 2dly: James Wheaton, of Providence, a saddler. Had one dau., III. Hannah, 722. b. 1800. m. Noah Smith.

713. VI. Paul, b. Aug. 23, 1762. d. Feb., 1866.

714. VII. Aaron, b. Nov. 29, 1764. d. July 8, 1818. m. Oct. 25, 1791, Amelia Sweet.

715. VIII. Lewis, b. May 3, 1767. d. Nov. 2, 1843. m. Lucy Orme, Sep. 25, 1788. She d. Nov. 22, 1847, aged 79 years.

716. IX. Ellis, b. Dec. 26, 1769. d. Aug. 26, 1851. m. Apr. 20, 1789, Lydia Miller. Children: — I. Arad, 723. m. Catherine Luther, of Spencer. II. Newell, 724. III. Lyman, 725.

717. X. James, b. Apr. 16, 1772. d. Nov. 10, 1856.

718. XI. Nancy, b. Nov. 5, 1775. d. Mar. 7, 1847. m. Titus, of Newton.

719. XII. Hannah.

709. Josiah. (132. Josiah, 17. James, 7. James, 2. James, i Thomas.) Eldest s. 2d child of Josiah Draper and Sarah Ellis, m. Mary, dau. of Dr. Berzolecl Mann, of Attleboro, and his wife Bebee, a dau. of Ezekiel Carpenter, of Attleboro (b. Oct. 1732. d. Oct. 1793)She was b. 1754. d. May 2, 1808. Dr. B. Mann was a celebrated physician in his lifetime.

CHILDREN, ALL B. IN ATTLEBORO, MASS.:

726. I. Preston, b. Nov. 29, 1777.

727. II. Polly, b. Mar. 15, 1779. m. 1st Gilman. One child, Zolide,

739. III. 2dly: George Nicolas. Children by 2d husband: Jerusha, 740, Joseph, 741, Nelson, 742, Francis, 743.

728. III. Herbert M., b. Feb. 3, 1781. d. Dec. 10, 1809.

729. IV. Tirzah, b. Oct. 11, 1782. d. in infancy.

730. V. Benjamin, b. Oct. 15, 1784. d. Oct. 12, 1802.

731. VI. Tirzah 2d, b. May 6, 1786. d. Nov. 1, 1865.

732. VII. Noah, b. May 14, 1788. d. Oct. 3, 1867.

733. VIII. Virgil, b. Jan. 4, 1789. d. Apr. 6, 1867.

734. IX. Fanny, b. Oct. 25, 1791. d. Aug. 3, 1880.

735. X. Susan R., b. Apr. 7, 1793.

736. XI. Bebee, b. May 2, 1796. m. the widower, Alfred Ware, of Franklin. He d. Mar. 11, 1855, aged 67. (No issue.)

737. XII. Amanda M., b. Jan. 13, 1798. d. Oct. 13, 1865. (Unmarried.)

738. XIII. Eunice M., b. Dec. 3, 1799. d. Mar. 2, 1869.

726. Preston. (709. Josiah, 132. Josiah, 17. James, 7. James, 2. James, 1. Thomas.) Eldest s. and child of Josiah Draper and Mary Mann. m. the widow Catherine (Hedden) Hudson.

CHILDREN:

744. I. Abby W., b. May 25, 1806. m. George Morse.

745. II. Elisia A., b. Feb. 3, 1809. m. Jason Guild.

746. III. Virgil, b. July 24, 1814.

747. IV. Louisa, b. (Jilted, and died of a broken heart.)

746. Virgil. (726. Preston, 709. Josiah, 132. Josiah, 17. James, 7. James, 2. James, 1. Thomas.) 3d child and only s. of Preston Draper and Catherine Hudson, m. his cousin, Anne Whiting, 967, dau. of Samuel Origin Draper, 962, and Nancy Whiting. She was b. Oct. 26, 1817.

CHILD:

748. I. Oscar M. m. 1st: Reliance Russell. 2dly: Hetty Woodward. Children by 1st wife: I. Oscar S., 749. b. June 19, 1856. II. Charles

750. b. May 30, 1867. III. Annie, 751. b. Dec. 25, 1870. Child, by 2d wife: Raymond, 752. b. June 13, 1887. All children b. at N. Attleboro.

728. Herbert M. (709. Josiah, 132. Josiah, 17. James, 7. James, 2. James, 1. Thomas.) 2d s., 3d child of Josiah Draper and Mary Mann. m. Sally, 878, dau. of John Draper, 710, and Sarah Hatch, his cousin.

CHILD:

753. I. Milton, b. July 10, 1808. d. June 12, 1884. m. Catherine, dau. of Nathan and Susan Lawrence, Jan. 28, 1839. She d. Nov. 1, 1885. Children: I. Susan L., 754. b. May 4, 1842. d. May 18, 1883. II. Mary E., 755. b. June 5, 1846. d. in infancy. III. Mary E. 2d, 756. b. June 6, 1849. IV. Hattie, 757, d. aged 17.

Susan L., 754, m. Jan. 19, 1865, Edwin Richards. Children: I. Carrie M., 758. b. May 30, 1869. d. Nov. 6, 1873. II. Irma T., 759. b. Oct. 19, 1875. III. Piercies E., 760. b. July 21, 18 —. d. May 17, 1887.

Mary E. 2d, 756. m. Nicholas B., s. of Nicholas W. Johnson and Mary Sprague, May 23, 1865. He died Mar. 17, 1886. Child: I. Herbert A., 761. b. Oct. 29, 1866.

731. Tirzah 2d. (709. Josiah, 132. Josiah, 17. James, 7. James, 2. James, 1. Thomas.) 3d dau., 6th child of Josiah Draper and Mary Mann. m. James, s. of William Page and Elizabeth Mason. (She was the 2d child of the same name, the 1st having d. in infancy.) Her husband was b. Dec. 2, 1781. d. Aug. 26, 1849.

CHILDREN, ALL B. IN ATTLEBORO:

762. I. Albert William, b. Mar. 24, 1812. d. Jan. 30, 1891.

763. II. Mary Mann, b. Nov. 3, 1813. m. John, s. of Joel and Susannah Metcalf.

764. III. Edwin Virgil, b. Nov. 25, 1815. d. Key West, Fla., Feb. 11, 1861.

765. IV. James Draper, b. Oct. 19, 1820. d. in infancy.

766. V. James Draper 2d, b. Sep. 18, 1822. d. Nov. 29, 1885.

768. VI. Elizabeth M., b. Mar. 22, 1826. d. in infancy.

769. VII. Elizabeth M. 2d, b. July 24, 1828. d. Dec. 15. 1870.

732. Noah. (709. Josiah, 132. Josiah, 17. James, 7. James, 2. James, 1. Thomas.) 4th s., 7th child of Josiah Draper and Mary Mann. m. 1st: Lucy, dau. of George Nicholas, m. 2dly: Nov. 12, 1828, Aurilla Graves. She was b. Sunderland, Mass., Nov. 8, 1804. d. Apr. 29, 1885.

Noah Draper, in early manhood, spent some years at the South, mostly in and around Charleston, S. C. Returning to New England, he was engaged for several years as a machinist in the construction of the mining gear in the first cotton mills erected in Providence, R. I., and in the very infancy of the cotton manufacture in this country. From there, about the year 1815, he removed with his family to Whitestone, in Oneida Co., N. Y. Pursuing the bent of his mind, he became a constructor of machinery adapted mostly for operating in the manufacture of cotton and woolen fabrics. Having purchased the cotton mills at Rome, he took up his residence at that place, running the mills, and at the same time carrying on a large mercantile business there. The lands he purchased at Rome have since become the most valuable portion of that city. Disposing of property, since become worth millions, he came to Chautauqua Co., in 1832, and settled at Dunkirk, where he engaged in the foundry business. He also had charge of the construction of that section of the Erie Railway (on the old track), terminating in Dunkirk, and laid the first ties and rails. He planned and caused to be built The Loder House, at Dunkirk, a large brick structure, which was burnt some 25 years since. In the year 1847 he removed to a small town called Cordova, and superintended the iron works then opened by Genl. Crosby. In 1856 he came to Fredonia, N. Y., where he had his residence until his death. He always sustained the character of an energetic, industrious, intelligent citizen, whose honesty and integrity were never questioned. It was with him a trait, peculiar and advantageous to himself and family, that he never misused his leisure hours. These were devoted to acquiring knowledge or to domestic society. He kept himself well informed on the events of the day, taking in his range the transactions of the world at large, as well as those of his own country. Though identifying himself with the Republican organization, he was never a partisan in the narrow sense of the word, but held the broader views of enlarged statesmanship, and always maintained his sentiments with the same modesty and honest consistency which characterized his conduct throughout a quiet career. In his last moments his mental faculties were possessed in all their freshness and activity.

CHILDREN, BY 1ST WIFE:

770. I. John Nicholas, b. June 6, 1812. d. 1866, Stillville, N. Y. (Unmarried.)

771. II. Herbert Mann, b. Dec. 26, 1813. d. St. Louis. He was Quarter

master under Genl. Lyon, and was with him at the battle of Wilson's Creek, July 10, 1861, when he, Genl. Lyon, was killed. He was a warm friend of Genl. Lyon's.

772. III. James Allen, b. Jan. 1, 1816. d. Erie, Aug. 27, 1847. m. Annie Kimball. Child: — I. Ella 783 — now Mrs. Hequembourg, of Buffalo. —

773. IV. Noah, Jr., b. Feb. 26, 1818. m. Eliza Hilton. Children: — I.Elinor,

784 (deceased). II. Silas Seymour, 785. III. Mrs. James Holstein, 786, of Dunkirk. IV. Mrs. Frank Allen, 787, of Bradford, Pa. He d. July 4, 1865, Sheridan, N. Y. Noah was engineer on the Erie R. R. for a time, and had charge of a squad of trackmen.

774. V. William, b. Dec. 26, 1819. d. Aug. 15, 1844. James and William enlisted on board the U. S. ship "Columbus" for a three years' voyage; went to the Mediterranean and the coast of Brazil.

775. VI. Horace, b. Aug. 10, 1821. d. as a child.

776. VII. George Josiah, b. Mar. 28, 1824. d. Aug. 3, 1864, Dunkirk, m. Emily Haight.

CHILDREN, BY 2D WIFE:

777. VIII. Horace Graves, b. Dec. 3, 1826. d. as a child.

778. IX. Orange Hanson, b. Mar. 3, 1829. m. Mary Elizabeth Wardwell.

Children: — I. Leila Foster, 788. II. Charles Wardwell, 789. He d. Mar. 27, 1867.

779. X. Lucy Aurilla, b. Apr. 3, 1831. m. Major George A. Camp, of Minneapolis, a millionaire, and veteran of the Civil War. She d. Aug., 1891. Children: — I. Charles Henry, 790. II. Charles. III. Ada Bell, 791. IV. Lucy May, 792. All deceased but Lucy M. She m. Henry von Wendelsteadt. Child: — Henry Albert, 793.

780. XI. Henry Thompson, b. July, 1833. d. as a child.

781. XII. Charles, b. June, 1836. m. Mary Wardwell, widow of his brother Orange. Child: — Harriet Taylor, 794.

782. XIII. Mary Augusta, b. July, 1838. Lives in Fredonia, N. Y.

Of this lady, the "Binghamton Leader," in a recent article, speaks thus highly: — "Miss Mary A. Draper, of Fredonia, was one of the speakers at the State Convention W. C. T. U., held in this city. Miss Draper is an educated lady earnest and enthusiastic in everything she undertakes, and well fitted for a public lecturer."

733. Virgil. (709. Josiah, 132. Josiah, 17. James, 7. James, 2. James, 1. Thomas.) 5th s., 8th child of Josiah Draper and Mary Mann. m. Eliza, dau. of Joseph Holmes and Mary Bullard, of Attleboro. She d. Rome, N. Y., July 3, 1872.

He had previously located at Whitesboro, Oneida Co., N. Y., where he was employed by his uncle, Newton Mann, a cotton manufacturer. Subsequently he removed to Rome, N. Y., where he owned and operated a cotton mill for many years. His brother Noah was for a time associated in this latter business with him. He was Vice Presdt. of the Fort Stanwix Bank, when he died.

CHILDREN, ALL B. ROME, N. Y.;

795. I. Anne Frances, b. Dec. 1, 1822.

796. II. Mary Bullard, b. Jan. 5, 1827.

797. III. Julia Holmes, b. Sep. 15, 1828.

795. Anne Frances. (733. Virgil, 709. Josiah, 132. Josiah, 17. James, 7. James, 2. James, 1. Thomas.) Eldest dau. of Virgil Draper and Eliza Holmes, m. Joseph A. Dudley, who accumulated a fortune in New York City in the drug business.

CHILDREN:

798. I. Eliza Holmes, b. 1850, Rome, N. Y. m. William S. Lyon, New York City. d. Nov. 10, 1879, New York. He d. New York, Apr. 22, 1884.

799. II. Charles Virgil, b. New York. m. Whitingsville, Mass., Sep. 19, 1878, Eliza A. Pollock. Children: — I. Frances O., 801. b. July 10, 1880. II. Eliza P., 802. b. July 17, 1883. III. Gladys, 803. b. Aug. 8, 1886. All b. Whitingsville, Mass.

800. III. William B., b. Brooklyn, N. Y., Nov., 1857. m. New York, Oct. 7, 1884, Ellie W. Roberts. She d. New York, Dec, 1890. Child:— I. Virgil Robert, 804. b. Westfield, N. J., June 20, 1887.

796. Mary Bullard. (733. Virgil, 709. Josiah, 132. Josiah, 17. James, 7. James, 2. James, 1. Thomas.) 2d dau. and child of Virgil Draper and Eliza Holmes, m. 1st: Henry S. Hill, druggist, Apr. 1, 1850. He d. Mar. 10, 1854. They had one child: Henrietta S., 805. b. Mar. 26, 1854, Rome, N. Y. She m. James P. Soper, Rome, N. Y., Nov. 16, 1882. He was a large lumber dealer in Chicago. Their children are: — I. Geraldine Draper, 811. b. Mar. 13, 1885, Chicago. II. James P., 812. b. Chicago, June 13, 1888.

Mary Bullard m. 2dly: Henry Kirke White, Rome, N. Y., Aug. 8, 1860, and had 5 children, all b. Rome, N. Y.:— I. Henry K., 806. b. June 11, 1861. d. Feb. 22, 1862. II. Anna E., 807. b. Feb. 22, 1864. d. Jan. 30, 1868. III. Harry Draper, 808. b. Oct. 2, 1865. IV. Jesse B., 809. b. Dec. 10, 1867. V. Emma E., 810. b. May 28, 1870.

797. Julia Holmes. (733. Virgil, 709. Josiah, 132. Josiah, 17. James, 7. James, 2. James, 1. Thomas.) 3d dau. and child of Virgil Draper and Eliza Holmes, m. Rome, N. Y., Nov. 6, 1854, Sidney R., s. of Dr. Roswell Kinney and Abby Mann, who was a granddau. of Newton Mann, a brother of Mary Mann, who m. Josiah Draper, 709. Mr. S. R. Kinney graduated at Hamilton College in 1850. d. Rome, N. Y., Sep. 21, 1861.

CHILDREN:

813. I. Henry Roswell, b. Sep. 2, 1855, Rome, N. Y. d. Brooklyn, N. Y., Nov. 2, 1858.

814. II. Frances Dudley, b. Oct. 16, 1857, Rome, N. Y. m. Rome, N. Y., Dec. 22, 1880, Oswald Prentice Backus, Counsellor at Law. Children: — I. Waldermine Draper, 815. b. Rome, N. Y., May 3, 1882. II. Oswald Prentice, 816. b. Bridgewater, Conn., Oct. 20, 1883. III. Sidney Kinney, 817. b. Rome, N. Y., June 29, 1887.

734. Fanny. (709. Josiah, 132. Josiah, 17. James, 7. James, 2. James, 1. Thomas.) 9th child, 4th dau. of Josiah Draper and Mary Mann. m. Nov. 6, 1813, Ira, s. of Calvin Richards and Lydia Richards.

CHILDREN:

818. I. Harriet D., b. Nov. 5, 1814. m. Dr. James W. Foster, June 27, 1839. He was b. Nov. 16, 1813. Children: — I. Jane F., 822. b. Jan. 22, 1 841. m. Edward E. Barrows. He was b. Feb. 16, 1839. II. James R., 823. b. May 2, 1844. m. Eva Phillips, June 19, 1879. III. Henry W., 824. b. May 27, 1847. d. July 17, 1848. IV. Henrietta, 825. b. July 14, 1849. m. Walter G. Clark, Nov. 17, 1874, s. of Dr. John L. Clark and Ann E. Milbur.

819. II. Edmond Ira, b. Nov. 27, 1815. d. May 15, 1882. m. Lucy Maria, dau. of Stephen Pitt Morse and Betsy Tingley, May 10, 1840. Children: — I. Anna Leslie, 826. b. Oct. 9, 1842. m. John Augustus, s. of Dr. Edwin A. Tweedie, Dec. 26, 1866. II. Ira, 827. b. May 3, 1845. d. July 23, 1846. III. Hattie Tingley, 828. b. June 21, 1847. IV. Edmond Ira, Jr., 829. b. June 26, 1852.

820. III. Josiah. m. Elizabeth Draper.

821. IV. Henrietta, m. Henry Barrows.

735. Susan R. (709. Josiah, 132. Josiah, 17. James, 7. James, 2. James, 1. Thomas.) 10th child, 5th dau. of Josiah Draper and Mary Mann. m. Hosea, s. of Abel Carpenter and Hannah Wilmerth, July 18, 1825, Rome, N. Y. He was b. Leyden, Vt.

CHILDREN:

830. I. Elira A., b. June 10, 1826, Providence, R. I. m. John M. Eddy, of E. Middleboro, Mass., Nov. 23, 1852. He d. Mar. 17, 1886. Children: — I. Florence, 836. b. Middleboro, May 4, 1855. m. Rainhard Jederman, Aug. 28, 1889,01 St. Paul, Minn. (Children: — I. Friedhelm E., 838, and II. Margaretta M., 839, twins, b. Oct. 1, 1890. d. in infancy.) II. Mary Morton, 837. b. May 24, 1861, E. Middleboro.

831. II. Herbert Mann, b. Jan. 13, 1828, Providence, R. I. m. there Kate G. Ladd. Children: — I. Frank, 840. (d. in infancy.) II. Henry L., 841. III. Edwin L., 842. (d. in infancy.)

832. III. Susan A., b. Dec. 13, 1829, Providence, R. I. m. there June, 1856, Dr. Horace H. Carpenter, who was b. Leyden, Vt., and is dead. Child:— I. Herbert E., 843. b. June, 1857, Derby, Vt. m. Lilian Andrew, of Providence, R.

I., in Minneapolis. (Children: — I. Paul Draper, 844. H. Leslie F., 845. III. Charles H., 846. b. Derby, Vt., Feb., 1862.)

833. IV. Andrew J. d. in infancy.

834. V. Richard M. J. & 835. VI. George W. (twins), d. in infancy.

738. Eunice M. (709. Josiah, 132. Josiah, 17. James, 7. James, 2. James, 1. Thomas.) 13th child, 8th dau. of Josiah Draper and Mary Mann. m. Oriskany, N. Y., Jan. 9, 1821, Ebenezer Rumford, s. of Captain Ebenezer Thomson and Rhoda Putnam, of Medford, Mass. He was a near relative of Genl. Israel Putnam. He graduated at Harvard College in 1816. d. Nov. 9, 1880.

CHILDREN

847. I. Henry & 848. II. Henrietta, (twins) d. Rome, N. Y., in infancy.

849. III. Louisa Capron, b. Warren, O., 1822. m. William W. Brigham, of Dunkirk, N. Y. (No issue.)

850. IV. Margaret Marion, b. Jan. 12, 1824, Warren, O. d. Dunkirk, N. Y., Sep. 9, 1858. (Unmarried.)

851. V. Julia King, b. Dec. 15, 1831, Dunkirk, N. Y. m. Julien Taintor Williams, 1851. Children:— I. Henrietta Clarke, 854. b. July 3, 1853. m. 1875, Walter Scott, of Philadelphia. (Children:— I. Walter R., 861. b. Feb. 3, 1876. II. Geraldine W., 862. b. Feb. 13, 1878. III. Maxwell W., 863. b. Feb. 3, 1880. IV. Adelaide L., 864. b. Feb. 9, 1882.) II. Henry Kirk, 855. b. Dunkirk, N. Y., 1856. m. May Elizabeth Willis, Oct., 1889. III. Jessie Carlyle, 856. b. Jan. 28, 1858. m. Charles W. Hinkley, of Chicago, June, 1884. (Child:— I. Gerald Watson, 865. b. Feb., 1889.) IV. Geraldine Emmeline, 857. b. Oct., 1860, d. May, 1867. V. Adelaide Thomson, 858. VI. Mabel Walton, 859. b. 1865. VII. Gerald Bismarck, 860. b. Apr. 1, 1870.

852. VI. Adelaide Amanda, b. May 6, 1833, Dunkirk, N. Y. m. Byron W. Clarke, 1851. She d. Dunkirk, 1864. Children:— I. Julia Eldridge, 866. b. Dec. 28, 1853, Dunkirk, d. 1857. II. Charles Cortland, 867. b. Dec, 1855, Buffalo, N.Y. III. Katie Lee, 868, and IV. Addie Thomson, 869 (twins), b. Sep. 9, 1858, Dunkirk. (Katie d. Brooklyn, N. Y., 1882; Addie d. 1880.) V. Camille Louise, 870. b. Apr., 1861, Dunkirk. Resides in Brooklyn, N. Y.

853. VII. Ebenezer Kirk, b. Nov., 1839, Dunkirk, N. Y. m. Mary Ann Waters, of Philadelphia, Dec, 1859. Children: — I. Louise Dudley, 871. b. Dunkirk, 1860. II. Emma Waters, 872. b. Dunkirk, 1862. III. Ebenezer Francis, 873. b. Dunkirk, 1865. IV. Henry Kirk, 874. b. Titusville, Pa., 1868. V. Arthur Rumford, 875. b. Titusville, Pa., 1871. All live in Titusville.

710. John. (132. Josiah, 17. James, 7. James, 2. James, 1. Thomas.) 3d child, 2d s. of Josiah Draper and Sarah Ellis, m. Sarah, dau. of Nathan Hatch and Amory Stanley.

CHILDREN:

876. I. Paul, b. Mar. 12, 1778. d. Mobile, 1819.

877. II. Lemuel, b. N. Attleboro, Jan. 15, 1780. d. July 29, 1866.

878. III. Sally, b. Oct. 23, 1781. m. Herbert M., 728, s. of Josiah Draper, 709, and Mary Mann, her cousin.

879. IV. Clarissa, b. Dec. 14, 1784. (Unmarried.)

880. V. Harriet L., b. Attleboro, Aug. 31, 1788. d. Aug. 14, 1869.

881. VI. John, b. Feb. 20, 1790. d. June, 1830.

882. VII. Horatio, b. Mar. 12, 1795. d. in infancy.

883. VIII. Horatio N., b. Mar. 13, 1797. m. Dec. 24, 1836, his cousin, Clementine, 1102, dau. of James Draper, 717, and Sally Perry. Child: — Carry, b. Aug. 15, 1843. d. 1861.

884. IX. Alonzo, b. Dec. 7, 1798. d. in infancy.

885. X. Barton Ingraham, b. July 25, 1800. d. Feb. 5, 1887.

876. Paul. (710. John, 132. Josiah, 17. James, 7. James, 2. James, 1. Thomas.) Eldest child, eldest s. of John Draper and Sarah Hatch, m. Feb. 26, 1800, Mary Tingley, of Providence, R. I. She d. Attleboro, Mass., 1816, aged 38 years.

CHILDREN, ALL B. ATTLEBORO, MASS.:

886. I. Mary Ann, b. 1801. d. 1861. m. Virgil Morse. Child: — I. Alonzo Draper, 891. d. 1864. (Unmarried.)

887. 11. Alonzo, b. 1803. d. 1846. (Unmarried.) Was a member of the firm of Thomas Hunt & Co., cloth importers, of New York.

888. III. Caroline, b. 1807. d. 1809.

889. IV. Charles Tingley, b. 1811. d. 1880.

890. V. Caroline 2d, b. 1812. d. 1841. (Unmarried.)

889. Charles Tingley. (876. Paul, 710. John, 132. Josiah, 17. James, 7. James, 2. James, 1. Thomas.) 4th child, 2d s. of Paul Draper and Mary Tingley. m. Ellen Childs, of Falmouth, Mass.

He was for many years a New York City merchant, and was the Draper of "Draper, Clarke & Co.," wholesale dealers in hats, caps and furs. He was well known for his amiable disposition and domestic habits and tastes, and was much beloved by his neighbours and friends.

CHILDREN:

892. I. Charles Albert, b. 1855. (Unmarried.) Is Paymaster and Purchasing Agent of the N. Y. O. & W. R.R. Co. Also Secretary and Purchaser of the "Mohegan Barite Co."

893. II. Minnie Tingley, b. 1857. (Unmarried.)

894. III. Alonzo, b. 1858. Is a practicing lawyer of Sing Sing, N. Y.

895. IV. Paul, b. 1864. d. 1890. (Unmarried.)

896. V. Benjamin L'Hommedieu, b. 1876. d. 1886.

877. Lemuel. (710. John, 132. Josiah, 17. James, 7. James, 2. James, 1. Thomas.) 2d s. and child of John Draper and Sarah Hatch, m. Portsmouth, N. H., Aug. 1, 1807, by Rev. Joseph Buckminster, Hannah Cotton Rogers. She was b. N. Attleboro, July 2, 1781, d. Mar. 1, 1847.

CHILDREN:

897. I. Caroline Rogers, b. Apr. 10, 1808. d. Aug. 6, 1885. m. Dover, N. H., May 20, 1830, by Rev. Hubbard Winsloe, the Rev. Amos Blanchard. He d. Jan. 14, 1870. Children: — I. Amos, 905. b. Apr. 12, 1831. II. Hannah Draper, 906.

b. Mar. 23, 1832. m. June, 1862, Horace Webster. III. Edward, 907. b. Sep. 17, 1837. d. May 26, 1838. IV. Edward 2d, 908. b. Sep. 8, 1841. d. Aug. 21, 1842.

898. II. Daniel Rogers, b. Oct. 19, 1809. d. July 10, 1839.

899. III. Hannah Rogers, b. Aug. 1, 1811. m. Dover, N. H., May 26, 1835, by Rev. David Root, Eli French. He d. July 21, 1868. Children: — I. William Rogers, 909. b. May 30, 1836. II. Hannah Draper, 910. b. Apr. 1, 1839. m. Oct. 21, 1862, in New York, Dr. James H. Wheeler. III. Samuel Gates, 911. b. May 25, 1843. m. Nov. 4, 1874, in New York, Bessie M. Arthur. She d. Oct. 22, 1880. He m. 2dly: Katherine Calnor, Apr. 3, 1889. IV. Elizabeth Rogers, 912. b. July 5, 1847. d. Aug. 27, 1847. V. George Rogers, 913. b. Dec. 9, 1849. d. Dec. 6, 1889.

900. IV. William Cotton, b. Aug. 31, 1812. d. Oct. 26, 1812.

901. V. George Rogers, b. Sep. 7, 1813.

902. VI. Anna A. Rogers, b. Sep. 23, 1814. m. New York, by Rev. Amos Blanchard, June 18, 1837, John S. Taylor. Children:—I. Sarah Louisa, 914. b. July 22, 1838. II. John Sidney, 915. b. Sep. 5, 1840. III. William Chester, 916. b. Sep. 2, 1842. d. Sep. 25, 1844.

IV. Hannah Rogers, 917. b. Aug. 17, 1844. d. July 15, 1885.

V. Lemuel Rogers, 918. b. Apr. 10, 1847. d. Feb. 10, 1849. VI. Frank Rogers, 919. b. Mar. 24, 1848. d. June 2, 1848. VII. Caroline Blanchard, 920. b. Oct. 20, 1850. d. Aug. 7, 185 1. VIII. Anna Emery, 921. b. Feb. 24, 1853. d. Sep. 2, 1853.

903. VII. William Cutter, b. Oct. 12, 1815. d. June 15, 1861. m. by Rev. James Tyng, at Brooklyn, N. Y., Oct. 18, 1848, Sarah E. Atkins. Children:— I. Hannah Rogers, 922. b. Aug. 22, 1849. II. William Dudley, 923. d. young. III. Leopold Frederick Augustus, 924. d. young. IV. Margaret Higginson, 925. d. young.

904. VIII. John Lemuel, b. Dec. 15, 1816. d. Jan. 19, 1864. m. by Rev. Brown Emerson, Oct. 17, 1849, at Salem, Mass., Caroline Augusta Sprague. She d. Aug., 1855. Children: — I. George Sprague, 926. b. Feb. 28, 1851. d. July 28, 1852. II. John Lemuel, Jr., 927. b. Nov. 3, 1852. d. same day. III. Caroline Augusta, 928. b. Aug. 4, 1855. m. John N. Woodfin.

880. Harriet L. (710. John, 132. Josiah, 17. James, 7. James, 2. James, 1. Thomas.) 5th child, 3d dau. of John Draper and Sarah Hatch, m. 1815, Javez Lorett.

CHILDREN:

929. I. Sarah Ann, m. Francis A. Fisher. She adopted Caroline, 928, the dau. of her first cousin John L. Draper, 904. Children: — I. Francis Egerton, 935. II. Alice Townsend, 936. III. Howard Fisher, 937. IV. John Draper, 938.

930. II. Louisa Matilda, d. unmarried.

931. III. Elizabeth Cornell, m. Charles A. Townsend, of Brooklyn, N. Y. Children:— I. Alice, 939. m. Lieut. Commander Miller, U. S. N. II. Emma, 940, deceased.

932. IV. William Sterry, d. aged six years.

933. V. Henrietta Frances, m. James R. Ludlow, Judge of the Court of Common Pleas, Philadelphia, Pa. Children: — I. Anna Kathleen, 941 (deceased). II. Clarissa Draper, 942. m. Charles Gibbins, Jr., of Philadelphia, Pa. III. Harriet

Louisa, 943. m. Dr. Joseph S. Neff. IV. Elizabeth Fisher, 944. m. Jacob L. Van Dewenter, of Netherwood, N. J.

934. VI. William Henry (deceased).

881. John. (710. John, 132. Josiah, 17. James, 7. James, 2. James, 1. Thomas.) 6th child, 3d s. of John Draper and Sarah Hatch, m. N. Providence, R. I., May 9, 1824, Harriet W. Tisdale. She was b. Feb. 5, 1805. d. Oct. 18, 1883.

CHILDREN:

945. I. Harriet Elizabeth, b. Aug. 6, 1826. m. Jan. 19, 1847, Josiah Draper Richards. d. Jan. 11, 1891. Her husband was b. July 7, 1827. d. July 18, 1890. Child:— Ira, 947. b. Mar. 25, 1852. m. Jan. 2, 1879, Lydia R. Raynord, of New Bedford. (Children:— I. Ira, 948. b. Sep. 20, 1879. II. Marion, 949. b. Feb. 3, 1881.)

946. II. Sarah Ann, b. Dec. 4, 1827. m. 1850, Charles E. W. Sherman, a direct descendant of Miles Standish, 8 generations removed. Children: — I. Helen, 950. b. Aug. 22, 1851. II. William W., 951. b. July 21, 1853. m. Harriet C. Solace, of Bridport, Vt., Oct. 10, 1878. (Child:— I. Charles H., 952. b. Apr. 4, 1880.)

885. Barton Ingraham. (710. John, 132. Josiah, 17. James, 7. James, 2. James, 1. Thomas.) Youngest child, 7th s. of John Draper and Sarah Hatch, m. Nov. 28, 1833, Julia, dau. of Joseph Holmes (b. June 8, 1765. d. Dec. 23, 1813,) and Mary Bullard (b. Oct. 30, 1764. d. Dec. 21, 1815). She was b. Feb. 18, 1802. d. July 22, 1845.

Mr. Draper having been born and brought up on a farm, naturally preferred the active life of a farmer, and receiving with an older brother, by will, the old homestead, which had been in the family for several generations, he followed this pursuit with energy and success. He was also largely interested in wood land and in brick making. He was a sympathetic and generous man and repeatedly assisted younger townsmen less fortunate in business. He took a deep interest in all matters appertaining to his native town of Attleboro, State and country, yet he never sought nor held office. He was known for his scrupulously upright life and abstemious habits.

CHILDREN:

953. I. Ellen Maria, b. Attleboro, Dec. 3, 1832. m. Nov. 27, 1851, Ward Dennis Cotton, of Hartland, Vt. Children:— I. Julia, 956. b. Nov. 19, 1852. m. Jan. 2, 1873, Edgar Le Roy Hixon. II. George, 957. b. Sep. 2, 1855. m, Jan. 4, 1886, Cora Rhodes, of Wrentham. (They have one child. I. Gladys, 958. b. Dec. 9, 1876.)

954. II. Eliza H., b. Dec. 16, 1834. (Lives on the old homestead left her by her father. Unmarried.)

955. III. Martha Ann, b. Jan. 30, 1837. d. Mar. 7, 1846.

711. Mille. (132. Josiah, 17. James, 7. James, 2. James, 1. Thomas.) 4th child, 2d dau. of Josiah Draper and Sarah Ellis. She m. Samuel Draper, 336, s. of Joshua Draper, 130, and Abigail Fairbanks, of Spencer, Mass. He was her own 1st cousin.

CHILDREN, ALL B. ATTLEBORO:

959. I. Milly & 960. II. Abigail (Twins), b. Mar. 11, 1788. Milly m. Aug. 3, 1813, James W. Vose, of Boston.

961. III. Sarah, b. Dec. 16, 1789.

962. IV. Samuel Origen, b. Aug. 7, 1792.

963. V. Josiah, b. Mar. 23, 1795. d. Aug., 1861.

964. VI. Nancy Wheaton, b. Apr. 12, 1797. m. July 30, 1823, Ebenezer Vose, of Boston.

965. VII. Herbert M., b. June 16, 1800. m. 1844, Mary P. Stanton. Child:— I. Herbert, 966. b. 1846. d. 1852.

962. Samuel Origen. (336. Samuel, 130. Joshua, 17. James, 7. James, 2 James, 1. Thomas.) 4th child, eldest s. of Samuel Draper, 336, and Mille Draper, 711. m. Nancy Whiting.

(The ancestry will be carried back for the descendants of Mille Draper, 711, through Samuel Draper, 336, and his father, Joshua Draper, 130, instead of through the mother, Mille, and her father, Josiah Draper, 132. The reason for doing this is because the ancestry is carried through the male line, but as Samuel and Mille Draper's children and their descendants have always lived in Attleboro, the author has thought it best to place them among the other Attleboro Drapers.)

CHILDREN:

967. I. Ann Whiting, b. Oct. 26, 1817. m. her cousin Virgil, 746, s. of Preston Draper, 726, and Catherine Hudson.

968. II. Samuel Willard & 969. III. Origen William (Twins), b. Jan. 8, 1819.

970. IV. Abby S., b. May 19, 1820.

971. V. Millie M., b. Mar. 28, 1823. d. Sep. 12, 1824.

972. VI. LaFayette, b. July 12, 1824. m. Sarah S., dau. of Willard and Lydia Haskell, Feb. 22,1846. Child: — I. Ida Estelle, 977. b. Attleboro, Dec. 7, 1848. (m. Claramon, s. of Washington and Nancy Hunt, May 30, 1870. Child: — I. Harry Draper, 978. b. Dec. 27, 1874. His mother d. same day.)

973. VII. Thomas S., b. Dec. 12, 1825. d. Apr. 12, 1827.

974. VIII. Mille Maria, b. Mar. 28, 1828.

975. IX. George Henry, b. May 7, 1829.

976. X. Halsey Walcott, b. Apr. 9, 1835.

969. Origen William. (962. Samuel O., 336. Samuel, 130. Joshua, 17 James, 7. James, 2. James, 1. Thomas.) 3d child, 2d s. of Samuel Origen Draper, 962, and Nancy Whiting, m. Lucy Darling.

CHILDREN:

979. I. Leonard.

980. II. Theodore, m. Adelia May. Children:— I. Eldora, 982. II. Hobart Augustus, 983 (deceased). III. Jessie, 984. IV. Roy, 985 (deceased). V. Theodore, Jr., 986. VI. Miriam, 987.

981. III. Nanny.

975. George Henry. (962. Samuel O., 336. Samuel, 130. Joshua, 17. James, 7. James, 2. James, 1. Thomas.) 9th child, 5th s. of Samuel Origen Draper and Nancy Whiting, m. Apr. 1, 1853, Emily Miller.

CHILDREN:

988. I. George Daniel, m. Dora Toms. Have one child: I. Clara, 990. b. Oct. 16, 1886.

989. II. Willard Halsey.

976. Halsey Walcott. (962. Samuel O., 336. Samuel, 130. Joshua, 17. James, 7. James, 2. James, 1. Thomas.) 10th child, 6th s. of Samuel Origen Draper and Nancy Whiting, m. Mary A. Wilson.

CHILDREN:

991. I. Leonora M., b. 1877.

992. II. Margaret W., b. 1886.

993. III. Frances Forbes, b. Sep., 1888.

963. Josiah. (336. Samuel, 130. Joshua, 17. James, 7. James, 2. James, 1. Thomas.) 5th child, 2d s. of Samuel Draper and Mille Draper, m. Mandara Everett.

Mr. Draper grew up, in the quiet country town of Attleboro, an intelligent lad with quiet tastes but much strength of purpose. He came, when quite young, with his father from Attleboro to N. Attleboro, where Samuel Draper, 336, ran a tannery on Elms Street, where John P. Bonnetts' factory now stands, and the family lived close by for several years, until Mr. Draper bought the Orme House, which stood on the present estate of F. H. Barrows. The house was removed to Ralph Street where it still stands. About 1825 Josiah Draper, with John Tifft, began the manufacture of plated jewelry in one end of a blacksmith's shop belonging to Mr. Tifft's father. Later they built a factory and did a good business in watch cases and steels. Several parties were associated with them for different periods, the firm being at these times, "Draper, Tifft & Co." In 1850 the firm became "Draper, Tifft & Bacon." A year later Mr. Tifft died, and his son, Frank L., and Mr. Draper's son, Frank, 995, became connected with the business. Mr. Draper lived ten years longer, dying Aug., 1861. He was a man who took an interest in all that was going on about him, but never sought notoriety or office; firm in his convictions and decided in expressing them, he retained the good will of all by his courteous ways. He was a constant attendant at the Universalist Church and a firm believer in the great destiny of the Republican party.

CHILDREN, ALL B. N. ATTLEBORO:

994. I. Celestine Walcott, b. Mar., 1828. m. E. W. Davenport. Child: — I. Annie, 998.

995. II. Francis S., b. Nov. 8, 1830. d. Aug. 15, 1886.

996. III. Ellen, b. 1834. d. Apr. 15, 1881. m. C. E. Smith. (No children.)

997. IV. Dora, b. 1837. d. Aug. 25, 1867. m. Louis Barrows. (No children.)

995. Francis S. (963. Josiah, 336. Samuel, 130. Joshua, 17. James, 7. James, 2. James, 1. Thomas.) Only s., 2d child of Josiah Draper and Mandara Everett, m. Eliza Robinson.

Nearly a century has elapsed since the manufacture of jewelry was first introduced at Attleboro, Mass., but it was not until 1821 that labor and capital were largely devoted to the industry. In that year, the father of Francis S. Draper, 995, and a Mr. Tifft, under the name of "Draper & Tifft," established the first large manufactory, and from that date the business gradually increased, until Attleboro became the centre of jewelry manufacturing in New England. Francis S. Draper, 995, became an apprentice in the jewelry firm of "Tifft, Whiting & Co.", and at the expiration of three years, his father retired from business, leaving his son a member of the firm of "Draper & Tifft." From this date, 1850 to 1857, the business was successful and the financial crisis of the following year found the firm able to meet it. Mr. Draper retired from business in 1860, and the year after joined the Union Army as First Lieut, in the 47th Mass. Regt. In nine months he was promoted to the rank of Captain. In Feb., 1863, he was appointed on the staff of General Banks, and went with him to New Orleans. There he served as Acting Commissary and Ordnance Officer, Quartermaster, Provost-marshal, and Disbursing Officer of the Sanitary Fund. After the surrender of General Lee's army in 1865, he resigned his commission, and in the Spring of 1866 returned to N. Attleboro. He then formed the firm of "Draper, Pate & Bailey," and resumed the manufacture of jewelry. In a year and a half, the firm found it necessary to enlarge their factory, to meet the increasing business. In Jan., 1875, Mr. Pate sold out his interest, and the firm became "S. F. Draper & Co." In this business Mr. Draper remained until his death. He was also the father of the present system of waterworks in N. Attleboro, which is considered one of the best in the country.

Samuel Francis Draper of Attleboro, Mass.

CHILDREN:

999. I. Josiah Everett, b. New Orleans, Jan. 1, 1852. m. Emma R., dau. of Jabez and Lizzie Walcott, July 28, 1878. They have: I. Josiah, 1001. b. May 6, 1880. II. Harold Walcott, 1002. b. May 8, 1884.

1000. II. Frank Eugene, b. N. Attleboro, Aug. 5, 1864. m. Henrietta Edith, dau. of Ephraim Wood and Sarah Spring Adams, of Wellesley, Mass. Child: — I. Harriet Eliza, 1003. b. June 4, 1889.

714. Aaron. (132. Josiah, 17. James, 7. James, 2. James, 1. Thomas.) 7th child, 4th s. of Josiah Draper and Sarah Ellis, m. Oct. 25, 1791, Amelia Sweet. Shed. Mar. 21, 1839.

Mr. Draper graduated from Brown University in 1790, but never prosecuted a learned profession.

CHILDREN:

1004. I. Henry S., b. Aug. 13, 1793. d. May 21, 1839.

1005. II. Mary A., b. Feb., 1798. d. Dec. 10, 1800.

1006. III. Jonathan G., b. Mar. 10, 1801. d. 1887.

1007. IV. Edward, b. Apr. 22. 1804. d. Aug, 18. 1831.

1008. V. Mary A. 2d, b. Mar. 11, 1806. d. Sep. 26, 1835. m. Virgil Morse.

1004. Henry S. (714. Aaron, 132. Josiah, 17. James, 7. James, 2. James, 1. Thomas.) Eldest s. and child of Aaron Draper and Amelia Sweet, m. Sybil Martin.

CHILDREN, ALL B. ATTLEBORO:

1009. I. Albert H., b. Aug. 29, 1816.

1010. II. Aaron,

1011. III. Joseph.

1012. IV. Frances.

1013. V. Mary A., d. Dec. 20, 1851. m. Dec, 1849, Augustus Ellis. Child: — I. Ella, 1017. d. in infancy.

1014. VI. Anna E., b. June 2, 1831. m. Dec. 28, 1852, Charles M., s. of Samuel and Catherine Newell. He d. Mar. 5, 1864. Child: — I. Alice, 1018. b. Attleboro, Oct. 28, 1854. m. Dec. 15, 1877, Frank H. Sadler. (Children: — ^I. Ada W., 1019. b. Dec. 6, 1878. II. Irma D., 1020. b. May 3, 1880.)

1015. VII. Edward.

1016. VIII. A child.

1009. Albert H. (1004. Henry S., 714. Aaron, 132. Josiah, 17. James, 7. James, 2. James, 1. Thomas.) Eldest child and s. of Henry S. Draper and Sybil Martin, m. Providence, R. I., Apr. 20, 1837, Nancy E., dau. of Jonathan Read and Nancy Bicknell. She d. June, 1871.

CHILDREN:

1021. I. Frederick Albert, b. New York, Apr. 3, 1838.

1022. II. Kate B., b. Attleboro, May 9, 1840. m. Feb., 1858, Stephen Betts, s. of William Samuel and Aurelia Sherman Whiting, of Connecticut. Children:— I. Clara Minetta, 1026. b. Alton, Ill., Nov. 8, 1859. m. June 16, 1886, at Pottsville, Pa., Willard Hunsiker. She d. Athens, Pa., Sep. 29, 1887. (Child: — I. Harold Whiting, 1032. b. Sep. 19, 1887.) II. Charles Wilcox, 1027. b. Camden, N. J., Apr. 8, 1863. m. Oct. 15, 1889, Mary Clinton. (Child:— I. Dorothy, 1033. b. Nov. 6, 1890.) III. Walter Sherman, 1028. b. Camden, N. J., Apr. 11, 1866. IV. Albert Draper, 1029. b. Camden, N. J., June 1, 1869. V. Howard Earle, 1030. b. Pottsville, Pa., July 23, 1871. VI, Stephen Edgar, 1031. b. Pottsville, Pa., Apr. 26, 1874.

1023. III. Henry Read, b. Attleboro, Mar. 5, 1842. m. Oct. 22, 1868, Etta Carmichael.

1024. IV. Alice B., b. Attleboro, Feb. 14, 1846. d. Oct., 1846.

1025. V. Edwin Frank, b. Brooklyn, N. Y., Nov. 13, 1854. Mr. Draper is a printer engaged with Messrs. Rand, McNally & Co., Map Publishers, of Chicago, Ill. (Unmarried.)

1021. Frederick Albert. (1009. Albert Henry, 1004. Henry S., 714. Aaron, 132. Josiah, 17. James, 7. James, 2. James, 1. Thomas.) Eldest child and s. of Albert Henry Draper and Nancy E. Read. m. Nashville, Tenn., Nov. 26, 1866, Mary Ellen, dau. of John Burman Harris and Sarah Brunette Humphreys.

CHILDREN:

1034. I. Walker H., b. Nashville, Tenn., Jan. 25, 1869.

1035. II. Nettie E., b. Nashville, Tenn., Sep. 22, 1871.

1036. III. Ollie B., b. Nashville, Tenn., Sep. 27, 1873.

1037. IV. Annie M., b. Nashville, Tenn., May 15, 1876.

1038. V. Minnie L., b. Bowling Green, Ky., Aug. 31, 1879.

1039. VI. Bessie F., b. Nashville, Tenn., Dec. 11, 1881.

1040. VII. Katie B., b. Nashville, Tenn., Oct. 3, 1886.

1041. VIII. Albert T., b. Nashville, Tenn., Aug. 17, 1888.

715. Lewis. (132. Josiah, 17. James, 7. James, 2, James, 1. Thomas.) 8th child, 5th s. of Josiah Draper and Sarah Ellis, m. Sep. 25, 1788, Lucy Orme. She d. Jan. 2, 1847, aged 79 years.

CHILDREN:

1042. I. Lanard.

1043. II. Lyman, b. Mar. 9, 1799.

1044. III. Lewis Laprelate, b. Mar. 25, 1801. d. Sep. 15, 1890.

1045. IV. Emily, b. Feb. 1, 1806. m. Olney D. Cook. Children: — I. Lycurgus, 1047. II. Lucius W., 1048. III. Marcus D., 1049. IV. Dwight, 1050. V. Emmeline, 105 1.

1046. V. Maria, m. Levi B. Hall.

1043. Lyman. (715. Lewis, 132. Josiah, 17. James, 7. James, 2. James, 1. Thomas.) 2d child and s. of Lewis Draper and Lucy Orme. m. 1st: 1819, Sally, dau. of Levi and Caroline Balou. She was b. 1793. d. Mar. 2, 1827. He m. 2dly: 1830, Mary Ann Hall. She was b. Pelham, May 2, 1809.

CHILDREN BY 1st WIFE, B. PELHAM:

1052. I. Sarah Ann, b. Feb. 20, 1821. m. Feb. 24, 1843, Samuel Flinn.

Child: — I. Ellen Matilda Draper, 1059. b. May 15, 1846. m. Nov. 27, 1874, Charles Oscar Howes. (Child: — I. Grace Adele, 1061. b. June 25, 1878.) Mrs. Flinn m. 2dly: Nov., 1853, John Holmes, and had: II. Jenny Eliza, 1060. b. Oct. 29, 1857. m. May 28, 1878, William B. Billings. (Children, b. Amhurst: — I. Harry, 1062. b. Jan. 1, 1882. II. Susan Buxton, 1063. b. Jan. 1, 1883. III. Clara May, 1064. b. May 1, 1886.)

1053. II. Albert Lyman, b. Apr. 18, 1826.

CHILDREN BY 2D WIFE, B. PELHAM:

1054. III. Adeline Orme, b. Oct., 1832. m. Sep. 5, 1855, David Glines. Children, b. Ware, Mass.: — I. Grace, 1065. b. Jan. 1, 1856. m. Nov. 4, 1880, Frank M. Sibley. (Children, b. Ware, Mass.:— I. Edith Orilla, 1067. b. Apr. 2, 1882. II. Theo. Delia, 1068. b. Apr. 2, 1884. III. Irene Glines, 1069. b. Jan. 26, 1887.) II. Emma Orilla, 1066. b. Nov. 12, 1861. m. May 4, 1887, Andrew J. Davis. (Children, b. Ware, Mass.: — I. Grace Glines, 1070. b. Jan. 20, 1889. II. Esther Helen, 1071. b. Sep. 19, 1891.)

1055. IV. Henry Oscar, b. Jan. 19, 1836. m. Nov. 8, 1877, Martha A. Serevance.

1056. V. Emma Jean, b. Dec. 31, 1839. m. Oct. 24, 1860, John H. Storrs. Children, b. Ware, Mass.:— I. Delia, 1072. b. Sep. 5, 1861. II. John Frink, 1073. b. Apr. 13,1863. III. John Henry, 1074. b. Nov. 4, 1864. m. Nov. 16, 1887, Gertrude M. Tyler. (Child: I. John Tyler, 1078. b. Ware, Mass., Aug. 19, 1889.) IV. George Draper, 1075. b. Sep. 19, 1866. V. Mabel Orme, 1076. b. Jan. 5, 1870. VI. Mary Ballou, 1077. b. Feb. 22, 1873.

1057. VI. Edgar LeRoy, b. Nov. 15, 1843. m. Oct. 8, 1868, Alice W. Bemis. Children:— I. Edith Pickering, 1079. b. July 25, 1869. II. Louise Bemis, 1080. b. Jan. 20, 1874.

1058. VII. George Lemuel, b. Feb. 5, 1846.

1053. Albert Lyman. (1043. Lyman, 715. Lewis, 132. Josiah, 17. James, 7. James, 2. James, 1. Thomas.) 2d child and s. of Lyman Draper and his 1st wife, Sally Balou. m. July 4, 1845, Lavinia Cook.

CHILDREN, B. PELHAM:

1081. I. Charles Clinton, b. Sep. 17, 1850. d. Oct. 4, 1854.

1082. II. Ella Louisa, b. Mar. 25, 1856. d. Dec. 14, 1874.

1083. III. Lizzie Jane, b. Oct. 31, 1857. m. Aug. 28, 1884, John Williams. Children: — I. Garren Foster, 1085. b. July 15, 1884. II. Mabel Eliza, 1086. b. Sep. 22, 1890. (Both b. Amhurst.)

1084. IV. John Ward, b. July 11, 1859. m. Minnie Livermore, Apr. 30, 1884.

1044. Lewis Laprelate. (715. Lewis, 132. Josiah, 17. James, 7. James, 2. James, 1. Thomas.) 3d s. and child of Lewis Draper and Lucy Orme. m. 1st: July 4, 1827, Margaret Henry. She d. June 12, 1838. He m. 2dly: Nov. 28, 1839, Eliza Kellog. She d. May 20, 1872.

CHILDREN BY 1st WIFE:

1087. I. Emmeline, b. Pelham, Oct. 25, 1828. d. Aug. 7, 1868. m. Dec. 1, 1847, Charles Royal Ingram. He d. May 21, 1874. Children, all b. Fon-du-lac, Wis.:— I. Edward Adolphus, 1092. b. Dec. 29, 1851. d. Nov. 21, 1883. m. Alice McLean. II. Dwight Bradford, 1093. b. July 15, 1855. m. 1882, Mary E. Sherwin. (Child:— I. George Lewis, 1097. b. Aug. 7, 1883.) III. George Lewis, 1094. b. Apr. 29, 1861. m. Lora Ett Stead, Apr. 2, 1883. IV. Charles Lincoln, 1095. b. Jan. 25, 1863. V. Mary Emmeline, 1296. b. July 20, 1868.

1088. II. Emerson Henry, b. Pelham, Nov. 2, 1831. m. Nov. 6, 1886, Luthera King.

1089. III. Mary Elizabeth, b. Shutesburg, Apr. 18, 1836. m. Apr. 9, 1863, William Dickinson Grey. Child:— Nellie Eliza, 1098. b. Geneseo, Ill., July 10, 1868.

1090. IV. John Luther, b. Amhurst, Apr. 17, 1838. m. Jan. 11, 1872, Susan Hall.

CHILD BY 2D WIFE:

1091. V. Antoinette Orme, b. Amhurst, Mass., Sep. 20, 1840. d. Nov. 13, 1861. m. Sep., 1858, Rev. John Peterson.

717. James. (132. Josiah, 17. James, 7. James, 2. James, 1. Thomas.) roth child, 7th s. of Josiah Draper and Sarah Ellis, m. Dec. 15, 1796, Sally Perry. She d. Oct. 7, 1849, aged 78 years.

Mr. Draper came to Attleboro with a farmer named Bicknell, and there remained.

CHILDREN, B. ATTLEBORO, MASS.:

1099. I. Amanda, b. Oct. 3, 1797. d. N. Attleboro, Oct. 21, 1885. (Unmarried.)

1100. II. Adeline, b. Jan. 9, 1799. d. N. Attleboro, Sep. 24, 1883. (Unmarried.)

1101. III. Lucian, b. Oct. 30, 1800. d. Providence, R. I., Oct. 27, 1886.

1102. IV. Clementine, b. June 23, 1803. d. Sep. 27, 1889. m. Dec. 25, 1836, her cousin, Horatio N. Draper, 883, s. of John Draper, 710, and Sarah Hatch. Child: — I. Carrie, 1106. b. Aug. 15, 1843. Sep. 22, 1861.

1103. V. Nathaniel P., b. June 21, 1806. d. Nov. 7, 1875.

1104. VI. Lorenzo, b. Nov. 19, 1811.

1105. VII. Ann Janet, b. Oct. 17, 1814. d. Aug. 11, 1890. m. Oct. 27, 1839, Elisha G., s. of Tully May and Hannah Gay. No issue. He d. Jan. 28, 1892.

1101. Lucian. (717. James, 132. Josiah, 17. James, 7. James, 2. James, 1. Thomas.) 3d child, eldest s. of James Draper and Sally Perry, m. Dec. 9, 1841, Mrs. Lucy Armington Dyke, dau. of Robert Sterry Burrough and Esther Armington.

Mr. Draper spent his boyhood in farm work, and received, during the time, a common school education. When about 20, he went to Providence, and worked with his cousin, Alonzo Draper, 887. He did not like this, and went into the dry goods store of William Russell. He there remained for a number of years, finally launching out into the wholesale dry goods business. He retired therefrom with a comfortable competency, and did not engage in any special specific business thereafter, but was interested in a number of enterprises. In these and all matters with which he was connected, he was an acknowledged embodiment of probity, honor and reliability. His advice was often sought, but rarely volunteered. He was Deacon of the First Congregational Unitarian Church for some years.

CHILDREN, B. PROVIDENCE:

1107. I. Anna F., b. Nov. 13, 1851.

1108. II. Robert J., b. Dec. 17, 1853.

1103. Nathaniel P. (717. James, 132. Josiah, 17. James, 7. James, 2. James, 1. Thomas.) 5th child, 2d s. of James Draper and Sally Perry, m. Oct. 8, 1835, Mrs. Frances Leonard, widow of Henry F. Leonard and dau. of Robert Burrough and Esther Armington.

CHILDREN:

1109. I. Antoinette E., b. July 20, 1838.

1110. II. Robert S., b. July 6, 1840. d. Apr. 1, 1848.

1104. Lorenzo. (717. James, 132. Josiah, 17. James, 7. James, 2. James, 1. Thomas.) 6th child, 3d s. of James Draper and Sally Perry, m. Oct. 28, 1842, Harriet W., dau. of Loring C. Shaw and Jemima Mason.

CHILDREN:

1111. I. Emma F., b. July 23, 1843. m. Dec. 10, 1873, Samuel D., s. of Moses Mason and Eliza Dunstan.

1112. II. Charles T., b. Nov. 4, 1845. m. Fanny, dau. of Isaac Staples. Children: — Roy, 1114. Carrol, 1115.

1113. III. Herbert L., b. Sep. 2, 1852. m. May 8, 1878, Stella May, dau. of Isaac Peck and Sarah Burdeck, of Providence, R. I. She was b. Oct. 10, 1854. Child:— I. Nathalie Peck, 1116. b. Brooklyn, N. Y., Aug. 26, 1888. d. Montclair, N. J., July 2, 1889.

137. Abijah. (17. James, 7. James, 2. James, 1. Thomas.) 11th child, 8th s. of James Draper and Abigail Child, of Dedham. (3d s. of this name, the two others dying in infancy.) m. 1st: Alice, dau. of John Eaton and Elizabeth Lovering, of Purgatory, Dedham, Apr. 8, 1762. She was b. Jan. 31, 1741. d. Jan. 22, 1777. He m. 2dly: Mar. 25, 1778, Desire, the widow of Nathaniel Metcalf. She was a dau. of Ebenezer Foster and Desire Cushman. b. Attleboro, Aug. 12, 1746. d. Dedham, Oct. 23, 1815.

Abijah Draper and both wives are buried in the cemetery in Dedham village, and the epitaphs on their graves are as follows:

"Ah, why so soon from me he's fled,
Laments the widow, orphan, friend.
You must not say, 'too soon he's dead,'
Who stayed to answer Life's great end."

On Desire's tombstone is the following:

"She sleeps in Jesus,
Wipe the falling tear.
She lives in glory —
Strive to meet her there."

Abijah Draper succeeded his father. Captain James Draper, 17, in his landed estate at Green Lodge, Dedham. He was an active, energetic man, of large executive ability, public spirited, and always ready to take part in every public enterprise. He was one of three chosen by the citizens of Dedham to erect a monument to William Pitt, in 1766. The base of this monument still exists in Dedham village, and is called the "Pillar of Liberty."

The inscriptions thereon, read as follows:

To the Honor of William Pitt, Esq., and other Patriots,
Who saved America from impending slavery, and confirmed our most loyal Affections to King George III., by procuring the repeal of the Stamp Act, 18th March, 1766.
Erected here, July 22, 1766, by Dr. Nathl. Ames, 2d, Col. Ebenr. Battle, Major Abijah Draper, and other patriots, friendly to the Rights of the Colonies at that day.
Replaced by the Citizens, July 4, 1828.

Mr. Draper held every office in the Militia to that of Major, and commanded in the latter capacity, a body of minute men at Roxbury, under Washington. Whilst there he was exposed to the small-pox, and it was supposed carried it to his home on one of his furloughs, as his 1st wife, Alice, d. of that disease.

CHILDREN, BY ALICE:

1117. I. Abijah, b. June ii, 1763. d. Dec. 16, 1774.
1118. II. Ira, b. Dec. 24, 1764. d. Jan. 22, 1848.
1119. III. Rufus, b. Nov. 27, 1766. d. Nov. 18, 1788, at Norfolk, Va.
1120. IV. James, b. Apr. 14, 1769. d. Jan. 22, 1777.
1121. V. Alice, b. Apr. 13, 1771. d. Jan. 27, 1852.
1122. VI. Abijah 2d, b. Sep. 22, 1775. d. Mar. 26, 1836.

CHILD, BY 2D WIFE:

1123. VII. Lendamine, b. Mar. 30, 1780. d. Oct. 26, 1823.

It is related of these children that Ira lived to a great age, and had a large family. Rufus d. early at Norfolk, Va., where he is buried. He had gone there in pursuit of his younger brother, James, having first sought vainly for him in New York City. Proceeding by vessel to Norfolk, he there sickened and d. of endemial fever. The brother James, whom he had sought in vain, had been apprenticed to a currier in Roxbury street, Dedham, and being ill-treated by the man, he ran away to New York, and probably from thence to the South. At any rate, he was never heard of again.

1118. Ira. (137. Abijah, 17. James, 7. James, 2. James, 1. Thomas.) 2d child and 2d s. of Major Abijah Draper and Alice Eaton, m. 1st: May 31,1786, Lydia, dau. of Lemuel and Rebecca Richards. She was b. Jan., 1768. d. Sep. 18, 1811. He m. 2dly: Mar. 9, 1812, Abigail (called Nabbie), his 1st wife's sister. She was b. Sep. 12, 1783. d. 1847.

In 1775, during the retreat of the British after the battles of Lexington and Concord Bridge, he was present with his father, who had taken part in the fighting. During the early part of the century, he removed from Dedham to Weston, Mass., and later to Saugus. Beginning life with a handsome property for the time, he expended most of it in the care and education of his large family, he having had sixteen children by his two wives, and also in the development of his mechanical inventions, which proved more profitable to the community than to himself. He is said to have invented the first threshing machine of which there is any record, but it was never introduced extensively. He also invented the "fly shuttle hand loom," which was considered to possess decided advantages over those formerly in use. He invented the first machine for road scraping, and machines of his identical pattern were in use very recently in the vicinity of Boston. The invention of his which went into most general use, was the "revolving temple" for keeping cloth extended in weaving. This was adopted in the larger part of the looms both in this country and abroad, and formed the basis of a profitable business, carried on both by him, his sons, his grandsons, and his great-grandsons afterwards. Under the administration of John Quincy Adams, he was a prominent candidate for U. S. Commissioner of Patents. He was a man of large natural intelligence, mechanical ingenuity, and progressive thought. He was one of the early Unitarians, and d. in that faith.

CHILDREN, BY 1st WIFE, ALL B. IN DEDHAM:

1124. I. James, b. May 28, 1781. d. Dec. 5, 1870.

1125. II. Ira, b. Jan. 4, 1789. d. June 18, 1845.

1126. III. Rufus, b. Aug. 30, 1790. d. in infancy.

1127. IV. A dau., b. Aug. 7, 1791. d. in infancy.

1128. V. A son, b. Dec. 17, 1793. d. in infancy.

1129. VI. Lucy Chickering, b. 1797. d. Sep. 15, 1801.

1130. VII. Rufus Foster, b. July 12, 1800. d. 1841.

1131. VIII. Abijah, b. Jan. 5, 1802. d. Oct. 4, 1802.

1132. IX. Abijah 2d, b. Nov. 15, 1803. d. Oct. 4, 1828. m. Mary . One child that d. in infancy.

CHILDREN, BY 2D WIFE:

1133. X. Ebenezer Daggett, b. June 13, 1813. d. Oct. 20. 1887.

1134. XI. Lydia, b. Mar. 31, 1815. d. Apr. 3, 1847.

1 135. XII. George, b. Aug. 16, 1817. d. June 7, 1887.

1136. XIII. Abigail, b. Oct. 24, 1819. d. July 22, 1847. m. William W. Cook, Feb. 2, 1842. Child: — A son, b. May 10, 1844. d. June 9, 1846. Mr. Cook m. 2dly: her niece, Nancy Marion, 1166.

1137. XIV. Lemuel Richards, b. Saugus, Dec. 1, 1823. d. Jan. 10, 1891.

1138. XV. Lucy Rebecca, b. Dec. 22, 1826. d. July 1, 1827.

1124. James. (1118. Ira, 137. Abijah, 17. James, 7. James, 2. James, 1. Thomas.) Eldest s. and child of Ira Draper and Lydia Richards, m. 1st: Jan. 14, 1809, Elizabeth, dau. of Nathaniel Sumnor and Elizabeth Smith. She was b. Dec. 31, 1786. d. Nov. 25, 1825. He m. 2dly: June 15, 1827, Nabbie, dau. of Josiah Allen and Deborah Day. She wash. Jan. 16, 1782. d. Jan. 16, 1868.

Until his marriage, his life had been spent on his father's farm. At this time he came to East Sudbury, having purchased what is now the Bryden farm in

Wayland, and erected new buildings thereon. During the War of 1812, he was enthusiastic in its prosecution, executing large contracts to supply the Charlestown Navy Yard with ship timber, and in 1814 he enlisted as a soldier and was stationed for duty at Fort Warren. The general appearance of his estates bore evidence of his ambition to excel, and of his skill in agricultural practice. One way in which his energy spent its force, was in purchasing estates in order to demolish old buildings and erect new ones, or remodel and renovate others, thirteen instances of which occurred during his lifetime. About the time of his second marriage, he made vigorous and successful efforts to introduce into the cloth factories of the Eastern and Middle States the "revolving temple," an invention of his father. He ranked among the leaders of public sentiment in the community. Accustomed to dwell on the bright and hopeful side of things, his presence tended to give a cheering glow wherever he moved. His daily motto was, "It will all come out right." His gift of $500 to the town in 1863, for a permanent library fund, attests his public spirit in that direction. In State and national affairs he was remarkably well informed. Next to religious duties in importance, he placed those of the citizen to his country. His general political policy may be inferred from the facts that, in 1808, he voted for James Madison for President, and for J. Q. Adams in 1824. In 1840, he was a delegate to the National Convention to nominate W. H. Harrison, and he was with the National Republicans through the Civil War. In early life he united with a church of Calvinist creed, but evidently held the doctrines in abeyance; in the time of free discussion, he took the liberal side. He filled the position of deacon in the First Church, in Wayland (Unitarian), 43 years. His devotion to the interests of religion was earnest and sincere. He gave the First Parish $500 as a permanent fund. On the tablets of memory his name will represent sterling integrity, persistent energy, and broad beneficence.

CHILDREN, BY 1st WIFE (NO ISSUE BY 2D):

1139. I. James Sumnor, b. Aug. 18, 1811, at Wayland.

1140. II. Newmann, b. June 17, 1817. d. Jan. 19, 1822.

1141. III. Elizabeth Allen, b. Dec. 15, 1822. d. Oct. 31, 1846. m. Chester Drake, of Holleston, May 11, 1843. (No issue.)

1139. James Sumnor. (1124. James, 1118. Ira, 137. Abijah, 17. James, 7. James, 2. James, 1. Thomas.) Eldest s. and child of James Draper and Elizabeth Sumnor. m. Aug. 18, 1834, Emmeline Amanda, dau. of Nathaniel Reeves and Miliscent Rice. She was b. June 10, 1810. d. Aug. 4, 1875.

He was educated in the common schools of his native town with the addition of two academical terms. Farming has been his chief occupation, although he taught school when a young man, and occasionally engaged in land surveying. He has taken an active interest in the public schools and in the Wayland Public Library, of which he was librarian for twenty years. While in this position he did much to promote its interests, and the results of his valuable services will long be remembered. He has been closely identified with public improvements and with plans instituted for the promotion of the business enterprise and thrift of the community. A letter written by him to a gentleman in Barre in 1867, was said to be the initial step which resulted in the organization of the Central Massachusetts Railroad Company. During twelve years he was a member of the Board of Directors and devoted his best efforts to the construction of the road. He has written occasionally for the press and edited the work entitled "Wayland in the Civil War," of which mention is made elsewhere in this volume. He has been much interested in researches relating to the history of his native town, results of which have been occasionally published. In politics he was first a Whig, then a member of the Free Soil party while that party existed, and in 1860 became a National Republican. During the Civil War he was an uncompromising Unionist, although previously opposed, on principle, to the use of armed force in the settlement of disputed questions. In matters of reform he has been of the liberal school. In 1833 he was an ardent anti-slavery man, and he has been, and still is, an advocate of "woman's rights." In religious matters he has been nominally associated with the Unitarian denomination, but has also been known as an enthusiastic Spiritualist. Concerning this he states: "During more than forty years I have carefully investigated the merits of Spiritualism and I am in full belief of the truth of its most important claims and of their value to man in his present stage of existence." He still further says: "A peculiar feature in my mental structure became prominent from the earliest independent action of my mind, to wit, an inclination not to rest satisfied with present conditions, and a correlative disposition to be on the lookout for the newer, and, as I believe, the better unfoldings that relate not only to man's external life, but to the interior — the immortal." He has been three times commissioned Justice of the Peace, and has held various offices of responsibility and trust in his native town.

CHILDREN:

1142. I. James Austin, b. Oct. 16, 1835.
1143. II. Charles Herbert, b. Mar. 22, 1838.
1144. III. Frank Winthrop, b. Feb. 25, 1843.
1145. IV. Ella Elizabeth, b. Feb. 26, 1849.
1146. V. Wallace Sherwin, b. Sep. 7, 1851.

1142. James Austin. (1139. James Sumnor, 1124. James, 1118. Ira, 137. Abijah, 17. James, 7. James, 2. James, 1. Thomas.) Eldest s. and child of James S. Draper and Emmeline A. Reeves, m. 1st: Oct. 16, 1856, Abby, dau. of Leonard D. Hart and Abby Drury. She was b. June 3, 1835. d. Jan. 17, 1876. m. 2dly: Anne Wheeler, dau. of Joseph Wellington and Keziah Haines, Oct. 17, 1877. She was b. Oct. 17, 1839, and at her marriage was the widow of William Dexter Draper, 1174.

Mr. Draper's occupation has chiefly been farming. He enlisted on July 31, 1861, in Comp. D, 35th Massachusetts Infantry Volunteers, and continued actively with his Regt. until honorably discharged, March 28, 1863. He has resided in Wayland, Mass., most of his life, and has been several times elected to positions of responsibility and trust in that town.

CHILDREN, BY 1ST WIFE:

1147. I. James Herbert, b. July 28, 1857. m. Elizabeth Louise, dau. of William Shaw and Elizabeth C. Clarke. She was b. Oct. 25, 1861.

1148. II. Elizabeth Brigham, b. Oct. 2, 1859. m. George Benjamine, s. of Benjamine M. Folsom and Abigail Pillsbury, Nov. 24, 1881. He was b. Dec. 2, 1858. Child:— Wallace Herbert, 1155. b. Dec. 29, 1884.

1149. III. Alfred Perry, b. Aug. 8, 1861. m. Cora Alice, dau. of Jesse L. Wilson and Lucy Locke. She was b. June 2, 1861.

1150. IV. Paul Turner, b. Oct. 6, 1863. m. Nellie Jane, dau. of Edwin Augustus Dudley and Harriet Miller, Nov. 17, 1886. She was b. Feb. 12, 1863. Child:— Edna Wildred, 11 56. b. Oct. 19, 1887.

1151. V. Gertrude Abby, b. Nov. 22, 1866.

1152. VI. Emma Drury, b. Apr. 19, 1868.

1153. VII. Leonard Drury, b. Dec. 1, 1869.

CHILD, BY 2D WIFE:

1154. VIII. Ernest Sparrell, b. Feb. 19, 1883.

1143. Charles Herbert. (1139. James Sumnor, 1124. James, 11 18. Ira, 137. Abijah, 17. James, 7. James, 2. James, 1. Thomas.) 2d s. and child of James S. Draper and Emmeline Reeves, m. Eliza James, dau. of Isaac Bell and Charlotte Brigham, Oct. 9, 1860. She was b. Jan. 16, 183-.

Mr. Draper attended the schools of his native town of Wayland, also private schools in Waltham, Mass. After spending two years as a clerk in Boston retail stores, he commenced the life of a bank clerk in the Faneuil Hall Bank in Boston in 1857. Two years later he obtained a position in the Safety Fund Bank, which was reorganized in 1864 as the First National Bank of Boston. From that date to 1881 he was Assist. Cashier, and was then promoted to the Cashier's position, an office that he now holds. He has also been elected a Director of the bank each year since 1886. He resides in Brookline, Mass., and is a member of the Board of Sinking Fund Commissioners of that town since 1886.

CHILDREN:

1157. I. Charles Bell, b. Mar. 11, 1863. d. Apr. 30, 1863.

1158. II. Frank Sumnor, b. Sep. 21, 1865. d. Jan. 2, 1888.

1159. III. Charlotte Brigham, b. May 9, 1868. d. June 16, 1874.

Of Mr. Draper's son, Frank Sumnor, may be said that he was a young man of great promise. He had been an engineer on the "Atchison, Topeka «& Santa Fe R. R." in Kansas, from which he returned to take a position in the First National Bank of Boston, which he held until he died. President William B. Strong, of the "A., T. & Santa Fe R. R.," said of him: "That he was one of the best young men that he had ever known."

1144. Frank Winthrop. (1139. James Sumnor, 1124, James, 11 18. Ira, 137. Abijah, 17. James, 7. James, 2. James, 1. Thomas.) 3d s. and child of James S.

Draper and Emmeline A. Reeves, m. Nov. 1, 1870, Fanny Victoria, dau. of Dr. William H. Jones and Catherine Brigham. She was b. Mar. 9, 1840.

Dr. Frank Draper attended the public schools of his native town, receiving at the High School a classical education which fitted him to enter Brown University when he was fifteen years old. He took the four years course at college and received the degree of A. B. with the class of 1862. In 1865, upon his return from service in the Army, the college conferred upon him the degree of A. M. Upon completing his studies at the University, he enlisted among the Volunteers of Wayland and was enrolled Comp. D, 35th Regiment of Massachusetts Infantry, Aug. 10, 1862. A month later (Sep. 17, 1862) the regiment was hotly engaged in the battle of Antietam. Dec. 13, 1862, it was under sharp fire at the battle of Fredericksburg. In the Spring of 1863 it was transferred to Kentucky, where it was occupied in attending to guerillas. In June of that year the North Army Corps, of which the 35th Mass. Regiment was a part, was assigned to Gen. Grant's army and was occupied in the entrenchments around Vicksburg until the surrender of that town July 3, 1863. The command then marched into the interior of Mississippi under Gen. Sherman and was engaged in the battle at Jackson. Here Private Draper, as the result of great exposure and privation during a very hot midsummer campaign, became disabled by serious sickness; he was sent north to a military hospital at Covington, Ky. Later, while convalescing, he was on duty at Lexington, Ky. While at this post he went before an Army Examining Board, and as the result of his examination was promoted to the grade of Captain of United States Volunteers, and was assigned in April, 1864, to the command of a Company in the 39th Regiment of United States Colored Troops then organizing at Baltimore, Md. With his new command Capt. Draper participated in the Wilderness campaign and in the various movements in the transfer of the Army of the Potomac from the Potomac river to the front of Petersburg. In June, 1864, he was appointed Aide-de-Camp to the Brigade Commander, and in this position took part in the battle of Petersburg, July 30. In October of that year he became Acting Assist. Adjutant General of his Brigade, and continued in that office till he resigned his commission, June 22, 1865, just after the close of hostilities. He was with his Brigade at the battle of Hatcher's Run in October, 1864, and in the military operations in North Carolina under Generals Schofield and Sherman near the end of the war.

Returning home, he began the study of medicine, at the Harvard Medical School, and graduated with honors in the Spring of 1869. After a trip to Europe and to the West, he settled in Boston for the practice of his profession, and is still located there. He joined the Massachusetts Medical Society in July, 1869; was Recording Secretary of the Society from 1873 to 1875; Treasurer from 1875 to 1891; a member of the Council from 1875 to the present; Anniversary Orator in 1892. He was Assist. Editor of the Boston Medical and Surgical Journal from 1872 to 1876. He edited the Massachusetts Registration Reports from 1874 to 1878. He was Assist. Surgeon at the Boston City Hospital during the year 1872-3, and was Visiting Physician upon the staff of that institution from 1874 to 1886. At present he holds the position of Medico-Legal Pathologist to the hospital. He was Medical Inspector on the Board of Health of Boston from 1873 to 1877, resigning that office to accept the original appointment of Medical Examiner for Suffolk County, in June, 1877, under the new Massachusetts law relating to inquests— a position which he still retains. In the Harvard Medical School, he was Lecturer on Hygiene from 1875 to 1878; Lecturer on Forensic Medicine from 1878 to 1884; Assist. Professor of Legal Medicine from 1884 to 1889, and Professor of Legal Medicine since 1889. He was a trustee of Tufts College from 1881 to 1883. He was appointed a member of the Massachusetts State Board of Health upon the reorganization of the Board in 1886, and is still active there. He is a member and Senior Vice-Presdt. of the Obstetrical Society of Boston; member of the Boston Society for Medical Improvement (President in 1885 and 1886); member of the American Public Health Association; member of the Boston Society of the Medical Sciences; member of the American Statistical Association; President of the Mass. Medico-Legal Society; Fellow of the American Academy of Arts and Sciences; Corresponding Member of the New York Medico-Legal Society; Vice-President of the Mass. Emergency & Hygiene Association; Companion of the Massachusetts Commandery of the Military Order of the Loyal Legion.

Dr. Draper has made numerous contributions to the literature of his profession, his writings embracing over fifty distinct medical essays, published in medical journals, besides many reviews and editorial articles without his name attached to them. His attention has been devoted chiefly to subjects of sanitary and Medico-Legal interest.

CHILDREN:

1160. I. Shirley Potter, b. Nov. 9, 1871.

1161. II. Arthur Derby, b. Aug. 30, 1874.

1146. Wallace Sherwin. (1139. James Sumnor, 1124. James, 1118. Ira, 137. Abijah, 17. James. 7. James, 2. James, 1. Thomas.) 5th child, 4th s. of James S. Draper and Emmeline Reeves, m. Aug. 26, 1873, Grace, dau. of diaries M. Campbell and Sarah Heard. She was b. Nov. 23. 1850.

He was educated in the public schools of Wayland. his native town, and, on graduating, commenced business life in Boston with Mr. Eben. D. Draper, at that time treasurer of the "American Steam Safe Co." After several years' experience in that business, he accepted a position in the Blackstone National Bank of Boston. He was soon thereafter offered a higher position in the Third National Bank of Boston; and still later another offer came to him from the Merchants' National Bank of Boston, where he remained until 1889. He was then appointed cashier of the National Bank of North America, Boston, a position which he now holds.

1125. Ira. (1118. Ira, 137. Abijah, 17. James, 7. James, 2. James, 1. Thomas.) 2d s. and child of Ira Draper and Lydia Richards, m. Nancy Bullard in 1809.

She was b. Oct. 22, 1784. d. Nov. 27, 1827. m. 2dly: Eunice, dau. of Joseph Rutter, June 3, 1828. She was b. in 1790. d. Nov. 4, 1869.

CHILDREN, BY 1ST WIFE:

1162. I. Warren, b. Oct. 31, 1810. d. Jan. 9, 1849.

1163. II. Ira Bullard, b. Aug. 3, 1813. d. Jan. 25, 1885.

1164. III. Dexter, b. Oct. 6, 1817. d. Feb. 24, 1825.

1165. IV. Lucy Ann, b. Apr. 14, 1820. d. July 17, 1851. m. Ephraim S., s. of William and Lucy Bemis, Oct. 15, 1844. He was b. 1819. d. July 29, 1870. Children:— I. Marshall M., 1169. b. Nov. 26, 1845. II. Charles E., 1170. b. 1848. d. March 20, 1884. III. Melvin, 1171. b. 1850.

1166. V. Nancy Marion, b. Mar. 17, 1823. m. William W. Cook, Nov. 2, 1849. One s.: Edwin, 1172. b. Mar. 29, 1857.

CHILDREN, BY 2D WIFE:

1167. VI. Joseph Rutter, b. June 30, 1830. d. Aug. 5, 1885.

1168. VII. Lydia Rutter, b. Oct. 19, 1833. m. Sept. 26, 1867, Rev. Alfred Sereno, s. of Martin N. Hudson and Maria Reed. He was b. Nov. 20, 1839.

1163. Ira Bullard. (1125. Ira, 1118. Ira, 137. Abijah, 17. James, 7. James, 2. James, 1. Thomas.) 2d s. and child of Ira Draper and Nancy Bullard. m. Mar. 20, 1838, Louisa, dau. of Paul and Abigail Loper. She was b. Feb. 15, 1813. d. Aug. 6, 1871.

CHILDREN:

1173. I. Nancy Louise, b. Sep. 22, 1839. d. Sep. 16, 1840.

1174. II. William Dexter, b. Aug. 19, 1840. d. Dec. 19, 1864. m. May 29, 1861, Annie Wheeler, dau. of Joseph Wellington and Keziah Haines. After her husband's death, she m. his cousin, James Austin Draper, 1142. William Dexter was a soldier in the War of 1861-5. Child:- William, 1177. b. Feb. 19, 1862.

1175. III. Curtis Warren, b. Sep. 27, 1846. Was a soldier in War of 1861-5.

1176. IV. Charles Rich, b. Dec. 29, 1849. m. Ida F., dau. of William N. and Fanny S. Wright, Apr. 26, 1877. She was b. May 2, 1855. Children:— I. Dexter Wright, 1178. b. May 23, 1881. II. Everett H., 1179. b. July 3, 1885.

1167. Joseph Rutter. (1125. Ira, 1118. Ira, 137. Abijah, 17. James, 7. James, 2. James, 1. Thomas.) Eldest child and only s. of Ira Draper and his 2d wife, Eunice Rutter. m. Nov. 22, 1855, Mary Jane, dau. of Calvin Fuller and Abigail Rutter. She was b. Sep. 2, 1824.

He graduated from Williams College in 1851, and from the Berkshire Medical College in 1860. He entered the army during the Civil War, and subsequently settled in South Boston, Mass., where he remained in practice until his death. He was succeeded in his practice by his s., Dr. Joseph Rutter, Jr.

CHILDREN:

1180. I. Mary Louise, b. June 18, 1858. d. Aug. 8, 1858.

1181. II. Joseph Rutter, b. May 22, 1862. m. Nellie Hall, dau. of Dr. Liberty D. Packard and Lucy Kingman, May 14, 1890. She was b. Dec. 16, 1863.

Dr. Draper graduated from Williams College in the Class of 1885, and received his degree of M.D. from Harvard University in 1888. He succeeded to his father's practice in S. Boston, Mass., where he resides.

Child:— Lillian Packard, 1182. b. June 24, 1891.

1130. Rufus Foster. (1118. Ira, 137. Abijah, 17. James, 7. James, 2. James, 1. Thomas.) 7th child and 5th s. of Ira Draper and Lydia Richards, m. Polly, dau. of Daniel Hemenway and Priscilla.

CHILDREN:

1183. I. Daniel, b. Nov. 20, 1826. d. Oct., 1887. m. 1st: Harriet Bickford. 2dly: Mary E. Daniel Draper was a soldier in the Civil War.

1184. II. James Dexter, b. Oct. 24, 1827.

1185. III. Rufus, b. 1829. m. in 1860, Mary Frances Hickox. Children: — I. James, 1187. b. Apr., 1862. II. Rufus, 1188. b. 1863. III. Jenny, 1189. b. 1873.

1186. IV. Jane. b. 1836. d. Mar. 1, 1861.

1184. James Dexter. (1130. Rufus Foster, 1118. Ira, 137. Abijah, 17. James, 7. James, 2. James, 1. Thomas.) 2d s. and child of Rufus F. Draper and Polly Hemenway. m. 1st: Feb. 28, 1850, Caroline P. Pratt. She was b. Jan. 26, 1833. d. Mar. 13, 1855. He m. 2dly: Apr. 3, 1862, Mary E. Newell. She was b. Apr. 25, 1843. Mr. Draper served gallantly in the Civil War, reaching the grade of First Lieutenant.

CHILDREN, BY 1st WIFE:

1190. I. Emma Caroline, b. Mar. 11, 1851.

1191. II. Ida Lorene, b. Aug. 2, 1852. m. Jan. 14, 1878, George H. Chamberlain. Child: — Gertrude, 1198. b. Jan. 13, 1880.

CHILDREN, BY 2D WIFE:

1192. III. William Newell, b. Jan. 2, 1865.

1193. IV. Charles Eugene, b. Mar. 24, 1868.

1194. V. Hubble Irving, b. Apr. 29, 1870.

1195. VI. James Dexter, Jr., b. Apr. 30, 1874.

1196. VII. Ernest Wilfred, b. Dec. 26, 1879.

1197. VIII, Rose, b. Mar. 24, 1880.

1133. Ebenezer Daggett. (1118. Ira, 137. Abijah, 17. James, 7. James, 2. James, 1. Thomas.) Eldest child and s. of Ira Draper and his 2d wife, Nabbie Richards, m. Anna, dau. of Benjamin and Anna Thwing, Sep. 11, 1834. She wash. Dec. 23, 1814. d. Jan. 30, 1870.

Ebenezer D. Draper was b. in Weston, Mass., where his father, Ira Draper, then resided. In his youth the family removed to Saugus, Mass., where Ira Draper carried on an extensive farm. At the age of 16, after a district school education, he was employed in the cotton mills at North Uxbridge, Mass., and soon became overseer of weaving. There he boarded at the house of Benjamin Thwing, where he met Miss Anna Thwing, who became his wife. Some time later he went into the business of making and selling temples for weaving, which were invented by his father, Ira Draper, and improved by his brother, George Draper. This business had been done previously both by Ira Draper, his father, and James Draper, his older brother. The business continued to grow under Ebenezer D. Draper's management, and, in 1853, his brother, George Draper, the inventor of the improvement above mentioned, became a partner in the firm of E. D. & G. Draper, which did an increasingly large and prosperous business for many years.

When the Fraternal Community at Hopedale was established, E. D. Draper and his wife became original members, and for many years he was its president. This Community depended, for such pecuniary success as it had, largely upon E. D. Draper's ability, and the business which he brought there to be done. In 1855 it became evident to him that the enterprise could not be financially successful, and he withdrew his capital, guaranteeing, however, the debt of the Community, which was paid dollar for dollar, with interest. From this time till 1868 he remained in partnership with his brother, George Draper, and acquired a handsome fortune. After retiring from this business he was, for some years, the Treasurer of the American Steam Fire Proof Safe Company, of Boston.

After his wife's death, Mr. Draper was again m., Oct. 18, 1872, to Mrs. Mary Boynton, who survives him. He had no children by either marriage, but adopted several, one of whom was the Rev. Chas. Henry Eaton, now pastor of the Church of the Divine Paternity in New York City, succeeding the celebrated Dr. Chapin.

Mr. Draper was a total abstainer and strong anti-slavery man; also a believer in non-resistance. He carried this latter belief to such an extent that he took no voluntary part in civil government, for the reason that all civil government is founded on physical force. He was a Universalist in religious belief. During the years of his prosperity he made it a rule to give away each year as much as or more than he expended for his living.

1134. Lydia. (1118. Ira, 137. Abijah, 17. James, 7. James, 2. James, 1. Thomas.) 2d child and eldest dau. of Ira Draper and his 2d wife, Nabbie Richards, m. John, s. of Lott Edmands and Esther Burrill, by Rev. Sylvanus Cobb, Feb., 1835. He was b. Maiden, Mass., Jan. 17, 1811. He m. 2dly: Phoebe Feny, in 1847, and d. Jan. 7, 1886.

CHILDREN, ALL B. SAUGUS, MASS.:

1199. I. George Draper, b. Apr. 9, 1836. m. Newport, R. I., Sep., 1867, Annie A., dau. of Thomas and Sarah E. Chambers. She was b. Newport, Mar. 6, 1838. d. Mar. 25, 1885. Children: — I. Roy, 1205. b. and d. Oct. 29, 1872. II. Florence Bryer, 1206. b. June 6, 1874.

Mr. Edmands served in the Navy, during the Civil War, as Assist. Engineer. He was an expert mechanic.

1200. II. Artemus Bradford, b. Dec. 3, 1837. m. 1st: Dec. 27, 1855, Margaret Matilda Glover. She was b. Feb. 12, 1836. d. July 11, 1872. He m. 2dly: Nov. 25, 1873, Lucinda E. Dow. She was b. Oct. 10, 1856. Children, by 1st marriage: — I. Kate, 1207. b. Feb. 28, 1860. II. Ida, 1208. b. Aug. 28, 1863. Children, by 2d marriage: — III. Frank, 1209. b. June 29, 1874. IV. George, 1210. b. Feb. 19, 1876. V. Arthur Bradford, 1213. b. May 18, 1878. VI, Fanny, 1214. b. Feb. 3, 1883.

Mr. Artemus B. Edmands is now Supt. of the Hopedale Machine Co., Hopedale, Mass., which employs several hundred men. Like his brother George, he is a mechanic of unusual skill, and has occupied positions of responsibility in the employ of others, and has also carried on business for himself in the manufacture of special machinery. He is a prominent Mason and Knight Templar, and is now Eminent Commander of the Milford Commandery.

1201. III. Esther Minerva, b. Nov. 23, 1839. m. by Rev. A. D. Sargeant, Aug. 3, 1861, Isaac Russell, s. of Isaac and Mary Cook. He was b. Parishville, N. Y., Apr, 24, 1828. d. Dec. 20, 1888. Children:— I. George Elmes, 1215. b. May 17, 1862. m. Addie O. Knolton, of W. Nottingham, d. Nov. 23, 1890. II. Frank Russell, 1216. b. Feb. 21, 1864. d. July 14, 1890.

1202. IV. Sarah Melissa, b. Feb. 19, 1842. m. Aug. 26, 1860, Hiram Sylvanus, s. of Asa and Sarah (Burrill) Grover. He was b. Saugus, Mass., Dec. 27, 1838. Children: — I. Jennie Gertrude, 1217. b. Dec. 29, 1861. m. Herbert L. Gilman, June 11, 1887. II. Fred. Grover, 1218. b. Dec. 19, 1863. m. Alice R. Grendall, May 2, 1888.

1203. V. Lydia Huldah, b. Sep. 30, 1844. m. Ebenezer Paine, s. of Lott and Sarah (Paine) Edmands, Dec. 27, 1868. He was b. July 13, 1845. Child: — Lulie Evylin, 12 19. b. Sep. 22, 1870.

1204. VI. Margaret Ellen, b. Jan. 30, 1847. Unmarried. (Adopted by her father's brother and wife, Artemus and Margaret Edmands.)

1135. George. (1118. Ira, 137. Abijah, 17. James, 7. James. 2. James, 1. Thomas.) 2d s. and 3d child of Ira Draper and his 2d wife, Nabby Richards, m. Hannah, dau. of Benjamin and Anna Thwing, of Uxbridge, Mar. 6, 1839. She was b. Jan. 1, 1817. d. Dec. 30, 1883. In the next November he m. 2dly: Mrs. Pamelia B. Blunt, of Milford, Mass., who survives him.

George Draper was b. Weston, Mass. Up to his fifteenth year he lived there, and in Saugus, Mass., on his father's farm, attending school Winters and doing farm work Summers. Though his years of schooling were brief, he acquired at school, and in later studies at home, a most excellent mathematical education — better than that possessed by most college graduates. At the age of fifteen he left home to take a position under his brother in the weaving department of the cotton mills at North Uxbridge, Mass. He remained there two years, and then was made superintendent and manager of a small cotton mill at Walpole, Mass. From there he went to Three Rivers, Mass., becoming overseer of weaving in what was then one of the largest fine mills in the country. While there he devised an improvement in a temple for weaving, which had been invented by his father, and placed the same in the hands of his brother, Ebenezer D. Draper, who made a business of making and selling these articles. In 1839, owing to a general depression in manufacturing business, caused by a progressive reduction of the tariff, he was thrown out of employment, as were a large part of the skilled operatives in New England. He looked vainly for work as an overseer or superintendent, used up his small savings, ran into debt several hundred dollars, and finally accepted a position as an operative in the Massachusetts Cotton Mills, of Lowell, at the remuneration of $5.00 per week. His experience at that time convinced him of the advantage to laboring men of a protective tariff, and he never forgot it.

With a change in the country's policy, manufacturing improved, and he soon became an overseer again. In 1843 he accepted a position as designer of the celebrated Edward Harris cassimeres at Woonsocket, R. I. In 1845 he was appointed superintendent of one of the mills of the Otis Company at Ware, Mass., and later he had charge of the entire corporation. In 1853 he removed from Ware to Hopedale, Mass., going into partnership with his brother, Ebenezer D. Draper, and soon after joined the Hopedale Community. In 1855, when the Community broke up as a financial institution, he joined his brother, E. D. Draper, in guaranteeing and paying its debts. From this time his career was one of uninterrupted material prosperity. His business increased until it became one of the most important in the State. In 1868 his brother, E. D. Draper, retired, and he took into partnership his oldest son, William F. Draper, and, later, his sons, George A. and Eben S. Draper; and two of his grandsons became partners.

George Draper of Hopedale, Mass.

He was a man of large inventive capacity, and took out probably not less than a hundred patents in the United States Patent Office. Among his inventions were devices for self-acting temples, eveners for railway heads, parallel motions for looms, shuttle guards for looms, self-lubricating bearings for spindles and warpers for beaming yarn. He also made a specialty of introducing to the manufacturing public the inventions of others which he had purchased, or which he managed for the inventors. His name is a "household word" among manufacturers, both of the New and the Old World, and the inventions which he introduced in textile manufacturing were among the most important of the century. The power-saving and rapidly running spindles of the Sawyer and Rabbeth varieties were perhaps the most important of these improvements. They have doubled the production of spinning, greatly reduced the power required to make cloth, and save millions of dollars annually to the community in the cost of textile fabrics.

He acquired a large fortune, despite the fact that his charities were unusual in amount and variety. He was always a strong temperance man and a total abstainer, and prior to the war was a Garrisonian Abolitionist. During the war he was an ardent Union man, and worked earnestly for the cause. He organized several companies of volunteers, paying their preliminary expenses, and making personal gifts to each man. He was active in recruiting, and a member of Gov. Andrew's private Advisory Board. After the war he was a firm friend of the soldier, and greatly interested in the Grand Army organization. His gifts thereto were frequent, and he made an annual donation to the Massachusetts Soldiers' Home at Chelsea.

As before stated, he was an earnest believer in a protective tariff, and founded the celebrated Home Market Club, which represents the protective sentiment of New England. In early life he was a Whig, then a Free Soiler, and from the birth of the Republican party till his death, a thorough and enthusiastic Republican. He was frequently a member of committees and a delegate to conventions, but never would accept public office, feeling that he could serve the public better in the management of his large business than in any other way.

He was from early manhood a Unitarian in faith, and never wavered in his views. He wrote much on political topics, both in pamphlets and newspaper articles, and his style was eminently clear and concise. He presided frequently on public occasions, and was a forcible and convincing speaker. During the latter years of his life he travelled much, both at home and abroad, giving up, to a large extent, his business cares.

He was active in the formation of the new Town of Hopedale, in 1886, and built and presented to that town its town hall, which is one of the finest in the State.

CHILDREN:

1220. I. William F., b. Apr. 9, 1842, at Lowell, Mass.
1221. II. Georgiana T., b. June 30, 1844, Lowell, Mass. d. July 23, 1844.
1222. III. Helen L., b. July 11, 1845, Lowell, Mass. d. Aug. 10, 1847.
1223. IV. Frances E., b. July 26, 1847, Ware.
1224. V. A son, b. Dec. 15, 1850. d. in infancy.
1225. VI. Hannah T., b. Apr. 11, 1853, Ware.
1226. VII. George A., b. Nov. 4, 1855, Hopedale.
1227. VIII. Eben S., b. June 17, 1858, Hopedale.

1220. William Franklin. (1135. George, 11 18. Ira, 137. Abijah, 17. James, 7. James, 2. James, 1. Thomas.) Eldest child and s. of George Draper and Hannah Thwing. m. 1st: Lydia W. Joy, Sep. 15, 1862. She was b. Aug. 31, 1843. d. Feb. 18, 1884. m. 2dly: Miss Susan Christy Preston, May 22, 1890. She was b. Nov., 1853, and was the dau. of Maj.-Gen. Preston, of the Confederate Army, formerly Minister to Spain under Buchanan.

Gen. William F. Draper, who is now in the meridian of manhood, has had a varied and successful career. Born in Lowell, Mass., 49 years ago, he received a common high school and academic education, and then spent several years in machine shops and cotton mills, learning both the theoretical and practical parts of the manufacture of machinery and cotton goods. The outbreak of the war aroused his patriotism, and, forsaking his business, he immediately entered the service, and remained until near its close, when he returned incapacitated for duty on account of wounds. He entered as a private in the 25th Mass. Regt. at the age of 19, and his extraordinarily quick series of promotions may be imagined, when it is stated that, before attaining his twenty-third year, he had, on several occasions, commanded a brigade. He was in active service in nearly all the Southern States; was signal officer for General Burnside in his North Carolina campaign; was commissioned in the 36th Mass., which he afterwards commanded; took part in the Maryland and Fredericksburg campaigns; also in the campaign in Kentucky; then in the Vicksburg and Jackson campaigns in Mississippi; then in the East Tennessee campaign, including the Siege of Knoxville; and finally in the Wilderness campaign in 1864. He was shot through the body in the Wilderness, but later returned and commanded a brigade at the Weldon Railroad engagement. Returning to his home, he was employed by his father and uncle, and subsequently became his father's partner in the manufacture of cotton machinery.

Gen'l William F. Draper of Hopedale, Mass.

This business has grown to large proportions at Hopedale, and Gen. Draper has been the head of it since his father's death in 1887. He is also president or director in some twenty railroad, banking or manufacturing corporations outside his business at Hopedale. He has been influential and active politically, though he has never held political office. He served three years as Aide-de-Camp on the staff of Gov. Long; was a delegate to the Republican National Convention at Cincinnati that nominated President Hayes; was Chairman of the Committee on Resolutions at the Massachusetts Republican State Convention in 1887; was a candidate for Governor before the Convention in 1888; and was chosen Presidential Elector at Large at that Convention, casting his vote for President Harrison. He has spoken in political campaigns considerably on the tariff issue, and has written many communications and essays on that subject. He is now President of the Home Market Club, which includes representatives of all the great industries of New England, and is devoted to the cause of protection. With all his other duties he has been eminently a social man, and is a member of a large number of clubs and other organizations, both in this country and on the other side of the water, where he has frequently travelled. Among these organizations are the Union and Algonquin Clubs, Boston; the Hope Club, Providence; Century Club, London; and the Loyal Legion.

Like his father and grandfather, he possesses much inventive ability, and has taken out many patents, both in the United States and foreign countries. His first invention was an effective device for preventing the formation of thick or thin places in cloth, during the process of weaving. This he disposed of for a substantial sum of money. Other inventions were improvements in spindles, spinning rings and looms, machinery manufactured by his firm. He is to-day counted the leading expert in spinning machinery in this country. He has testified frequently in important suits relating to such machinery, and his pamphlet on the "History of Spindles" is accepted as an authority.

His first wife, Miss Lydia W. Joy, was the adopted dau. of the Hon. David Joy of Nantucket, Mass., and a descendant of a brother of Gen. Warren, who fell at Bunker Hill.

CHILDREN, BY 1ST WIFE:

1228. I. William Franklin, b. Dec. 17, 1865.
1229. II. George Otis, b. July 14, 1867.
1230. III. Edith, b. Feb. 18, 1874.
1231. IV. Arthur Joy, b. Apr. 28, 1875.
1232. V. Clare Hill, b. Oct. 4, 1876.

CHILDREN, BY 2D WIFE:

1233. VI. Margaret Preston, b. Mar. 18, 1891.

1223. Frances E. (1135. George, 1118. Ira, 137. Abijah, 17. James, 7. James, 2. James, 1. Thomas.) 4th child and 3d dau. of George Draper and Hannah Thwing. m. Feb. 20, 1868, Charles H. Colburn, of Milford, now of Hopedale, Mass., a large manufacturer of boots and shoes.

Outside her home duties she has been very greatly interested in Sunday school work, and has written a question book for Sunday schools that is in general use by the Unitarian denomination.

CHILDREN:

1234. I. Helen, b. Nov. 9, 1868.
1235. II. Alice Draper, b. Jan. 7, 1875.

1225. Hannah Thwing. (1135. George, 11 18. Ira, 137. Abijah, 17. James, 7. James, 2. James, 1. Thomas.) 6th child and 4th dau. of George Draper and Hannah Thwing. m. Jan. 20, 1881, Edward Louis Osgood, then of the celebrated publishing firm of Jas. R. Osgood & Co., Boston, now retired.

CHILDREN:

1236. I. Edward Dana, b. Jan. 2, 1882.

1237. II. Fanny Colburn& 1238. III. Hannah Draper (Twins), b. Dec. 27, 1882.

1239. IV. George Draper, b. Apr. 25, 1888.

1226. George Albert, (1135. George, 1118. Ira, 137. Abijah, 17. James, 7. James, 2. James, 1. Thomas.) 7th child and 3d s. of George Draper and Hannah Thwing. m. Nov. 6, 1890, Jessie Preston, of Lexington, Ky., dau. of Gen. Preston before mentioned, and sister of Susan Preston, who m. his elder brother, Gen. Draper, 1220.

George A. Draper, like his older brother, was educated by his father with a special view of becoming his partner in manufacturing machinery. He attended school locally, and took a course in the Massachusetts Institute of Technology, and later in the machine shops at Hopedale. He was admitted to the firm of George Draper & Sons soon after his twenty-first birthday. He is a man of marked mechanical ability, and inherits largely also the inventive talent of his father and grandfather. He has been for several years a member of the Massachusetts Republican State Central Committee.

CHILD:

1240. I. Wickliffe Preston, b. Aug. 9, 1891.

1227. Eben Sumner, (1135. George, 1118. Ira, 137. Abijah, 17. James, 7. James, 2. James, 1. Thomas.) 8th child and 4th s. of George Draper and Hannah Thwing. m. Nov. 21, 1883, Nanny Bristow, dau. of Gen. Benj. H. Bristow, of New York, Secretary of the United States Treasury under Grant, and candidate for the Presidency in 1876.

He received a similar education to that of his brother George, 1226, like him taking a course at the Massachusetts Institute of Technology, in mechanical engineering, and spending some time in machine shops and cotton mills, in acquiring a knowledge of the making and running of cotton machinery. He was admitted to the firm of George Draper & Sons, Jan. 1, 1880. As a business man he has shown exceptional ability. He has charge of the selling department of the firm, and is a director in several outside enterprises. Though personally popular, he has not as yet entered political life. He is much interested in religious matters, and has been for several years Supt. of the Hopedale Sunday School.

CHILDREN:

1241. I. Benj. Helm Bristow, b. Feb. 28, 1885.

1242. II. Dorothy, b. Nov. 22, 1890.

1137. Lemuel Richards, (1118. Ira, 137. Abijah, 17. James, 7. James, 2. James, 1. Thomas.) 6th child and 3d s. of Ira Draper and his 2d wife Nabby Richards, m. Jan. I, 1845, Lydia M., dau. of David and Esther Mansfield. She was b. Dec. 25, 1824.

While his older brothers left home to engage in other lines of business, he remained at home with his father, carrying on the home place, which he inherited after his father's death. About 1850, having disposed of the place, he went into the livery and teaming business in Milford, Mass., and later, for a few years, he sold manufacturers' supplies in Worcester. Prior to 1860 he returned to Milford, and purchased the Woonsocket Stage Line, and later came into possession and management of four or five stage lines, with Milford as a centre, and also carried on a large livery and teaming business. About 1870 he gave up this business, and for several years was a contractor in building bridges and heavy mason work for railroads. About 1885 he removed to Hayden Rowe, Mass., and there ended his days. Like his brothers he was a Republican in politics, a Unitarian in religion, and shunned public life. At the time of his death he was at the head of the Hopkinton Grange. He was a man of fine physique and great personal strength, and possessed the strong will and ability to manage men that were such marked qualities in his elder brothers.

CHILDREN:

1244. I. Edward Mansfield, b. Apr. 10, 1846. d. Sep. 9, 1848.
1245. II. Annetta Louise, b. Sep. 28, 1847.
1246. III. Oscar Eugene, b. Apr. 12, 1850.
1247. IV. Eva Richards, b. Aug. 31, 1854. d. Apr. 1, 1884.
1248. V. Minnie Eliza, b. Mar. 1, 1857. d. Jan. 12, 1860.
1249. VI. William Lemuel, b. Aug. 29, 1861. m. Feb. 28, 1883, Emma Louise Smith. She was b. Aug. 6, 1858. (No issue.)

1245. Annetta Louise. (1137. Lemuel, 1118. Ira, 137. Abijah, 17. James, 7. James, 2. James, 1. Thomas.) 2d child and eldest dau. of Lemuel Draper and Lydia Mansfield, m. Nov. 30, 1871, Jonas Hale Carter.

CHILDREN:

1250. I. Lemuel Draper, b. Oct. 25, 1872.
1251. II. Eva Louise, b. Apr. 6, 1881.
1252. III. Lucie Hale, b. Oct. 7, 1884.

1246. Oscar Eugene. (1137. Lemuel, 11 18. Ira, 137. Abijah, 17. James, 7. James, 2. James, 1. Thomas.) 3d child and 2d s. of Lemuel Draper and Lydia Mansfield, m. Oct. 12, 1869, Emma Lucy Hunt. She was b. May 16, 1849. d. Dec. 8, 1876. He m. 2dly: Sep. 21, 1879, Emma E. J. Sturtevant. She was b. Mar. 31, 1851.

CHILDREN, BY 1ST WIFE:

1253. I. Laura Adelaide, b. Dec. 12, 1870.
1254. II. Hiram Eugene, b. Sep. 15, 1872.
1255. III. Clarence Percival, b. Aug. 12, 1874.

CHILD, BY 2D WIFE:

1256. IV. Oscar Griswold, b. Apr. 11, 1886.

1121. Alice Draper. (137. Abijah, 17. James, 7. James, 2. James, 1. Thomas.) 5th child, eldest dau. of Major Abijah Draper and Alice Eaton, m. Mar. 6, 1793, Ebenezer Daggett. He was b. Oct. 2, 1762. d. Sep. 11, 1812.

CHILDREN:

1257. I. Carlos, b. Dec. 2, 1793.

1258. II. Sally, b. May 8, 1797. d. Jan., 1800.

1259. III. Herman, b. Mar. 27, 1800. d. Dec. 12, 1838.

1260. IV. Albert Pliny, b. Oct. 13, 1805. d. Oct. 15, 1827.

1261. V. Susanna, b. Feb. 16, 1809. d. Nov. 17, 1825.

1257. Carlos Daggett. (1221. Alice, 137. Abijah, 17. James, 7. James, 2. James, 1. Thomas.) Eldest child and s. of Alice Draper and Ebenezer Daggett, m. Mary Child, of Weston. She was b. Apr. 5, 1799.

CHILDREN:

1262. I. Edward Child, b. Aug. 29, 1817. d. Dec. 18, 1848.

1263. II. Ebenezer, b. Mar. 7, 1820.

1264. III. Charles Henry, b. Mar. 21, 1822. d. Mar. 23, 1827.

1265. IV. Mary Susanna, b. July 16, 1824.

1266. V. Albert Pliny, b. July 21, 1827. d. Mar. 26, 1837.

1267. VI. Herman, b. May 6, 1831. d. Mar. 18, 1837,

1268. VII, George, b. Apr. 4, 1834. d. Apr. 20, 1837.

1269. VIII. Charles Herman, b. Mar. 2, 1838.

1270. IX. Albert Pliny 2d, b. Apr. 16, 1841.

1122. Abijah. (137. Abijah, 17. James, 7. James, 2. James, I.Thomas.) 6th child, 5th s. of Major Abijah Draper and Alice Eaton, m. Lavinia Tyler, of Attleboro, Jan. 12, 1807. She was b. Mar. 25, 1778. d. May 22, 1864.

He graduated at Brown University in 1797, and taught school at "Green Lodge," during college vacations. He located himself as a physician at West Roxbury, Mass. His mother, Mrs. Desire Draper, kept house for him till he married. During a period of sixty years he and his son. Dr. Abijah Weld Draper, were practicing physicians in West Roxbury. Dr. Abijah Draper, Sen., collected some material for a family history. It was never published. He was a member of the Massachusetts Medical Society and Worshipful Master of a Masonic Lodge.

CHILDREN, ALL B. AT WEST ROXBURY:

1271. I. Abijah Weld, b. Jan. 25, 1808. d. Feb. 19, 1874.

1272. II. Augusta. d. Sep. 4, 1877. 1273. &III. Amanda (Twins), b. July 21, 1810. (d. Apr. 26, 1879. (Said to have d. of a broken heart.)

1271. Abijah Weld. (1122. Abijah, 137. Abijah, 17. James, 7. James, 2. James, 1. Thomas.) Eldest child of Dr. Abijah Draper and Lavinia Tyler, m. 1st: Lydia Frances Swain, Jan. 20, 1839, at Philadelphia, Pa. She was b. Nantucket, Mass., Jan. 18, 1812. d. at W. Roxbury, Apr. 29, 1846. He m. 2dly: the widow Sarah Hawes (Hewins) Reynolds, Apr. 26, 1848. She was b. at S. Boston, Mar. 19, 1819.

Dr. Abijah Weld Draper taught school in his early life, before entering upon his profession. He removed to Philadelphia about 1837, where he was established as a dentist, but remained there but a few years, returning to West

Roxbury to practise as a physician. During the Civil War he was one of the surgeons at Army Square Hospital, Washington, D. C. Failing health compelled him to relinquish the practise of his profession a few years before his death. He was a member of the Massachusetts Medical Society and of the New England Historic Genealogical Society. He was deeply interested in the history of the Draper family, and the author is indebted to him for copious notes on this subject. He was also much interested in the history of his native town of Roxbury. Dr. Draper made it his duty, as well as pleasure, to watch over and care for the old graves of the family in the Eustis Street, West Roxbury, Cemetery. Amongst these are the graves of James the 1st, called the "Puritan," and Miriam Stansfield, his wife; James 2d and Abigail Whiting; James 3d and Abigail Child; Captain Jonathan and Sarah Jackson, and others. In Nov., 1877, the family of Dr. Draper removed to Milton, Mass.

CHILDREN, BY 1ST WIFE:

1274. I. William Marshall, b. June 28, 1840, at Philadelphia, d. W. Roxbury, July 19, 1870.

By 2d wife:

1275. II. Abijah Weld, Jr., b. W. Roxbury, Apr. 18, 1849. In 1880, bought a farm in the town of Foxborough, and removed there.

1276. III. Lydia Frances, b. W. Roxbury, July 21, 1852.

1277. IV. Miriam Stansfield, b. W. Roxbury, Nov. 19, 1854.

1274. William Marshall. (1271. Abijah Weld, 1122. Abijah, 137. Abijah, 17. James, 7. James, 2. James, 1. Thomas.) Only child of Dr. Abijah Weld Draper and Lydia Frances Swain.

Was a druggist by profession. Enlisted, Oct. 5, 1861, as a private in Company G, 22d Mass. Volunteers. Discharged for disability, Nov. 26, 1862. For nine months Chief Clerk and Hospital Steward for the Medical Director of the Third Army Corps, and one year Acting Medical Cadet in Armory Square Hospital, Washington, D. C. Also, held the position of Hospital Steward in charge of the Chief Quartermaster's Hospital of Washington. Appointed Oct. 14, 1864, Hospital Steward U. S. Army, with rank as Sergt. of Ordnance, in full charge of Hicks Hospital, Baltimore, Md. Discharged from the army Oct. 14, 1867, at expiration of service, and engaged in business in Baltimore, Md., but, being too ambitious for his strength, by overwork incurred disease of the spine, of which he d. after a long and painful illness.

1275. Abijah Weld, Jr. (1271. Abijah Weld, 1122. Abijah, 137. Abijah, 17. James, 7. James, 2. James, 1. Thomas.) Eldest child, only s. of Dr. Abijah Weld Draper and his 2d wife, Sarah H. Reynolds, m. Ella Josephine Howard, of Sharon, June 9, 1886. She was b. Feb. 18, 1857. They reside in Foxborough.

CHILDREN:

1278. I. Alice Eaton, b. Feb. 24, 1889.

1279. II. Howard, b. Sep. 16, 1890.

1272. Augusta. (1122. Abijah, 137. Abijah, 17. James, 7. James, 2. James, 1. Thomas.) 2d child and eldest of the twin daus. (Augusta and Amanda) of Dr. Abijah Draper and Lavinia Tyler, m. Chauncy Woodward, of Brookline, Mass., Nov. 25, 1847. Resided in W. Roxbury. He d. Feb., 1872.

CHILDREN:

1280. I. Herbert Chauncy, b. Oct. 21, 1849.
1281. II. Marion Lavinia, b. Mar. 3, 1851.
1282. III. William Henry, b. Sep. 28, 1852. d. Jan., 1860.

1123. Lendarmine. (137. Abijah, 17. James, 7. James, 2. James, 1. Thomas.) Only child of Major Abijah Draper and his 2d wife. Desire Metcalf. m. Calvin Guild, of Dedham, Apr. 6, 1800.

He was a hatter, auctioneer, and sheriff in Dedham.

CHILDREN:

1283. I. Frances, b. Sep. 4, 1801.
1284. II. Lendarmine Draper, b. Sep. 29, 1803.
1285. III. Amasa, b. Oct. 12, 1805. d. in infancy.
1286. IV. Emeline, b. Jan. 17, 1807. d. Dec. 11, 1809.
1287. V, Calvin, b. Nov. 22, 1808.
1288. VI. Cornelia, b. Mar. 29, 1810.
1289. VII. Nathanial Metcalf, b. July 21, 1811.
1290. VIII. Abigail, b. Aug. 9, 1814.
1291. IX. Nancy, b. Oct. 20, 1818,
1292. X. Lucretia, b. Mar. 3, 1823. d. June 2, 1832.

18. Gideon. [*] (7. James, 2. James, 1. Thomas.) 6th child, 4th s. of James Draper, 7, and Abigail Whiting, m. Roxbury, Apr. 22, 1713, Abigail Aldis.

[*] Note: In reference to the descendants of Gideon Draper, 18, the author desires to say, that they have become so widely scattered, and the majority are so indifferent to genealogical matters, that it has been with the utmost difficulty that any connecting lines could be established. The use so generally, in this branch, of the name of Gideon, has also tended to greatly confuse and delay the work, and it may be said that at least three times as much labor has been done to collect the following data as that devoted to any other branch of the family, and if there are errors, the reader will please blame those whose duty it was to supply the information, and who neglected to do so, although repeatedly urged.

CHILDREN:

1293. I. Abigail, b. Dedham, May 26, 1714. d. there Dec. 4, 1729.
1294. II. James, b. Dedham, Sep. 29, 171 5. d. there Jan. 7, 1719.
1295. III. John, b. Dedham, July 29, 1717.
1296. IV. Ruth, b. Dedham, Nov. 29, 1718.
1297. V. Gideon, b. Dedham, Aug. 25, 1722. d. Dover, N. Y., 1778.

1298. VI. Nathanial, b. Dedham, Feb. 17, 1724. d. 1827-30. m. Grace. She outlived her husband many years, and was a Federal pensioner. He was a Major in the Revolutionary War.

1299. VII. Nathan, b. Apr. 9, 1725. Lived in Shaftesbury.

1300. VIII, William, b. Feb. 10, 1727.

1301. IX. Caesar, b. Feb. 14, 1729.

1302. X. Mary, b. Nov. 30, 1731. d. Dec. 21, 1731.

1297. Gideon. (18. Gideon, 7. James, 2. James, 1. Thomas.) 5th child, 3d s. of Gideon Draper, 18, and Abigail Aldis. m. about 1740-50, Dolly Bassett.

Gideon Draper went from Roxbury, Mass., to Dover, N. Y. During the time he lived at Dover the territory was transferred to N. Y. State, and was called the Connecticut Gore.

CHILDREN:

1303. I. William.

1304. II. Joseph, m. Miss Benson. Had a s. named Louis, 131 5, and a dau., 1316, who m. a cutler of Sullivan Co., N. Y.

1305. III. Reuben, m. (No issue.)

1306. IV. John.

1307. V. Ebenezer, m. Hannah Worcester, Children: — Gideon, 131 5. John,

1316. Amos, 1317,

1308. VI, Benjamin.

1309. VII. Ezekiel. (Unmarried.)

1310. VIII. Gideon.

1311. IX. Nathan.

1312. X. Millie, m. Oliver Briggs,

They joined the Quakers. Had a large family,

1313. XI, Abigail, m. Caspar Elster.

He was one of the Hessians of Burgoyne's army, but would not return to Europe,

1314. XII. A son.

1303. William. (1297, Gideon, 18. Gideon, 7. James, 2. James, 1. Thomas.) Eldest s, and child of Gideon Draper and Dolly Bassett.

He was a Quaker at the time of the Revolution and did not serve on that account. He went, instead, on his wife's persuasion, to Long Island.

CHILDREN:

1318. I. Gideon, b. Connecticut, 1769. d. Aug., 1850.

1319. II. Daniel.

1320. III. Nathanial.

1321. IV. William.

1322. V. David. Lived at Akron.

1318. Gideon. (1303. William, 1297. Gideon, 18. Gideon, 7. James, 2. James, 1. Thomas.) Eldest s. and child of William Draper, m. Dierus Hollister, of Vermont.

He was called "Hatch," having learnt harness making from a man of that name. In 1795 he settled near Saratoga, Fulton Co., N. Y. In 1820 lived near Broad Albia. From there he went to Akron.

CHILDREN:

1323. I. Harrison, b. 1797. d. young.

1324. II. Harriet, b. 1799. m. Joseph Perkins.

1325. III. Maria, b. 1801, m. Samuel Eighma, a Methodist preacher.

1326. IV. Clarissa, b. 1803. m. S. Lighthall.

1327. V. Hiram, b. 1804. d. 1842. m. Sophia Smith. Settled in New York City, and practised medicine.

1328. VI. Laura, b. 1806. m. Miniot Smith. They settled in New Canaan, Conn.

1329. VII. Aheimas E., b. 1808. d. Mar. 26, 1888. m. 1831, Lorenda S. Hodges. She was b. Sep. 6, 1812. d. Sep. 12, 1876. They settled in Erie Co., N. Y. Children: — I. William C, 1330. b. 1832. m. Harriet Canett, 1854, and settled in Portsmouth, O. (Children: — I. Francis Edgar. 1340. b. 1857. m. Pattie Nichols, 1879. Settled in Kansas City, Mo, II, Jessie, 1341. b. 1861. III. Nellie, 1342. b. 1869. m. Wells A. Hutchins, Jr., 1891. Settled in Portsmouth, O. IV, Hattie, 1343. b. 1873.) IIBeulah M., 1331. b, 1833. d. unmarried. III. John W., 1332, b. 1835. (Unmarried.) IV. Sylvanus, 1333. b. 1836. d, in infancy, V, Micah S., 1334. b, 1838. m. Helen Smead, 1862, Settled in the old homestead, Erie Co., N, Y. (Children: — I. Gideon W„ 1344, b. 1863. II. Egbert M., 1345. b, 1866, III. Carrie, 1346. b. 1869. All three m. and live with their father on the old homestead). VI. Francis A., 1335. b, 1840, m, Jenny Adams, 1868. Settled in Cincinnati, -O, (Child: — Walter S., 1347. b. 1870.) VII, Cephas, 1336. b. 1841. d. in infancy. VIII, Laura D., 1337. b. 1843. (Unmarried.) IX. Edgar F., 1338. b. 1846. m. Mary E. Adams, 1869. Settled in Portsmouth, O. (No issue.) X. Hiram S., 1339. b. 1848. (Unmarried.)

1317. Nathanial. (1303. William, 1297. Gideon, 18. Gideon, 7. James, 2. James, 1. Thomas.) 3d child, 3d s. of William Draper.

CHILDREN:

1348. I. Nathanial. Lived at High River Junction. Moved to Rochester, N. Y., in 1860, m. Rachel Casten, of Milo, Yates Co., N. Y. (No issue.)

He was a teacher in the High School, a farmer and J. P., and made a great deal of money by the appreciation of real estate in Rochester.

1349. II. Thomas Penniman, m. Sarah Parmenter. Children: — I. Charles T., 1356. d. aged two years. H. George Parmlee, 1357. b. Aug. 9, 1833. m. Was a lawyer in Rochester, N. Y. III. Samuel, 1358. m. Lived in Charleston, N. H. Children: — I. Ezra, 1359. II. Nathanial, 1360. III. Eli, 1361. IV. John, 1362.

1350. III. Samuel.

1351. IV. Grace.

1352. V. Anna.

1353. VI. Mary.

1354. VII. Sallie.

1355. VIII. Betsey.

1306. John. (1297. Gideon, 18. Gideon, 7. James, 2. James, 1. Thomas.) 4th child, 4th s. of Gideon Draper and Dolly Bassett. m. Miss Stewart.

CHILDREN:

1363. I. Samuel, d. about 1814.

He was a Presiding Elder in the Methodist Episcopal Church. He lived in the township of White Hall, Lake Champlain, and was on circuit between 1810 and 1814, the circuit being the Methodist Churches in the N.W. part of the State of Vermont or Stow circuit. He was a large man, red face and nose, and weighed about 240 pounds. A robust, resolute, energetic man, and an extraordinary preacher for his time, so much so that tradition largely preserves it. He had a horse given him when a colt, which he named "Gratis," which he rode for many years, a very smart, vigorous animal. One of the traditional anecdotes of Elder Samuel is, that in a sermon, he spoke thus of dancing: "That folks would stitch catgut over a shingle and go to see-sawing and dancing, hopping up like peas on a hot shovel; that if they saw their cattle behave so, they would think the devil was in them."

1364. II. Isaac.

1365. III. Gideon, b. 1784. d. Clifton Springs, N. Y., 1862,

1366. IV. James.

1367. V. Andrew,

1368. VI. Alonson.

1369. VII. Jacob Lane, b. Jan. 27, 1792. d. Brooklyn, N. Y., Apr. 4, 1867.

1370. VIII. William, b. Duchess Co., N. Y., Aug. 27, 1795.

1371. IX. Jesse.

1372. X. Sallie.

1373. XI. Polly.

1365. Gideon. (1306. John, 1297. Gideon, 18. Gideon, 7. James, 2. James, 1. Thomas.) 3d child, 3d s. of John Draper and Miss Stewart, m. Elizabeth Croniz. She was b. in Maryland, d. Clifton Springs, N. Y., 1862, a week before her husband. He was a Methodist minister.

CHILDREN:

1374. I. John C, b. 1826. A banker of Canandaigua.

1375. II. Gideon, b. Manchester, N. Y., 1828. d. Yokohama, Japan, Dec. 8, 18—. m. Charlotte Brown, of New York City. Has a s. living in Japan, Rev. Gideon F. Draper, 1381, at whose house he d. The latter m. Mira, dau. of the late Bishop E. O. Haven, of the M. E. Church.

Dr. Gideon Draper, 1375, graduated at Dartmouth College in 1849. For several years he practised law at Canandaigua, N. Y. He went to Europe in 1853, and after three years of study and travel in Egypt, the Holy Land, etc., he returned to New York, and in May, 1857, joined the New York Conference. Entering the Methodist Episcopal Church he became a D.D. He spent about 25 years in the active ministry, including one year as Professor in Genesee College. He made several tours to Europe, and was one year pastor of the American Church in Geneva, Switzerland. In 1885-6 he served as pastor of a church in London. Dr. Draper was deeply interested in the cause of Christian missions, and was always prepared to speak or write instructively concerning them. He had become very widely known through his journeys and his writings, and was everywhere beloved.

1376. III. Mary S., m. George Dunkle, of Hopewell.

1377. IV. Caroline Wesley, m. Hopewell, N. Y., Feb. 28, 1836, D. D. Dayton, M.D. They both d. at Geneva, N. Y. Children:— I. George Draper, 1381. b. Clifton Springs, N. Y., Mar. 6, 1857. m. Dec. 17, 1878, at Eddytown, N. Y., Emma Willard Chadwick. (Children:- I. Davis Draper, 1386. b. Geneva, June 11, 1880. II. Carrie W., 1387. b. Geneva, N. Y., Feb. 5, 1883. III. George Nelson, 1388. h. Worthington, Minn., Aug. 3, 1886. IV, Josephine, 1389. b. Worthington, Minn., Apr. 26, 1889.) Mr. Dayton resides at Worthington, Minn., where he is President of the following associations: The Minn. Loan & Investmt. Co., Bank of Worthington, the Worthington Mill Co., and the Minn. Northern Rw. Co. II. Josephine Elizabeth, 1382. m. Rev. J. Easter. III. Caroline Amanda, 1383. d. aged 16. IV. Benjamin Bonney, 1384. (Entered the church, d. and was buried at sea.) V. Edson Carr, 1385. (A clergyman.) Three others who d. in infancy.

1378. V. Amanda, m. Rev. Thomas Carlton. (Deceased.)

1379. VI. Pamelia A., m. Rev. Woodruff Post, of Olean, N. Y.

1380. VII. Laura Jane, m. Rev. Charles Shilling. (Deceased.)

1368. Alonson. (1306. John, 1297. Gideon, 18. Gideon, 7. James, 2. James, 1. Thomas.) 6th child, 6th s. of John Draper and Miss Stewart.

He was a Baptist preacher. Married and located in Shelly, Orleans Co., N. Y., between 1840-50.

CHILDREN:

1390. I. Horace.

1391. II. Isaac W. He served in the Union Army.

1392. III. Ann Eliza, m. C. C. Richtmeyer.

1393. IV. Jacob, m.

1369. Jacob Lane. (1306. John, 1297. Gideon, 18. Gideon, 7. James, 2. James, 1. Thomas.) 7th child, 7th s. of John Draper and Miss Stewart, m. 1835, Semantha, dau. of Philip and Fanny Valentine, of Suffolk Co., L. I.

CHILDREN:

1394. I. Gilbert Arnold, b. New York City, 1835. m. Louise, dau. of Ichabod and Minerva Sherman. Children: — I. Eloise, 1397. m. William B. Varnum, [of Brooklyn, N. Y. (They have: I. Harold, 1399. II. Marjorie, 1400. Ill, Gilbert, 1401.) II. Florence, 1398.

When the call for troops to suppress the Rebellion was issued, Mr. Gilbert A. Draper was Supt. of James Mission, a suburban offshoot of Somerville Methodist Church, and also Assist. Foreman of the Brooklyn Fire Department. He immediately opened a recruiting office, and soon added a company to John Cockrane's Regt. of Chasseurs, then forming in New York City. After the first battle of Bull Run the Regt. was attached to the Army of the Potomac. Gilbert Draper commenced service as a 2d Lieut., and they participated in the eight days' campaign on the Peninsular, under McClellan, at the termination of which Capt. Draper, promoted, returned to Brooklyn on furlough to recruit from injuries received. He was soon thereafter occupied in recruiting for a new regiment, which took the field under Col. Edward Molyneux, as the 159th N. Y. S. V., Capt. Draper ranking as Lt.-Col. They were attached to the command of Gen. Banks, and Col. Draper was shot through the heart while his brigade was, with fixed bayonets, charging the enemy who were located behind trees in a wood near Irish Bend, Bayou Tache, Ia. His body was there interred, but subsequently exhumed, and transferred to its final resting place in Greenwood Cemetery, Brooklyn, N. Y. Col. Draper was a man of remarkable memory and physique.

1395. II. Jacob K.

1396. III. Semantha, m. James Nelson Edgar, of Brooklyn, N. Y. They have:

Eugene Ashley, 1402, m. (Who has a s., Lawrence Thurston, 1403.)

1370. William. (1306. John, 1297. Gideon, 18. Gideon, 7. James, 2. James i Thomas.) 8th child, 8th s. of John Draper and Miss Stewart, m. Elizabeth '-. She was b. Aug. 23, 1798,

CHILDREN:

1404. I. James Lane, b. 1823. m. 1845, Emma, dau. of Philip and Fanny Valentine, of Long Island, N. Y. Children:— I. James Nelson,

1401. b. 1850. m. (Had two or more children.) II. Ellen Jane,

1402. b. 1854. m. Darius Hollenbeck. III. Delia Elizabeth, 1403. b. 1855. m. William Ray.

1405. 11. Theodore William.

1406. III. Nelson, b. 1831. m. and has a family in California.

1315. Gideon. (1307. Ebenezer, 1297. Gideon, 18. Gideon, 7. James, 2. James, 1. Thomas.) s. of Ebenezer Draper and Hannah Worcester, m. 1st: Sep. 14, 1797, Elizabeth Chapman, of Dover, N. Y. She was b. Oct. 13, 1777. d. Dec. 25, 18/5 He m. 2dly: Dec. 6, 1818, Mrs. Huldah (Cutler) Wilder. She was b. Mar. 24, 1776. d. 1 (No issue by 2d wife.)

CHILDREN, BY 1ST WIFE, B. SHELDON, VT.:

1407. I. Alonson, b. July 9, 1800. d. Apr. 30, 1875.

1408. II. Israel Chapman, b. Apr. 11, 1802.

1409. III. Lyman, b. Aug. 16, 1806.

1410. IV. Esther, b. Sep. 4, 1808. d. Aug. 8, 1811.

1411. V. Lorenzo, b. Aug. 31, 1810. d. Aug. 9, 1859.

1412. VI. Wilson, b. May 3, 1812. d. Nov. 14, 1840.

1413. VII. Horace, b. Apr. 2, 1814. d. Oct. 25, 1838.

1414. VIII. Elizabeth, b, Dec. 3, 1815, d. May 27, 1876. m. M. Lock. (Several Children.)

1407. Alonson. (1315. Gideon, 1307. Ebenezer, 1297. Gideon, 18. Gideon, 7. James, 2. James, 1. Thomas.) Eldest s. and child of Gideon Draper and Elizabeth Chapman, m. Oct. 12, 1823, Phoebe Fish, of Ferrisburg, Vt. She was b. Mar. 15, 1800.

CHILDREN:

1415. I. John Fish, b. Dec. 3, 1826. m. Azinath Randall. Child: — Allan Martin, 1421.

1416. II. Allan Martin, b. Dec. 11, 1830. d. Dec. 14, 1850.

1417. III. Wilson, b. Aug. 25, 1834. m. Martha Kimball. Child: — Fred Wilson, 1422. b. Aug. 12, 1858.

1418. IV. Helen, b. July 24, 1837. d. Aug. 24, 1837.

1419. V. Horace, b. Oct. 15, 1838.

1420. VI. An infant, b. Apr. 1, 1840. d. Apr. 6, 1840.

1408. Israel Chapman. (1315. Gideon, 1307. Ebenezer, 1297. Gideon, 18. Gideon, 7. James, 2. James, 1. Thomas.) 2d child, 2d s. of Gideon Draper and Elizabeth Chapman, m. Miranda Wilder. She was b. Mar. 8, 1808.

CHILDREN:

1423. I. Nelson Cutter, b. Mar., 1831. d. May, 1835.

1424. II. Celia.

1425. III. Israel C.

1409. Lyman. (1315. Gideon, 1307. Ebenezer, 1297. Gideon, 18. Gideon, 7. James, 2. James, 1. Thomas.) 3d s., 3d child of Gideon Draper and Elizabeth Chapman, m. 1st: Aug., 1831, Olive Hill. She was b. Aug. 20, 1809. d. Nov. 24, 1858. m. 2dly: Anna Fairbanks.

CHILDREN, BY 1st WIFE (NO ISSUE BY 2D):

1426. I. Susan Elizabeth, b. Apr. 23, 1832. d. May 8, 1832.

1427. II. Elizabeth Hill, b. Aug. 27, 1833. d. Dec. 5, 1839.

1428. III. Nelson C, b. Fairfax, Vt., Sep. 4, 1835. d. Sep. 12, 1883.

1429. IV. Isaac Hill, b. Apr. 17, 1840. d. Feb. 20, 1863. m. Feb. 9, 1859, Mary T. Evarts. She was b. July 1841. Child: — Olive Jane, 1431. b. May 13, 1861. d. Aug. 19, 1889. She m. Simpson Dunlop, of Oak Park, Ill. (Children: — I. Hannah, 1432. II. Samuel Draper, 1433.)

1430. V. Olive Hill, b. Aug. 20, 1846. d. Feb. 18, 1881.

1428. Nelson C. (1409. Lyman, 1315. Gideon, 1307. Ebenezer, 1297. Gideon, 18. Gideon, 7. James, 2. James, 1. Thomas.) 3d child, eldest s. of Lyman Draper and Olive Hill. m. Nov. 18, 1858, Azinath M. Ballard, of Georgia, Vt.

Previous to his marriage Mr. Draper had settled at Marine Mills, Minn., where he was engaged for about four years in the grocery and lumber business. He then moved to Hastings, Minn., where he was engaged in general merchandise. During this last residence he was twice elected to represent his district in the State Senate. In 1868 he removed to Chicago, and was there engaged in the wholesale grocery business. Part of the time the firm was "Lockwood & Draper," and later "Gould, Draper & Co." He was Federal Inspector of tea for the Port of Chicago; was one of the originators of the Northwestern Travelling Men's Association, being its second president; was a member of Damascus Commandery, Knights Templar, of St. Paul, Minn., and had taken the 32d Masonic degree; he was a member of the Calumet,

Commercial and Union League Clubs of Chicago; was also identified with the association of the Sons of Vt. of Chicago.

CHILDREN:

1434. I. Arthur Nelson, b. Marine Mills, Minn., Oct. 9, 1859. m. 1890, Anna M. Schlund.

Mr. Draper has enjoyed the benefits of the common schools, and has been in the banking business, being now cashier of Dunlop Bros.' Bank at Oak Park, Ill. He is a member of the Royal Arcanum and of the Knights of Pythias.

1435. II. Olive Emma, b. Apr. 9, 1861. d. Dec. 19, 1861.

1436. III. Nellie Louise, b. Sep. 2, 1862. d. Aug. 4, 1863.

1437. IV. Herbert Lyman, b. Hastings, Minn., July 19, 1864.

He was educated in the Chicago schools and at Williams College. In 1884 he went into the grain commission business in the Chicago Board of Trade. After three years of this he went into the employ of the Excelsior Stone Co., and when this was merged in the Western Stone Co. he was cashier and is now secretary. He is a member of the Zeta Psi and of the Royal Arcanum.

1411. Lorenzo. (131 5. Gideon, 1307. Ebenezer, 1297. Gideon, 18. Gideon, 7. James, 2. James, 1. Thomas.) 5th child, 4th s. of Gideon Draper and Elizabeth Chapman, m. 1st: Sep. 16, 1832, Lucinda Westover Duclos. She was b. Apr. 1, 1809. d. Oct. 20, 1848. He m. 2dly: Mrs Electra Heines.

CHILDREN, BY 1ST WIFE (NO ISSUE BY 2D):

1438. I. Gideon Frank, b. Apr. 21, 1834. d. July 13, 1856. (Unmarried.)

1439. II. Luna Duclos, b. May 18, 1837. m. Oct. 14, 1857, Alonson L. Withers. He was b. 1838.

1440. III. Lucinda Westover, b. Feb. 28, 1841.

1441. IV. Caroline Mary, b. Sep. 10, 1843.

1442. V. Hiram L., b. Feb. 7, 1845. d. Apr. 30, 1846.

1443. VI. Mary E., b. Nov. 29, 1846. d. May 31, 1848.

1310. Gideon. (1297. Gideon, 18. Gideon, 7. James, 2. James, 1. Thomas.) 8th child, 8th s. of Gideon Draper and Dolly Bassett. m. Mary, dau. of Josiah Thayer and Mercy Darling, of Dover. She d. at Hopewell, but outlived her husband many years, and m. 2dly: about 1815, Lawrence Knickerbocker.

Gideon Draper kept an inn at Dover during the Revolution, and was often visited by Washington and his officers. He was drafted into the Continental Army, but did not serve, as he was immediately taken ill and died.

CHILDREN:

1444. I. Gideon, b. Nov. 28, 1771, Dover, Duchess Co., N. Y. He entered the Methodist Church. Emigrated from Dover, N. Y., to Sheldon, Franklin Co., Vt., about 1794. d. Apr. 1, 1858.

1445. II. Sarah, b. 1773. m. Mr. Barlow, d. about 1858. Had a son named Friend, 1447.

1446. III. Friend, b. Dover, N. Y., Nov. 28, 1775. d. Jan. 4, 1867.

1446. Friend. (1310. Gideon, 1297. Gideon, 18. Gideon, 7. James, 2. James, 1. Thomas.) 3d child, 2d s. of Gideon Draper and Mary Thayer, m. 1st: Aug. 21, 1796, Mary A. Nase. See was b. Apr. 14, 1763. He m. 2dly: a dau. of the Rev. Abner Chase, P. E., Dec. 18, 1836. She was b. Benton Centre, Sep. 8, 1806.

Friend Draper became a travelling preacher in Albany County, N. Y., in 1803. On Apr. 17, 1808, on Chatham Circuit, he preached his first sermon in Claverack, the next at Hillsdale, and so on daily, and sometimes two or three times. His circuit was 400 miles, and for two years he preached from 40 to 50 times in four weeks. His next circuit was the Buckland, in Mass., just above Deerfield; then the Granville Circuit, from Hartford up to Springfield and Westfield. 1811, from Granville to Pittsfield Circuit. 1812, the barracks were just above him at Pittsfield, Rhinebeck Circuit, most part of which was in New York State, including Sharon and Canaan in Connecticut. 1814, Chatham Circuit. 1815, Petersburg Circuit, N. Y. 1816, Lebanon, Columbia Co., where he owned a farm and had his home. 1817, Cambridge, N. Y. Circuit. 1818 and 1819, Saratoga Springs Circuit. 1820, Montgomery Circuit, N. Y. 1821, Beme Circuit, N. Y. 1822, Coeyman's Circuit, Albany County, N. Y. He resided at Cairo, W. Catskill, for two months, where his wife died with yellow fever, brought back by a man who had visited New York City. 1823, Sullivan Circuit. 1824, Petersburg Circuit again. 1825, located at White Creek, N. Y., and farmed. Sep., 1826, moved to Manchester Village, 1833, on Milo Circuit. 1834, Benton Circuit.

CHILD, BY 1ST WIFE:

1448. I. Philip Nase, b. Dover, N. Y., Apr. 15, 1797. d. Manchester, N. Y., Dec. 15, 1827. m. May 14, 1823, Sila Ann, dau. of Dr. Post, with whom he had commenced practise as a physician at White Creek. He was a graduate of the University of Michigan, both in literature and the medical department. Children: — I. James Friend, 1452. b. Washington Co., N. Y., July 15, 1825. m. June 23, 1855, Adelaid Haywood, at Saline, Mich. (Child:— Frank James, 1454. b. Chicago, Sep. 13, 1857. Unmarried. Lives Salt Lake City, Utah.) Mr. J. F. Draper's wife dying, hem. 2dly: Oct. 30, 1861, Mary Ann Hutchins. (Children, by 2d wife:— I. Allan H., 1455. b. Chicago, Aug. 14, 1863. II. Mary Lucy, 1456. b. Victor, N. Y., Oct. 30, 1865. III. Mabel, 1457. b. Victor, June 13, 1870.) H. Lucy Maria, 1453. b. Oct. 14, 1827, d. in childhood.

CHILDREN, BY 2D WIFE:

1449. II. Gideon B., b. Benton Centre, 1839. d. 1863. (Unmarried.)

He entered the Union Army, and was wounded at the Battle of Yorktown, 1861.

1450. III. Maria L., b. June, 1827. d. Feb., 1838.

1451. IV. Sabra, m. Mr. Reeves, d. Penn Yan, 1877. Children:— I. Emma Winifred, 1458. b. Penn Yan, 1868. II. Marion Edith, 1459. b. 1872. III. William Judson, 1460. b. Penn Yan, 1875.

19. Ebenezer. (7. James, 2. James, 1. Thomas.) 5th s., youngest child of James Draper and Abigail Whiting, m. 1st: Dorothy, dau. of Joshua Child and

Elizabeth Morris, of Brookline, Mass., May 2, 1723. She was a sister of Abigail, who m. James Draper, 17, and was b. May 25, 1701. d. Aug. 2, 1748. He m. 2dly: Sibyl, dau. of William and Esther Avery, of Dedham, Mass., Nov. 16, 1749, by Rev. Sam. Small. She was b. Jan. 3, 1720. d. Feb. 16, 1816.

Mr. Draper and his 1st wife were admitted to full communion at the First Church of Roxbury, Jan. 26, 1724. He was dismissed to the church in Dedham, Nov. 14, 1734. He was a farmer by occupation, and after leaving his father's home at Roxbury, passed his subsequent life at the family -place. Green Lodge, near Dedham.

CHILDREN, BY 1st WIFE:

1461. I. Dorothy, b. Roxbury, Feb. 1, 1724. m. by Rev. Samuel Dexter, Nov. 23, 1744, Joseph, s. of Joseph and Mehetable Colburn. He was b. July 7, 1718. Children: — I. Joseph, 1478. b. Aug. 21, 1745. II. Mary, 1479. b. Oct. 1, 1747. III. Dorothy, 1480. b. Aug. 12, 1750. IV. Levie, 1481. b. June 3, 1753. V. Simeon, 1482. b. Oct. 29. 1755.

1462. II. Anna, b. Roxbury, May 16, 1725. d. July 19, 1729.

1463. III. Keziah, b. Roxbury, Sep. 25, 1726. m. Apr. 25, 1745, Edward Pitcher, of Attleboro. Children: — I. Keziah, 1483. b. Mar. 10, 1746. II. Mary, 1484. m. Rev. Peter Reed. III. Eunice, 1485. m. Dr. Walcott, of Cumberland. IV. Nabbie, 1486, m. Mr. Harding. V. Rufus, 1487. VI. Edward, 1488. VII. Chloe, 1489. m. Jere Ingram.

1464. IV. Ebenezer, b. Roxbury, Mar. 23, 1729. m. June 7, 1753, by Rev. Samuel Dexter, Mary Deane, of Taunton, Mass. Lived in N. Attleboro. (No issue.)

1465. V. Anna 2d, b. Roxbury, Sep. 12, 1731. d. there Jan. 11, 1736.

1466. VI. Prudence, b. Green Lodge, Apr. 13, 1734. m. 1st: May 23, 1751, Ebenezer Battle, m. 2dly: July 3, 1777, Joshua Whiting, m. 3dly: Sep. 1, 1784, Major Jonathan Day. Children, by 1st marriage: — I. Prudence, 1490. b. July 25, 1752. d. Aug. 10, 1752. II. Prudence 2d, 1491. b. Feb. 27, 1756. m. Dec. 16, 1775, Timothy Stow. III. Abigail, 1492. b. May 6, 1758. d. Apr. 1, 1759. IV. Sarah, 1493. b. July 26, 1760. V. Joseph, 1494. b. Apr. 23, 1763. VI. Lucy, 1495. b. Dec. 10, 1764. VII. Anna, 1496. b. Jan. 1, 1768. m. Apr. 7, 1786, Jonathan Fisher, of Needham.

1467. VII. Isaac, b. Green Lodge, July 27, 1736.

1468. VIII. Miriam, b. Green Lodge, Mar. 26, 1739. d. Sep. 26, 1831. m. 1st: by Rev. Andrew Tyler, June 28, 1758, Captain Joseph, s. of Joseph Guild and Hannah Curtis. Capt. Guild was an honest, upright, energetic citizen of Dedham. b. May 11, 1735. d. Dec. 28, 1794. In 1775, he was a captain of a company of minute men, a member of the Committee of Safety, muster master, a Selectman of Dedham and Representative to the General Court. Children:— I. Joseph. 1497. b. Mar. 14, 1760. II. Calvin, 1498. b. July 6. 1775mApr. 6, 1800, his cousin, Lendermine, dau. of Major Abijah Draper, 1123, and Desire Metcalf. III. Reuben, 1499. b. Aug. 18, 1762. IV. Ebenezer, 1500. b. Feb. 6, 1765. 1469. IX. Stephen, b. Green Lodge, Feb. 23, 1742.

CHILDREN BY 2D WIFE, ALL B. GREEN LODGE, DEDHAM:

1470. X. Sibyl, b. Sep. 21, 1750. m. by Rev. Thomas Balch, May 23, 1770, Captain Daniel Fisher, Jr. Children:— I. Daniel, 1501. b. Dedham, Jan. 2, 1771. II. Elizabeth, 1502. b. Dedham, May 1, 1774. III. Polly, 1503. b. Dedham, Nov. 24, 1779. IV. Andrew, 1504, b. Dedham, Oct. 1, 1781. V. Hannah, 1505. b. Dedham, Sep. 3, 1783. VI. Debby Ames, 1506. b. Dedham, Sep. 20, 1785.

1471. XI. Rebecca, b. Sep. 7, 1751. d. Sep. 29, 1751.

1472. XII. William, b. Sep. 23, 1752.

1473. XIII. Rebecca 2d, b. Aug. 19, 1754. m. Nov. 15, 1780, John, s. of John Colburn and Mary Smith, of Needham.

1474. XIV. Jemima, b. Nov. 7, 1756. d. Sep. 14, 1856. m. by Jonathan Metcalf, Esq., Mar. 17, 1782, James Turner, of Dedham. Children:— I. Joel,' 1507. b. May 13, 178-. II. Ebenezer, 1508. b. May 8, 1784. m.' Mar. 22, 1816, Sally Draper, of Roxbury. III. Nancy, 1509. b. Jan. 15, 1790. d. Feb. 12, 1881. m. May 22, 1816, at Dedham, Nathaniel Sumner, of Canton, Mass. He was b. Dec. 4, 1787, at Dedham. (Children:— I. James Turner, 15x2. b. Canton, Feb. 10, 1820. d. Sep. 8, 1884. m. May 18, 1843, Sarah Everett, dau. of John and Ruth (McKendry) Gerald. Children:— I. Sarah Draper Turner, 1515. b. Nov. 11, 1844. m. T. B. Draper (26, of Canton Draper Branch). II. Larra Wentworth, 1516. b. Mar. 6, 1847. III. Eliza Ann, 1517. b. July 24, 1853. IV. Alice Maria, 1518. b. Nov. 19, 1855. II. Nathaniel, 1513. b. Dec. 8, 1824, d. Mar. 30, 1853. III. George Frederick, 1514. b. June 7, 1830.) IV. Danford, 1510. b. Oct. 7, 1796. V. Eliza, 151 1, b. Dec. 24, 1802. m. by Rev. Alvan Lamson, June 2, 1830, Captain Luther Eaton, of Dedham. 1475XV. Mary, b. Apr. 5, 1760. m. July 26, 1787, Ezekiel Kingsbury, of Dedham. Children:— I. Caty, 1519. b. Oct. 28, 1788. m. David, s. of Benjamin and Lucy May, of Winchendon, May 11, 1813. II. Daniel, 1520. b. June 19, 1790. m. Abigail B. Locke, Aug. 19, 1812. III. George, 1521. b. July 13, 1797. m. Eliza McElroy, Mar. 25, 1820. He was drowned Feb. 13, 1830. She d. May 13, 1844. IV. Mary Draper, 1522. b. Mar. 9, 1805. m. Nov. 28, 1833, Judah Wetherbee.

1476. XVI. Catherine, b. Dec. 16, 1761. m. Nathanial Thayer, of Medway, Mass., Jan. 14, 1779.

1477. XVII. Anna 3d, b. June 15, 1764. d. June 18, 1766.

1467. Isaac. (19. Ebenezer, 7. James, 2. James, 1. Thomas.) 7th child, 2d s. of Ebenezer Draper and Dorothy Child, m. Miss Tingley.

Isaac and his brothers, Ebenezer (1464) and Stephen (1469), went from Dedham to Attleboro, and must have had, for that time, quite a competence, as each invested considerable capital when they started in business in their new homes. Isaac built a comfortable house, and started a tannery in the village of S. Attleboro, and was very successful in this business, which was carried on by his son, Ebenezer (1523), and his grandsons, George (1531) and Isaac (1530). The site of the old tannery is still used for the same purposes by William Campe & Co.

CHILDREN, B. ATTLEBORO:

1523. I. Ebenezer.

1524. II. Dorothy, m. Jabez Ellis.

1525. III. Ira, b. Jan. 3, 1772. d. Feb. 3, 1860.

1526. IV. Chloe, m. Comfort Tififany.

1527. V. Charlotte. Unmarried.

1528. VI. Prudence. Unmarried.

1523. Ebenezer. (1467. Isaac, 19. Ebenezer, 7. James, 2. James, 1. Thomas.) Eldest s. and child of Isaac Draper and Miss Tingley. m. Sep. 26, 1793, Sarah Capron, of Attleboro.

He succeeded his father in the tannery business in S. Attleboro.

CHILDREN:

1529. I. Austice, b. Nov. 21, 1794.

1530. II. Isaac, b. July 28, 1796.

1531. III. George, b. Dec. 22, 1800, d. Oct. 30, 1876.

1532. IV. Ebenezer H., b. Jan. 5, 1803. d. Sep. 4, 1830.

1533. V. Sallie, b. Nov. 24, 1805.

1534. VI. Chloe T., b. Feb. 28, 1809.

1535. VII. Seth M., b. Nov. 7, 1811.

1530. Isaac. (1523. Ebenezer, 1467. Isaac, 19. Ebenezer, 7. James, 2. James, 1. Thomas.) 2d child and s. of Ebenezer Draper and Sarah Capron. m. Elisia Adams.

CHILDREN:

1536. I. George A., b. Dec. 19, 1818.

1537. II. Seth, b. Rome, N. Y., July 3, 1820. d. Taunton, Mass., Oct. 9, 1876.

1538. III. Lucy A., b. Aug. 18, 1822. m. H. F. Tingley, of Providence, R. I.

1539. IV. Isaac, b. Jan. 4, 1824.

He was a surgeon in the Russian Army during the Crimean War, and d. at Sebastopol.

1540. V. Elizabeth, b. June 11, 1826. d. Aug. 20, 1827.

1541. VI. James H., b. Aug. 27, 1827. m. Georgina B. Children: — I. Arthur E., 1545. b. Feb., 1885. d. Nov. 8, 1885. II. Merton E., 1546. b. 1887. d. Mar. 1, 1889. III. Pearl E., 1547. b. 1888. d. Mar. 10, 1889. IV. Alexander, 1548. b. Apr. 8, 1890.

1542. VII. Henry, b. Sep. 22, 1829. d. July 24, 1868.

1543. VIII. Edward P., b. July 15, 1833. d. Dec. 14, 1833.

1544. IX. Stella F., b. Oct. 9, 1836. m. Sep. 16, 1862, Joseph C, s. of Joseph and Berthia M. Whiteman, of Boston.

1537. Seth. (1530. Isaac, 1523. Ebenezer, 1467. Isaac, 19. Ebenezer, 7. James, 2. James, 1. Thomas.) 2d s. and child of Isaac Draper and Elisia Adams, m. Apr. 16, 1856, Mary Elizabeth, dau. of Ulysses Whiteman, Ex-Mayor of Boston, and Mary Elizabeth Hadwen, a descendant of Isaac Hadwen, of England.

CHILDREN:

1549. I. Hadwen, b. Jan. 17, 1857. d. Apr. 14, 1864.

1550. II. Edward Hadwen, b. Feb. 19, 1860.

1551. III. Mary E., b. Mar. 16, 1862. d. Mar., 1863.

1552. IV, Helen Elizabeth, b. Mar. 10, 1867.

1531. George. (1523. Ebenezer, 1467. Isaac, 19. Ebenezer, 7. James, 2. James, 1. Thomas.) 3d child and s. of Ebenezer Draper and Sarah Capron. m. June 3, 1829, by Rev. Jesse Fisher, Harriet, dau. of Jonathan Lee and Jerusha Frink. She was b. Windon, Conn., Jan. 7, 1800.

CHILDREN:

1553. I. Dwight, b. Mar. 12, 1830. d. Mar. 6, 1845.

1554. II. George Lee, b. Mar. 11, 1832. m. Henrietta E., dau, of Carlos and Cynthia Barrows, of Attleboro. He joined, in 1861, the 1st Light Infantry of Providence, R. I., commanded by Col. Burnside; was at the battles of Bull Run, Roanoke Island, Newberne and Morris Island, and at the siege of Charleston and Fort Sumter; was at the expedition against Kingston and Goldsboro. He was disabled from the effects of the war, and is a U. S. pensioner.

1555. III. John L., b. Jan. 21, 1834. m. June 22, 1861, Jane F., dau. of Nathanial F, and S. Potter, of Attleboro. Child:— Harriet L., 1558. b. Dec. 18, 1862.

1556. IV. Mary Lucretia, b. Dec. 20, 1835. m. June 29, 1859, Edward P., s. of John and Olive S. Tiffany.

1557. V. Harriet Anna, b. Feb. 4, 1842. d. Feb. 28, 1845.

1469. Stephen. (19. Ebenezer, 7. James, 2. James, 1. Thomas.) 9th child, 3d s. of Ebenezer Draper and Dorothy Child, m. by Rev. Benjamin Caryl, Apr. 4, 1764, Elizabeth, dau. of Jonathan and Mary Fisher, of Dedham. She was b. Sep. 11, 1740.

He came to Attleboro from Dedham and purchased 30 acres of land, where he built his house and tannery. The date of this deed of purchase is Apr. 17, 1772. His tannery was one of the largest in the country, and he was very successful in his business, building other tanneries in Connecticut and Rhode Island. He also wove cloth, and had nail machinery. Mr. Draper was a man of uncommon energy and integrity, and was a very straight-laced Puritan. The home that he built is still occupied by his descendants, although the house was taken down and another one built on its site in 1885; and to this day, through all the years, the family have met there to celebrate Thanksgiving in large numbers. The old tannery buildings were torn down in 1858.

CHILDREN, B, IN S. ATTLEBORO:

1559. I. Fisher, b. Mar. 29, 1765. d. May, 1839.

1560. II. Paul, b. Sep. 19, 1767. Lost at sea.

1561. III. Anna, b. July 11, 1770,

1562. IV, Betty, b. Dec. 31, 1772.

1563. V. Stephen, b. Apr. 29, 1775.

1564. VI. Mary, b. Aug. ii, 1777.

1565. VII. Catherine, b. Jan. 14, 1780.

1566. VIII. Joseph, b. July 24, 1782. d. Aug. 1, 1782.

1567. IX. Ebenezer, b. Jan. 14, 1784. d. May 23, 1851.

1568. X. Miriam, b. Dec. 31, 1790. m. Mr. Eaton. Had several children. One dau., 1569, m. Mr. Carpenter. Lived in Brookfield, Mass., and had a large family, who are supposed to be all dead. Another dau., 1570, m. Chaffie. Lived in Pennsylvania. Another, 1571, m. Mr. Kransky, and had two sons, who both changed their names from Kransky to Draper, by Act of Legislature. Their names are George, 1572, and John, 1573. Both are m. and have children. Another dau., 1574, m. Mr. Titus. Had two sons, and went to Canada to live.

1559. Fisher. (1469. Stephen, 19. Ebenezer, 7. James, 2. James, 1. Thomas.) Eldest child and s. of Stephen Draper and Elizabeth Fisher, m. Mar. 5, 1789, Hannah Maxey, of Wrentham, Mass,

CHILDREN, ALL B. ATTLEBORO:

1575. I. Ursula, b. Jan. 3, 1791. d. Lynn, Mass., Nov. 21, 1871. m. Capt. Oliver R. Wellman, of Salem, Mass. Children: — I. Oliver, 1580. b. Salem, Mass., Mar. 15, 1810. d. Mar., 1869. m. Mehetable Wilson, of Salem. II. Benjamin, 1581. b. Jan. 7, 1812. m. Josephine Gotea, of Philadelphia. III. Ursula, 1582. b. Apr. 22, 1815. m. Richard Hill, of Salem. IV. Samuel, 1583. b. Feb. 8, 1817. m. Mary Hill, of Salem. V. Sarah, 1584. b. Feb. 17, 1820. m. Robert Weston, d. Lynn, Mass., Jan. 9, 1862.

1576. II. Horace, b. 1793. d. in infancy.

1577. III. Susanna Maxey, b. Apr. 21, 1795. d. Sep. 19, 1865. m. Apr. 19, 1833, Jabez, s. of Samuel Newall and Philena Tiffany, of Attleboro. Children: — I. Abigail, 1585. b. Aug. 19, 1834. II. Caroline W. b, Apr. 4, 1837. III. Catherine M., 1586. b. Sep. 24, 1839. d. Aug. 9, 1842.

1578. IV. Horace 2d, b. Apr. 19, 1797. d. unmarried.

1579. V. Hannah, b. Feb. 28, 1807. d. unmarried, Apr. 19, 1832.

1560. Paul. (1469. Stephen, 19. Ebenezer, 7. James, 2. James, 1. Thomas.) 2d s. and child of Stephen Draper and Elizabeth Fisher, m. Oct. 21, 1790, Mary Sweet. She was b. in Providence, R. I., Mar. 31, 1768. d. Mar. 2, 1853.

Mr. Draper graduated at Brown University in 1789 with the honorable degree of A.M. He went to sea as a purser in the U. S. Navy, and was never heard from again. He, presumably, was drowned in 1800.

CHILDREN:

1587. I. Nehemiah Sweet, b, Oct. 28, 1795. d. June 18, 1871.

1588. II. Julia Ann.

1589. III. Louise.

1590. IV. Carmilliles.

1591. V. Mary Ann.

1587. Nehemiah S. (1560. Paul, 1469. Stephen, 19. Ebenezer, 7. James, 2. James, 1. Thomas.) Eldest child and only s. of Paul Draper and Mary Sweet, m. 1st: Feb. 8, 1820, Newport, R. I., Martha Matilda Moore. She was b. Sep. 19,

1800. d. Oct. 4, 1833. m. 2dly: Oct. 8, 1835, Mary Harris Hooper, of Brooklyn, N. Y. She was b. Dec. 16, 1804. d. June 24, 1867.

CHILDREN, BY 1ST MARRIAGE:

1592. I. Harriet Louise, b. July 23, 1823. d. Jan. 3, 1858.

1593. II. Mary Elizabeth, b. Mar. 4, 1825. m. June 17, 1852, Francis J., s. of Edward Sheldon and Mary Wray. Children:— I. Frank Augustus, 1604. II. Hattie, 1605. III. Louise, 1606.

1594. Ill, Frederick A., b. Sep. 21, 1828. d. Mar. 24, 1868.

1595. IV. Edward, b. Mar. 25, 1832. d. Sep. 19, 1832.

1596. V. Charles Edmond, b. July 30, 1833. d. Sep. 14, 1833.

CHILDREN, BY 2D MARRIAGE:

1597. VI. Eliza Harris, b. July 10, 1836. d. Sep. 24, 1836.

1598. VII. Charles Edward, b. Sep. 3, 1837. d. Aug. 8, 1839.

1599. VIII. Benjamin H., b. June 10, 1841. d. May 27, 1862.

1600. IX. Edward, b. Dec. 5, 1842. d. Jan. 8, 1843.

1601. X. Francis, b. Jan. 2, 1849. d. July 18, 1850.

1602. XI. Edwin, m. Mary E., dau. of Dexter and Mary Stone, of Pawtucket, R.I. She was b. 1847. d. Apr. 1, 1875. Child: — Nettie Elizabeth, 1607. b. and d. Feb. 11, 1871.

1603. XII. Leonard H., m. Oct. 9, 1879, Ella, dau, of S. W, and Laura Whiting, of Troy, N. Y.

1563. Stephen. (1469. Stephen, 19. Ebenezer, 7. James, 2. James, 1. Thomas.) 3d s., 5th child of Stephen Draper and Elizabeth Fisher, m. 1st: Fanny Capron. She d. Mar. 19, 1799. m. 2dly: Catherine Fisher, of Fisherville, Mass., Sep. 27, 1801.

CHILDREN, BY 2D MARRIAGE:

1608. I. Eliza,

1609. II. Seth (?). m. Sep. 2, 1844, Mary L. Greeman. Lives in Thomson, Conn.

1610. III. Edwin. Resides in Grovedale, Conn.

1611. IV. Albert, b. Foster, Conn., Nov, 29, 1808.

1612. V. Stephen, b. Killingley, Mar. 19, 1811. d. Mar. 19, 1890.

1613. VI. Daniel F. Resides in Rochdale, Mass,

1614. VII, Fanny C, m. ___ Hunt.

Lives in Plainfield, Conn., with her son Joel, 1615.

1611. Albert. (1563. Stephen, 1469. Stephen, 19. Ebenezer, 7. James, 2. James, 1. Thomas.) 4th child, 3d s. of Stephen Draper and Catherine Fisher, m. 1833, Mary C, dau. of Joseph and Martha Clarice, of Newport, R. I.

CHILDREN:

1616. I. Emily F., born Newport, Oct. 10, 1834. m. New York City, Sep. 30, 1855, Dr. John H. Vere.

1617. II. Catherine F., b. Newport, Nov. 8, 1836. m. 1856, O. G. Langley.

1618. III. Joseph Clarke, b. June 6, 1840. d. Foo Chow, China, Aug. 9, 1864. Unmarried.

1619. IV. Elizabeth B., b. Newport, Mar. 1, 1842. d. Brooklyn, N. Y., Oct. 28, 1882. m. Feb. 22, 1863, Frederick Stafford, of Brooklyn.

1620. V. Charles Henry, b. Newport, May 12, 1845. m. Delia Putnam, of Brooklyn.

1621. VI. William, b. Newport, Aug. 15, 1847. d. Newport, Oct. 3, 1851.

1622. VII. Albert, b. Brooklyn, May 21, 1853. m. Amelia Arnold. Children: — I. Albert, 1624. II. Catherine, 1625. III. Charles H., 1626.

1623. VIII. George, b. New York City, May 28, 1856.

1612. Stephen. (1563. Stephen, 1469. Stephen, 19. Ebenezer, 7. James, 2. James, 1. Thomas.) 5th child, 4th s. of Stephen Draper and Catherine Fisher, m. 1st: 1840, Harriet, dau. of Captain T. Eliot, of Sutton, Mass. She d. Sep. 5, 1850. He m. 2dly: Wealthy Cutting, of Leicester, Mass., Nov. 15, 1851. She d. Mar. 19, 1889.

Mr. Draper was apprenticed to a tanner when but 12 years old, but left that when still a young man, and engaged in the manufacture of scythes in Greenville, Mass., the firm being Draper, Brown & Chadsey. He removed to Troy, N. Y., in 1847, and conducted the business there very successfully, until the invention of mowing machines compelled the firm to make a change. He then was engaged in the manufacture of twine and fish lines, which he conducted to within a few months of his death.

CHILDREN, BY 1st WIFE:

1627. I. William Henry, b. June 24, 1841.

1628. II. Frederick Eliot, b. Oct. 12, 1843.

1629. III. Harriet Augusta, b. Dec. 12, 1845.

1630. IV. Charles Eugene, b. Aug. 14, 1850.

CHILDREN, BY 2D WIFE:

1631. V. Edward Cutting, b. Sep. 5, 1855. d. Feb. 11, 1856.

1632. VI. Catherine Fisher, b. Jan., 1859. d. June, 1859.

1627. William Henry. (161 2. Stephen, 1563. Stephen, 1469. Stephen, 19. Ebenezer, 7. James, 2. James, 1. Thomas.) Eldest s. and child of Stephen Draper and his 1st wife, Harriet Elliot. m. Nov. 15, 1864, Magdalene Livingstone, of Schenectady, N. Y.

CHILDREN:

1633. I. Andrew Livingstone, b. Jan. 23, 1865. m. Oct. 15, 1891, Mary Ruth Thompson, of Lockport, N. Y.

1634. II. Grace Mary, b. Nov. 7, 1870. d. May 17, 1871.

1635. III. George Frederick, b. Sep. 22, 1872. d. Dec. 19, 1873.

1636. IV. Edward Eliot, b. June 9, 1876.

1637. V. Bessie Magdalene, b. Aug. 15, 1881.

1628. Frederick Eliot. (1612. Stephen, 1563. Stephen, 1469. Stephen, 19. Ebenezer, 7. James, 2. James, 1. Thomas.) 2d child and s. of Stephen Draper and his 1st wife, Harriet Eliot, m. Troy, N. Y., Dec, 1871, Jenny Woodcock.

Mr. Draper enlisted, when scarcely 18 years old, in the 11th N. Y. Battery, a company formed in Albany. In 1864 he re-enlisted, and remained until the close of the war in 1865.

CHILDREN:

1638. I. Fred. Eliot, Jr., b. Apr. 3, 1873.
1639. II. Philip Henry, b. Apr. 3, 1875.
1640. III. Louis le Grand, b. Aug. 28, 1878.

1630. Charles Eugene. (1612. Stephen, 1563. Stephen, 1469. Stephen, 19. Ebenezer, 7. James, 2. James, 1. Thomas.) 4th child and s. of Stephen Draper and Harriet Eliot, m. Dec. 18, 1876, Jenny Pile, of Troy, N. Y. She d. Apr. 14, 1886. He m. 2dly: Nov. 4, 1891, Lucy G. Gushing.

CHILDREN, BY 1ST WIFE:

1641. I. Charles Stephen, b. and d. 1881.
1642. II. Jenny Louise, b. July 30, 1882.

1567. Ebenezer. (1469. Stephen, 19. Ebenezer, 7. James, 2. James, 1. Thomas.) 9th child, 5th s. of Stephen Draper and Elizabeth Fisher, m. Beulah, dau. of Joel Bradford and Alsey Mosier, of Smithfield, R. I. She was b. Jan. 20, 1790. d. Attleboro, Sep. 20, 1868.

CHILDREN, B. ATTLEBORO:

1643. I. Alsey Almenia, b. Oct. 6, 1807. d. Apr. 25, 1821.
1644. II. Joseph, b. Oct. 25, 1808.
1645. III. Arnold, b. Apr. 27, 1810. d. Salem, Mass., Apr. 7, 1860.
1646. IV. Paul, b. Dec. 31, 1811. d. Apr. 25, 1885.
1647. V. William Henry, b. Apr. 17, 1813. d. Nov. 24, 1885.
1648. VI. Cornelia, b. Oct. 9, 1816. m. Aug. 29, 1837, J. Herbert, s. of John S. Stanley and Juliet Marsh. He was b. Dec. 10, 1811. Mr. Stanley has been quite a traveler. His first voyage was on a whaling expedition of 1% years round the world. Returning from this he married and settled down to work on his farm at Attleboro in 1849. He then took a trip to California, via Cape Horn, returning in 1850. Between then and 1858 he made two trips to California via the Isthmus of Panama. Returning from the last one, he settled in Kansas, removing from thence in 1860 to Irvington, N. J. Leaving there in 1867, he returned to Attleboro, where he and his wife celebrated their golden wedding, Aug. 29, 1887. Children, all b. in Attleboro: — I. Delia M.,1657. b. Sep., 19, 1838. II. Linnaeus H., 1658. b. Nov. 30, 1840. m. Mar., 1864, Pauline, dau. of Adolphus Bagulen and Anna Taxter. III. Emmeline A., 1659. b. Oct. 11, 1844. m. Dec. 6, 1877, Edwin F., 1660, s. of Francis B. Kent and Abigail S. Lewis. IV. Arthur W. b. Sep. 30, 1847. m. Sep. 17, 1873, Eunis S., dau. of Henry F. May and Elizabeth Cushman.
1649. VII. James Otis, b. June 29, 1818. d. Pawtucket, R. I., Oct. 14, 1891.

1650. VIII. Celia Augusta, b. Aug. 13, 1820. d. Pawtucket, Jan. 1, 1883. Unmarried.

1651. IX. Louisa, b. July 22, 1822. m. Oct. 28, 1847, Robert S., s. of Samuel Cushman and Sophie George, of Attleboro. Children: — I. Ellen, 1661. b. Oct. 17, 1852. m. May 15, 189 1, R. Anthony Gage. 11. Josephine, 1662, b. July 18, 1859. d. Oct. 28, 1863. III. Louisa, 1663. b. Apr. 20, 1861. IV. Robert, 1664. b. July 9, 1864,

1652. X. Charles Francis, b. Nov. 6, 1824. d. Attleboro, Mar. 6, 1839.

1653. XI. Elizabeth, b. Apr. 9, 1826. d. Attleboro, May 16, 1826.

1654. XII. Lydia Ann, b. Sep. 22, 1827. m. May 21, 1851, Abner, s. of Joshua Attwood and Hannah Thomas. He was b. May 5, 1825.

He learnt the trade of machinist in Taunton, where he lived until 1858, then removed, first to Bedford, where he was associated with his brother-in-law, James O. Draper (1649), in business, and then to Pawtucket, R. I., where they remained in business together until 1866. He then went into the firm of Cushman, Philips & Co., bobbin manufacturers, in which he is still an active member, although the firm is now known as the Attwood, Crawford Co.

1655. XIII, Gamalial Bradford, b. May 16, 1831. (Unmarried.) In 1849, two of his brothers having preceded him to California, he rounded Cape Horn on a sailing vessel, and joined them in 1850 in the southern mines. But as they left him within a few months to return East, he moved to the northern mines, and did not learn of their return to California for over a year after their arrival. In 1858, having spent over 8 years in the mines, he returned to the old homestead in S. Attleboro, where he still resides. In 1887 he was elected a Selectman, and has since served the town of N. Attleboro as Selectman, Assessor and Overseer of the Poor. He has been largely instrumental in the collection of the data belonging to this branch of the family, and has taken a lively interest in the same.

1656. XIV. Hannah Maria, b. Sep. 4, 1833. m. May 2, 1873, Jesse Brown, s. of Samuel and Penelope Chamberlain, of Noretown, N. J. Lives in Attleboro. Child: — Alice Draper, 1665. b. Sep. 10, 1874.

Mr. Brown served in the 29th N. J. Volunteers nine months and in the 12th N. J. Volunteers three years.

1644. Joseph. (1567. Ebenezer, 1469. Stephen, 19. Ebenezer, 7. James, 2. James, I, Thomas.) 2d child, eldest s. of Ebenezer Draper and Beulah Bradford, m. June 23, 1833, Lucilola B., dau. of David M. Makepeace and Lucilla Bishop, of Attleboro.

Mr. Draper learnt the trade of a machinist, at which he worked in various places. In 1836 he moved to Greenville, Ill., where his brother, William H. (1647), had preceded him, and, buying an adjoining farm, they lived through the hardships of a new settlement until 1844, when, owing to a very sickly season, where all were sick and many died, both brothers returned to Massachusetts. Joseph bought a farm in E. Norton, where he, his wife and son still reside.

CHILDREN:

1666. I. Joseph Ormond, b. Attleboro, July 17, 1834. d. Pawtucket, R. I., July 4, 1864. m. May 19, 1861, Ellen A., dau. of William Bartlett and Anna Sanderson. She was b. Central Falls, R. I., Feb. 14, 1833. Child: — Frank Ormond, 1670. b. Central Falls, Sep. 5, 1862. m. 1890, Ida A., dau. of Richard C. Tiffany and Rebecca Pratt, of New London, Conn.

He is a graduate of Brown University and Principal of the Garden Street School at Pawtucket, R. I.

1667. II. Samuel Atherton, b. Greenville, Ill., June 15, 1837.

1668. III. Elizabeth T., b. Greenville, Ill., Nov. 15, 1840. d. there Aug. 23, 1841.

1669. IV. George W., b. Greenville, Ill., Aug. 14, 1843. d. there Sep. 9, 1844.

1667. Samuel A. (1644. Joseph, 1567. Ebenezer, 1469. Stephen, 19. Ebenezer, 7. James, 2. James, 1. Thomas.) 2d s. and child of Joseph Draper and Lucilola Makepeace, m. Dec. 24, 1863, in Norton, Mary E., dau. of Robert Kirk and Sylvia A. Claflin, of Attleboro.

CHILDREN, ALL B. NORTON:

1671. 1, Emma de Witt, b. Oct. 12, 1864.

1672. II. Frederick M., b. Feb. 23, 1867. m. Sep. 23, 1890, Susie L., dau. of Francis Maurey and Anna Seera, of Norton. She was b. Columbus, O., Mar. 13, 1864.

1673. III. Joseph, b. Mar. 28, 1870.

1674. IV. Elizabeth, b. June 19, 1875.

1645. Arnold. (1567. Ebenezer, 1469. Stephen, 19. Ebenezer, 7. James, 2. James, 1. Thomas.) 3d child, 2d s. of Ebenezer Draper and Beulah Bradford, m. Pawtucket, R. I., Feb. 12, 1842, Caroline Sibyl, dau. of Willard Bullard and Harriet Thompson, of Dedham. She was b. Dedham, Nov. 4, 1817.

He learnt the trade of a carpenter, and about 1839 became a member of the firm of French & Draper, of Newport, R. I., engaged in the manufacture and pressing of straw bonnets. About 1840 he engaged in the same business in Salem, Mass., until his death. His family still reside there.

CHILDREN, ALL B. AT SALEM:

1675. Maria Louise, b. Jan. 25, 1844. d. Boston, May 24, 1875. m. in Salem, Apr. 25, 1872, Dr. Francis Webster, s. of Ezekiel Goss and Almira Dwelley Hatch. Child: — Francis Draper, 1679. b. Boston, July 23, 1873. d. Jan. 16, 1879.

1676. II. Charlotte Elizabeth, b. May 9, 1846. Unmarried.

1677. III. Annie Caroline, b. Aug. 22, 1848. Unmarried.

1678. IV. William Pinneo, b. July 25, 1850. m. Springfield, June 2, 1885, Alice Elizabeth, dau. of Samuel Ruggles Newall and Augusta Hine.

1646. Paul. (1567. Ebenezer, 1469. Stephen, 19. Ebenezer, 7. James, 2. James, 1. Thomas.) 4th child, 3d s. of Ebenezer Draper and Beulah Bradford, m. Sep., 1835, Charlotte, dau. of Timothy George and Betsy Capron. She was

b. Wrentham, Mass., 1809. d. Salem, Mass., Aug. 23, 1845. He m. 2dly: Maria G., dau. of Thomas D. Sadler and Sarah Leonard, of Attleboro.

CHILDREN, BY 1ST MARRIAGE B. ATTLEBORO (NO ISSUE BY 2D):

1680, I. Anne Frances, b. Jan. 3, 1839. m. Nov. 23, 1859, George D., s. of Henry Cunliffe and Mary Sargeant, of Bellville, N. J. Children: —

I. Harry, 1682. b. Attleboro, Feb. 10, 1862. d. Wappinger's Falls, N. J., Aug. 14, 1869. II. Charles S., 1683. b. Wappinger's Falls, July 7, 1867. m. May 20, 1891, Winifred N. Carlyle, of Clinton, Mass. III. Maud, 1684. b. Wappinger's Falls, Sep. 2, 1869. m. July 29, 1889, Irving V., s. of Charles O. Sweet, of Attleboro. (Child:— Elsa E., 1685. b. Attleboro, Oct. 27, 1890.) 1681. II. Henry B., b. Salem, Feb. 9, 1842. d. Taunton, Mass., Apr. 16, 1869.

1647. William Henry. (1567. Ebenezer, 1469. Stephen, 19. Ebenezer, 7. James, 2. James. 1. Thomas.) 6th child, 5th s. of Ebenezer Draper and Beulah Bradford, m. Jan. 28, 1835, Huldah, dau. of Dr. Richard Briggs, of Worthington, Mass. She was b. Worthington, Apr. 1, 1811. d. Greenville, Ill., Aug. 20, 1844. He m. 2dly: Mar. 31, 1847, Charlotte, dau. of James Ide and Betsy George. She was b. Wrentham, Mass., Feb. 25, 1815. d. Wrentham, Dec. 17, 1875.

Mr. Draper learnt shoe making, and in 1835 removed to Greenville, Ill. In the Summer of 1844, when malarial fevers prostrated old residents and new comers alike, he buried his wife and four children in the space of two weeks. In the following Spring, he, with his only surviving son Ebenezer (1687), moved to Massachusetts, where he married again. He was living at Wrentham, Mass., at the time of the discovery of gold in California. Crossing the Isthmus in 1849, he joined his brother, James O. (1649), and brother-in-law, J. S. Stanley, who had preceded him via Cape Horn, and were joined by his youngest brother, Gamalial B. (1655), in May, 1850. After one year in the mines they all returned to Massachusetts, except Gamalial. But within a year they again returned to California. After Mr. Draper's wife returned East in 1856, he bought a farm near Shepherdsville, Wrentham, and there resided until his death. He was a deacon of the Congregational Church in Wrentham for many years.

CHILDREN, BY 1ST WIFE, B. GREENVILLE, ILL.:

1686. I. William Henry, b. Oct. 23, 1836. d. Greenville, Aug. 28, 1844.

1687. II. Ebenezer, b. Jan. 14, 1838. d. Wrentham, Mass., Aug. 23, 1877.

He enlisted, Aug. 14, 1862, into Company D, 40th Regt. Mass. Volunteer Infantry, for three years. Mustered out June 16, 1865. Promoted Sergeant, May 21, 1864, and 1st Sergt., Dec. 1, 1864; Adjutant, Jan. 6, 1865,

1688. III. Charles Francis, b. Apr, 7, 1839. d. Greenville, Oct. 23, 1841.

1689. IV. James, b. Jan. 15, 1841. d. Greenville, Sep. 1, 1844.

1690. V. Emerson O., b. Oct. 19, 1842. d. Greenville, Aug. 13, 1844.

1691. VI. Helen J., b. May 25, 1844. d. Greenville, Sep. 1, 1844.

CHILDREN, BY 2D WIFE:

1692. VII. Charlotte Ella, b, Attleboro, Jan, 3, 1848. m. Oct. 20, 1881, Wrentham, Mass., George Leland, s. of Lowell R. Blake and Betsy Young, He was b. Jan. 29, 1852. d. Attleboro, June 11, 1886.

1693. VIII. William Francis, b. Wrentham, Feb. 18, 1852. m. Montgomery, N. Y., Mar. 14, 1883, Lemma, dau. of Christopher J. Mould and Martha Bull. Child: — William Bradford, 1695. b. Montgomery, Nov. 26, 1883.

1694. IX. George Ide, b. Wrentham, Mass., Sep. 26, 1859. m. New York City, Jan. 13, 1881, Augusta A. Wolfge.

1649. James Otis. (1567. Ebenezer, 1469. Stephen, 19. Ebenezer, 7. James, 2. James, 1. Thomas.) 7th child, 5th s. of Ebenezer Draper and Beulah Bradford, m. Attleboro, Nov. 18, 1840, Mary G., dau. of Galen C. Carpenter and Mary George. She was b. Wrentham, Nov. 17, 1817. d. Central Falls, R. I., Apr. 10, 1866. He m. 2dly: Emmeline Babitt, of Taunton, May 1, 1867. She d. Dec. 1, 1875. He m. 3dly: the widow Belinda (Salla) Mowrey, dau. of Alfred Salla and Prudence A. Alexander. She was b. Dec. 1, 1837, and m. Spencer B. Mowrey, Oct. 26, 1862. He d. Nov., 1865.

Mr. Draper received such limited education as the country districts afforded, and worked on his father's farm until he went to Abingdon, when a youth, where he learnt shoemaking. At twenty he went to Mobile, and was in the produce business. He then returned home and worked at his trade in Wrentham. In Apr., 1849, he started for California via Cape Horn in the ship "Aretus," Capt. James Woolley, and was six months in making the voyage. He returned in 1850, and went back in 1852, remaining until Apr., 1855, when he came home again. He met with success in mining, paid all his indebtedness, and had sufficient to make a new start in life. He went to live in Foxboro, where he engaged in the manufacture of soap, and in 1858, in company with his brother-in law, Abner Attwood, of Pawtucket, engaged in that business in Bradford, Mass. They removed to Pawtucket in 1861, where the business was carried on under the firm name of Draper & Attwood, until 1867, when Mr. Attwood retired, and Mr. Draper continued alone until 1871, when his nephew, Arthur W. Stanley, was admitted as a partner under the well-known firm name of J. O. Draper & Co. The establishment is one of the largest of the kind in the country, and the varieties of soaps manufactured, from the lowest to the highest and finest grades, are numerous. Mr. Draper was a public-spirited citizen, and contributed willingly to all worthy enterprises. In politics he was a strong Republican, with temperance proclivities.

(The author of this history had been in correspondence with Mr. James O. Draper relative to family data for several weeks prior to his death. About ten days before this occurred the author received a letter from him, giving a great deal of family history, which was concluded by a postscript, in which he said that he would have been glad to have known of his descent, but that he was an old man, and did not expect to live long enough to ascertain it. A few days thereafter the author was able to write and tell him who his ancestors were, in direct descent to himself, thereby gratifying his wish. This letter was received by Mr. Draper on Tuesday, Oct. 13, 1891. He was much pleased, and sent for several of his family, who passed that evening with him, discussing the family history, and making plans for collecting all available data for this work. He died at half-past two the following morning.)

CHILDREN, BY 1ST WIFE:

1696. I. Bradford, b. Abington, Sep. 18, 1841. d. Feb. 17, 1842.

1697. II. M. Elizabeth, b. Abington, Apr. 25, 1843. m. Dec. 9, 1855, at Bedford, Mass., John W., s. of William Clarke, of Bedford. Children: —

I. Willie E., 1702. b. Bedford, Mass., Sep. 26, 1861. m. Margaret E., dau. of Thomas Sim, of Carlton, N. B. (Children: — I. Olive B., 1708. b. Feb. 2, 1884. II. Allen W., 1709. b. Nov. 8, 1887.)

II. Alice Louise, 1703. b. Cambridge, Mass., Sep. 8, 1865. d. June 18, 1873. III. Beulah Bradford, 1704. b. Cambridge, Mass., Sep. 30, 1867. IV. John Spencer, 1705. b.' Cambridge, Feb. 1, 1873. V. Susan Sprague, 1706. b. Cambridge, Jan. 28, 1878. VI. Mary George, 1707. b. Jan. 4, 1881.

1698. III. Anna A., b. Attleboro, Oct. 26, 1844.

1699. IV. James A., b. Foxboro, Mass., July 5, 1855.

1700. V. Galen C, b. Foxboro, Mass., Feb. 10, 1858. d. Pawtucket, May 8, 1882. (Unmarried.)

1701. VI. George B., b. Bedford, Mass., Dec. 30, 1859.

1699. James A. (1649. James Otis, 1567. Ebenezer, 1469. Stephen, 19. Ebenezer, 7. James, 2. James, 1. Thomas.) 4th child, 2d s. of James Otis Draper and Mary G. Carpenter, m. Pawtucket, R. I., Harriet C, dau. of Nehemiah W. Randall and Mary E. Salusbury, of Pawtucket. She was b. Valley Falls, R. I., Apr. 17, 1854.

CHILDREN:

1710. I. Florence, b. Pawtucket, Oct. 1, 1876,

1711. II. Beulah, b. Pawtucket, June 27, 1877. d. Terre Haute, Ind., Apr. 23, 1882.

1712. III. Ida F., b. Pawtucket, June 20, 1878.

1713. IV. Mary E., b. Pawtucket, Apr. 13, 1879. d. Terre Haute, Ind., Apr. 22, 1882.

1714. V. Ernest B., b. Terre Haute, Nov. 28, 1881. d. there June 15, 1882.

1715. VI. Helen B., b. Terre Haute, Mar. 26, 1883. d. there July 2, 1883.

1716. VII. Galen C, b. St. Louis, Mo., July 14, 1884. d. there Aug. 2, 1884.

1717. VIII. Leroy S., b. St. Louis, Mo., Dec. 15, 1886.

1701. George B. (1649. James Otis, 1567. Ebenezer, 1469. Stephen, 19. Ebenezer, 7. James, 2. James, 1. Thomas.) 6th child, 4th s. of James Otis Draper and Mary G. Carpenter, m. Nov. 30, 1882, Sarah M., dau. of Squire Z. Phinney and Sarah W. Grey, of Providence, R. I.

CHILDREN, B. PAWTUCKET, R. I.:

1718. I. G. Bradford, b. Oct. 29, 1884.

1719. II. Frederick Z., b. Mar. 21, 1886.

1472. William. (19. Ebenezer, 7. James, 2. James, 1. Thomas.) 3d child, only s. of Ebenezer Draper and his 2d wife, Sibyl Avery, m. 1st: Jan. 9, 1785, by Rev. Jason Haven, Lydia Smith. She d. Jan. 25, 1790.

The following epitaph is on her tombstone:

> "Time was, like you
> I Life possest.
> And Time shall be,
> When you must rest."

He m. 2dly: Aug. 23, 1790, by Rev. Jason Haven, Polly Jones.

CHILDREN, BY 1st WIFE:

1720. I. Ebenezer, b. Dedham, May 12, 1786. d. Feb, 20, 1788.

1721. II. Catherine, b. Dedham, June 1, 1789.

CHILD, BY 2D WIFE:

1722. III. William, b. Dedham, July 14, 1796, m. by Rev. William Coggeswell, May 1, 1815, Elizabeth B. Columbia. Child:— I. Caroline, 1723, b. Dedham, May 24, 1816.

8. John. (2. James, 1. Thomas.) 5th child, 2d s. of James Draper and Miriam Stansfield. m. 1st: Sep. 3, 1686, Abigail, dau. of John and Mary Mason. She was b. Dedham, "6th of 11th month, 1659." d. Jan. 23, 1704-10. He m. 2dly: June 12, 1711, Judith Rogers. Shed. Mar. 30, 1730. He m. 3dly: Nov. 26, 1730, Elizabeth Wright Mason, widow of Joseph Mason, and dau. of Joseph Daniel and his 1st wife, Mary Fairbanks. She was b. 1679.

Mr. Draper removed early from Roxbury to the neighboring township of Dedham, where he resided all his life as a farmer. It is generally supposed that his property was a farm in what is now known as Dover, though at that time it was part of the township of Dedham.

CHILDREN, BY 1ST WIFE, B. DEDHAM (NO ISSUE BY 2D AND 3D):

1724. I. Abigail, b. Dec, 1686. m. Jan. 19, 1711, John, s. of John Battelle and Hannah Holbrook. Children: — I. Abigail, 1732. b. July 12, 1713. II. John, 1733. b. Apr. 30, 1718. III. Mary, 1734. b. Dec. 14, 1721. IV. James, 1735. b. Sep. 19, 1728.

1725. II. Susanna, b. Aug. 1, 1687. m. John PHmpton, of Medfield, Mass., 1707. He d. 1730. She m. 2dly: Stephen Sabin, Town Treasurer and Schoolmaster of Medfield. He "owned a fine farm and an Indian boy, the latter valued at ^9. Stephen d. 1737; Susanna was his 2d wife. Soon after she m. 3dl)': Joseph Plimpton, a brother of her 1st husband. He was a Selectman of Medfield six years, and Representative to the General Court in 1720 and 1731. He d. 1740. Children, by her 1st husband (no issue by her 2d and 3d husbands): — I. John, 1736. b. 1708. II. James, 1737. b. 1709. d. 1785. Settled in Foxboro, Mass. m. Lydia Lovell, 1736. III. Daniel, 1738. b. 1721. d. 1778. Settled in Sturbridge, Mass., where he was a very prominent citizen; Colonel in the Militia, and held many town offices in Revolutionary times. IV. Elizabeth, 1739. b. 1726. d. 1757. (A number of children are supposed to have come between James, 1737, and Daniel, 1738.)

1726. III. John, b. Feb. 20, 1690. d. Apr. 13, 1766.
1727. IV. Mary, b. Oct. 22, 1693. d. Aug. 25, 1700.
1728. V. Hannah, b. Aug. 7, 1695. d. Aug. 24, 1700.
1729. VI. Joseph, b. June 3, 1699.
1730. VII. James, b. Jan. 29, 1701. d. Jan. 7, 1719.
1731. VIII. Mehetable, b. Jan. 14, 1704.

1726. John. (8. John, 2. James, 1. Thomas.) 3d child, eldest s. of John Draper and Abigail Mason, m. Boston, Sep. 18, 1724, by Samuel Checkley, Esq., Moriah, dau. of Thomas and Abigail Hall, of Dedham. She was b. May 8, 1701. d. Apr. 13, 1766. He was a farmer in Dover (part of Dedham).

CHILDREN, B. DOVER:

John, b. Aug. 8, 1725. d. Dover, Feb. 3, 1805.
1724:. Children: — I. Samuel, 1748. b. Feb. 21, 1753.
1749. b. Oct. 1, 1755. III. Jason, 1750. b. Aug. 31, 1758. IV.

1741. II. Mary, b. July 7, 1727. m. May 15., 1753^ by Rev. Samuel. Dexter, Samuel, s. of Eleazar and Mary Fairbanks. He was b. June 10, 1724. Children:— I. Samuel, 1748. b. Feb. 21, 1753. II. Laben, 1749. b. Oct. 1, 1755. III. Jason, 1750. Mary, 1751. b. Apr. 8, 1761.

1742. III. A daughter, b. and d. Mar. 6, 1730.

1743. IV. Thomas, b. June 26, 1732. m. May 14, 1766, Lydia Cheney. She was b. Dedham, Feb. 1, 1741. Child: — Esther, 1752. b. Dedham, July 26, 1767.

1744. V. Moses, b. June 29, 1734. d. Feb. 1, 1741.
1745. VI. Jonathan, b. Apr. 18, 1737.
1746. VII. Moriah, b. Aug. 27, 1739.
1747. VIII. Susanna, b. Mar. 12, 1748.

1740. John. (1726. John, 8. John, 2. James, 1. Thomas.) Eldest s. and child of John Draper and Moriah Hall. m. by Rev. Samuel Dexter, Oct. 3, 1751, Abigail, dau. of John Cheney and his 2d wife, Elizabeth Currig. She was b. Dedham, Aug. 20, 1727. d. Dover, Oct. 6, 1809.

CHILDREN:

1753. I. Elizabeth, b. Feb. 15, 1752.
1754. II. Moses, b. Feb. 9, 1754. Left for parts unknown.

1755. III. Lydia, b. May 22, 1756. d. Aug. 31, 1846. m. Oct. 11, 1776, Benjamin, s. of Jonathan Wright and Margaret Fairbanks, of Medfield. He was b. 1720. d. 1800. (His mother, Margaret, lived to be 103 years old.)

1756. IV. Josiah, b. Aug. 2, 1758.
1757. V. Aaron, b. Jan. 13, 1761.
1758. VI. Daniel, b. Feb. 20, 1763. d. Dec. 9, 1834.

1759. VII. Abigail, b. May 2, 1765.

1760. VIII. Miriam, b. 1766. m. Oct. 13, 17 —, Josiah Knolton, of Sherburne.

1761. IX. Mary, b. June 12, 1767.

1756. Josiah. (1740. John, 1726. John, 8. John, 2. James, 1. Thomas.) 4th child, 2ds. of John Draper and Abigail Cheney. m. Keziah Knolton. She wash. 1765. d. Dover, of dropsy of the heart, Oct. 13, 1843.

CHILDREN:

1762. I. Polly, b. July 4, 1788. m. Feb. 14, 1811, Elnathan Hammond, of Bridgewater, N. S.

1763. II. Moses, b. Oct. 29, 1792. d. Apr. 2, 1885.

1764. III. Abigail, b. Mar. 28, 1802. m. Dec. 14, 1826, Willard Mann, of Dover.

1763. Moses. (1756. Josiah, 1740. John, 1726. John, 8. John, 2. James, 1. Thomas.) Eldest s., 2d child of Josiah Draper and Keziah Knolton. He lived to be 92 years, 5 months and 4 days. m. 1st: Dec. 2, 1819, Maria Wilbur, of Medfield. She was b. 1798.

d. Sep. 9, 1871. He m. 2dly: the widow Ann Hussey, of Spencer. (No issue by this marriage.) She d. Dorchester, 1886.

CHILDREN, ALL B. DOVER:

1765. I. Elizabeth, b. June 7, 1821. m. Albert, s. of John Mann and Sallie Jackson. He was b. Apr. 27, 1817. d. Oct. 7, 1862. Children: — I. Albert Chester, 1771. b. May 5, 1846. II. A child, 1772. b. July 30, 1851. d. Aug. 30, 1851. III. Edna Endora, 1773. b. July 31, 1852. d. Mar. 8, 1872. IV. George Melvyn, 1774. b. Mar. 25, 1855. V. Oscar Eugene, 1775. b. July 6, 1857. m. Kate Casey. VI. Leonard Draper, 1776. b. June 7, 1861. d. Jan. 11, 1863.

1766. II. Leonard, b. Jan. 6, 1823. m. Caroline F., dau. of David Chickering and Orpha Burbanck, of Dover, Oct. 13, 1846. (No issue.)

1767. III. Alfreda, b. Jan. 17, 1825. d. Apr. 11, 1825.

1768. IV. Maria, b. Jan. 9, 1827. d. Oct. 2-3, 1828.

1769. V. Anna Maria, b. Mar. 29, 1830. d. Dec. 13, 1878. m. Nov. 30, 1848, Oliver Everett, s. of John Mann and Sallie Jackson. He d. July 18, 1876. Children: — I. Herbert, 1777. b. Sep. 2, 1849. d. Jan. 13, 1878. II. A son, 1778, who d. in infancy. III. Minnie L., 1779. d. in infancy. IV. Albert Lester, 1780. b. June 2, 185 1. m. Ella Bacon. V. Bertha, 1781. d. June 19, 1878. m. B. B. Otis. VI. Ada, 1782. d. in infancy.

1770. VI. Adeline, b. June 5, 1834. m. 1st: Simon Macdonald, of Nova Scotia. He d. June 20, 1873. She m. 2dly: William, s. of Aaron Schofield and Emily Benjamin, of N. Alton, Kings Co., N. S. Children, by 1st marriage (no issue by 2d): — I. Arthur L., 1783. b. Feb. 22, 1857. m. Nov. 9, 1881. II. Flora J., 1784. b. Sep. 3, 1861. m. June 10, 1891. III. Georgie W., 1785. b. Oct. 10, 1869. d. June 22, 1879.

1757. Aaron. (1740. John, 1726. John, 8. John, 2. James, 1. Thomas.) 5th child, 3d s. of John Draper and Abigail Cheney, m. by Rev. Mr. Haven, Dec. 30, 1784, Martha Little, of Dedham.

CHILDREN, B. DEDHAM:

1786. I. Moses, b. July 24, 1815.

1787. II. Aaron, b. June 17, 1818.

1788. III. Mary E., b. June 22, 1819. m. Apr. 25, 1852, Isaac Collier.

1789. IV. Lucy, b. Apr., 1822.

1790. V. Lydia, b. July 15, 1824.

1786. Moses. (1757. Aaron, 1740. John, 1726. John, 8. John, 2. James, 1. Thomas.) Eldest s. and child of Aaron Draper and Martha Little, m. Oct. 1, 1845, at E. Medway, Cynthy Irene, dau. of Amariah Ware and Betsy Ware. She was b. Franklin, Mass., June 1, 1820.

CHILDREN, B. W, DEDHAM:

1791. I. Irene Watson, b. Aug. 15, 1846. m. James Albert, s. of Albert Billings and Harriet Boyden, of Walpole, Mass. Children: — I. Albert Ellis, 1800. b. Aug. 8, 1866. m. Sep. 14, 1889, Emma Moreton, of Taunton. II. Cora Estelle, 1801. b. Nov., 1868. m. Newtonville, Mass., Jan. 13, 1889, Charles Henry Taintor. (Child: — Chester Arnold, 1802. b. May 5, 1890.)

1792. II. Ellis, b. Aug. II, 1848. m. Jenny Tibbitts.

1793. III. Frances Ella, b. Oct. 4, 1849. m. Jan. 3, 1870, James White, s. of Job White Dupee and Clarissa Myria, his wife. He was b. Oct. 17, 1849. Children: — I. Claudia Francis, 1803. b. N. Wrentham, Feb. 18, 1871. m. Taunton, Harry Stevens Allan, Oct. 8, 1891. II. Charles Herbert, 1804. b. Taunton, July 8, 1873. III. Eugene White, 1805. b. Taunton, Sep. II, 1875. d. Sep. 9, 1877. IV. Maud Ella, 1806. b. Taunton, May 21, 1881. V. George Eugene, 1807. b. Taunton, Nov. 21, 1884. VI. Elsie White, 1808. b. Taunton, Jan. 10, 1886. d. Jan. 11, 1890.

1794. IV. Edson, b. Apr. 8, 1851. d. Sep. 8, 1853.

1795. V. Edna & 1796. VI. Eldora (Twins), b. Apr. 21, 1855. (Edna d. Sep. 11, 1855. Eldora d. May 9, 1890, m. Nov. 15, 1873, Thomas Marshall Smith.)

1797. VII. Eugene, b. June 12, 1856.

1798. VIII. Orene Ware, b. Mar. 13, 1858. d. June 4, 1869.

1799. IX. Elmar Austin, b. Aug. 5, 1862.

1758. Daniel. (1740. John, 1726. John, 8. John, 2. James, 1. Thomas.) 6th child, 4th s. of John Draper and Abigail Cheney, m. by Rev. Thomas Thacher, May 14, 1793, Naomah, dau. of Joseph and Hannah Deane, of Dedham. She was b. May 24, 1774. d. Sep. 1, 1833.

Daniel Draper, called "Daniel of High Rock," built a house at High Rock, W. Dedham, in 1813, and the sixth generation from him are now living in it. He was noted for his wonderfully powerful voice, which was heard, on one occasion, a distance of two miles.

CHILDREN, B. W. DEDHAM:

1809. I. Sarah, b. Dec. 6, 1793. d. Aug. 11, 1795.

1810. II. Joseph, b. Aug. 5, 1796, d. Jan. 19, 1838.

1811. III. Martin, b. Mar. 7, 1797. d. Nov. 21, 1879,

1812. IV, Willard, b. Nov. 2, 1800. d. Mar. 28, 1877,

1813. V. Mary, b. Aug. 21, 1803. d. Sep. 4, 1819.

1814. VI. Sarah, b. July 1, 1809. d. Nov. 10, 1831. m. Mar. 4, 1829, Nathanial Noyes. He was b. Mar. 10, 1810. Child, 1815. b. Pembroke, N. H. d. in infancy.

1810. Joseph. (1758. Daniel, 1740. John, 1726. John, 8. John, 2. James, 1. Thomas.) Eldest s. and 2d child of Daniel Draper and Naomah Deane. m. Medfield, Nov. 19, 1818, Polly, dau. of Phineas and Lucy Colburn. She was b. W. Dedham, Apr. 14, 1792. d, there 1866.

They lived in Medfield the first year of their marriage, and Joseph erected a dam and fulling mill on the present site of Frendis's mill, and there, for several years, carried on the business of his English ancestors, of fulling and making cloth. He subsequently sold the mill and business to Abner Mason, and moved his family to W. Dedham, where he and his wife died and are buried.

CHILDREN:

1816. I. Ellis Dwight, b. Medfield, Aug., 1819. d. Norwood, Mass., Dec. 21, 1887.

1817. II. Mary, b. Medfield, Feb., 1821. m. 1844, Samuel R. Leland, of Worcester. He d. 1854. Was a music dealer and noted musician in Worcester. Children, b. Worcester: — I. Frank Augustus, 1824, b. Apr. 23, 1846. m. Nov. 3, 1873, Hattie Mowry Lapham. (Child: — Hattie May, 1826, b. Feb. 27, 1879.) HJulietta Elizabeth, 1825. b. Mar. 8, 1848. d. June 11, 1851.

1818. III. Joseph Loring, b, Medfield, 1823. d. 1853. m. Hattie Bowne, of Sandwich, Mass.

1819. IV. Francis William, b. Medfield, Apr., 1825. d. W. Dedham, 1845.

1820. V. Lucy Ellis, b. Dover, Sep. 3, 1828. d. Worcester, May 22, 1873. m. Worcester, Apr. 20, 1853, Dr. Frank H., s. of Michael B. and R. A. Kelly. He was b. New Hampton, N. H., Sep. 9, 1827. d. Worcester, Oct., 1890. Dr. Kelly was for several terms Mayor of the City of Worcester and a practising physician in that city; Fellow of the Massachusetts Medical Society, and author of "Reminiscences of New Hampton, N. H.," which contains the genealogies of the Kelly and Simpson families. After the death of his wife, he m, Mrs. Jenny P. Martin, dau. of Edward A. and Marian S. Pratt, of Princetown. (No issue by 2d marriage.) Children, by Lucy Ellis Draper: — I. Frank H., 1827. d. in infancy. II. George Draper, 1828. d. in infancy. III. Frank H. 2d, 1829. b. Dec. 8, 1862. m. May 20, 1886, Jean L. Richardson, of New Haven, Conn. (Children: — I. Jessie Kelly, 1831. b. May 23, 1889. d. in infancy. II. Frank H., Jr., 1832. b. Feb. 26, 1890.) IV. George Draper 2d, 1830. b. June 6, 1866. Graduated as M. D. from Harvard.

1821. VI. Rufus Heminway, b. Feb. 3, 1830, m. May 4, 1871, Charlotte S. Lyman, of Dubuque, Ia.

1822. VII. George Dean, b. Jan. 2, 1832. d. May 7, 1866.

1823. VIII. Sarah Noyes, b. Mar. 18, 1834. m. June 5, 1856, Louis, s. of Paul and Sallie Ellis, of Dedham. He was b. Feb. 1, 1833. Children: — I. Grace Antoinette, 1833. b. W. Dedham, Aug., 1857. m. Mar. 15, 1881, George Edward Munro. (Child:— George Ellis, 1836. b. Mar. 30, 1882.) II. Frank Louis, 1834. b. Feb., 1859. d. Aug., 1859. III. Kate Heminway, 1835. b. Aug., 1867.

1816. Ellis Dwight. (1810. Joseph, 1758. Daniel, 1740. John, 1726. John, 8. John, 2. James, 1. Thomas.) Eldest s. and child of Joseph Draper and Polly Colburn. m. Ann, dau. of Elijah Hursey and Nancy Harding. She was b. Dedham, Feb. 28, 1819.

Mr. Draper, at the age of 16, apprenticed himself to Abijah Colburne, of W. Dedham, who carried on a small furniture shop, and at 23 he established himself at Pawtucket, R. I., in the furniture business. He gave up the business there, but went into it again at Norwood, in company with Curtis G. Morse, and remained with the firm until 1 861. At that time he went into the foundry business at W. Dedham with his brother, Rufus H. Draper, 1821. After various changes in the firm names he finally sold his business to other parties in 1871, and started a new foundry in Norwood, taking in his son Frank (1837) as partner, under the firm name of E. D. Draper & Son, and continuing a successful business until his death.

CHILDREN:

1837. I. Frank D., b. Pawtucket, R. I., Sep. 30, 1846. m. Sarah K. Colburn, of Walpole, Nov. 10, 1875. Children: — I. Mary F., 1840. b. Norwood, Dec. 5, 1878. II. George E., 1841. b. Apr. 10, 1881.

1838. II. Martha A., b. Norwood, Aug. 8, 1849. m. Apr. 16, 1873, James A. Davis, of Wynn, Me. Children: — I. Alfred D., 1842. b. Norwood, Mar. 30, 1874. II. Annie E., 1843. b. Norwood, Oct. 1, 1878.

1839. III. George E., b. Norwood, Mar. 15, 1852. d. there July 16, 1877. m. Nettie, b. Norwood, Dec. 31, 1860, d. there Mar. 10, 1887.

1822. George Dean. (1810. Joseph, 1758. Daniel, 1740. John, 1726. John, 8. John, 2. James, 1. Thomas.) 7th child, 5th s. of Joseph Draper and Polly Colburn. m. May 2, 1855, Fanny Ellis, dau. of Elusha Baker and Elizabeth Sanford, of W. Dedham. She was b. there July 13, 1834.

CHILDREN, B. W. DEDHAM:

1844. I. Fannie E., b. May 11, 1856. m. June 7, 1888, Frederick J. Baker, of Dedham.

1845. II. George L., b. Dec. 15, 1858. m. Jan. 18, 1878, Lizzie A. Reed, of Worcester, Mass.

1846. III. Mary, b. June 29, 1865. d. May 24, 1866.

1811. Martin. (1758. Daniel, 1740. John, 1726. John, 8. John, 2. James, 1. Thomas.) 3d child, 2d s. of Daniel Draper and Naomah Deane. m. July 12, 1818, Sally, dau. of Elijah Fisher, of Canton. She was b. Aug. 6, 1799. d. Apr. 9, 1885.

When Martin Draper was 8 or 9 years old he went to live with Deacon Samuel Fales, a farmer, residing in the easterly part of Dedham, about 5 miles from High Rock. It was a custom of those days with some to place children in a family to be "brought up," as it was called, or live until they were of age, and his was an instance of the kind. The deacon became much attached to him. He worked on the farm, and in Winter was allowed to attend the district school for a few weeks. When 21 years old he received from the deacon a "freedom suit" of clothes and two hundred dollars in money.

Near the close of the year 1816 there came to live in the family of Deacon Fales a young woman named Sally Fisher, who was not quite 18. She was skilled in the various duties of housekeeping, and in addition thereto could sew, knit, spin and weave, and do many other things of a similar nature. She had been carefully taught by her aunt, Rachel Cobb. Her charms, accompanied by these qualifications and characteristics all combined, were too much for the young man of 21; they overpowered him, and they were married by Rev. Mr. White. She proved herself to be a real helpmeet to her husband. Bringing up a family of 7 children, spinning, weaving, knitting, sewing, making most, if not all, their clothes until they were quite large. As an instance of her readiness to meet difficulties and her ability to overcome them, I will mention an incident in her history. One cold wintery afternoon Mr. Draper loaded a team with wood, and, as was his custom, proposed to start with it for the market at Roxbury or Boston during the small hours of the next morning. When he came in at early evening he found that he had no mittens. Mistress Sally brought out her knitting needles and yarn, and before retiring that night she knit a pair of mittens, and they were worn by him the next morning. When about 65 years of age she had a severe stroke of paralysis, and after that was but a wreck of her former self. She died at the home of her daughter in Roxbury, aged 85 years, 8 months, 3 days.

Martin Draper continued to live with Deacon Fales until 1824, carrying on the farm upon shares. Afterwards he worked for Mr. Eliphalet Pond, who was a farmer; also carried on the business of making potash and soap, and of sending milk to market. After moving, in 1825, to what was known as the "Farrington Place," and afterwards to the "Fisher Place," in the Spring of 1831, he bought the High Rock Farm, containing about 75 acres. He had a strong and vigorous constitution, and splendid physical development. At the head of his military command his finely proportioned form, so erect and stately in its bearing, made as perfect a figure as was ever seen on a training day.

Martin Draper was one of the early pioneers in the Temperance Reform Movement. In those days it was the universal custom of society to treat friends and visitors with strong drink. It was used on all festive occasions, at military parades, fairs, shows, etc., at weddings and funerals, raisings and huskings. Farmers thought they could not get through their planting and haying without it; in fact its use was universal. Mr. Draper refused to drink or to invite his friends to do so. He tried publicly to discourage it, as the following incident will illustrate. In the year 1831 he built a barn (raised May 9th and 10th), now standing on the old homestead farm at High Rock. The usual invitations were given out, with the understanding that no intoxicating drink would be used on the occasion. This was contrary to all precedents in those days. The announcement caused much gossip. The knowing ones shook their heads at this departure, and said it could not be done. It was done, an acknowledged success, and the barn stands to this day a monument of triumph in the cause of temperance.

In 1831 he changed his residence to the farm in W. Dedham. This was about four miles from his church. Through the heat of Summer and the cold and snow drifts of Winter, it was all the same to him. His duty was at the church, and there he was always found. His persistency in doing what he thought to be his duty is illustrated by an incident that occurred some time after he moved to W. Dedham.

There was a terrible snow storm one Saturday, continuing until Sunday morning. The four miles of road between his house and the church was badly blocked with snow, trackless much of the way, and in many places impassable, except to shovel through the drifts. With horse, sleigh and shovel he fought his way through, after a severe struggle, to the church, and there found Dr. Burgess, who had done the same thing from his own residence, which was about equally distant in another direction. These and Comfort Weatherbee, the sexton, constituted the whole congregation that Sunday. For many years he was not absent once from his accustomed seat in the House of God on the Sabbath. He was a teacher in the Sabbath School, and attended many of the other meetings connected with the church. Between Mr. Draper and Dr. Burgess a strong and enduring attachment and friendship was formed, which continued to the end of life. Martin Draper united with the church in 1829. Six years later, in 1835, he was elected deacon, which office he held to the end of his life— about 44 years.

The last time that he worshipped in the church will long be remembered by many of his friends. It occurred not many months before his death. The only surviving son of his old pastor, Edward P. Burgess, wished to give his aged friend an occasion of especial enjoyment and happiness, and desired that he might worship once more, and sit with him again at the table of their common Lord and Master, and partake of the sacred emblems of Christ's love. Mr. Burgess called for him and returned him to his home in W. Dedham.

Mr. Draper was much interested in military affairs, and joined the Dedham Light Infantry, a military company belonging to the First Regiment of the Second Brigade, First Division, Mass. Militia. After filling several noncommissioned offices, he was elected Ensign, May 20, 1822, being commissioned by Gov. John Brooks. He was elected Lieutenant, Sep. 23, 1824, and Captain, Aug. 16, 1826. At his own request he was honorably discharged from the office of Captain in the regiment aforesaid Mar. 10, 1828. He was one of the Board of Selectmen of Dedham during the following years:— 1843, 1844, 1845, 1846, 1847, 1848, 1855, 1856, 1857, 1858 and 1859. He was also one of the Assessors all of these years, except 1846 and 1847; and for many years was one of the Board of Overseers of the Poor, and also held other public offices.

A few days before his death one of his sons, in conversation with him, said: "Father, if you knew that you could never be any better, should you feel willing and ready to go?" He, without hesitation, replied: "Yes, I long to go. I know in whom I believe; I am ready to depart; I wait my Lord's coming." Then, though suffering from extreme weakness, he summoned his remaining strength, as in broken accents he sang to the old tune of "Lenox" the words so familiar to him:

"How long, dear Saviour, O how long,
Shall this bright hour delay?
Fly swifter round, ye wheels of time,
And bring the welcome day."

CHILDREN, B. W. DEDHAM:

1844. I. Warren Fales, b. Dec. 12, 1818. m. May 24, 1848, Irene Patience Rowley, of Wrentham. She was b. Jan. 25, 1824. d. Lansing, N. Y.

Warren F. Draper

The early years of his life were spent on High Rock Farm at W. Dedham. At the urgent solicitation of Dr. Ebenezer Burgess, his father's pastor, Warren entered Phillips Academy, Andover, Mass., graduating from that institution in 1843, and from Amhurst College in 1847. He then entered the Theological Seminary, Andover, to prepare for the ministry, but was obliged to leave on account of his health. During his academic and collegiate courses Mr. Draper taught public school in the towns of Andover, Holliston, Medfield and Canton, and engaged in other work for means to defray his expenses. Returning to Andover in the Spring of 1849, Mr. Draper engaged in the book selling and publishing business as successor to the firm of Allen Morrill & Wardwell. For upwards of 40 years he has been closely identified with the business, educational and religious, interests of Andover. For nearly 40 years he was the leading bookseller, which branch of his business he disposed of in 1887. He is still engaged in the publishing of works for the special use of theological students and clergymen, and it has always been his aim to publish a line of books, every one of which should be of sterling and permanent value.

From his press have come Greek and Hebrew text-books, critical commentaries, classical and miscellaneous works. He also published 36 volumes representing as many years of the Bibliotheca Sacra, the most prominent Theological Quarterly in the country, edited by Professors Edwards and Park, of Andover Seminary, and other prominent scholars, and he prepared and published a full general index to the first 30 volumes of this work. For about 15 years he published and partly edited the "Andover Advertiser," a local weekly newspaper.

Being thus closely associated with the Andover institutions, Mr. Draper has felt a deep interest in them, and with the cordial co-operation of his wife, has aided them from time to time with his benefactions. He established a Scholarship in the Theological Seminary, and about 25 years ago gave a fund for Prize Speaking in Phillips Academy, and more recently $2,500 for a Scholarship in the same institution.

For about 15 years Mr. Draper has been deacon and treasurer of the Seminary Church, and when the stone chapel was erected in 1876, he contributed $500 towards it. For 24 years he has provided, in his wife's name, for an Annual Reading in Abbot Academy; also a Scholarship in the same.

On the occasion of his 70th birthday, Mr. Draper gave the First Congregational Church, Dedham, Mass., a fund as a memorial to his father. Deacon Martin Draper, who was deacon of that church for 44 years. The income from that fund to be used to aid a member of the church to prepare for the ministry, or it may be used to help the poor of the church.

In 1868 Mr. Draper was elected a trustee, and during the past 15 years has held the office of treasurer of Abbot Academy, and for the last 5 years has devoted the greater part of his time to the interests of that institution. When the new administration building of Abbot Academy was formally opened, in January, 1891, it was, by vote of the trustees, named "Draper Hall," not only because Mr. Draper gave the largest single item, $25,000, towards its completion, but because of the interest, care and unceasing devotion he, as well as his wife, have shown towards Abbot Academy.

Mr. Draper has also taken an active share in local town affairs. For some years he carried on an annual spelling match, giving prizes open for competition to all the pupils in the town schools. He often served on committees on lecture courses and other objects; also for several years as trustee and treasurer of the Memorial Hall Library, etc.

Thus Mr. Draper has rounded out a busy life of more than threescore years and ten, and is still active and vigorous, esteemed by his townsmen and a wide circle of friends.

1845. II. Daniel Fisher, b. June 10, 1822, d. Feb. 10, 1874.

1846. III. Martin, b. Oct. 26, 1823. d. Aug. 27, 1889.

1847. IV. Sarah Elizabeth, b. May 31, 1832. d. June 21, 1883. m. Sep. 27, 1856, George Shepherd Rawlins. He was b. Sep. 1, 1833. d. June 7, 1876. Children: — I. Lily Florence, 1851. b. Oct. 24, 1859. d. Aug. 26, 1884. m. Sep. 11,

1879, Joseph William Cox. He was b. Mattapan, Oct. 16, 1858. II. Emma Josephine, 1852. b. Apr. 22, 1862. d. Aug. 15, 1862.

1848. V. George Bradford, b. Aug. 5, 1834. d. Roxbury, Dec. 10, 1875. (Unmarried.) Resided at High Rock Farm, and carried on dairy business with his brother, Charles Edward. He was a man of rare abilities and beloved by all. Town Assessor for several years and a member of the School Committee. He was a member of the Constellation Lodge F. and A. M. At his death he bequeathed $1,000 to the so-called Damon Donation.

1849. VI. Charles Edward, b. July 18, 1836.

1851. VII. Abigail Burgess, b. Apr. 15, 1841. m. Apr. 19, 1860, Francis, s. of Francis Thurston Pond and Lucy Tolman. He was b. W. Dedham, May 19, 1836. d. Nov. 13, 1889. Children: — I. Frank Eldridge, 1853. b. W. Dedham, Oct. 24, 1865. d. June 16, 1868. II. Aylmer, 1854. b. W. Dedham, Apr. 15, 1868. III. Jenny Tolman, 1855. b. Boston Highlands, Oct. 15, 1869.

1845. Daniel Fisher. (1811. Martin, 1758. Daniel, 1740. John, 1726. John, 8. John, 2. James, 1. Thomas.) 2d child and s. of Martin Draper and Sally Fisher, m. May 1, 1847, the widow Mary Ann (Collins) Merrill, of Portland, Me. She was b. Salem, Jan. 27, 1817. d. Cambridge, Apr. 3, 1889,

Mr. Draper left the old homestead when 16 years of age, entering Phillips Academy at Andover. After this he studied his profession of dentistry, and taught in Dedham High School. His health was very poor, he being threatened with lung disease all his life, and his profession was therefore very hard upon him. But his business was successful, and he managed with prudence to accumulate quite a large property. During the latter part of his life he spent most of his Winters in Florida on account of his health. He was a man of excellent judgment, of few words, and these to the point, and of honorable character. His wife, with long years of nursing, became, prior to her death, a confirmed invalid.

CHILDREN:

1856. I. Mary Adeline, b. Apr. 10, 1848. m. Jan. 29, 1879, Edward Howard, s. of Edward White Cobb, who was a direct descendant of Peregrine White, the first white child born in New England. Mr. Cobb is a graduate of Harvard in the class of 1878. Shortly after graduating he became a teacher of Chemistry and Physics at the Friends' Academy, New Bedford, Mass. He has taught at the Roxbury High School and the Laurence School, in Boston. Children:— I. Ruth Draper, 1860, b. Dec. 4, 1883. H. Winifred Draper, 1861. b. Aug. 18, 1885.

1857. II. William Burgess, b. May 16, 1852. m. Sep. 5, 1882, Carrie M. Drew.

Children: — I. Warren Fales, 1862. b. Aug. 9, 1884. II. Elwyn Burgess, 1863. b. Oct. 28, 1890.

1858. III. Daniel Francis, b. July 28, 1853. d. Dec. 18, 1856.

1859. IV. Ella Frances, b. Apr. 7, 1861.

1846. Martin. (1811. Martin, 1758. Daniel, 1740. John, 1726. John, 8. John, 2. James, 1. Thomas.) 3d s. and child of Martin Draper and Sallie Fisher, m.

Aug. 15, 1848, Sarah, dau. of Nathanial P. Morrison, of Somerville, Mass. She was b. Jan. 24, 1824.

Martin Draper had attended the district schools in the different parts of Dedham where he had lived, and thus had acquired the rudiments of an education. In 1843, becoming convinced that there was an easier way of obtaining a living than by farming, he entered Phillips Academy, Andover, Mass., to fit himself for teaching. After teaching a district school in Dover, Mass., during the Winter of 1843-4, and again in 1844-5, he returned to Andover, and continued his course, being there, in all, four terms. December, 1845, he commenced as teacher of the Walnut Hill School, Somerville, Mass., and Sep. 28, 1846, was elected Principal of the Prospect Hill Grammar School, Somerville. Mr. Draper was a very successful teacher, painstaking, and thorough in his methods of instruction and a superior disciplinarian. After remaining Master of the Prospect Hill School for five years, he resigned and became associated with his brother, Warren F. Draper (1844), in the printing and publishing business at Andover, under the name of Draper & Brother. At the end of two years, severing his connection with his brother, he entered the Grocers' Bank, Boston, as bookkeeper. After filling that position for two years, Apr. 15, 1856, he entered the National Bank of North America, Boston, as messenger, and remained an officer of that institution until his death in 1889 — a continuous service of over 33 years.

Mr. Draper was a resident of Cambridge in 1858, and was a member of the Somerville School Committee during the years 1857 and 1858, and also served on the Cambridge School Committee in 1867 and 1868.

In 1879 he compiled and copyrighted an interest table for computing interest on daily balances, which is invaluable to bank bookkeepers. In 1864 he purchased an estate on North Avenue in North Cambridge, and there he lived until his death.

Mr. Draper was a great lover of music, especially of oratorio and church music. He had a very keen ear and a fine appreciation of musical harmonies. For 20 years or more he was a member of the Handel and Haydn Society, Boston, in whose concerts and festivals he took an active part and greatly enjoyed.

CHILDREN:

1864. I. Susan Amelia, b. Somerville, Mar. 9, 1850.

1865. II. Warren Martin, b. Cambridge, Apr. 14, 1859.

1849. Charles Edward. (1811. Martin, 1758. Daniel, 1740. John, 1726. John, 8. John, 2. James, 1. Thomas.) 6th child, 5th s. of Martin Draper and Sally Fisher, m. Dec. 18, 1862, Aspacia Priscilla, dau. of Benjamin Holbrook Tubbs and Aspacia Euphrosina Priscilla Pitman, of W. Dedham. Mr. Draper lives in Roxbury, but owns and occupies, for part of the season. High Rock Farm at W. Dedham. He is engaged in the milk and dairy business, in which his brother, George Bradford (1848), was, previous to his death, in partnership with him. Mr. Draper is a member of Washington Lodge F. and A. M.; Past High

Priest Mt. Vernon R. A. Chapter; Principal Conductor of Work in Roxbury Council of R. and S. M.; Captain General in Joseph Warren Commandery, Knights Templar; a Scottish Rites Mason, and has taken 32 degrees.

CHILDREN:

1866. I. Walter Holbrook, b. W. Dedham, May 25, 1866.

1867. II. Fred. Bradford, b. W. Dedham, June 13, 1868.

1868. III. Charles Martin, b. W. Dedham, Nov. 1, 1869.

1869. IV. Herbert George, b. Roxbury, Oct. 19, 1871. d. Dec. 10, 1872.

1812. Willard. (1758. Daniel, 1740. John, 1726. John, 8. John, 2. James, 1. Thomas.) 4th child, 3d s. of Daniel Draper and Naomah Deane. m. Nov. 2, 1826, by Rev. Samuel Adiin, Louisa, dau. of Abijah and Hannah Smith, of Walpole, Mass. She was. b. Walpole, Aug. 9, 1806. d. Dedham, June 19, 1883.

Mr. Draper lived all his life at High Rock Farm, W. Dedham, in the house built there by his father, and was for 30 years deacon in the West Baptist Church.

CHILDREN, ALL B. W. DEDHAM:

1870. I. Henry Sidney, b. July 18, 1828.

1871. II. Francis Willard, b. Aug. 7, 1829.

1872. III. Whiting Smith, b. Jan. 11, 1832. d. Dec. 21, 1886.

1873. IV. Louisa Antoinette, b. June 22, 1835. d. Apr. 13, 1875. m. Dec. 15, 1861, Stephen C., s. of David Rawlins and Betsy Fuller Thompson. He was b. Greensboro, Vt., Feb. 8, 1839. Child: — Endora Antoinette, 1879. b. Somerville, Mass., June 10, 1867.

1874. V. Abijah Smith, b. May 16, 1838. d. Aug. 28, 1866. m. July 15, 1861, Mary Jane, dau. of Robert G. Mahan and Mary A. Jones. She was b. Detroit, Sep. 3, 1841. At the death of her husband she m. 2dly: Mr. McLeod. Child, by 1st marriage: — Jenny Gertrude, 1880. b. Feb. 19, 1864. d. Oct. 16, 1890.

1875. VI. Hannah Mariah, b. Apr. 18, 1840. d. Sep. 18, 1864. (Unmarried.)

1876. VII. Mary Elizabeth, b. Feb. 2, 1843. d. June 1, 1860. (Unmarried.)

1877. VIII. Ellen Endora, b. Apr. 27, 1845. d. Apr. 30, 1866. m. Oct., 1865, William W. Leonard, of Chiltenville.

1878. IX. Edwin Leicester, b. Dec. 9, 1847. d. Oct. 23, 1870. (Unmarried.)

1870. Henry Sidney, (1812. Willard, 1758. Daniel, 1740. John, 1726. John, 8. John, 2. James, 1. Thomas.) Eldest s. and child of Willard Draper and Louisa Smith.

m. 1st: Nov. 14, 1849, Catherine Aris, of Lisbon, Me. She d. Dec. 25, 1860. He m. 2dly: Jan. 8, 1861, Hattie Maria, dau. of Samuel and Emmeline Butler, of Turner, Me. She was b. Mexico, Me., Nov. 13, 1843.

Mr. Draper is a large dairyman, and lives at W. Dedham. A well known, highly respected and prosperous man.

CHILDREN, BY 1st MARRIAGE, ALL B. W. DEDHAM:

1881. I. Julia Edna, b. Jan. 12, 1852. m. James W. Armstrong, of St. Johns, Neb.

1882. II. Lucy Aurilla, b. Dec. 23, 1854. m. George C. Williams, of Gardner, Me.

1883. III. Martha Elizabeth, b. Nov. 16, 1857. m. Fred. E. McIlroy, of Boston.

CHILDREN, BY 2D MARRIAGE, B. W. DEDHAM:

1884. IV. Sydney Waldo, b. Feb. 18, 1862.

1885. V. Florence Isabel, b. May 5, 1868.

1886. VI. Willard Sheppard, b. Nov. 22, 1870. m. Oct. 12, 1890, Ella, dau. Of Daniel and Elmira Holt. She was b. Weld, Me., Feb. 18, 1871.

1887. VII. George Henry, b. Jan. 26, 1880.

1871. Francis Willard. (1812. Willard, 1758. Daniel, 1740. John, 1726. John, 8. John, 2. James, 1. Thomas.) 2d child and s. of Deacon Willard Draper and Louisa Smith, m. Oct. 10, 1850, Louisa, dau. of Louis Ellis and Louisa Guild. She was b. Norwood, Mass., July 19, 1830.

Mr. Draper is a dairyman farmer at High Rock, W. Dedham. He is a deacon of the W. Dedham Baptist Church, and has been Supt. of the Sunday School for 20 years.

CHILDREN, B. W. DEDHAM:

1888. I. Minella Louisa, b. July 25, 1851.

18S9. II. Hattie Naomah, b. Mar. 20, 1855. m. June 2, 1872, Frederick Standish, s. of Francis Soule and Maria Colburn, of W. Dedham. He was b. W. Dedham, Oct. 3, 1851. Children: — I. George Wyngate, 1893. b. Dec. 2, 1872. II. Herbert Melville, 1894. b. Nov. I, 1875. d. Jan. 7, 1889. III. Maria Louisa, 1895. b. July ir, 1878. IV. Grace Angelina, 1896. b. Nov. 24, 1888. V. Sydney Edward, 1897. b. Aug. 20, 1890.

1890. III. Abbot Wallace, b. Oct. 10, 1859. d. June 17, 1861.

1891. IV. Frank Ellsworth, b. July 15, 1861. m. Nov. 30, 1882, Lucy Anna, dau. of William L. Smith, Jr., and Sarah E. Cushing, of Charlotte, Me. She was b. there Nov. 2, 1857. Child: — Annie Maud, 1898. b. Sep. 29, 1883.

1892. V. Alice Estelle, b. Aug. 28, 1869. m. Sep. 29, 1891, Fred. A., s. of Charles R. Baker and Sarah E. Smith, of W. Dedham. He was b. Oct. 6, 1866.

1872. Whiting Smith. (1812. Willard, 1758. Daniel, 1740. John, 1726. John, 8. John, 2. James, 1. Thomas.) 3d s. and child of Deacon Willard Draper and Louisa Smith, m. W. Dedham, May 6, 1855, by Rev. J. Chaplin, Harriet Adelaide, dau. of Jesse Fairbanks and Burridell Mason. She was b. Walpole, Mass., Aug. 18, 1834.

CHILDREN:

1899. I. Fred. Emerson, b. W. Dedham, Aug. 20, 1856.

1900. II. Eva Frances, b. Waltham, Aug. 11, 1862.

1901. III. William Noyes, b. Waltham, Aug. 29, 1864. d. there Dec. 18, 1868.

1902. IV. Ernest Mason, b. Waltham, June 9, 1874. d. there Aug. 19, 1875.

1729. Joseph. (8. John, 2. James, 1. Thomas.) 6th child, 2d s. of John Draper and Abigail Mason, m. Jan. 27, 1725, in Boston, by Samuel Checkley, Esq., Deborah, dau. of Samuel Ellis and Deborah Lovell, of Medfield.

CHILDREN:

1903. I. Deborah, b. Jan. 23, 1727. m. by Rev. Samuel Dexter, Mar. 1, 1753, Nathanial, s. of Nathanial and Ann Smith, of Dedham. He was b. May 7, 1723.

1904. II. Hannah, b. Aug. 25, 1728.

1905. III. Olive, b. Nov. 17, 1729. m. by Rev. Samuel Dexter, Oct. 12, 1749, John Gay, of Natick.

1906. IV. Joseph, b. June 9, 1731.

1907. V, James, b. Feb. 20, 1732. d. Apr. 6, 1785.

1908. VI. Sarah, b. Nov. 9, 1735.

1906. Joseph. (1729. Joseph, 8. John, 2. James, 1. Thomas.) Eldest s., 3d child of Joseph Draper and Deborah Ellis, m. Mar. 1, 1759, Lydia, dau. of Michael and Abigail Bacon, of Dedham. She was b. Dec. 21, 1734.

CHILDREN:

1909. I. Deborah, b. Dover, Dec. 1, 1759. m. Captain David, s. of Peletiah Morse and Esther Allen, of Sherburne.

1910. II. Enoch, b. May 8, 1763. d. Jan. 24, 1822.

1911. III. Michael, b. May 9, 1765. d. Natick, Apr. 18, 1825.

1912. IV. Joseph, b. Nov. 8, 1767. d. Oct. 6, 1770.

1913. V. Cato, b. Oct. 4, 1770.

1914. VI. Joseph 2d, b. Oct. 15, 1773. d. Warwick, Mass., Jan. 12, 1855.

1910. Enoch. (1906. Joseph, 1729. Joseph, 8. John, 2. James, 1. Thomas.) Eldest s., 2d child of Joseph Draper and Lydia Bacon, m. Hannah, dau. of John and Hannah Clarke. She was b. Sherburne, 1762. d. Sep. 24, 1851.

Mr. Draper leased what was known as the Hill Farm, owned by one Tom Pegan, an Indian, from whom the hill derived its name, and the early settlers secured their titles. Pegan Hill, in the southeastern part of Natick, commands one of the finest views for miles around — a distance of 50 miles, and on fair days as far as the White Mountains can be seen. In the year 1792 Enoch Draper became owner of the property, and to this day a part of the original farm is occupied by his descendants to the fifth generation.

CHILDREN, B. NATICK, MASS.:

1915. I. Reuben, b. Mar. 20, 1789. d. Sep. 6, 1853.

1916. II. Joannah, b. Apr. 21, 1793. d. Needham, Mar. 29, 1862. (Unmarried.)

1917. III. Catherine, b. Jan. 27, 1795. m. by Rev. Ralph Sanger, John, s. of John Esty and Louisa Champney, of Stowe. She d. Needham, Aug. 27, 1855.

1918. IV. Calvin, m. Dec. 12, 1825, Judith Fisher, of Dedham. Children: — I. William, 1919. II. Alger, 1920.

1915. Reuben. (1910. Enoch, 1906. Joseph, 1729. Joseph, 8. John, 2. James, 1. Thomas.) Eldest s. and child of Enoch Draper and Hannah Clarke, m. Nov. 18, 1811, Lydia, dau. of Adam Morse and Lydia Bacon, of Natick. She was b. Oct. 15, 1792. d. Jan. 21, 1884.

Reuben, who succeeded his father on the Pegan Hill Farm, made it most remunerative. He took a deep and intelligent interest in the affairs of the country, and, having access to a good library, he was in the habit of reading aloud in the evening to his family, awakening thus in them "a great interest in history and other literature. He was very much respected and beloved.

CHILDREN, B. NATICK:

1921. I. Lucy Clarke, b. Feb. 9, 1812. d. July 15, 1885. (Unmarried.)

1922. II. Henrietta, b. June 4, 1814. (Unmarried.) She was for many years a teacher, and for more than 30 consecutive years in one school in Boston.

1923. III. James Dallas, b. Jan. 18, 1817.

1924. IV. Catherine Louisa, b. Apr, 12, 1819. d. Oct. 23, 1879. m. by Rev. Ralph Sanger, Charles, s. of John Morse and Betsy Rice, of Natick. He was b. Aug. 6, 1814.

1925. V. Eunice Anna, b. Dec. 1, 1823. d. Mar. 23, 1862. (Unmarried.)

1926. VI. Enoch Ellis, b. Jan 1, 1827. d. Nov. 16, 1854. m. Jan. 1, 1852, Eliza A. Kidder. She was b. July 16, 1829. d. Dec. 11, 1861. Child: — Reuben Franklin, 1928. b. Mar. 20, 1854. d. Apr. 6, 1854.

1927. VII. Eliza Sanger, b. Sep. 16, 1834. d. Mar. 14, 1836.

1923. James Dallas. (1915. Reuben, 1910. Enoch, 1906. Joseph, 1729. Joseph, 8. John, 2. James, 1. Thomas.) 3d child, eldest s. of Reuben Draper and Lydia Morse, m. June 18, 1843, by Rev. Charles Robinson, at Medfield, Mary Olive, dau. of Elijah Bullard and Mary Collins Temple, of Medfield. She was b. Medfield, Feb. 13, 1819.

Mr. Draper has continued to farm on part of the old place on Pegan Hill, and still resides there.

CHILDREN:

1929. I. Ellen Eliza, b. June 30, 1846. m. Sep. 30, 1869, by Rev. Horatio Alger, Joseph Franklin, s. of Mason Richards and Harriet Mills, of Dover, He was b. Needham, Oct, 26, 1843, Child: — Sybil Louise, 1935. b. Boston, Feb. 23, 1881.

1930. II. George Reuben, b. June 9, 1849. d, Feb. 3, 1878.

1931. III, Susan Gertrude, b. July 10, 1851, Is a graduate from Bridgewater Normal School, and has been teaching for 12 years.

1932. IV. James Abbot, b. May 10, 1853. m. Oct. 31, 1878, by Rev. A. J. Canfield, Mary E. Morrill, of Chelsea. Child: — Blanche Eugenia, 1936. b. Chelsea, Oct. 24, 1879. Mr. Draper is a dentist by profession, and has located himself in St. Johns, N. B. He m. 2d: June 9, 1891, by Rev. L. G. Macneil, Mrs. Margaret Wilson Barker, of St, Johns, N. B., dau. of Rev. Mr. Wilson, of Glasgow, Scotland.

1933. V. Ida Betsey, b. Feb. 9, 1855. m. June 18, 1876, by Rev. J. P. Sheafe, Jr., Dana Childs, s. of William P. Hanchett and Ede R. Childs, of Dracut. Children: — 1, Olive Gertrude, 1937, b. June 12, 1877. II. Dana Childs, Jr., 1938, b. Dec. 26, 1878. III. Ellen Draper, 1939. b. May 12, 1881. IV. George Draper, 1940. b. May 12, 1883. V. James Malcolm, 1941. b. Mar. 6, 1887,

1934. VI. Laura Ann, b. Jan. 21, 1857. m. Oct. 15, 1889, E. Hale Dean, s. of William and Elizabeth Dean, of Windsor. He was b. Windsor, May 9, 1857.

1911. Michael. (1906. Joseph, 1729. Joseph, S. John, 2. James, 1. Thomas.) 3d child, 2d s. of Joseph Draper and Lydia Bacon, m. May 1, 1794, by Rev. Benjamin Caryl, Hannah, dau. of Jabez and Hannah Baker, of Dedham. She was b. Apr. 26, 1773. d. Jan. 6, 1823. Both are buried in the cemetery at Dover, Mass.

CHILDREN, B. DOVER:

1942. I. Charles, b. Jan. 7, 1795. d. May 9, 1852. m. Nancy Everett, 1821.

She was b. Jan., 1792. d. Dec. 17, 1876. (She m. 2dly: Clement Bartlett, of Dedham.) Charles and his wife are both buried in the cemetery at Dover. Children: — I. Nancy Everett, 1946. b. Mar. 19, 1822. d. Sep. 3, 1845. II. Harriet Everett, 1947. b. Jan. 24, 1825. d. Sep. 24, 1825. III. Sarah Everett, 1948. b. Feb. 8, 1831.

1943. II. Hannah, b. Sep. 10, 1797. m. Apr. 3, 1823, Alexander Soule. He was b. July 14, 1795. d. Apr. 15, 1878. Children: — I. Charles Otis, 1949. b. Oct. 27, 1823. d. June 22, 1826. H. Martha, 1950. b. Apr. 2, 1826. m. 1st: Linus Bliss. He d. Oct. 17, 1872. m, 2d: Moses Blanchard. (They have 7 children.) III. Eliza Draper, 1951. b. Dec. 29, 1828. m. Lowell Colburn, of Natick. (Have had 3 children.) IV. Mary Baker, 1952. b. Feb. 10, 1831. m. May 5, 1851, Ephraim Wilson. (Children: — I. Nancy Draper, 1953. II. Henry, 1954. III. Herbert, 1955. IV. James, 1956. V. Edward, 1957. VI. Lilian Mary, 1958. VII. Eliza, 1959.)

1944. III. Mary, b. Sep. 21, 1801. d. Feb. 28, 1839, of consumption. (Unmarried.)

1945. IV. Eliza, b. Feb. 1, 1806. d. Mar. 6, 1831. m. Feb. 3, 1828, Jabez Everett. He d. Jan. 28, 1831.

1914. Joseph 2D, (1906. Joseph, 1729. Joseph, 8. John, 2. James, 1. Thomas.) Youngest child, 4th s. of Joseph Draper and Lydia Bacon, m. Jan. 1, 1801, Anna Field. She was b. June 8, 1775. d. Oct. 16, 1838. Joseph Draper kept an inn and farmed.

CHILDREN, B. DOVER:

1960. I. Anna, b. Sep. 28, 1801. d. Warwick, May 5, 1856. m. Sylvanus, s. of Ashbel Ward. He was b. Jan. 25, 1802. d. Warwick, May 5, 1856. Children:— I. Anna, 1964. b. Oct. 23, 1828. d. Apr. 8, 1856. II. Augusta Maria, 1965. b. June 4, 1830. m. 1870, Rev. O. Bissell. III. Artemus Draper, 1966. b. Dec. 20, 1837. m. Sep. 15, 1867, Mrs. Susan E. Boyd. IV. Justin Edwards, 1967. b. May 27, 1847. m. Nov., 1873, Jenny E. Capen.

1961. II. Harriet, b. May 6, 1803. d. Feb. 14, 1820.

1962. III. Ira, b. June 11, 1805. d. Bellows Falls, Vt., Aug. 24, 1882.

1963. IV, Catherine Field, b. Warwick, Feb. 8, 1814. d. Athol, Mass., Aug. 13, 1889. m. Joseph, s. of Joel Pierce, of Warwick. He d. June 14, 1888, Child:— Mary Pierce, 1968. b. July 3, 1846.

1962. Ira. (1914. Joseph, 1906. Joseph, 1729. Joseph, 8. John, 2. James, 1. Thomas.) Only s. and 3d child of Joseph Draper and Anna Field, m. Nov. 10, 1831, Emily, dau. of David Ball and Eunice Conant, of Warwick. She was b. June 25, 1809. d. Bellows Falls, Vt., Nov. 27, 1888.

Ira Draper was a man of sterling worth, and greatly esteemed by the people of the Town of Warwick, where he lived most of his life. He held public office almost all his life, and represented the town in the Massachusetts Legislature in 1847 and 1848.

CHILDREN, B. WARWICK:

1969. I. Joseph, b. Feb. 16, 1834. m. Jan. 23, 1863, Mary Jane, dau. of Benjamin G. Putnam and Sylvia Smith, of Warwick.

He graduated at the Jefferson Medical College in 1858, and has since followed his profession of a physician. He has been engaged in the care of the insane since 1859; was Assistant Physician at the Vermont Asylum for the Insane from 1859 to 1865; at the Worcester Lunatic Hospital from 1865 to 1870; at the New Jersey Asylum at Trenton from 1870 to 1873, when he was appointed Superintendent of the Vermont Asylum, which position he now holds. He is considered one of the greatest authorities on the disease of insanity and the care of the insane. The doctor and his wife have no children.

1970. II. Harriet, b. Mar. 17, 1835. d. Nov. 1, 1859. m. Alfred N., s. of Sylvanus N. Atwood and Harriet King, of Warwick, Mar. 15, 1858. They lived in Chicago. (No children.)

1971. III. Mary, b. Apr. 8, 1840. m. Aug. 21, 1879, Dr. Olney W., s. of Alexander S. Phillips and Laura Waterman, of Waitsville, Vt. They live at Bellows Falls, Vt., and have one child: — Olive Draper, 1972. b. Brattleboro, Vt., Jan. 22, 1881.

1907. James. (1729. Joseph, 8. John, 2. James, 1. Thomas.) 5th child, 2d s. of Joseph Draper and Deborah Ellis, m. Apr. 1, 1767, Louise Adams, of Wrentham. She d. Sep. 28, 1818. They are both buried at Dover, Mass.

CHILDREN, B. DOVER, MASS.:

1973. I. Chloe, b. Mar. 15, 1768. d. Aug. 17, 1776,

1974. II. James, b. Nov. 21, 1771. d. Nov. 18, 1789.

1975. III. Mehetable, b. Oct. 18, 1773. d. Sep. 19, 1775.

1976. IV. Lois, b. Oct. 26, 1776. m. her cousin, Jesse Draper, 2007, s. of Joseph, 2001, and Hannah Draper.

1977. V. William, b. Feb. 12, 1780.

9. Moses. (2. James, 1. Thomas.) 6th child, 3d s. of James Draper and Miriam Stansfield. m. 1st: July 7, 1684, Hannah, dau. of John Chandler. She was b. Sep. 9, 1669. d. July 9, 1692. He m. 2dly: Nov. 3, 1692, Mary Thacher, of Boston.

Moses Draper "confessed Jesus Christ" in 1683; was received into full communion and baptized "month 12, day 17;" Hannah, his wife, on "month 1, day 30," 1684, at the First Church, Roxbury. Hannah is buried in the Eustis Street or Eliot Burial Ground at Roxbury. The small gravestone is marked:

"Hannah Draper, ye wife of Moses Draper.
Aged 22 years, 8 Mos. 21 Das.
Dyed June ye 9, 1692."

A grant was made by the Town of Dedham to Moses Draper, near Stony River bridge, by Dedham road, for a blacksmith's shop for him and his successors, for this use and no other. He also had a blacksmith's shop in Boston, and it is generally supposed a small store there also. Mr. Draper died young, and of his children but one lived to grow up, or at least there are no authentic records of any descendants. The following are the official records relative to the settlement of his estate and administration of the same for his children:

Suff. Records, Lib. 13, Fol. 140. (Index Vol. 2.)

Letters of administration granted to Mary Draper, relict, wid. &c. On the estate of her late husband, Moses Draper, late of Boston, county of Suffolk, blacksmith, deceased. Letters granted the 9th day of November, 1693.

Ibid. Fol. 141. Inventory (Index Vol. 2), taken this 22d day of August, 1693, commences with household furniture— "item. One cow £1 15."; then follows shop tools; "One crank at Roxbury, weighing 18 lbs.", is one of the items, &c. &c., making £161, 18, I.

And then follows "An inventory of his estate at Roxbury, taken the 25th day of Oct. 1693."

His dwelling house & barne	£90		
The shop with the land adjoining	10		
The hay in the barne	2	10	
1 pr. bellows £2, 5s. 1 vice 18s	3	3	
1 brass kettle £1, 10s. 1 plough, 8s	1	18	
1 acre of meadow at Beare Marsh	4		
1 acre more at Hollison	2	10	
7 acres of land at Dorchester	3		
His first wife's wearing cloathes & child bed linnen	6	3	
	123	4	
	161	18	1
Approved, Nov. 9th, 1693.	£285	2	1

Lib. 13, Fol. 355, Settlement of acct. Dec. 26, 1695.

Lib. 13, Fol. 323.

Letters of guardianship appointing James Draper (7) to be guardian unto Hannah, the daughter of his brother, Moses Draper (9) of Boston, deceased, "being a minor about 7 years of age." Granted 1st. day of August, 1695.

Lib. 17, Fol. 73.

Roxbury, Moses Draper, son of late Moses Draper (9), blacksmith, being upwards of 16 years, having nominated and appointed my honord. uncle, Joshua Gee of Boston, shipwright, to be my guardian.

June 27th, 1710.

Lib. 21, Fol. 33.

Settlement of acct. of the estate of Moses Draper, late of Boston, deceased, merchant.

Nov. 10th, 1718.
Lib. 18, Fol. 212.

Joseph Grant of Boston, Shipwright, and Samuel Gore, of Roxbury, yeoman, appointed administrators of the estate of Moses Draper, shopkeeper, late of Boston. Granted 19th January, 1714.
Lib. 19, Fol. 22, Index 3d. vol.

Inventory, dated Boston, March 29, 171 5, beginning with 2 doz. combs at 4s., &c. amounting to;^24 17 6.

Appraisers:

John Kilby, Seth Dwight,

Then follows an inventory dated Roxbury, ____, 1715, of the real estate of Moses Draper, late of Roxbury.

Housing & lambs in Roxbury, one dwelling house, one out house, one smith's shop, adjoining to the dwelling house, five acres of land, being planted out with an orchard, being formerly the land of Jacob Newel, as may appear from a deed from P. Newel to Moses Draper, of Roxbury, deceased. £,^°-

One small piece of land lying upon Meeting House hill, bounded towards the north, "heirs of John Ruggles, late of Rox. deceased," containing 24 feet square, as by deed from Sarah Allen & Wm. Cleaves to said Draper. _;^3.

One acre of fresh meadow, lying in Beases Marsh, as may appear by deed.

One acre of freash meadow lying within the range of lot, known by the name of Morrel's lot, bought of Capt. Timothy Stevens. £^.

Seven acres of land lying in the township of Dorchester, near a place commonly called Mother Brooks, bought of Baraciah Lewis, his part in it. ^^4.

Item. Said Draper's interest & right with his sister's Hannah Gore, in two 19 acre lots, lying in Woodstock, in part of it commonly called the Old Town, half, with the after right his part, £10.

Signed: Edward Bridge, Josiah Holland, Thomas Mory.

Approved, January, 16th, 1715.

CHILDREN, BY 1ST WIFE:

1978. I. Hannah, b. Roxbury, Apr. 8, 1686. m. John Gore.

The Probate Court appointed her uncle, James Draper, 7, her guardian on Aug. 1, 1695, after the death of her parents.

1979. II. Elizabeth, b. Roxbury, 1687. d. Nov. 5, 1687.

1980. III. Elizabeth 2d, b. Roxbury, Nov. 17, 1688. d. Nov. 17, 1688.

CHILDREN, BY 2D WIFE:

1981. IV. Moses, b. Boston, Sep. 12, 1693. Bap. Second Church, Boston, Sep, 17, 1693.

On June 27, 1710, being then 16 years old, he chose his uncle, Joshua Gee, shipwright, of Boston, as his guardian. (He is supposed to have m. Mary Allen or Aldis, of Boston, Nov. 26, 1743.This is not at all authentic, and there are no traces of any descendants.)

10. Daniel. (2. James, 1. Thomas.) 7th child, 4th s. of James Draper and Miriam Stansfield. m. Nov. 16, 1691, Elizabeth Brackett.

CHILDREN, B. ROXBURY:

1982. I. Elizabeth, b. Sep. 9, 1692. d. Sep. 12, 1692.

1983. II. Daniel, b. Nov. 6, 1695. d. Sep. 17, 1703.

1984. III. Mary, b. Nov. 5, 1698. d. Oct. 25, 1775. m. Apr. 4, 1722, by Rev. Jacob Belcher, Captain Hezekiah Allen, s. of Joseph Allen and Hannah Sabin, of Dover. He was b. 1692. d. Aug. 16, 1775. Both are buried in Dover, Mass. They lived first in Medfield, moved from there to Weston, and finally settled in Dover. Children: — I. Hezekiah, 1990. b. Apr. 15, 1724. II. Mary, 199 1. b. July 2, 1727. III. Timothy, 1992. b. Aug. 31, 1729. d. Nov*-. 23, 1736. IV, Elizabeth, 1993. b. Aug. 7, 1731. V, Hannah, 1994, b. Nov. 21, 1733. VI. Mehetable, 1995. b. Apr. 30, 1736. VII. Abigail, 1996. b. Mar. 22, 1742.

1985. IV. Miriam, b. July 16, 1701. d. same day.

1986. V. Mehetable, b. June 19, 1705.

1987. VI. Daniel 2d, b. Nov. 3, 1707. d. Feb. 2, 1764.

1988. VII. Timothy, b. Apr. 12, 171 1. d. Feb. 10, 1774.

1989. VIII. Elizabeth 2d, b. 17 — . d. Sep, 15, 1728.

1983. Daniel 2D. (10. Daniel, 2. James, 1. Thomas.) 2d s., 6th child of Daniel Draper and Elizabeth Brackett. m. Rachel, dau. of Jabez and Mary Pond, of Dedham. She was b. "Feb. ye i," 1709-10. d. 1764.

CHILDREN:

1997. I. Daniel, b. Sep. 18, 1730. d. Feb. 2, 1764. m. Sarah. Child: — Rachel, 2006. b. Jan. 15, 1764.

1998. II. Mary b. July 19, 1732. d. Sep. 21, 1741.

1999. III. Eliphalet, b. Feb. 10, 1735. d. Aug. 31, 1741.

2000. IV. Abigail, b. July 1, 1737. m. Mar. 1, 1763, by Rev. Benjamin Caryl, Dr. Alexander Shepherd, of Newtown.

2001. V. Joseph, b. Mar. 2, 1740.

2002. VI. Eliphalet 2d, b. Jan. 12, 1742. d. Jan. 1, 1744.

2003. VII. Mary 2d, b. Sep. 26, 1744. m. May 19, 1767, Benjamin Fairbanks, of Dedham.

2004. VIII. Elizabeth, b. Jan. 16, 1747. — ^^., P\ JWt^'1^JuL(/\J

2005. IX. Catherine, b. Nov. 14, 1751.

2001. Joseph. (1983. Daniel, 10. Daniel, 2. James, 1. Thomas.) 5th child, 3d s. of Daniel Draper and Rachel Pond. m. 1st: by Rev. Andrew Tyler, Sep. 29, 176S, Hannah Whiting. She was b. 1736. d. Oct. 23, 1776. He m. 2dly: Mary Robbins.

CHILDREN, BY 1st WIFE:

2007. I. Jesse, b. Dedham, Feb. 26, 1771. d. Dover, July 31, 1833.

2008. II. Joseph, b. Feb. 12, 1773. d. in infancy.

2009. III. Eliphalet, b. Dec. 28, 1774. d. Jan. 1, 1775.

2010. IV. Daniel, b. Dec. 2, 1775. d. Dec. 5, 1775.

CHILDREN, BY 2D WIFE:

2011. V, Joseph 2d, b. Sep. 11, 1780. d. Nov. 7, 1833.

2012. VI. Hannah, b, Oct. 20, 1781. d. July 27, 1783.

2013. VII. Polly, b. Oct. 6, 1782. d. Nov. 22, 1862. m. 1st: by Rev. Jason Haven, Apr. 16, 1804, Asa, s. of Asa Hamant and Peinanah Clark, of Medfield, Mass. He was b. 1763. d. Dec. 29, 1843. Children: — I. Hannah, 2020. b. Feb. 12, 1805. d. June 20, 1864. m. 1845, John A. Gould, of Walpole. (One child, 2026. b. Mar. 17, 1847, m. 1864, L. Albert Guild, of Norwood.) II. Emmeline, 2021. b. Apr. 29, 1807. d. June 14, 1811. III. Polly Draper, 2022. b. July 22, 1810. m. 1832, Daniel P. Russell. (They had:— I. Abigail, 2027. b. Aug. 13, 1834. m. 1883, John Clark, of Medway. II. Charles H., 2028. b. 1836. m. 1874, Rhoda Clark, of Medway. III. Walter G., 2029. b. 1843. m. 1866, Catherine Bruce, of Medfield.) IV. Charles, 2023. b. Nov. 23, 1812. m. 1st: Mary Bosworth, 1841. (Child: — Mary B., 2030. b. May 23, 1843. m. 1863, Willard Harwood.) She d. 1844, and he m. 2dly: Harriet S. Hunt, of Medway. (Child:— Alice E., b. 1850. m. 1885, Henry W. Austin.) V. Daniel Draper, 2024. b. Sep. 9, 1815. d. 1887. m. Cynthia Harding, 1841. (They had:— George Draper, 2031. b. 1842. m. 1869, Jennie A. Estey, of Canton. Marietta, b. 1843. d. Sep. 10, 1853.) VI. Lydia Adams, 2025. b. June 29, 1817. m. 1841, Wm. D. Rowe, of Boston. He d. Mar., 1884. (Child:— Mary Adelaide, 2032. b. Mar. 29, 1843. m. May 3, 1864, Wm. Marshall, of Boston. Children:— I. Willie R., 2033. b. Mar. 4, 1865. II. Henry E., 2034. b. July 12, 1872.) Polly (Draper) Hamant m. 2dly: John Clark, of Medway.

2014. VIII. Hannah 2d, b. Jan. 19, 1784. m. David, s. of John Smith and Jemima Pales, Apr. 28, 1809. He was b. 1768. d. 1857. (No issue.)

2015. IX. Rebecca, b. Feb. 19, 1787. m. John Woods, of Ashburnham, Mass., 1831. She d. Medfield, Mass., Dec. 25, 1870. (No issue.)

2016. X. Daniel, b. Nov. 20. 1788. d. June 1, 1867.

2017. XI. George, b. Dec. 28, 1792. d. Jan. 4, 1851.

2018. XII. Dolly, b. Jan. 1, 1794. d. W. Dedham, June 1, 1826.

She was an invalid and never married. Was considered the genius of the family, as she wrote poetry and painted.

2019. XIII. Catherine, b. Sep. 18, 1800. d. Medway, May 31, 1861. m. June 20, 1818, Horace, s. of Joseph and Anna Richardson, of Medfield, and grandson of Dr. Abijah Richardson, who served as surgeon all through the war of the Revolution, and was very noted in his profession until his death. Horace Richardson d. Millis, Dec. 25, 1856. Children: — I. George Draper Joseph, 2035. m. Sylvia Bullen. II. Horace Robbins, 2036. m. Hannah Daniels. III. Emma Catherine, 2037. m. Elbridge T. Prentiss, of Chicago, Sep. 12, 1867. He d. Aug. 12, 1876. (No children.)

2007. Jesse. (2001. Joseph, 1983. Daniel, 10. Daniel, 2. James, 1. Thomas.) Eldest s. and child of Joseph Draper and his 1st wife, Hannah Whiting, m. by Rev. Benjamin Caryl, Mar. 25, 1797, Lois, 1976, dau. of James Draper, 1907, and Deborah Ellis, of Dover, his cousin.

He moved to Southboro, where he was a Justice of the Peace. After his death, his wife and children went to Dorchester to live.

CHILDREN, B. DOVER, MASS.:

2038. I. James, b. May 3, 1798. m. Lucy Dana. Children: — I. Lucius D., 2048. II. James, 2049. III. William, 2050. IV. Lucy Anna, 2051.

2039. III. Caroline, b. Apr. 21, 1800.

2040. IV. Jesse, b. Aug. 20, 1802.

2041. V. Joseph, b. 1804. m. Maria Houghton. Children: — I. Albert F.,

2052. II. Lois M., 2053. III. Jesse L., 2054.

2042. V. William, b. May 8, 1806. m. Anna Morrison. Child: — Caroline, 2055.

2043. VI. Lucinda, b. July 13, 1808. m. Nathanial Dunbar. (No issue.)

2044. VII. Francis & 2045. VIII. Frances Ann (Twins), b. Jan. 28, 1811.

Francis m. Sarah Simmons. Children: — I. Frank, 2056. II, Harry, 2057. III. Frances Ann, 2058.

Frances Ann m., Aug. 21, 1838, Nathanial Dunbar, of Canton, Mass., her sister Lucinda's widower. Children: — I. Frank, 2059. II. William, 2060. III. Anna, 2061. IV. Louisa, 2062.

2046. IX. Hannah Smith, b. Aug. 17, 1813. m. William Plimpton, of Walpole. Child: — William, 2063.

2047. X. Daniel Adams, b. Sep. 23, 1818.

2040. Jesse. (2007. Jesse, 2001. Joseph, 1983. Daniel, 10. Daniel, 2. James, 1. Thomas.) 3d child, 2d s. of Jesse Draper and Lois Draper, m. Mary Herrick, of Brighton, Mass.

CHILDREN, B. BRIGHTON, MASS.:

2064. I. Charles Henry, m. Abby Adams, of Bangor, Mass. Children: — I. Charles Henry, 2067. b. E. Cambridge, Mass., May 23, 1851. m. Louise Halliwell Smith. She was b. Edgewater, N. J., Aug. 29, 1852. (Children, b. Brooklyn, N. Y.: — I. Edith Louise, 2069. b. Feb. 19, 1874. II. Stuart Winship, 2070. b. Aug. 16, 1877. III. Jennie Christina, 2071. b. Nov. 1, 1883. IV. Alice Adams, 2072. b. Sep. 28, 1885.) II. George Edward, 2068. b. E. Cambridge, Oct. 30, 1852.

2065. II. George Francis.

2066. III. Emma Amanda.

2011. Joseph 2D. (2001. Joseph, 1983. Daniel, 10. Daniel, 2. James, 1. Thomas.) Eldest s. and child of Joseph Draper and his 2d wife, Mary Robbins. m. Nov. 12, 1826, Amy, dau. of Silas Bullard and his 2d wife, Thankful Adams. She was b. Dedham, Nov. 30, 1792. d. Aug. 20, 1859.

CHILDREN:

2073. I Mary Robbins, b. July 28, 1828.

2074. II. Joseph, b. Oct. 14, 1831. d. Jan. 16, 1881.

2016. Daniel. (2001. Joseph, 1983. Daniel, 10. Daniel, 2. James, 1. Thomas.) 5th child, 2d s. of Joseph Draper and Mary Robbins. m. 1st: — Sep. 18, 1817,

Medfield, Mass., Hannah, dau. of Isaiah Smith and Sally Clark. She was b. Medfield, Jan. 26, 1793. d. there May 11, 1825. He m. 2dly: Mar. 1, 1826, Nancy, dau. of Warner Clafflin and Nancy Pond. She was b. Roxbury, Mass., Sep. 1, 1803. d. Boston, Dec. 11, 1878.

Daniel Draper, formerly a merchant in Boston, Mass., early in life was very poor, but by perseverance and industry accumulated a fortune. He became a dealer in cattle, and afterwards formed the firm of Draper & Hudson, dealers in West India fruits and Mediterranean products; later the firm of Daniel Draper & Sons, who were the largest shipowners and merchants in Mediterranean and South American products in Boston, and also ice merchants. He was one of the founders of the Boston Ice Company. Mr. Draper died at the age of 78 years. He was a strong Democrat, but never aspired for or held any political office.

The following is an editorial notice in the "Boston Post" of June 3, 1867:—

"The death of Mr. Daniel Draper was announced in the evening papers on Saturday. He died at his late residence in this city, the morning of that day, at the advanced age of 78 years and 6 months. Mr. Draper was distinguished for enterprise and sagacity as a business man, and accumulated a very large fortune. He was remarkable for his self-reliance and freedom of thought, expression and action. As a citizen he was faithful to all his obligations, in his friendships constant, and in every domestic relation affectionate and indulgent. Among our oldest and most successful merchants he will be remembered as a striking example of what intelligent and constant labor is capable of accomplishing, and as a citizen, friend and relative, as one whose long life has been crowned with respect and tender regard."

CHILDREN, BY 1st WIFE:

2075. I. Daniel Robbins, b. Boston, Aug. 6, 1818. d. Brighton, Mass., Mar. 19, 1822.

2076. II. David Smith, b. Boston, Apr. 15, 1820. d. New York, Apr. 3, 1885.

2077. III. Mary Robbins, b. Brighton, Mass., Mar. 5, 1822. m. at Purchase St. Church, Boston, Dec. 22, 1846, Adolphus, s. of Abner Davis and Nancy Cobb, of Barnstable, Mass. Mr. Davis was b. Barnstable, Mass., Mar. 23, 1810. d. Arlington, Mass., Nov. 2, 1885. Children: — I. Daniel Abner, 2086. b. Boston, Sep. 22, 1847. m. New York, June 1, 1882, Minnie Estelle, dau. of Dr. Frank Hastings Hamilton and Mary Gertrude Hart. She was b. Buffalo, N. Y., June 7, 1855. He came to New York in 1868, and 5 years later became a member of the firm of Converse, Stanton & Davis, until 1886. Then he became a partner in the present firm of Deering, Milliken & Co. (Child: — Frank Hamilton, 2089. b. New York, Dec. 6, 1883.) II. Mary Eliza, 2087. b. Boston, Sep. 14, 1850. m. Arlington, Mass., Sep. 17, 1873, John Edward, Jr., s. of John Edward Devlin and Martha Josephine Day. (Children: — I. Marjorie Standish, 2090. b. Arlington, June 13, 1874. II. John Edward, 2091. b. Wilton, N. H., July 24, 1876.) III. Julia Draper, 2088. b. Boston, Dec. 5, 1852. m. New York, Mar. 27, 1878, Frank Hall, s. of William Clement Scott and Maria Frances Crawford. He was b. Terre Haute, Ind., Apr. 7, 1848. (Children: — I. Donald, 2092. b. New York, June 4, 1879. II. Clement, 2093. b. New York, Nov. 16, 1880.)

2078. IV. Daniel Augustus, b. Brighton, Mass., Feb. 2, 1825. d. there July 9, 1825.

CHILDREN, BY 2D WIFE, B. BOSTON, MASS.:

2079. V. Julia Eliza Clafflin, b. Nov. 21, 1826. d. Apr. 30, 1849.

2080. VI. Daniel Draper, Jr., b. Mar. 2, 1829. d. Apr. 7, 1840.

2081. VII. William Perkins, b. Jan. 28, 1831.

2082. VIII. Noel Byron, b. Jan. 13, 1833. d. May 13, 1833.

2083. IX. Ada Augusta Byron, b. May 8, 1835. d. Florence, Italy, Apr. 9, 1888.

2084. X. George, b. Sep. 15, 1837. d. New York, Apr. 4, 1891.

He graduated at Harvard College, and was a member of the firm of Daniel Draper & Sons. Retired from business about 1869.

2085. XI. Warner Clafflin, b. May 7, 1839. d. Philadelphia, Nov. 14, 1864.

2076. David Smith. (2016. Daniel, 2001. Joseph, 1983. Daniel, 10. Daniel, 2. James, 1. Thomas.) 2d child and s. of Daniel Draper and his 1st wife, Hannah Smith, m. New York, Apr. 15, 1851, Jane Beekman Thompson.

He came to New York when a young man; was a clerk for some time, and then formed the firm of Draper & Devlin, shipowners and merchants in Mediterranean products. He retired about 1862, and went to Great Barrington, Mass., to live. He returned from there, however, several years later, and settled in New York City. He was Vice-President of the Housatonic R.R. at his death.

CHILDREN:

2094. I. Jenny Thompson, b. Brooklyn, N. Y., Feb. 20, 1852.

2095. II. Frank, b. Marseilles, France, Oct. 14, 1854. d. same clay.

2096. III. David Smith, Jr., b. Brooklyn, N. Y., Jan. 5, 1858.

2097. IV. Charlotte Sherwell, b. Brooklyn, N. Y., May 29, 1861.

2081. William Perkins. (2016. Daniel, 2001. Joseph, 1983. Daniel, 10. Daniel, 2. James, 1. Thomas.) 3d child, 2d s. of Daniel Draper and his 2d wife, Nancy Clafflin. m. S. Boston, Mass., June 2, 1857, Helen M., dau. of Hall Jackson How and Eliza Parsons Waldron.

He was formerly with the firm of Daniel Draper & Sons, and retired from business about 1869.

CHILDREN:

2098. I. A child. 2099. II. Nellie. 2100. III. Ada A.

2101. IV. William Perkins, Jr.

2085. Warner Clafflin. (2016. Daniel, 2001. Joseph, 1983. Daniel, 10. Daniel, 2. James, 1. Thomas.) 7th child, 5th s. of Daniel Draper and his 2d wife, Nancy Clafflin. m. June 5, 1862, Charlotte Hyde, dau. of Col. Andrew Reeder Chambers and Sarah Ann Hyde, of Philadelphia. She was b. Philadelphia, Dec. 10, 1844.

Mr. Draper went to Philadelphia when quite a young man, and was a merchant in Mediterranean products.

Child: 2102. I. Sally Clafflin, b. Philadelphia, Pa., Feb. 18, 1863. m. Philadelphia, Apr. 15, 1884, Herman Adelbert, s. of George Albert Lewis and Ann Cornelia Larcombe, of Philadelphia. He was b. Philadelphia, Nov. 1, 1856. They have: — I. Barbara Carter, 2103. b. Germantown, Pa., July 31, 1885. II. Margaret Charlotte, 2104. b. Germantown, Pa., Nov. 18, 1886. III. George Draper, 2105. b. Germantown, Pa., Sep. 5, 1888.

2017. George. (2001. Joseph, 1983. Daniel, 10. Daniel, 2. James, 1. Thomas.) 7th child, 3d s. of Joseph Draper and Mary Robbins. m. Polly, dau. of Jonathan Metcalf and Mary Adams, of Franklin, Nov. 26, 1820. She was b. 1793. d. 1846. He m. 2dly: June 1, 1850, Mrs. Cordelia (Merrifield) Colburn, the widow of James Perrin Colburn. She was b. Dover, Me., Apr. 28, 1825, and was the dau. of William Merrifield and Louise Thayer.

CHILDREN, BY 1ST WIFE:

2106. I. Horace, b. W. Dedham, Nov. 8, 1821.

2107. II. Jonathan M., b. June 5, 1824. d. Aug. 31, 1891.

2108. III. Caroline Adams, b. Sep. 6, 1827. d. Oct. 22, 1831.

2109. IV. George, Jr., b. May 27, 1833. d. Quincy, Mass., June 3, 1891.

2110. V. Albert, b. W. Dedham, Mar. 20, 1836.

CHILD, BY 2D WIFE:

2112. VI. Caroline Adams 2d, b. W. Dedham, Nov. ri, 1851.

2106. Horace. (2017. George, 2001. Joseph, 1983. Daniel, 10. Daniel, 2. James, 1. Thomas.) Eldest s. and child of George Draper and Polly Metcalf. m. May 13, 1847, Eliza, dau. of Joseph Ellis and Polly Willett, of Walpole, Mass. She was b. July 20, 1823.

CHILD:

2113. I. Marion Ellis, b. W. Dedham, Feb. 22, 1848. m. Boston, June 30, 1870, Howard Appleton, s. of Isaac Henderson Pickering and Sarah Ann Goodrich, of Portsmouth, N. H. He was b. Aug. 30, 1839. They have: — I. Eva Draper, 2114. b. Boston, May 10, 1871. II. Joseph Appleton, 211 5. b. Walpole, Apr. 26, 1878.

2107. Jonathan M. (2017. George, 2001. Joseph, 1983. Daniel, 10. Daniel, 2. James, 1. Thomas.) 2d s. and child of George Draper and Polly Metcalf. m. Jan. 1, 1851, Louisa Lovett, dau. of Jonathan Bowditch. She was b. Boston, Aug. 14, 1834. d. Mar. 14, 1886.

CHILDREN:

2116. I. George Eugene, b. Chelsea, Mass., Jan. 8, 1852.

2117. II. Charles Granville, b. Boston, Oct. 27, 1854. d. Feb. 20, 1873.

2118. III. Alice Louise, b. Dedham, Dec. 23, 1864. m. Feb. 28, 18S9, Arthur Stockin. He was b. Berwick, Me., Apr. 19, 1864.

2119. IV. Lucy Isabel, b. Quincy, Mass., Oct. 2, 1867. m. Mar. 31, 1890, Charles Clark Perkins. He was b. Charlestown, Mass., Aug., 1867. Child: — Ruth Isabel, 2120. b. Charlestown, Mass., Mar. 17, 1891.

2116. George Eugene. (2107. Jonathan M., 2017. George, 2001. Joseph, 1983. Daniel, 10. Daniel, 2. James, 1. Thomas.) Eldest child and s. of Jonathan M. Draper and Louisa Lovett Bowditch. m. 1st: Aug. 26, 1878, Nancy Symmes Richardson, of Charlestown, Mass. She was b. Charlestown, 1858. d. Oct., 1887. He m. 2dly: Boston, Jan. 8, 1890, Sarah Abbie Stiles. She was b. Buxton, Me., Nov. 17, 1853.

CHILDREN, BY 1ST WIFE:

2121. I. Clarence Eugene, b. Watertown, Mass. d. in infancy.
2122. II. Ethel Gertrude, b. Watertown, Mass., June 16, 1881.
2123. III. Roy Wellington, b. Roxbury, Mass., Nov. 4, 1886.

2109. George. (2017. George, 2001. Joseph, 1983. Daniel, 10. Daniel, 2. James, 1. Thomas.) 4th child, 3d s. of George Draper and Polly Metcalf. m. Mary Emma. dau. of George Washington Nash and Jane Patten, of Cambridge, Mass. She was b. Addison, Me., Feb. 12, 1837.

CHILDREN:

2124. I. Jenny, b. Boston, Dec. 18, 1861. d. same day.
2125. II. Jane Frances, b. Boston, Dec. 17, 1862.
2126. III. Horace Gilbert, b. Dedham, Jan. 23, 1864. d. Sep. 14, 1864.
2127. IV. Elizabeth, b. Dedham, Aug. 9, 1868. d. Oct. 4, 1870.
2128. V. Nancy Metcalf, b. Dedham, May 6, 1871. d. Aug. 19, 1872.
2129. VI. William Hill, b. Dedham, July 27, 1873.

2110. Albert. (2017. George, 2001. Joseph, 1983. Daniel, 10. Daniel, 2. James, 1. Thomas.) 5th child, 4th s. of George Draper and his 1st wife, Polly Metcalf. m. Nov. 2, 1858, Maria Ann Elizabeth, dau. of Thomas Charles Farrington and Ann Matilda Glass, of Nassau, N. P., West Indies. She was b. Gt. Cayman, West Indies, May 1, 1836.

CHILDREN:

2130. I. Lida Thomasine, b. Nassau, N. P., West Indies, Aug. 17, 1859.
2131. II. Albert Lewis, b. Boston, Mass., Feb. 1, 1862.
2132. III. Edward Farrington, b. Boston, Mass., Oct. 8, 1864.
2133. IV. Caroline, b. Boston, Mass., May 21, 1866.

1988. Timothy. (10. Daniel, 2. James, 1. Thomas.) 7th child, 3d s. of Daniel Draper and Elizabeth Brackett. m. Hannah, . She d. May 16, 1783.

He and his brother Daniel (1987) were admitted to membership in the Clapboard Tree Parish, Dedham, July 5, 1738. He was a private in Capt. Joseph Richards' Company of Militia, of which Daniel Draper (1987) was 1st Lieut. This company was raised in 1754, with a full complement of officers and 97 privates, amongst whom were eight Drapers. The company was formed to protect the settlement from the Indians.

CHILDREN, B. W. DEDHAM:

2134, I. Hannah, b. Feb. 25, 1733. d. Sep. 25, 1741,

2135. II. Timothy, b. June 15, 1735. d. Dec. 27, 1795.

He served in the Revolutionary War, for we find that on Nov. 5, 1777, he and Joseph Draper (2001) were each paid £6 for services in the war up to that date. We also find that he was a Sergeant in the 2d Company of Clapboard Tree Parish, and that Joseph Draper (2001) was a private. It is not known if Timothy Draper ever married, and he, presumably did not do so.

2136. III. Abigail, b. June 9, 1737. d. Sep. 21, 1741.

2137. IV. Stephen, b. Mar. 14, 1739.

2138. V. Jacob, b. June 21, 1740.

2139. VI. Hannah 2d, b. Nov. 3, 1742. d. Oct. 2, 1754.

2140. VII. Mercy, b. Apr. 4, 1745. d. Oct. 1, 1754.

2141. VIII. Abigail 2d, b. Apr. 13, 1747. d. Sep. 28, 1754.

2142. IX. Aaron, b. Feb. 1, 1751.

(There is a strong probability that this Aaron went to New Hampshire, and that he there m. 1st:Miss Metcalf; 2dly: Miss Heath. Reference is made to the descendants of Aaron Draper (2142) appended to this branch of the family.)

2143. X. Moses, b. Jan. 3, 1754. d. Sep. 18, 1754.

2144. XI. Ichabod, b. Aug. 24, 1757. d. Dec, 1827.

In the Continental Records we find the following in the return made of "Bounty" due for a detachment drafted to do duty as guards at Cambridge, commanded by Col. Jonathan Reed, by order of the General Court, in the service of the United States: — "Ichabod Draper — Sergeant. Time from Apr. 1, 1778, 'Bounty' £2. per month. Service, 3 months. Discharged, July 2. Total Bounty, £6. 2. 8." We find further that this same Sergeant Ichabod did further service of the same kind, under Col. Jacob Garrish, from "Aug. 1, to Sep. 12, 1778. Bounty, £22. Captain Nathanial Heath's Company." In a further return of the number of men drafted from the companies of Capts. Gore, Mayo, White and May, under the command of Lieut. Morton, to go to Nantasket to drive the ships out of the harbor, June — , 1776, we find that Ichabod Draper was one of the privates drafted — "3 days service; march — 20 miles." We find further that Ichabod graduated from Harvard University in 1783. He was the first minister of the Second Church at Amhurst, Mass.; ordained Jan., 1785; resigned Oct., 1809. He remained in Amhurst and d. there.

2145. XII. Philip, b. Mar. 2, 1757. d. Mar. 21, 1817. m. Mehitable, dau. of Jeremiah Kingsbury and Abigail Fisher, of Dedham. She was b. 1757. Mr. Draper received his M. D. from Harvard University in 1780, and was a practising physician in the South Parish of Dedham until his death. Children: — I. Jeremiah, 2146. b. Apr. 18, 1789. d. Dedham, Sep. 29, 1840. m. Sabrina Waite, of Montreal. He was a farmer, although he graduated from Harvard University, Class of 1808. II. Moses, 2147. b. Jan. 5, 1791. m. his brother Jeremiah's, 2146, widow.

He graduated from Harvard, Class of 1808. He was a practising lawyer in Boston, and resided in Dorchester. Had one son, John W., 2148. Was President of the Metropolitan Horse R.R. Co. in Boston, in 1872.

(Probably correct.)

2142. Aaron. (1988. Timothy, 10. Daniel, 2. James, 1. Thomas.) 9th child, 4th s. of Timothy and Hannah Draper, m. 1st: Miss Metcalf; 2dly: Miss Heath.

He was bound out to the cabinet makers' trade in Vermont. He was a self-made man entirely, and fought all through the Revolutionary War, although he never enlisted, being in a number of engagements. The family had for a long time in their possession an old powder-horn, with a wax end wound around the neck near the stopper, where a bullet struck it, taking out the stopper of the horn, which had belonged and was carried by Aaron Draper. During the War of 1812 and 1814, when the British forces attempted to capture Sackett's Harbor, N. Y., he, hearing the guns booming at Fort Tomkins, mounted his sorrel mare and started for the scene of action, 14 miles distant. When within four miles of there he met Gen. Allen, bareheaded, swinging his sword over his head, and saying that Sackett's Harbor had been taken. He told Aaron to hurry back and notify Adams to get the people out. Aaron's reply was: "Let us get a shot at the Britishers first!" Gen. Allen rode on himself to Adams, and Aaron Draper rode to the harbor, and was in time to see the British take to their boats and start for their ships, as badly frightened, perhaps, as Gen. Allen. Aaron fired a few shots after the boats and then went home again. An anecdote is told about him as follows: — He, with 15 others, fitted out a schooner, and, arming it as best they could, went privateering. During the Revolution they fell in with a British brig, a man-of-war, which attacked them, and they had quite a fight. The two vessels closed, the schooner throwing grappling-irons aboard the brig; then, when the schooner was in a sinking condition, her men boarded the enemy and captured her, casting their vessel adrift, which shortly sank out of sight.

Aaron Draper moved from Vermont about 1814, and settled in Ellisburgh, Jefferson Co., N. Y., buying and clearing up a farm near Adams. Mr. Draper was a strict temperance man, never using tobacco. He belonged to the Baptist Church, and is buried in the country cemetery, near Adams, N. Y.

CHILDREN:

2149. I. Betsy, b. Brattleboro, Vt. m. 1st: ___ ___. (She had a dau., 2152, who m. Josiah Standish.) On her husband's death, she m. 2dly: James Templeton. Child: — I. Sarah, 2152½. m. Marshall Clark. (They have: — I. Lovina, 2153. m. Alonzo Scott. II. Eliza, 2154. m. Mr. Graves. III. Aaron, 2155. m.)

2150. II. Samuel Heath, b. Brattleboro, Vt., Mar. 15, 1802. d. Jan. 28, 1882.

2151. III. Aaron, d. young, aged 20.

2150. Samuel Heath. (2142. Aaron, 1988. Timothy, 10. Daniel, 2. James, 1. Thomas.) 2d child, eldest s. of Aaron Draper and Heath, m. Harriet Smith. She was b. Bristol, R. I., Aug. 8, 1804. d. Jan. 6, 1883.

Mr. Draper worked on the farm with his father, and helped to pay for it. He taught school during the Winters, and also taught singing school and lead the choir in the Baptist Church at Lorraine, Jefferson Co., N. Y. His wife's (Harriet Smith) family date back to Sir William Compton, of England, a nephew of whom, with the same name, came to America, and married a sister of Benjamin Franklin. Mr. Draper carried despatches during the War of 1812-14, although but a lad. Later, he belonged to the State Militia, and was Commissary Sergeant to his regiment. He lived and died on the old farm now in the possession of his son. He was his own cooper, house and barn builder, agricultural implement maker, wagon and buggy maker, farmer, shoemaker, tailor, and built a small factory wherein he manufactured brown earthenware. He was also a well-educated man; originally a Whig in politics, and then a Republican, as is the whole family.

CHILDREN:

2156. I. William Henry, b. Dec. 30, 1829. m. 1857, Almeda M. Macomber, of Evans Mills, Jefferson Co., N. Y., and niece of Judge Macomber, of Jefferson Co., N. Y. Child: — Mary, 2161. m. D. Randall (had one child, a son, 2162).

Mr. Draper enlisted as Artificer in Battery C, 6th N. Y. Lt. Artillery. Served three years in the Civil War. Was at Gettysburg and other engagements. He lives on the old homestead.

2157. II. Hannah Richmond, b. July 28, 1835. d. Aug. 30, 1869. m. Geo. T. Pomeroy, of Milwaukee.

Mr. Pomeroy enlisted in the 186th Regt., N. Y. V. I. Was shot through the right eye at the taking of Petersburg, Va.

2158. III. Edward Compton, b. Mar. 5, 1837.

2159. IV. John Smith, b. Ellisburg, Jefferson Co., N. Y., June 14, 1840. m. Aug. 16, 1864, Charlotte A. Potter, of Watertown, N. Y. She d. Oakland, Cal., Oct. 22, 1890. Children: — I. Hattie E., 2163. b. Boonsboro, Iowa, 1868. m. Oakland, Cal., Feb. 18, 1889, Willard S. Woodruff. II. Frederick, 2164. b. Mendota, Ill., 1871. d. Oskaloosa, Iowa, aged 10 months. III. Mabel L., 2165. b. Chicago, Ill., Mar., 1876.

Mr. Draper was educated in the common schools, academy and college and engaged in commercial life in 1862 as a druggist, which business he conducted for over a quarter of a century in various places. While thus engaged at Boone, Ia., he wrote the book entitled, "Shams, or Uncle Ben's Experience with Hypocrites," which has had a large sale throughout the country. From that year, 1887, Mr. Draper has been connected with the publishing business. He is now one of the incorporators and Secretary and Treasurer of the Wheeler & Wheeler Publishing Co., of San Francisco., Cal.

2160. V. Jane, b. May 15, 1845. d. in infancy.

2158. Edward Compton. (2150. Samuel Heath, 2142. Aaron, 1988. Timothy, 10. Daniel, 2. James, 1. Thomas.) 3d child, 2d s. of Samuel Heath Draper and Harriet Smith, m. 1st: Feb. 25, 1863, Ophelia Ann Harville, of Clifton, Monro Co., Wis. She was b. Chestnut Hills, N. H., June 24, 1842. d. Gouverneur,

N. Y., Nov. 9, 1864. He m. 2dly: Sep. 5, 1871, in Chicago, Hulda Tarborg Marie Louise, dau. of Count Hjalmar Hammarsljold and Emily Holmberg (both famous singers), of Stockholm, Sweden. She was b. Charleston, S. C., Jan. 7, 1852.

Mr. Draper attended school until he was 17, and then apprenticed himself to the watchmaker's trade in Watertown, N. Y. He enlisted, May 7, 1861, in Company G, 35th Regt., N. Y. Volunteers. He went to Washington and assisted in building Fort Tillinghast about the time of the first battle of Bull Run. Becoming sick, he was discharged for disability. In the Spring of 1862, having recruited his health, he helped to raise the 93d Regt., N. Y. Volunteers. Before the Civil War he was a member of the Company A, 36th N. Y. S. M., and taught school in 1858, 1859 and 1860. He has been in the jewelry and watchmaking business in several parts of the country, Chicago, St. Louis, and so forth. He has also been in the drug, grocery and organ manufacturing trades. He has invented several useful things in connection with reed organs.

CHILD, BY 1ST WIFE:

2166. I. Isabel Ophelia, b. June 24, 1864.

CHILDREN, BY 2D WIFE:

2167. II. Birdie May, b. Cedar Rapids, Ia., May 1, 1873.

2168. III. Edwin H., b. Cedar Rapids, Ia., Feb. 3, 1876.

2169. IV. Frederick Compton, b. Chicago, Ill., Jan, 25, 1887. d. Chicago, May 25, 1896.

12. Jonathan. (2. James, 1. Thomas.) 9th child, 5th s. of James Draper and Miriam Stansfield. m. Sarah Jackson, of Newton, Mass. She was b. Nov. 8, 1680.

Jonathan inherited the old homestead in Roxbury. He was a Captain in the Trained Bands, and lived part of the time in what was then the southern portion of Newton, now a part of W. Roxbury. The old homestead had been owned successively by James (2), Jonathan (12), and was then bought by James Richards, sold to T. O. & S. Woodward. Abijah Draper then bought it, and his son, Dr. Abijah W. Draper, inherited it. It then became the property of D.Arnold and then of H. Russell. Another account of the old property states that James (2) gave a part of his farm to his youngest son, Jonathan (12), some years before his death. The estate has remained in the family until sold by David, a lineal descendant of Jonathan (12), to Dr. Stimson. Dr. Stimson stated to Dr. Abijah W. Draper that David Draper had told him that tradition stated that the house when built was considered equal, if not superior, to anything in the country. He did not say how old, nor by which of his ancestors it was built, but spoke of it as one of the oldest houses in the country. Dr. Abijah W. Draper's impression was that from its construction, the style of the roof, the lift on the rafter to carry the roof over the combing, the projection of the story at the end, the square window no doubt lead originally, and the sill, and many other things, all gave it an appearance of the greatest antiquity. It appears that it was built, or a part of it, in the time of James (2).

(After careful investigation of the various theories in reference to the original Draper house, a picture of which is contained in this history, the author is inclined to the belief that a part of this house was originally built by James Draper (2), and, as his family increased, it was built on to. A careful examination of the pictures of the building would tend to corroborate this theory. Jonathan's children inherited this house with the part of the farm which was his share, and doubtless always lived there, and his descendants after him.)

In the Suffolk Co. Records, Book 14, p. 356, there is a deed recorded of land from James (2) to his son Jonathan (12) in Roxbury, acknowledged Apr. 12, 1693. This tends to show that the farm, or part of it, was deeded by James (2) to his son a year before his death.

CHILDREN, B. ROXBURY, MASS.:

2170. I. Jonathan, b. Oct. 29, 1703.

2171. II. David, b. Sep. 27, 1706.

2172. III. Thomas, b. Mar. 14, 1709. d. 1769.

2173. IV. Samuel, b. June 14, 1713. d. June 12, 1744.

2174. V. Sarah, b. May 14, 1717. m. by Rev. Mr. Walter, Dec. 8, 1737, Josiah Sumner.

2175. VI. Moses, b. Aug. 11, 1721. d. Jan. 21, 1775.

2172. Thomas. (12. Jonathan, 2. James, 1. Thomas.) 3d s., 3d child of Jonathan Draper and Sarah Jackson, m. 1st: Relief . She d. 1758. Is supposed to have m. 2dly: Reliance.

Thomas Draper (2172) owned 100 acres of land in Newton in 1738. It was this property that he inherited from his father, and which is referred to in the biography of Jonathan (12) as being situated in the southern part of Newton, next the Roxbury line. Thomas sold it to James Richards, who then sold it to T. O. & S. Woodward, and so forth.

CHILDREN, BY 1ST WIFE, B. NEWTON:

2176. 1. Thomas, b. Oct. 30, 1732,

2177. II. John, b. Dec. 17, 1733. m. Apr. 8, 1757, Ann Worllyleek, of Roxbury. Child: — Nannie, 2191, b. Roxbury, Mar. 8, 1761.

2178. III. Aaron, b. Mar. 15, 1735, m. Feb. 21, 1760, by Rev. Andrew Tyler, Mary, dau. of Jonathan and Mary Fisher. She was b. Dec. 19, 1738. Child: — Mary, 2192. b. Roxbury, Jan. 25, 1761.

2179. IV. Sarah, b. Dec. 7, 1736.

2180. V. Moses, b. May 26, 1738. d. same year.

2181. VI. Thomas 2d, b. Dec. 19, 1739. d. same year.

2182. VII. Abigail, b. June 2, 1741. m. Feb. 23, 1762, by Rev. Mr. Walter, Ensign John Baker.

2183. VIII. Phoebe, b. Oct. 27, 1742. d. 1751.

2184. IX. Elizabeth, b. Mar. 26, 1744. m. Feb. 23, 1764, Jacob Robinson.

2185. X. Catherine, b. Nov. 29, 1745.

2186. XI. William, b. June 1, 1747. d. 1748.

2187. XII. Anna, b. July 28, 1749.

2188. XIII. Rebecca, b. Sep. 6, 1750. d. 1751.

2189. XIV. William & 2190. Rebecca (Twins) b. Mar. 7, 1752. William d. 1755.

2175. Moses. (12. Jonathan, 2. James, 1. Thomas.) 6th child, 5th s. of Jonathan Draper and Sarah Jackson, m. Mary Aldis, at the time the widow Allen.

CHILDREN, B. ROXBURY, MASS.:

2193. I. Moses, b. Aug. 26, 1744. d. Feb. 11, 1798.

2194. II. Samuel, b. Oct. 5, 1746. m. Sarah, dau. of Abraham and Mary Hyde, of Brookline, Mass. (No issue.) She d. Washington, N. H., Apr. 24, 1806. He m. 2dly: Nancy Miles, of Stodderd, Sep. 11, 1806. He was called Captain Samuel, and removed to Washington, N. H., prior to 1779.

2195. III. Sarah, b. June 5, 1748. m. ___ Prentiss, of Newton.

2196. IV. Jonathan, b. Dec. 18, 1750. d. Hudson, O., in his 98th year.

2197. V. Nathaniel, b. 175-.

2198. VI. David, b. June, 1762. d. Dedham, Mar. 25, 1842.

2193. Moses. (2175. Moses, 12. Jonathan, 2. James, 1. Thomas.) Eldest s. and child of Moses Draper and Mary Aldis. m. Apr. 21, 1770, Grace Hyde, of Dedham.

He was a Lieutenant in Captain Moses Whiting's 1st Roxbury Company of Minute Men at the Lexington alarm, Apr. 19, 1775, and was with his company when the troops assembled at Roxbury Neck. He commanded the Roxbury Company at the Battle of Bunker Hill, attached to Col. Gardner's Middlesex Regt. He also commanded a company of infantry in the suppression of Shay's Rebellion in the Fall of 1786, and was subsequently elected, in 1788, Colonel of the 1st Suffolk Regt. He kept a tavern in Dedham in 1786.

CHILDREN:

2199. I. Grace, b. Jan., 1771.

2200. II. Moses, b. July 24, 1774.

2201. III. Aaron, b. July 21, 1776. d. Jan. 5, 1802. m. Oct. 16, 1800, Polly Wild. (No issue.) His widow m. Feb. 14, 1807, Thomas Codman. She d. Apr. 9, 1859.

2202. IV. Jonathan.

2203. V. Nathanial.

2204. VI. Nathan.

2205. VII. David.

2200. Moses. (2193. Moses, 2175. Moses, 12. Jonathan, 2. James, 1. Thomas.) Eldest s., 2d child of Col. Moses Draper and Grace Hyde. m. May 11, 1796, Sarah Gurney.

CHILDREN:

2206. 1, Moses, b. May 7, 1797. d. July 26, 1797.

2207. II. Sarah, b. Nov. 25, 1798. d. Feb. 15, 1814.

2208. III. Benjamin Jackson Gurney, b. Aug. 3, 1800. d. Jan., 1862. m. in the First Church, Roxbury, Mass., by Rev. Ebenezer Burgess, May 1, 1825, Hannah Burrill, of Dedham.

2209. IV. David Allen, b. June 13, 1813. d. Jan. 3, 1816.

2203. Nathanial. (2175. Moses, 12. Jonathan, 2. James, 1. Thomas.) 5th child. 4th s. of Moses Draper and Mary Aldis. m. July 3, 178c, Anna Jones.

He moved from Roxbury, Mass., to Washington, N. H., prior to 1783, and resided there on Fason Hill.

CHILDREN, ALL (Except Grace) B. WASHINGTON, N. H.:

2210. I. Grace, b. Roxbury, Mass., Mar. 21, 1782, m. Nov. 15, 1804, Thomas Davis, of Washington, N. H.

2211. II. Anna, b. Jan. 25, 1784.

2212. III. Polly, b. Feb. 12, 1786.

2213. IV. Sally, b. Mar. 24, 1788.

2214. V. Nathanial, b. Dec. 28, 1790.

2215. VI. Samuel, b. Apr. 4, 1793.

2216. VII. Thomas P., b. Mar. 7, 1796.

2217. VIII. Eliza, b. May 5, 1798.

2218. IX. Nathan A., b. Apr. 3, 1802.

2198. David. (2175. Moses, 12. Jonathan, 2. James, 1. Thomas.) 6th child, 5th s. of Moses Draper and Mary Aldis. He went from Roxbury, Mass., to Washington, N. H., and there settled and m. Rebecca, dau. of John Healey, May 17, 1785. They lived on Draper Hill. His wife d. July 10, 1854, aged 88 years.

CHILDREN, ALL B. WASHINGTON, N. H.:

2219. I. Sally, b. Feb. 24, 1786. m. May 23, 1816, by Rev. Joshua Bates, Ebenezer Turner. He d. Aug. 15, 1858. They resided in Dedham, and she d. there Jan. 12, 1858. (No issue.)

2220. II. David A., b. Mar. 27, 1787. d. Nov., 1812.

2221. III. Samuel, b. Mar, 27, 1789. m. June 10, 1811, Hulda Thornton. They went to Illinois.

2222. IV. Ebenezer H., b. Oct. 20, 1791. d. Nov. 29, 1792.

2223. V. Betsy, b. May 1, 1793. m. First Church, Roxbury, Mass., by Rev. Ebenezer Burgess, June 19, 1839, Nathaniel Fisher, of Boston. She d. Sep. 3, 1870. They lived in Northboro, Mass.

2224. VI. Moses, b. Mar. 8, 1798. d. Sep. 14, 1823.

2225. VII. Lucy Sampson, b. Oct. 23, 1799. d. Oct. 4, 1820.

2221. Samuel. (2198. David, 2175. Moses, 12. Jonathan, 2. James, 1. Thomas.) 3d child, 2d s. of David Draper and Rebecca Healey. m. Caroline ____.

CHILDREN:

2226. I. Caroline Matilda, b. May 9, 1812.

2227. II. David Allen, b. Aug. 26, 1813.

2228. III. Samuel Healey, b. June 12, 1815.

2229. IV. Emmeline Melinda, b. Apr. 29, 1817,

2230. V, George Clinton, b. Apr. 21, 1819.

2231. VI. Lucy Sampson, b. Feb., 1821.

2196. Jonathan. (2175. Moses, 12. Jonathan, 2. James, 1. Thomas.) 4th child, 3d s. of Moses Draper and Mary Aldis. m. Silence Copeland. She was b. Apr, 30, 1755. d. Feb., 1804.

He lived in Washington, N. H., prior to 1778, and was a town officer there in that year. He was also an officer in the Continental army.

CHILDREN:

2232. I. Asa, b. Whitehall, May 18, 1789. d. Apr. 2, 1853.

2233. II. Luke, b. Whitehall, Mar. 2, 1791. d. Toledo, O., Oct. 18, 1866.

2234. III. Abel, d. in Michigan.

2235. IV. Samuel.

2236. V. Joel.

2237. VI. Polly, m. Fort Ann, N. Y., Daniel Stone. Both d. there.

2238. VII. Betsy, m. Whitman Vaughn.

2239. VIII. Moses, m. in New York.

2240. IX. Lucy, b. 1768. d. 1842. m. Elisha Chadwick. Children: — I. Elizabeth, 2241. m. Mr. Galer. (Children: — I. Polly, 2248. II. Jane, 2249.) II. Archibald, 2242. m. (Children: — I. Elisha, 2250. II. George, 2251. III. Luther, 2252. m. Children: — I. Alonzo, 2253. II. Sarah, 2254. III. Louise, 2255. IV. Lucy, 2256.) III. Lydia,

2243. m. her cousin. Dr. Lyman C. Draper, 2285. IV. Amelia,

2244. m. William Sutton. (Child:— Helen, 2257.) V. Phcebe,

2245. m. Steven Ranson. (Child: — Antoinette, 2258.) VI. George,

2246. m. (Child:— John Sumner, 2259.) VII. Mary A., 2247. b. Washington, N. Y., 1820. m. Lyman M. Bugbee, in 1840. (Children: — I. Parker Elisha, 2260. II. Lucy, 2261. III. Marietta A., 2262. IV. Eliza, 2263. m. 1st: Mr. Conway. 2dly: Abraham Crissey. Child: — Emma, 2264.)

2232. Asa. (2196. Jonathan, 2175. Moses, 12. Jonathan, 2. James, 1. Thomas.) Eldest s. and child of Jonathan Draper and Silence Copeland. m. Dec. 14, 1820, Margery Burk. She was b. May 25, 1796. d. Nov. 2, 1863.

CHILDREN:

2265. I. Polly, b. Dec. 20, 1821. m. Dec. 12, 1844, Morris Miller.

2266. II. Martin, b. Feb. 21, 1823. d. Aug. 15, 1823.

2267. III. Lydia, b. Apr. 3, 1827. d. May 24, 1891. m. Dec. 12, 1844, Henry E. Benson.

2268. IV. Luther Martin, b. Nov. 6, 1831. d. Feb. 5, 1890.

2269. V. Lucius, b. Jan. 11, 1834. m. Dec. 1, 1853, Mary Ann Richards. Children: — I. Minnie, 2271. II. Nettie, 2272. III. Millie, 2273. IV. Charlie, 2274.

2270, VI. Gilbert Coleman, b. Hudson, O., Mar. 28, 1839. m. Feb. 10, 1863, Sarah Angela Miller. Children: — Two who d. in infancy. Frank Burk, 2275, b. Aug. 23, 1868.

Mr. Gilbert C. Draper came to Michigan in 1855. Joined Michigan Conference of the M. E. Church in 1866. Served in regular pastorate until Feb., 1890, when transferred to the Austin Conference in Texas, and appointed Presiding Elder of the Fort Worth District, where he traveled over 10,000 miles in the discharge of his duties. He subsequently resigned and returned to Michigan.

2268. Luther Martin. (2232. Asa, 2196. Jonathan, 2175. Moses, 12. Jonathan, 2. James, 1. Thomas.) 2d s., 4th child of Asa Draper and Margery Burk. m. Nov. 25, 1852, Catherine Vashti Richards.

CHILDREN:

2276. I. Frank W., b. Sep. 18, 1853. d. Sep. 26, 1856.

2277. II. Fred B., b. Apr. 2, 1855. d. Mar. 22, 1883. m. Feb. 22, 1881, Alice Flower.

2278. III. William A., b. Aug. 2, 1857. m. May 20, 1885, Lena A. Sharp.

2279. IV. Anna R., b. Oct. 16, 1858. m. May 5, 1877, Horace Rogers.

2280. V. Jay B., b. Mar. 26, 1860, m. May 11, 1886, Alice Cozadd.

2281. VI. Mary B., b. Aug. 7, 1862,

2282. VII. Sidney D., b. Sep. 26, 1864.

2283. VIII. Louie F., b. June 18, 1868. m. Feb. 14, 1889, William Barnes.

2284. IX. Lillian, b. June 18, 1871.

2233. Luke. (2196. Jonathan, 2175. Moses, 12. Jonathan, 2. James, 1. Thomas.) 2d s. and child of Jonathan Draper and Silence Copeland. m. Virgenis, Vt., Aug. 25, 1813, Harriet, dau. of Job Hoisington and Sarah Knapp. She was b. Virgenis, N. Y., Apr. 16, 1796. d. Sylvania, O., Feb. 26, 1881.

Job Hoisington, father of Mrs. Draper (b. Aug. 10, 1765; m. Sarah Knapp, Dec. 31, 1792), fell in the defense of Buffalo, N. Y., against the British, Dec. 30, 1813, and was scalped by the British Indians.

Luke Draper moved to Buffalo soon after his marriage, although he had been there during the War of 1812. He was in partnership with Martin Dayley, keeping a dry goods store there. They were burnt out by the British, and Luke was taken prisoner and sent to Quebec. He was kept in prison there several months, and had a hard time, the prison being filthy and the food maggoted peas and mouldy biscuits. Those that had any money could obtain things by paying exorbitant prices. Luke succeeded in secreting his money, so that he was able to buy food, though at such high prices, as, for instance, one dollar for a pint of salt. They were forced to cast lots to see who should be exchanged first, and Luke, not being one of the lucky ones, had to wait before finally buying another man's chance for a hundred dollars. He then returned home.

CHILDREN:

2285. I. Lyman Copeland, b. Evans, Erie Co., N. Y., Sep. 4, 1815. d. Madison, Wis., Aug. 26, 1891.

2286. II. Charles Richard, b. Springfield, Pa., Sep. 17, 1818. d. Toledo, Feb. 7, 1875. (Unmarried.) He was all his life engaged in horse dealing.

2287. III. Warren Hoisington, b. Springfield, Pa., May 6, 1820. d. Toledo, O., Oct. 17, 1867. (Unmarried.)

He roamed a good deal over the country; went to California in 1856, and returned to Toledo in 1866. At one time he was in partnership with his brother, Marvin K. Draper, 2288.

2288. IV. Marvin K., b. Lockport, N. Y., Dec. 3, 1828.

2285. Lyman Copeland. (2233. Luke, 2196. Jonathan, 2175. Moses, 12. Jonathan, 2. James, 1. Thomas.) Eldest child and s. of Luke Draper and Harriet Hoisington. m. 1st: 1853, Lydia, 2243, dau. of Elisha Chadwick and Lucy Draper, 2240. She was b. at Queensbury, Warren Co., N. Y., May 2, 1811, and was the widow of Peter A. Remsen. She d. May 23, 1888. Dr. Draper m. 2dly: in Cheyenne, Wyo., Oct, 10, 1889, Mrs. Catherine T. Hoyt. She was b. about 1831. (No issue by either marriage.)

Probably no historical student within the basin of the Mississippi has been so generally known among men of letters as Dr. Lyman Copeland Draper. While his reputation has been chiefly that of a collector and editor of materials for history, rather than a writer, his work is quite as famous in its way as though his contributions to standard literature had been more numerous. Occupying a position quite unique in American scholarship, and regarded as an oracle on western topics amongst historical specialists the country over, but little is popularly known of his personality as to what sort of man this tireless worker was. Indeed, so retiring was his disposition, so modest his demeanor and of so shrinking a habit, it has been given to but few to understand the man as an individual.

When but three years of age, his parents removed from Erie Co., N. Y., to Erie Co., Pa., and three years later to Lockport, on the line of the Erie Canal. His father, Luke Draper (2233) was, by turns, grocer, tavern-keeper and farmer, and as soon as his son could be of use about the house, the store or the land, he was obliged to do his fair share of the labor; and so life went on with him, working first at one thing, then another, reading hard, and increasing his meagre curriculum of knowledge by the few books then obtainable on the frontier. Before long he acquired a reputation as a youth of letters. Even at that early age the lad's taste for Revolutionary lore was well developed. It seems to have been inherent; for at the family fireside, the deeds of Revolutionary heroes always formed the chief topic of conversation. In his boyhood there were still living many veterans of the Continental Army who were always welcome to the hospitality of the Draper household, while the War of 1812 was but an event of a few years before. The boy was early steeped in the facts and traditions of Anglo-American fights and western border forays, and with the pride of military lineage, he possessed a passion for obtaining information as to the events in which his ancestors took part. He saw in his youth Gen. Lafayette, Gov. Cass, De Witt Clinton, and other celebrities of that day, such as the Seneca Chief, Tommy Jimmy, and others of his tribe, Lafayette was the subject of his first school composition, whilst his first article for the press, published in the "Rochester Gem," for Apr. 6, 1833, was a sketch of Charles Carrol, of Carrolton, the last of the "signers" of the Declaration of Independence.

Peter A. Remsen, a cotton factor at Mobile, Ala., had married a cousin of Dr. Draper's, and to Mobile he went in the Fall of 1833. Whilst there he occupied himself in collecting information regarding the career of the famous Creek Chief, Weatherford. Leaving Mobile, he went to Granville College, O., and was an undergraduate there for two years. For a year after leaving there he was a student at Hudson River Seminary, Stockport, N. Y.; following this up with an extended course of private reading, chiefly historical, while resident with Mr. Remsen, whose home was then in Genesee Co., N. Y. It was in 1838 that Dr. Draper conceived the idea of writing a history of western pioneers. This at once became his controlling thought, and he entered upon its execution with an enthusiasm which never lagged through half a century, and which he deemed the mission of his life. From Mr. Remsen's home he began an extensive and long continued correspondence with prominent pioneers all along the border line. In 1840 he commenced the work of supplementing his correspondence with personal interviews with pioneers, and the descendants of pioneers and Revolutionary soldiers in their homes, and took in this quest long and dangerous journeys through New York, Ohio, Kentucky and the Virginian backwoods. The period of Dr. Draper's greatest activity in this direction was between 1840 and 1879; but he always continued this work of interviewing, more or less, until his death. Upon the shelves of his large individual library were several hundred portly volumes of MSS., the greater part of which was wholly original matter, covering the entire history of the fight for the Northwest, from 1742 to 1814. In 1840, while in the midst of his chosen task, he drifted to Pontotoc in northern Mississippi, where he became part owner and editor of the Mississippi "Intelligencer." The paper was not a financial success, and at the close of his first year in the office, his partner bought him out, giving in payment the deed to a tract of wild land in the neighborhood. He and Charles H. Larrabee, who had been a student with him at Granville, and was now a lawyer, united their fortunes and moved upon this tract of land. They were not very successful, and Dr. Draper, having received the offer of a clerkship under a relative who was the Erie Canal Superintendent at Buffalo, N. Y., returned north, leaving Larrabee in possession. The latter had a call to Chicago, and left the plantation, with its crop of sweet potatoes ungarnered, and their land to the mercy of the first squatter who passed along. Dr. Draper returned the following year to Pontotoc, but stayed only a short time, and then went to live in the family of Mr. Remsen at Baltimore, and finally in Philadelphia.

In the Spring of 1852 Mr. Remsen died, leaving Dr. Draper at the head of the little household. His old friend Larrabee, who had drifted from Chicago to the Badger State, had been corresponding with him, inviting his assistance in the management of the State Historical Society of Wisconsin, which had been organized at Madison in 1849. Larrabee now become a Judge, and one of its founders, knowing the scope of Dr. Draper's labors, had communicated with his associates, and they, with Gov. Farwell, heartily co-operated with him in endeavoring to obtain Dr. Draper's assistance. So that it came about that, in the middle of October of that year, he arrived in Madison with the family of Mr. Remsen, whose widow he married the following year. In January, 1853, he was chosen one of the executive committee of the Society. A year later he reorganized it, and was chosen Corresponding Secretary, and under his fostering care, aided by the Legislative annuity which was obtained in 1855, it has grown marvellously. Beginning with 50 volumes in 1854, the library now contains 120,000 priceless volumes, rich stores of MSS. and a splendid museum that annually attracts over 12,000 visitors. During the years 1858 and 1859, Dr. Draper served as Superintendent of Public Instruction. He was quite as efficient in this role as in that of an antiquarian collector. He found the affairs of his office in a chaotic state, but soon succeeded in inaugurating an admirable system of management, still in vogue. He made a very careful study of the workings of public school libraries wherever, he went, and as a result of this investigation, he secured the passage of an act by the Wisconsin Legislature of 1859, by which one-tenth of the State School Fund income was set apart as a township library fund, to which was added one-tenth of a mill tax on the assessed valuation of the State. During the first year the law was in operation nearly $89,000 was raised in the manner prescribed. But in 1861, when the Civil War broke out, the resources of the commonwealth were taxed to the utmost to support its troops at the front, and the well-digested library law was repealed, whilst the money already accumulated was transferred to other funds before a book could be purchased. State Supt. Draper won enthusiastic praise from Gov. Randall, legislative committees and prominent educators in different portions of the country. He was *ex-officio* a member of the Board of Regents of the University of Wisconsin and the State Normal Schools, and his services as well as his life-work in promoting the cause of historical literature was formally recognized by the State University in 1871 by the conferring upon him the title of LL.D. — Granville having made him an M.A. Just twenty years previous.

Dr. Lyman C. Draper

But all this tended to detract from his work as an historian, and Dr. Draper, finally heeding the urgent calls of his friends, the year 1860 found him back at his work in behalf of the State Historical Society. As Corresponding Secretary he was the executive officer, and in addition to this he edited the publications of the Society's Historical Collections. The collections constituted a vast mass of original material bearing upon the history of the State, all of it gathered by Dr. Draper. So complete has this work been done that it substantially covers all the information obtainable upon the pre-territorial history of the State. Their incalculable value has been frequently tested by the best of authorities.

Devoting his time so assiduously as he has to the interests of his Society, it is not at all surprising that Dr. Draper has not had the opportunity to give to the public more freely of his individual harvest of raw material, to which, in the midst of whatever duty for the moment at hand, he never forgot or neglected to add. He frequently contributed special articles to magazines and encyclopaedias, sketches of noted border heroes for the "Encyclopaedia of Biography," published by Appleton & Co., etc. He has also freely shared of his stores to other historians.

In 1869 we rather oddly find Dr. Draper preparing and publishing, in partnership with W. A. Croffut, a well-known writer, an exhaustive work of 800 pages, entitled "The Helping Hand: An American Home Book for Town and Country," devoted to stock and fruit raising, domestic economy, agricultural economics, etc.— a singular digression for a historical specialist. Nevertheless, competent critics declared the book to be one of great practical utility. The publication came eventually into the toils of a lawsuit, and the authors never realized anything from their labors. It was just as well, however, for had the "Western Plutarch" found agricultural writings a source of profit — his salary as secretary was very meagre in those days — he might have been tempted into that field to the detriment of the cause of historical literature.

Dr. Draper's great work, in his especial field of scholarship, has been his "King's Mountain and its Heroes," an octavo volume of 612 pages, published by Peter G. Thomson, of Cincinnati, in 1881. Unfortunately for the publisher and author, as well as the lovers of historical study, the greater part of the edition was consumed by fire soon after its issue, so that few copies are now extant. Aside from the border forays of whites and Indians, the really romantic portion of the history of the Revolution is confined to the Whig and Tory warfare of the Carolinas, which, for the first time, has been fully told in "King's Mountain." The book was well received by those most capable of forming a just estimate of its merits. George Bancroft declared it "a magnificent volume." "The amount of material gathered together," says Parkman, "is truly wonderful. Nothing but a lifetime of zealous research could have produced so copious a record of this very interesting passage of our history." "It is a delightful book apart from its usefulness," says George W. Childs; "it enchains the reader, and has the interest of Cooper's novels." "I find it," says

Gen. Joe E. Johnson, "the most interesting American historical work I have ever read." "The work deserves credit," wrote Gen. Sherman, "for accuracy and fullness." Writes Robert C. Winthrop: "It is an interesting and valuable work, exhibiting great research." Says the New England "Historic-Genealogical Register": "It is scarcely possible to speak in too high praise of the work." "It is," says the late Gov. Seymour, "a valuable contribution to the history of our country." "I am amazed," Gov. Ferry, of South Carolina, writes, "at the extent of the historical information it contains, reminding one of Homer's glowing accounts of similar contests between the Grecians and Trojans." The Boston "Literary World" declares the opinion that "the effort is a masterpiece." Prof. Phillips, of the North Carolina University, says: "The author has a gift for such work, and he may be styled 'The Lover of Patriots.' The marvellous tale of 'King's Mountain' has been told skillfully, charitably and yet fairly." Says the Hon. John M. Lea, of Tennessee: "The book will live. Its crowning virtue is that it seeks to tell the truth, doing equal justice to Whig and Tory."

These are but samples of the encomiums fairly showered upon Dr. Draper's great work.

He was a clear, forcible writer, with a pure and elevated style. He was possessed of a conscientious desire to do exact justice to all the actors who have moved on the stage of history. He scorned the too common literary habit of shaping facts to fit a theory, and considered a perversion of historical truth as the meanest of lies, because its baneful effects are the most widely permeated and lasting.

No living man is so well equipped, at every point, to write the history of the border forays of the Revolutionary period, and of the early days of western settlement. Dr. Draper's "King's Mountain," stupendous a work as it is, is but one dip into the well of his possessions, and a great body of students of American history have been keenly awaiting for years further progress in his work. George Bancroft, Sparks, Parkman, Shea, Lossing and others have watched for emanations from his pen. The venerable Bancroft once wrote to him: — "I look forward with eager and impatient curiosity for the appearance of your lives of Boone, of Clark, of James Robertson, and so many others. Time is short — I wish to read them before I go hence. Pray do not delay; the country expects of you this service."

Perhaps one of the greatest difficulties with Dr. Draper has been that he has — in a desire to inform the public, which is quite as keen as the desire of the public to hear from him — attempted too much. The variety of manuscript historical works which for some years past he had in various stages of preparation, is quite astonishing. But, instead of finishing them one at a time, he continually added to them all, never pausing in his zealous search for fresh details, and ever hesitating to close his story for fear that the next mail might bring some stray fact that would prove a missing link or throw an illustrative side-light. A less conscientious man would have brought his products to the market years before; but Dr. Draper never consented to publication so long as there was a stone in the path of his search yet unturned. This may possibly be deemed the excess of caution, but American scholarship will no doubt, in due time, reap the advantage of it.

One work of Dr. Draper's is a volume on the so-called Mecklenburg Declaration of Independence of May, 1775. This exhaustive and wonderfully painstaking monograph is destined to settle the vexed question for all time. A keenly interesting work on "Border Forays and Adventures," in the preparation of which he had the assistance of Mr. C. W. Butterfield — well known to readers of the "Magazine of Western History." — has also been published.

Dr. Draper mapped out a connected series of biographies of eminent border men — Gen. George Rogers Clark, "the Washington of the West;" Daniel Boone, the founder of Kentucky; Gen. Simon Kenton, the noted border fighter and companion of Boone and Clark, whose stirring career was filled with romantic adventures; Sumter, the revolutionary hero of South Carolina; while Brant, Tecumseh, Brady and the Wetzels are among those whom he desired to introduce in their true colors to the world of letters. A work on Dunmore's Indian War of 1774 was also among those which he had blocked out. This splendid series of histories, illustrative of early times on the border, Dr. Draper had clearly in view when he commenced to gather original matter for them, nearly a half century ago.

Short and slight of stature, Dr. Draper was a bundle of nervous activity. His delicately cut features exhibited great firmness of character, and the powers of intense mental concentration readily brightened with the most winning of smiles. By nature and by life habit he was a recluse. His existence has been largely passed among his books and manuscripts, and he cared nothing for those social alliances and gatherings which delight the average man. Long abstention from general intercourse with men with whom he had no business to transact, made him shy of forming acquaintances, and wrongfully gained for him a reputation of being unapproachable. To him who had a legitimate errand thither, the latch-string of the fire-proof library and working "den" — which was hidden in a dense tangle of lilacs and crab-trees in the rear yard of the bibliophile's residence lot — was always out, and the literary hermit found to be a most amiable gentleman, and a charming and often merry conversationalist, for few kept so well informed on public men, current events and standard literature. To know Dr. Draper was to admire him as a man of generous impulses, who wore his heart upon his sleeve, was the soul of honor, and did not understand what duplicity meant. But had he through life given himself more to the world, this tireless brain-worker could not have accomplished the wonders he has, nor have carved out for himself the eminent position which he will always maintain among the historical scholars of the country.

2288. Marvin K. (2233. Luke, 2196. Jonathan, 2175. Moses, 12. Jonathan, 2. James, 1. Thomas.) 4th child, 4th s. of Luke Draper and Harriet Hoisington. m.

Mar. 21, 1857, Christiana Kinney. She was b. Faxdile, Isle of Man, England, Nov. 1, ICS38.

Mr. Draper has been in various kinds of business, and has traveled and resided in many places in the Union. When a child his parents lived at what is now Toledo, then but a collection of several small villages. The Indians had not then been removed from that section, and the Indian boys were his first playmates. He is at present engaged in traveling for his sons, who are in the gold and silver plating business.

CHILDREN, ALL B. TOLEDO, OHIO:

2289. I. Miron Luke, b. Apr. 20, 1858. d. Toledo, May 8, 1861.

2290. II. Albert Kinney, b. Feb. 12, 1860, m. Mar. 11, 1885, Emma Sueawb, of Fulton, Ill. Child: — -Lorraine C, 2297. b. Aug. 21, 1886.

2291. III. Harriet, N., b. Dec. 14, 1861. m. Apr. 9, 1885, Sigel A. Warren, of Sylvania, O. He d. Jan., 1887. She m'. 2dly: Oct. 22, 1890, William Orr, of Benton Harbor, Mich. (No issue by 1st marriage.) Child, by 2d marriage: — Sarah L., 2298. b. Luketown, Ill., July 31, 1891.

2292. IV. Lyman, b. Feb. 17, 1866.

2293. V. Marvin Charles, b. Dec. 25, 1868.

2294. VI. Ella Belle & 2295. VII. Eva Bessie (Twins), b. Sep. 4, 1871. Ella B. d. Sep. 14, 1871. Eva B. d. Jan. 7, 1874.

2296. VIII. Linnie Hazel, b. Nov. 24, 1881.

2289. Albert. (2233. Luke, 2196. Jonathan, 2175. Moses, 12. Jonathan, 2. James, 1. Thomas.) s. of Luke Draper and Rachel Polley. b. Apr. 8, 1808. d. Aug. 14, 1883. m. Rachel Sparks, June 9, 1836. She was b. Apr. 15, 1815.

At about the age of 22, Albert Draper went with his uncles, Jonathan and Benjamin Polley, over the Alleghany Mountains, and helped to construct the Erie Canal. Afterwards they came to Indiana, and had a large contract on the canal that runs through Fort Wayne and Huntington. This contract, however, was thrown up; the Polleys went back East, but Albert remained at Huntington, and was the first white man married in Huntington Co. He subsequently built the first bridge across the Wabash River in Huntington Co. He and his wife, Rachel, were bap. Apr. 4, 1858, and were received into full fellowship as members of the regular Baptist Church, called the "Yankee-town" Church, in Rockcreek Township, Huntington Co., Ind.

CHILDREN:

2299. I. Riley, b. Sep. 24, 1837, m. Dec. 8, 1861, Sarah E. Hunt, at Markle, Huntington Co., Ind. Children: — I. Emma L., 2304. b. Markle, Ind„ Sep. 15, 1862. m. Aug. 20, 1883, Otto F. Booth. II. Carrie E., 2305. b. Markle, Ind., Aug. 14, 1864. III. Charles, 2306. b. Upper Alton, Ill., Feb. 28, 1866. IV. EfRe R., 2307. b. Surrey, Mo., Oct., 1867. V. Arthur, 2308. b. Surrey, Mo., Oct., 1869. VI. Jennie A., 2309. b. Surrey, Mo., May, 1871. m. Jan. 3, 1891, C. W. Stroud. VII. Albert G., 2310. b. Surrey, Mo., July 5, 1879. VIII. Everett, 231 1, b. Surrey, Mo., Nov. 7, 1883.

Riley Draper (2299) was the first white child born in Huntington Co., Ind.

2300. II. Mary, b. Mar. 14, 1842. m. June 3, 1859, David Divilbin. (Has 8 Children.)

2301. III. William, b. July 7, 1843. d. Dec. 25, 1848.

2302. IV. Solomon, b. Jan. 18, 1845. A lawyer.

2303. V. Benjamin, b. Nov. 19, 1846. Lives in Arkansas.

2304. VI. Rachel, b. Sep. 3, 1849. m. Mr. Bartlett. Has one dau.

2305. VII. Albert N., b. Apr. 2, 1855.

The Boston Drapers

This branch of the family, although in no ways, as far as the author can ascertain, connected with other branches of the Drapers in America, yet belonging to the parent or English stem, acquires large importance because they were connected with an event which has done more to revolutionize and build up the United States than perhaps anything else that has ever occurred. And it is but proper that a sketch of this enterprise should form a portion of this history.

About the year 1700 the Postmaster of Boston was one John Campbell, a Scotchman, and a son of Duncan Campbell, the organizer of the postal system of America. He was also a bookseller. In those early days the dissemination of news was in the hands of the postmaster of each city or town, and John Campbell on Monday, Apr. 24, 1704, issued the initial number of the Boston "News-Letter." It was an event not only in Boston, but throughout America, it being the first newspaper issued and printed in the Colonies. The first sheet of the first number was taken damp from the press by Chief Justice Sewall to show to President Willard, of Harvard University, as a wonderful curiosity. The "News-Letter" was printed sometimes on a single sheet, foolscap size, and oftener on a half sheet, with two columns on each side. The printer was Bartholomew Green, eldest son of Thomas Green, printer to Cambridge University, where the Greens had been located as such since 1649, and where Samuel Green printed the first Bible in America, not in English, but in the Indian language. A copy of this sold in 1872 in New York for $300.

Bartholomew Green was a member in good standing of the Old South Church, and when, in 1719, Campbell was removed from the post-office in Boston, it was evident that he must soon relinquish his control of it. This did not happen, however, until Dec. 31, 1721, when it passed into the hands of Bartholomew Green. When the latter assumed the management of the paper, he designed giving it a semi-religious character, which was more or less steadfastly adhered to until his death in 1733, when the paper passed into the hands of his son-in-law, John Draper, who continued to maintain the semi-religious character of its columns, until his death in 1762. He was succeeded by his son, Richard Draper, who changed the title of the paper to that of the Boston "Weekly News-Letter and New England Chronicle." The name was again changed to the "Massachusetts Gazette and Boston News-Letter." In 1768 it was united with the Boston "Postboy." The union was a mongrel affair, and did not last long. Although the united papers were called the "Massachusetts Gazette," each paper continued a separate publication. The "Postboy" as such appearing on Mondays and the "News-Letter" on Thursdays— one half being called by its own name and the other half by the name of the united concerns. One half was the official organ of the Government and published the laws. The contents of the other half were in accordance with the interests and opinions of each publisher. These Siamese Twins in journalism were separated in 1769, and Draper fell back on his old title and continued to publish the "News-Letter" till June 6, 1774, when he died, and was succeeded by his widow, Margaret Draper, and John Boyle, whom he had taken into partnership a month previously. John Howe afterwards assumed Boyle's share, and, with the widow Draper, carried on the paper till March, 1776, when, with the evacuation of Boston by the British troops, the "News-Letter," after a life of 72 years, ceased to exist. The only full file of the paper through the whole 72 years, now in existence, is in the possession of the New York Historical Society. The "News-Letter" was loyal to the Home Government, and was the only paper published in Boston during the siege of that city by Washington.

John Draper (10), a son of Richard Draper (2), a merchant of Boston, and his wife, Sarah Kilby, m. Deborah Draper, dau. of Bartholomew Green, printer. It was while serving his apprenticeship with Green that he met her. As already stated, on the death of his father-in-law, he succeeded him in the publication of the "News-Letter" and his printing house, which was in Newbury Street, Boston. Draper also commenced the publication in September, 1731, of the political paper called the "Weekly Rehearsal." It was printed on a half sheet of small paper, and was carried on at the expense of some gentlemen who had formed themselves into a political club and wrote for it. At the head of this club was the celebrated Jeremy Gridley, Esq., who was the real editor. The receipts of the "Rehearsal" about paid the expense of publication. He printed the paper about a year and a half, and it expired after a four years' life. In 1734 Mr. Draper printed the Laws of the Province, and he was printer to the Government and Council till he died. He printed Ames' famous Almanac, of which 60,000 copies were annually sold.

The "Historical Magazine," 2d edition, Vol. 7, p. 219, says, in speaking of John Draper: "Few names, early or late, connected with printing, have been more extensively known than Draper. A list of works containing their imprint would fill pages."

John Draper not only succeeded Bartholomew Green in his business, but he was heir to his calamities also. On the night of Jan. 30, 1734, the flames were seen to burst from his printing house; but too late for any effectual help to be afforded. The fire had broken out in the interior of the building, which was burnt to the ground, and nearly the whole of the printing material destroyed.

This last was in some measure repaired by the friendship of the brethren of the type, who loaned him a press and some fonts of letters till he could replace his own from England. He owned the house in which he lived on Cornhill, the east corner of the short alley leading to the church in Brattle Street. He was an industrious and useful member of society, and was held in estimation by his friends and acquaintances.

The following obituary is from the Boston "Evening Post," of Dec. 6, 1762:

"On Monday evening last departed this life, after a slow and hectic disorder, having just entered the sixty-first year of his age, Mr. John Draper, printer, who, for a long time, has been the publisher of a newspaper in this town, and by his industry, fidelity and prudence in his business, rendered himself agreeable to the public. His charity and benevolence, his pleasant and sociable turn of mind, his tender affection as a husband and parent, his piety and devotion to his Maker, has made his death as sensibly felt by his friends and relations as his life is worthy of imitation."

Richard (4), the son of John Draper (10) and Deborah Green, succeeded his father in his printing business and in the publication of the "News-Letter." He was brought up a printer by his father, and continued with him after he became of age, and for some years before his father's death was a silent partner with him. He was early appointed printer to the Council and Government, which he retained during life. Under his editorship the paper was devoted to the Government, and in the controversy between Great Britain and the Colonies, strongly supported the Royal cause and decorated the head of his paper with the King's Arms. Many able advocates of the Government filled the columns of the "News-Letter," but the opposition papers were supported by writers at least equally powerful and numerous.

The constitution of Richard Draper was very feeble, and he was often confined by sickness; so that soon after his father's death, he took his kinsman, Samuel Draper (17) (who was connected with Z. Fowle), into partnership, under the firm name of "R. & S. Draper." Samuel was not permitted to share in the honor of printing for the Government and Council, and in all work done for them, Richard's name alone appeared as printer. Richard Draper, having been successful in his business, erected a handsome brick house on a convenient spot in front of the old printing house in Newbury Street, in which he resided. He was attentive to his business, and was esteemed the best compiler of news of his day. He did alone very little book printing, but he was concerned with Edes & Gill and the Fleets in publishing several volumes of sermons, etc.

The Boston "Evening Post," of June 13, 1774, gives the following biography of Richard Draper: — "He was a man remarkable for the amiable delicacy of his mind and gentleness of his manners. A habit enfeebled and emaciated by remorseless disease and unremitted distress could never banish the smile from his countenance. A well founded confidence in the mercies of God, and the happy consciousness of a life well spent, smoothed the pillow of anguish and irradiated the gloom of death with the promise of succeeding joy. In every relation he sustained in life, his endearing manners and inflexible integrity rendered him truly exemplary."

He married Margaret Green, a granddaughter of Bartholomew.

Richard Draper was succeeded in the publication of the "News-Letter" by his widow Margaret, who continued in partnership with John Boyle until the beginning of the Revolutionary War. Boyle had been taken into partnership by Richard Draper a month previous to his death, but at the outbreak of hostilities, his sympathies being strong for the Continental cause, he was not agreeable to Widow Margaret, and was succeeded in the partnership by John Howe, who was a devoted loyalist, and continued with her until the final suspension of the paper, which occurred on the evacuation of Boston by the British troops, when Widow Margaret departed with the soldiers, going first to Halifax and thence to England, where she enjoyed a pension from the British Government for the remainder of her life.

Richard and Margaret were not blessed with any children. She is named in Sabine's "Loyalists," and in Trumbull's "McFingal," a satirical ode, as "Mother Draper."

Genealogy

CHILDREN OF JOHN (1. WILLIAM, 1. EDWARD.) AND RACHEL DRAPER:

I. John, b. Sep. 29, 1689. Bap. July 23, 1693.
II. Rachel, b. Nov. 9, 1691. m. Sep. 22, 1708, Adam Waters, of Boston.
III. William, b. Dec. 27, 1693. Bap. Dec. 31, 1693.
IV. Mary, b. Oct. 11, 1695. Bap. First Church, Oct. 13, 1695.
V. Keziah, b. Jan. 20, 1697. Bap. Dec. 26, 1698.

(No further record of this branch.)

2. Richard, (1. Edward.) s. of Edward and Ann Draper, b. near Banbury, Co. of Oxford, England, m. Boston, Mass., Oct. 22, 1689, by the Rev. Theodate Lawson, Sarah Kilby. He d. ____. She d. ____.

Richard Draper is supposed to have emigrated with his brother William (i) to the Colonies, and settled in Boston about 1680, He was a merchant in that city, and a well-known member of Old South Church. It is proven by the Boston records that Richard Draper and John Wentworth furnished the lumber from which "Faneuil Hall" was built, called the Cradle of Liberty. The following extract from his will is from the Suffolk County records:
Lib. 27, Fol. 22.

In the name of God, amen. 1, Richard Draper (2) of Boston, etc., son of Edward and Ann Draper, late of Great Britain, near Banbury, in the county of Oxford, in Great Britain, deceased, and only brother to (1) William Draper Senr. of Boston, gives to his wife Lydia, revision according to contract before marriage of house lives in.

Pue in Brattle St. Church is mentioned.

Gives to his daughter Sarah Mors (3).

I give to my two sons John (10) and Samuel (13) Draper, &c. and lands in joining Brookfield.

Presented for Probate, Jan. 25, 1728.

Lib. 27, Fol. 65.

Inventory of goods, &c., of Richd. Draper, Shopkeeper. £688. 15. 7.

Approved April 7, 1729.

CHILDREN (ALL BUT JOHN), B. BOSTON:

3. I. Sarah, b. Aug. 3, 1690. Admitted to Brattle St. Church May 3, 1701. m. Brattle St. Church Mar. 9, 1710, Nathanial Morse.

II. Ann, b. July 7, 1693. Bap. Old South Church, July 9, 1693. d. Feb. 5. 1703.

III. Esther, b. Jan. 13, 1694. Bap. Old South Church, Jan. 20, 1694.

IV. Rebecca, b. Nov. 21, 1696. Bap. Old South Church, Nov. 26, 1696.

V. Mary, b. Jan., 1697. Bap. Jan. 9, 1797.

VI. Richard, b. Sep. 9, 1699. Bap. Brattle St. Church, Dec. 8, 1699.

VII. Thomas, b. Jan. 1, 1700. Bap. Brattle St. Church, Jan. 5, 1700.

VIII. John, b. Roxbury, Oct. 29, 1702. Admitted to Brattle St. Church, Feb. 5, 1727. d. Boston, Nov. 29, 1762.

IX. William, b. July 9, 1703. Bap. July 16, 1703.

X. Edward, b. Sep. 9, 1705. Admitted to Brattle St. Church, Jan. 1, 1792.

XI. Samuel, b. Jan. 1, 1707. Bap. Brattle St. Church, June 8, 1707.

10. John. (2. Richard, i. Edward.) 8th child, 3d s. of Richard Draper (2) and Sarah Kilby. m. Deborah, dau. of Bartholomew Green. She d. Dec. 9, 1736, aged 39 years.

CHILDREN, ALL B. BOSTON:

I. Richard, b. Feb. 24, 1726-7. Bap. Feb. 26. d. June 4, 1774. m. Mar. 22, 1749, Margaret, dau. of John Green, (No issue.)

They were both admitted to full communion in the West Church, Boston, Nov. 3, 1765.

II. John, b. Aug., 1728, Bap. Brattle St. Church. III. Lydia, b. Dec, 1729. Bap. Brattle St. Church, Dec. 21, 1729, m. Sep. 4' 1755' John, s. of Bartholomew Green, Jr.

13. Samuel. (2. Richard, i. Edward.) 11th child, 6th s. of Richard Draper (2) and Sarah Kilby. Lived in Martha's Vineyard. (No details.)

CHILDREN:

17. I. Samuel, b. Martha's Vineyard, 1737. d. Boston, Mar. 21, 1767.

18. II. Richard, b. Martha's Vineyard, 17— . d. before 1810.

19. III. Edward, b. Martha's Vineyard, 1749. d. Nov. 15, 1831.

17. Samuel. (13. Samuel, 2. Richard, 1. Edward.) Eldest s. and child of Samuel Draper (13). m. May 14, 1762, Susanna Coburn, of Boston. She d. Mar. 2, 1812.

Samuel Draper was the nephew and apprentice of John Draper (10). Soon after he came of age he went into trade with Zachariah Fowle, who stood in much need of a partner like Draper; their connection was mutually advantageous. Fowle had been in business seven years, but had made no progress in the advancement of his fortune. Draper was more enterprising, but had not capital to establish himself as a printer. He was a young man of correct habits and handsome abilities, industrious and a good workman. The connection continued five years, during which they printed three or four volumes of some magnitude; a large edition of "The Youth, Instructor in the English Language;" another of the "Psalter;" also a variety of pamphlets, and Chapman's small "Books and Ballads." They so far succeeded in trade that they kept free of debt, obtained a good livelihood, and increased their stock. Their printing house was in Marlborough Street, at the south corner of Franklin Street, Boston. The articles of co-partnership contemplated a continuance of "Fowle & Draper," but the latter's uncle's death and the delicate health of his cousin, Richard Draper, who made liberal proposals to him, caused Draper to leave Fowle, and go into partnership with Richard Draper, where he remained till his death in 1767.

CHILDREN:

20. I. Susanna, b. Feb. 9, 1763. Bap. Feb. 13, 1763. d. Apr. 25, 1811.

21. II. Elizabeth, b. Feb. 22, 1765. Bap. Feb. 24, 1765. m. Eliphalet Casnell, Dec. 16, 1802. d. Aug. 13, 1849.

18. Richard. (13. Samuel, 2. Richard, i. Edward.) 2d child, 2d s. of Samuel Draper (13). m. Oct. 5, 1763, Ann Curryer.

Was a printer in Boston.

CHILDREN:

22. I. Richard, b. Sep. 25, 1765. d. Oct. 24, 1766.

23. II. Sarah, b. Feb. 12, 1766.

24. III. William, b. Feb. 28, 1767.

25. IV. Ann, b. 1768.

26. V. Ann 2d, b. 1771.

27. VI. Samuel, b. 1773.

19. Edward. (13. Samuel, 2. Richard, 1, Edward.) 3d s., youngest child of Samuel Draper (13). m. Jan. 7, 1776, Sarah L. Barbour. She d. Aug. 19, 1822.

Edward Draper was the oldest printer in Boston and lived in Brattle Street. In 1777 he printed in Newberry Street, probably in the place formerly occupied by the "News-Letter" establishment. Amongst the books that came from his press were David Osgood's "Sermons on Peter Thacher," in Brattle Street Church. He also printed for the newspapers. He was buried from the New North Church, Boston, 1831, aged 82.

CHILDREN:

28. I. Lydia, b. Mar. 8, 1776. d. Jan. 8, 1844.

29. II. Sally, b. Aug. 4, 1777. d. Aug. 2, 1778.

30. III. Samuel, b. July 21, 1779. d. May 21, 1787.

31. IV. Sally 2d, b. Dec. 8, 1780. d. May 21, 1787.

32. V. Rachel, b. July 30, 1783. d. June 1, 1787.
33. VI. Edward, b. Oct. 26, 1784. d. June 3, 1787.
34. VII. John Green, b. Oct. 15, 1785. d. June 19, 1787.
35. VIII. Samuel 2d, b. Sep, 8, 1787. d. Dec. 27, 1863.
36. IX. Edward 2d, b. Jan. 19, 1790. d. Apr. 26, 1796.
37. X. John Coburn, b. Mar. 30, 1791. Bap. Apr. 3, 1791. d. May 20, 1833.

35. Samuel. (19. Edward, 13. Samuel, 2. Richard, 1. Edward.) 8th child, 4th s. of Edward Draper (19) and Sarah L. Barbour, m. Mar. 9, 1821, Anna Tufts Jones, of Charlestown, Mass. She d. Dec. 23, 1882.

He was a merchant of Boston.

CHILDREN:

38. I. Catherine Jones, b. Feb., 1822. d. Dec. 15, 1874.
39. II. Edward L., b. Jan. 23, 1825. m. June 5, 1861, Emma A. Hunt. (No issue.)
40. III. Samuel, Jr., b. Oct. 15, 1826. d. Nov. 22, 1876. (Unmarried.)
41. IV. Sarah Mercy, b. Dec. 31, 1827.
42. V. George Bartlett, b. Nov. 26, 1829. d. in infancy.
43. VI. William A., b. Oct. 17, 1832. d. in infancy.
44. VII. Lucy A. d. in infancy.
45. VIII. Anna Elizabeth. (Unmarried.)

Capt. Samuel Draper's Descendants

In spite of long continued search and active enquiry in many directions, the mystery which surrounds Capt. Samuel (2) Draper is far from being satisfactorily solved. Miss Adelaid H. Draper (162), of Boston, has devoted many weeks of hard work and extensive correspondence in the effort to try and clear up this branch of the Draper family The author has also endeavored to do so, but has not met with any more success than his efficient assistant, Miss Draper. This is probably, in a large measure, due from first the utterly incomprehensible silence with which some of Capt. Drapers descendants, living in the State of New York, have seen fit to observe relative to the subject-presumably because they were trying to recover an alleged English estate and thought probably that other Drapers might have designs upon it, although assured to the contrary, and this history would probably have aided them in their search had they been willing to assist with the facts. Secondly, Capt. Samuel Draper lead so exceedingly roving a life, and sailed to so many ports of the world, that he left few or no records of himself.

The following information about Samuel Draper is largely conjectural. He is supposed to have been the wild son of a Church of England clergyman, one Thomas Draper of Halifax, Yorkshire, England. The young man ran away to sea, and never thereafter returned home. There is a vague tradition that he had a brother in Roxbury, Mass In course of time Samuel Draper became a captain of a ship, which it is more than probable was on buccaneering intent. Whilst in some port of the kingdom of Spain he carried off a Spanish girl, and it is presumed made her his wife. She thereafter always sailed with him. They had children, and it was the custom of the Captain to name his sons after the port in which they were born, or to which the ship was bound. We have, therefore, 3. Boston Draper, 4. Newburyport Draper, 5. New York Draper and, an exception, 6. James Draper. Legend gives us the names of New York and Newburyport Draper, but we have only authenticated, through old documents which have been available to us, the names of Boston and James.

Until a few years ago there existed some few relics of Capt. Samuel Draper, amongst which was a coat, probably an officer's uniform, as with it was a sword or sabre, and a military hat of the Continental style, but importance seems to have been attached only to the coat It was given by Capt. Samuel to his son Boston, with directions to preserve carefully as evidence, in case a fortune should be left to him or his posterity. The silver buttons on this coat bore a device, which was a ship, at the stern of which was a man's arm holding a cutlass. This device was probably one of the Captain's own devising another description of these buttons says they had a stag's head on them, but a third account says that the inscription on these said buttons was "Rex. A. D. and also the letters "C. K. S." and perhaps "R. I." Later, these buttons were taken from the coat and strung upon a string, and have presumably been lost. Some twenty years ago an English lawyer came to Boston and informed the descendants of Capt. Samuel Draper that, if they could prove the marriage of the Spanish woman to the sea captain, a large estate was theirs in England. This they were unable to do, and it is this same estate that the New York descendants are groping for. All the information that it has been possible to collect has been welded together in these pages of the sea captain's descendants, and it would have been much more complete if those most nearly connected could have seen fit to take a little trouble to aid Miss Adelaid Draper and the author.

The first record that we have of Boston Draper (3) is found in a paragraph in the history of Lexington, Mass. It is stated there, on page 380, that Boston Draper was a private in Capt. John Clapham's Company of troops furnished in the year 1759-60 from that town for the war between France and England in Canada. The next record is that he married, about the year 1767, Tryphena, daughter of Boz Brown, who was the original owner of the Draper homestead in Boxboro, at which the Continental soldiers assembled to start for Lexington in the Revolutionary War, and Miss Sarah M. Draper (82) still has the punch-bowl from which they drank. Boston Draper and his wife were married by a Justice of the Peace. He died in Boxboro, Mass., Dec, 15, 1784, aged 65 years, 11 months, 14 days, which would make his birth early in the year 1719, when it is presumed that about that date Capt. Samuel Draper was in or near the port of Boston. Tryphena, Boston's wife, died Jan. 11, 1829, in Boxboro, aged 82 years. Their gravestones still stand. Boston evidently settled in Littleton, which is a part now of the town of Boxboro, and there he had a homestead, at which all his children were born. It is also said by tradition that Boston, after he attained manhood, sailed one voyage with his father.

CHILDREN OF BOSTON DRAPER AND TRYPHENA BROWN:

7. I. Samuel, b. Aug. 8, 1770. d. Chesterfield, N. H., Dec. 3, 1841.

8. II. Tryphena, b. Sep. 24, 1773. d. Boxboro, Oct., 1845.

9. III. Boz Brown, b. Oct. 16, 1775.

10. IV. Mary, b. Sep. 5, 1777. d. Boxboro.

11. V. Sarah, b. Dec. 20, 1779. d. Sep. 3, 1861. m. Jan. 10, 1801, Reuben Worster. He was b. June 9, 1780. d. 1848. Children: — I. Sabria, 13. b. Feb. 20, 1802. m. Sep. 20,18 — , Calvin Newton. (Child: — Waldo, 23, d. in childhood.) II. Moses, 14. b. Dec. 6, 1805. m. Susan Howes. (Children: — Merrick, 24. Elizabeth, 25.) III. Emory, 15. b. Nov. 6, 1807. m. Almira Alcott. (Children: — Mira, 26. Mary, 27. Also several who d. in infancy.) IV. Reuben, 16. b. Sep. 2, 1809. d. 1840. m. Eliza Morse. (Child: — Charles, 28.) V. Lois, 17. b. Sep. 3, 1811. d. 1863-4. m. Dwight De Bell. He d. and she m. 2dly: George Rice. (Children, by 1st marriage: — Jonathan, 29. Louisa, 30. Fred, 31. Children, by 2d marriage: — George, 32. d. in childhood. John, 33.) VI. Sally, 18. b. July 21, 1813. d. 1886. m. Martin Wright. (Children: — Everson, 34, deceased. James L., 35. Silas, 36. d. 1885. Also several who d. young.) VII. Tryphena, 19. b. May 5, 1815. m. Frank Draper. VIII. Lydia, 20, b. July 17, 1817. d. Feb. 9, 1874. m. D. Emory Wright. He was b. Apr. 14, 1814. (Children: — Lydia C, 36. b. Nov. 30, 1834. d, Feb. 9, 1874. m. Sep. 27, 1855. John Hill. Mary O., 38. b. Aug. 14, 1837. m. Feb. 29, 1865, Andrew Litchfield. She d. Sep. 17, 1890. Cordelia L., 39. b. Oct. 25, 1838. m. July 28, 1860, James Kirkpatrick. Park E., 40. b. Mar. 12, 1840. m. Jan. 30, 1866, Mary Wheelock. Sarah D., 41. b. Nov. 16, 1842. d. Sep. 11, 1849. Reuben, 42. b. June 4, 1849, m. Feb. 16, 1875, Abbie Mann.) IX. Abel, 21, b. Mar. 8, 1820. m. Sep. 22, 1845, Harriet Beals. (Children:— Henry A., 43. b. May 5, 1847. d. Aug. 4, 1849. Carrie H., 44. b. June 23, 1849. m. Anthony H. Durant, Aug., 1868, Charles H., 45. b. June 3, 1852. m. Mar. 13, 1886, Annie L, Vickroy. Edward B., 46. b. Oct. 14, 1855. Lydia A., 47. b. May 17,1859. Lawrence M., 48. b, Dec. 25, 1860. Merton E., 49. b. Aug. 22, 1864.) X. Selim, 22. b. May 26, 1822. m. Lucy Ripley. (Children: — George, 50. b. Feb. 10, 1846. John, 51. b. Sep. 13, 1847. Waldo, 52. b. Oct. 21, 1849. Alden, 53. b. Oct. 17, 1852. Chios, 54. b. Nov. 26, 1854. Caroline, 55. b. Oct. 18, 1857. d. May 18, 1860. Miranda, 56. b. Nov. 20, 1859. William, 57. b. Mar. 19, 1861. Hattie, 58. b, Aug, 18, 1863. Cora, 59. b. Oct. 21, 1865, Henry, 60. b, Sep. 17, 1870.)

12, VI. Benjamin, b, July 12, 1782. d, Boxboro, Aug. 14, 1852.

7. Samuel. (3. Boston, 2. Samuel, 1. Thomas.) Eldest child and s. of Boston Draper and Tryphena Brown, m. Sep., 1793, Sarah Crouch. She was b. Harvard, Mass., July 3, 1762. d. Chesterfield, N. H., Dec. 19, 1863, aged 101 years, 5 months, 16 days.

Samuel Draper moved from Boxboro, Mass., to Chesterfield, N. H., in 1803 — the journey being performed in an ox-team. He spent the remainder of his life on the Hill Farm, on which he then settled. His wife, Sarah Crouch, attained to the great age recorded above. After using glasses for 50 years, her sight improved so that she discontinued their use, and at the age of 93 she could read several chapters of her coarse print Bible at a time without glasses, and her faculty to read continued until she was 98. The Crouch family were of Welsh extraction, and a long lived race — one sister of Sarah's living until she was 92 years old. The descendants of Samuel (7) were mainly farmers. The religious element predominated in this branch of the Draper family.

CHILDREN (ALL BUT ABRAM), B. BOXBORO, MASS.:

61. I. Samuel Lewis & 62. II. Sarah (Twins), b. Sep. 27, 1794. He d. Chesterfield, N. H., June 13, 1881. She d. Swanzey, N. H., Mar. 20, 1869.

Sarah, 62, m. W. Swanzey, N. H., Mar. 13, 1817, John Crouch. He was b. Mar. 13, 1796. d. Swanzey, Nov. 17, 1885. Children, all b. Chesterfield, N. H.:— I. Mary Ann, 67. b. Nov. 15, 1818. d. Aug 27, 1822. II. Abraham Lewis, 68. b. May 26, 1820. m. Rebecca Davis Taylor at Brattleboro, Vt., Apr. 22, 1846. She was b. Ashb5^ Mass., July 7, 1825. He d. White Rock, Kan., May 4, 1874. (They had: — I. Lewis Ellery, 72. b. Chesterfield, May 30, 1850. m. Aug., 1872. II, John Edgar, 73, b. Chesterfield, Oct. 13, 1853. m. III. William, 74. b. Jones Co., Ia., Feb. 23, 1856. m. Ida Adelaid. b. Jones Co., Ia., Oct. 6, 1861. m. Aaron Bromley.) III. Clarke Brown, 69. (Twin brother to Abraham Lewis, 68.) b. May 26, 1820. m. his twin brother's widow, Rebecca, in Townsend, Mass., Feb. 14, 1882, IV. Levi, 70. b. July 14, 1823. m. W. Swanzey, Mar. 7, 1848, Sarah Baley. She was b. W. Swanzey, Jan. 18, 1832, and d. there Oct. 5, 1878. V. Mary Ann 2d, 71. b. June 6, 1827.

63. III. Amy, b. June 2, 1797. d, Chesterfield, Nov. 25, 1871.

64. IV. Eunice, b. Mar. 30, 1799. d. Boston, July 10, 1801.

65. V. Eunice 2d. b. Sep. 5, 1802. d. W. Swanzey, Jan. 20, 1888. m. Chesterfield, Feb. 15, 1832, Ephraim Crouch. He was b. Chesterfield, Jan. 28, 1811. Children, all b. Chesterfield: — I. Eunice Semira, 75. b. June 4, 1833. II. Ephraim Augustus, 76. b. Oct. 13, 1835. Ill, John Luman, 77. b. Apr. 6, 1839. m. Keene, N. H., Sep. 17, 1865, Elmira Tarbox. She was b. Nelson, N. H., Feb. 24, 1841. (They have:— I. Elsie E., 78. b. Oct. 11, 1867. II. George L., 79. b. June 7, 1870. III. Charles A., 80, b. Jan. 18, 1873.)

66. VI. Abram, b. Chesterfield, Aug. 15, 1805. d. Swanzey, Sep. 7, 1884.

61. Samuel Lewis. (7. Samuel, 3. Boston, 2. Samuel, 1. Thomas.) Eldest child and s. of Samuel Draper and Sarah Crouch, m. his cousin, Laura, 132, dau. of Benjamin Draper, 12, in Boxboro, Mass., Dec. 26, 1821. She was b. Boxboro, Mass., Mar. 20, 1807. d. Chesterfield, Dec. 13, 1884.

Samuel Lewis lived nearly all his life on the same estate with his father Samuel (7), and there also his granddaughter, Sarah M. Draper (82), will end her days. Samuel Lewis served three months as musician in the War of 1812, and received a pension, which was transferred to his widow Laura after his death. A curious freak of nature presented itself in both Samuel Draper (7) and his son, Samuel Lewis, inasmuch as their teeth were all double, and they never shed them in childhood, the elder Samuel losing but one after he was 71 years old, and his son but three after he attained the age of 82 years.

CHILDREN:

81. I. Benjamin Lewis, b. Boxboro, Mass., June 13, 1824. d, Chesterfield, Oct. 10, 1859.

He was a merchant, and a close student all his life; a highly respected and eminently useful citizen, just, honest and upright in action. With superior mental endowments he won the respect and esteem of all with whom he had intercourse.

82. II. Sarah Mead, b. Boxboro, Feb. 24. 1827.

83. III. Laura Elvira, b. Chesterfield, May 2, 1830. d. there July 18, 1830.

84. IV. Laura Elvira 2d, b. Chesterfield, Apr. 25, 1834. d. Boston, Aug. 2. 1854.

She was a teacher.

66. Abram. (7. Samuel, 3. Boston, 2. Samuel, 1. Thomas.) 6th child and 2d s. of Samuel Draper and Sarah Crouch, m. at Alstead, N. H., Dec. 21, 1829, Sarah March. She was b. Alstead, July 29, 1803. (Is still living.)

CHILDREN:

85. I. George Washington, b. Chesterfield, Sep. 29, 1831. m. Dec. 16, 1852, Lydia Maria Bidwell. Child:— Emma L., 88. b. Mar. 12, 1859. d. July 2, 1878.

86. II. Abbie Ann, b. Chesterfield, Sep. 13, 1832. m. July 18, 1861, Enoch Howes.

87. III. Harriet Huntly, b. Alstead, Dec. 31, 1846. d. there Sep. 14, 1850.

9. Boz Brown. (3. Boston, 2. Samuel, 1. Thomas.) 3d child, 2d s. of Boston Draper and Tryphena Brown. Mr. Draper m. three times, and it is impossible to ascertain the order in which his children were born.

He moved to Herkeimer, N. Y., and had the following—

CHILDREN:

89. I. Sallie, b. Feb. 22, 1802. d. May 13, 1885. m. 1830, Richard Whitcombe. He was b. Oct. 2, 1801, at Slow, Mass. d. Sep. 16, 1877. Children:— I. Richard G., 101. b. Aug. 14, 1835d. Nov. 2, 1890. m. Apr. 26, 1853, Martha J. Wells, of W. Vienna, Oneida Co., N. Y. She was b. June 16, 1834. (Child -.—Abbie, 103. b. W. Vienna, Mar. 26, 1855. m. Nov. II, 1871, Addison West. They have 2 daus.: Mattie E., 104. and Clara M., 105.) II. Mary, 102. b. Sep. 26, 1841. m. 1860, Thomas M. Richie. He was b. Canada, Mar. 7, 1834, and d. Apr. 18, 1883. (They have:— Miron T., 106. b. May 18, 1865. Sarah L., 107. b. Oct. 30, 1862. Walter H., 108. b. May 3, 1867.)

90. II. Samuel. Had 7 children:— One called Mary Jane, 128. b. 1840. m. 1857, George F. Ballou, of Canastota, N. Y. (They had one child:— Ida. b.

1859. m. Canastota, 1883, Charles Hood, of Canastota. They had two sons:—109 and no.)

91. III. Jerome. (Supposed to be dead.) Has a s.:— Granville, in, now living in Rome, N. Y.

92. IV. Olive, b. Nov. 18, 1809. d. Sep. 26, 1879. m. Mar. 28, 1830, Daniel Bender. He was b. Mar. 27, 1808, and d. June 23, 1879. Children: — I. Mary E., 112. b. Jan. 14, 1831. II. Mary Ann, 113. b. June 5, 1832. III. George H,, 114. b. May 9, 1834. IV. Harriet D., 115. b. Nov. 18, 1835. V. Mary C, 116. b. Dec. 8, 1837. VI. Cynthia A., 117. b, Apr. 9, 1839. VII. Lucinda M., 118. b. Jan. 16, 1840. VIII. Lucy M., 119. b. July 8, 1842. IX. David A., 120. b. May 26, 1844. X. Charles H., 121. b. June 10, 1846. XI. Francis G., 122. b. Feb. 29, 1848. XII. David C, 123. b. Jan. 16, 1850. m. Delia L. Willard, Oct 19, 1871. (They have:—Willard C, 124. b. Oct. 15, 1877. Frederick C, 125. b. Aug. 23, 1879.) XIII. George P., 126. b. June 13, 1852. XIV, John F., 127. b. Aug. 31, 1856.

93. V. Mary Ann, b. Herkeimer.

94. VI. Franklin, m. Catherine ____.

95. VII. Benjamin.

96. VIII. Ari.

97. IX. Elizabeth, m. Jan. 31, 1849, Granville Draper, 139. She was b. Feb. 25, 1832. Children: — I. Amy, 129. b. Sep. 19, 1850. II. Madison M., 130. b. Nov. 20, 1852.

98. X. John. Lives in Philadelphia.

99. XI. Betsey, m. Isaac Hardy, and had children. Lived in New Hampshire.

100. XII. Tryphena.

12. Benjamin. (3. Boston, 2. Samuel, 1. Thomas.) 6th child, 3d s. of Boston Draper and Tryphena Brown, m. Amy Mead. She was b. Harvard, Mass., July 22, 1781, d. Boxboro, Aug. 29, 1849.

She was called "the little mother" by her children, and very much beloved.

CHILDREN, ALL B. BOXBORO:

131. I. Alonzo, b. July 10, 1805. d. Salem, Mass., Nov. 22, 1862.

132. II. Laura, b. Mar. 20, 1807. m. her cousin, Samuel Lewis Draper, 61, Dec. 26, 1821.

133. III. Amy, b. Feb. 14, 1808. d. Mar. 7, 1842, at Remsen, N. Y. m. Feb. 19, 1824, Jonas E. Horton. Children: — I. John Albert, 141. b. Chester Co., Feb. 2, 1827. m. Mar. 20, 1858, at Remsen, N. Y., Ellen Raymond. (Children: — Carrie Estella, 149. b. June 28, 1860, d. May II, 1891. Mary Adelaid, 150. b. July 3, 1866. m. June 24, 1883, George Godkin, d. Sep. 18, 1891. One child: — Jessie Anna, 151. b. July 26, 1871. m. Henry Losaby, Mar. 10, 1891. Francis Otis. b. Aug. 26, 1874. Charles Albert, 152. b. Jan, 26, 1877. d. May 11, 1877. Grace. 153. b. Oct. 26, 1879.) II. Alonzo Draper, 142. b. Mar. 5, 1828. d. Mar. 31, 1839. III. Otis Skinner, 143. b. Littleton, Mass., May 8, 1831. m. Delia Crist, of Mohawk, N. Y. IV. Syrena Mead, 144. b. Littleton, Mass., Aug. 25, 1832. m. Nov. 21, 1848, Daniel Bowman, of Mohawk, N. Y. V. Sebastian Stevens, 145. b. Littleton, Mass., May 12, 1835. d. 1837. VI. Erastus D., 146. b. July 22, 1839. m.

Cornelia Raymond. VII. Alpheus, 147. b. Feb. 5, 1841. m. and lives in Ohio. VIII. Mary A., 148. b. Feb. 27, 1842. m. William Kingsbury.

134. IV. Cynthia, b. June 27, 1809, d. Winchester, N. H., Jan. 20, 1853. m. 1825-6, John Russell. He was b. Marlboro, Mass., June 25, 1799. d. Ayer, Mass., Jan. 8, 1871. Children:— I. Aaron Howe, 154. b. Boxboro, Apr. 10, 1827. d. S. Boston, Jan. 18, 1892. m. 1st: Winchester, N. H., Sep. 8, 1855, by Rev. Mr. Abbott, Maria Everdon. b. Hartford, Vt., Dec. 30, 1832. (Child:— Frank Everdon. b. New Bedford, Mass., Mar. 10, 1857. m. Winchester, N. H., Apr, 30, 1888, Nellie I., dau. of Joseph Priest and Esther Ann Howard. She was b. Hinsdale, N. H., Oct. 21, 1857.) m. 2dly: Boston, Jan. 21, 1863, Laura Victorine Cook, of Maine. She d. Boston, June 3, 1890. (Child -.—Aaron, 159. d. Boston, aged 6 years.) II. Edwin F., 155. b. Westford, Mass., Aug. 29, 1828. m. 1st: Boston, Jan. 1, 1855, Adelaid Schultz. She d. Boxboro, Jan. 20, 1863. (Children:— Addie M., 160. b. May 25, 1828. Carrie W., 161. b. Sep. 12, 1860.) Edwin F. m. 2dly: Harvard, Mass., May 12, 1869, Charlotte Williston. She was b. Boxboro, 1830. III. Artemus W., 156. b. Westford, Mass., Apr. 9, 1830. d. Harvard, Apr. 30, 1831. IV. Artemus W. 2d, 157. b. Boxboro, Sep. 5, 1832. d. there Mar. 6, 1834. V. John E., 158. b. Swanzey, N. H., May 14, 1847. d. Ayer, Mass., Aug. 26, 1868.

135. V. Semantha, b. Nov. 2, 1810. d. Boxboro, June 23, 1884.

136. VI. Jerome, b. July 28, 1812. d. Boxboro, Aug., 1812.

137. VII. Benjamin Franklin, b. Aug. 28, 1814.

138. VIII. Simon Whitney, b. July 16, 1819. d. S. Braintree, Mass., May 21, 1875.

139. IX. Granville Whitney, b. May 26, 1821.

140. X. Reuben Mead, b. Dec. 21, 1824. d. Worcester, Mass., Sep. 25, 1880.

131. Alonzo. (12. Benjamin, 3. Boston, 2. Samuel, 1. Thomas.) Eldest child and s. of Benjamin Draper and Amy Mead. m. New Ipswich, N. H., Oct. 9, 1831, Hannah Vose, dau. of Benjamin Cram and Polly Vose." She was b. Lyndboro, N. H., Feb. 11, 1807, and d. S. Boston, Mass., Jan. 29, 1892.

Mr. Draper was a teacher of the piano and wind instruments. He had a very lovable disposition, which attracted children to him very greatly. He published a book of fife melodies, consisting of quicksteps, marches and hornpipes. He also wrote and arranged a great deal of music for military orchestras.

CHILDREN:

162. I. Adelaid Hannah, b. Keysville, N. Y., Aug. 3, 1833.

(The author is much indebted to this lady for almost all the information regarding the descendants of Capt. Samuel Draper.)

163. II. Alonzo Granville, b. Brattleboro, Vt., Sep. 6, 1835. d. Brazos, Santiago, Tex., Sep. 3, 1865.

164. III. Endora Mead, b. Waterville, Me., Aug. 30, 1842. m. Sep. 19, 1865, Henry, s. of Henry Faxon and Adaline Flynn, of Boston, Mass. He was b. Boston, Apr. 16, 1834. Henry Faxon, Sr., was in the service of the City of Boston for over 50 years; his last office being that of City Milk Inspector. Mrs. Endora

Faxon will graduate in the Class for 1892, Boston College of Physicians & Surgeons, and will take her degree as a practising physician. Children, all b. Boston: — I. Richard, 167. b. Mar, 12, 1867. II. Henry Mead, 168. b. Nov. 17, 1870. d. Orlando, Fla., Mar. 27, 1884. III. Endora Winifred, 169. b. May 1, 1877.

165. IV. Algernon & 166. V. Sidney (Twins), b. July 30, 1845. Sidney d. same day. Algernon d. Mar. 14, 1874.

163. Alonzo Granville. (131. Alonzo, 12. Benjamin, 3. Boston, 2. Samuel, 1. Thomas.) Eldest s., 2d child of Alonzo Draper and Hannah Vose Cram. m. Lynn, Mass., Aug. 24, 1856, Sarah Elizabeth, dau. of Gustavus Andrews, J. P., and Sarah Ann Lillie, of Boston. She was b. Boston, Dec. 23, 1838.

Alonzo Granville Draper evinced an intense thirst for knowledge, assailing his parents with torrents of questions concerning the meaning of words, and upon the various subjects of conversation that reached his ear, and he was pronounced a "lawyer in embryo" before he was eight years old. In 1843 his parents removed to Boston, where he received his education. He graduated from the Otis School in 1850, receiving the Franklin medal, and after spending one year as clerk, he entered the English High School, and graduated in 1854 with another Franklin medal and three prizes. His teacher said that he could not allow one boy to carry off all of the first prizes, but permitted him to choose between the literary and scientific departments. During a visit to Boxboro, when under fifteen years of age, he delivered a temperance lecture in the little town house, the people coming from miles around to hear "Uncle Ben Draper's" (12) grandson; and, at the age of fifteen, he helped to organize a temperance society in Boston, including both old and young, and for which he drafted the constitution and by-laws.

Gen'l Alonzo Granville Draper of Lynn, Mass.

Failing to see the way open to go through college as he had earnestly hoped to do, he commenced the study of law, which he pursued with his usual determination in such leisure as he could command from the efforts necessary for his own support. Marrying, with his father's consent, before he was twenty-one years old, and with the additional care of a little family, he never wavered in courage and purpose, and, at the time the Civil War broke out, he was prepared to enter the bar. He settled in Lynn, Mass., in 1857, and soon became interested in the condition of the industrial classes, and Mar. 19, 1859, he commenced the editorship of the "New England Mechanic," a paper advocating the interests of the journeymen shoemakers, and in 1860 he organized and led the "Shoemakers' Strike," which was the first movement of the kind of any magnitude in the country, and as such challenged general attention. The necessity for this movement was occasioned by an overstocked market, and a consequent depression of prices, for which the only remedy proposed was that they should, for a time, stop work, and thus reduce the supply. This plan was adopted by the advice of many of the manufacturers, who promised pecuniary and moral support, while others refused to submit to what they termed the dictation of the laboring classes. A Lynn paper of September, 1865, referring to the affair, states that "Draper was a man of ability, and conservative as a leader, invariably counselling moderation, and deprecating, at all times, any resort to violence." The strike was characterized by a great deal of sobriety and good humor, with but few acts to condemn, considering the multitude participating, Having instigated the movement, he next lent his energies to secure funds to keep the strikers from suffering while waiting to resume work. He was a fluent extemporaneous speaker, and the interest in the cause was so general that he was greeted in New York and elsewhere by large and enthusiastic audiences, and money was liberally subscribed. He also made appeals to the churches, and by various other methods was able, with the aid of voluntary contributions, to sustain the strike. A Lynn paper — the "Saturday Union," of Sep. 26, 1885, which devoted an entire number to a description of the "Lynn Strike" of 1860, copied from Boston papers, with illustrations from "Frank Leslie's," says: — "One of the features of the strike was a public demonstration, composed of the military and fire companies of Lynn and Marblehead, with the novelty of eight hundred ladies in line, followed by four thousand workmen. The Lynn City Marshal, fearing there might be a disturbance, telegraphed to Salem and Marblehead for assistance; but the people of those places were in sympathy with the 'jours,' and returned for answer, 'Fight your own battles.' The strike was general throughout New England, and embraced nearly twelve thousand shoemakers and over three thousand female stitchers and binders."

At the opening of our Civil War, Alonzo G. Draper was 25 years of age; by occupation Assistant City Marshal of Lynn, Mass. Among the first to respond to his country's call to arms, he raised a company in Lynn, and for two months he supplied a drillmaster, and supported his men by subscription until they were accepted, and he was mustered in with them as Captain of Company C, 1st Mass. Heavy Artillery, July 5, 1861. They were drilled both as an infantry and an artillery regiment, and were stationed along the Potomac for the defense of Washington; and Aug. 22, 1862, Capt. Draper was ordered by Brigadier-Gen. Whipple, as Instructor in Infantry and Artillery, to the 107th New York Volunteers. He was promoted to Major, Jan. 16, 1863, and placed in command of Fort Albany. While there he joined the Free Masons, and became a member of the Benjamin B. French Lodge, No. 15, of the District of Columbia. Entered Apprentice, passed to the degree of Fellowcraft, and raised to the sublime degree of Master Mason, Feb. 16, 1863, and was distinguished for his zeal and fidelity to the craft.

In reply to Gov. John A. Andrew, as to Major Draper's fitness to command colored troops. Col. Thomas B. Tannatt said he thought him a too severe disciplinarian for that race; but it proved one element of his success with them, as they soon learned that there was no distinction made between them and the white men who came under his authority, and their sense of justice was satisfied. He was honorably discharged to accept promotion, Aug. 1, 1863, and was mustered in on the same date at Newbern, N. C, as Colonel 2d N. C., Infantry, afterwards the 36th U. S. Colored Troops. Aug. 29, 1863, he was on board of the transports with his men in two hours after the order was received to leave Newbern, and he went to Portsmouth, Va., where he recruited the remaining six companies to fill his regiment. Gen. Butler, wishing to recruit colored soldiers from within the enemy's lines, the regiment was ordered to make an expedition into the interior of North Carolina. It proceeded beyond Elizabeth City, obtaining a large number of recruits and contraband families, and, on its return, was attacked by a large body of guerrillas at Indiantown, N. C, who were routed and their camp burned. Feb. 22, 1864, Col. Draper went to Point Lookout, in the Military District of St. Mary's, Md., where the regiment was employed as guard for the rebel prisoners' camp, and on Aug. 20, 1864, he assumed command of the district upon the relief of Gen. Hinks. From Point Lookout there were two raids into the interior of Virginia, in one of which they captured Burleigh, afterwards the noted Canadian raider, and broke up a party of torpedo setters on the banks of the Potomac. (It will be noticed that Col. Hart in his Notes mentions but one raid. The other, above mentioned, must have occurred before Col. Draper was transferred to the 36th Regt. in 1864.)

Two incidents of the North Carolina raids may here be noted. Col. Draper, on asking of a woman information concerning the location of the guerrilla camp, prudently took a different road from that indicated, and thus escaped marching into a pit which had been prepared in the roadway, where the guerrillas were lying in ambush on either side. On another occasion he kept a Southern lady as hostage for the lives of two of his men, since it was customary to brutally murder their colored captives instead of treating them as prisoners of war. While crossing a district under command of a New York Colonel, he and his hostage were invited to dine with him, when the latter took away Col. Draper's sword, with the intention of releasing the lady, but the latter immediately ordered his regiment to the rescue. He was sustained in the action when the affair came before Gen. Butler, who decided that the New Yorker had exceeded his authority.

Fearing that the war would be over without his having an active part in the struggle, he made a successful appeal to Major Gen. Butler, and reported to that officer in the field on the 7th of July, 1864. While in the Army of the James he commanded a brigade, doing arduous duty in the trenches, where he lost many men. Afterwards he was ordered to Deep Bottom, where he participated in the battle of New Market Heights, Sep. 29, 1864. This battle has been variously mentioned as being near Chapin's farm, Deep Bottom and New Market Heights. In this engagement Col. Draper, commanding 2d Brigade, 3d Division, 18th Army Corps, "carried his brigade in column of assault with fixed bayonets, over the enemy's works, through a double line of 'abattis,' after severe resistance. For incessant attention to duty, and gallantry in action, he was recommended to brevet rank as Brigadier General by Major Gen. Butler, and was promoted to rank of Brigadier General by Brevet, 28th day of Oct., 1864, for gallant and meritorious service in the attack on the enemy's works at Spring Hill, Va." The 2d Brigade participated in the engagement which followed the victory at Spring Hill, and resulted in the capture of Fort Harrison.

The following extract occurs in Gen. Butler's "General Orders," after the battle: — "Of the colored soldiers of the 3d Divisions of the 18th and 19th Corps, and the officers who led them, the General commanding desires to make special mention. In the charge on the enemy's works, by the Colored Division of the 18th Corps, at Spring Hill, New Market, better men were never led — better officers never led better men. With hardly an exception, officers of colored troops have justified the care with which they have been selected. A few more such gallant charges, and to command colored troops will be the post of honor in the American armies."

From his enlistment to July 7, 1864, Col. Draper's services were in constant requisition on military boards.

NOTES by Lieut.-Col. Wm. H. Hart, Late of the 36th Volunteers.

"Early on the morning of Sep. 29, 1864, the colored troops moved out from Deep Bottom, Va., and about daybreak engaged the enemy, who were strongly entrenched. The 1st Brigade was repulsed, after a sharp skirmish, and fell back. Immediately Draper's Brigade was sent to dislodge the Confederates. Forming in column by division, closed in mass, the brigade charged the enemy's rifle pits under a heavy musketry fire and a severe cross or enfilading fire, from gun batteries at either end of the rebel line. The troops, emulating the bravery of their intrepid commander, moved gallantly forward in the face of a galling fire, and impeded by the trunks and limbs of felled trees, charged the rebel works through a double line of abatis. Once, and only once, did our dusky warriors falter under the terrible ordeal of fire to which they were subjected, and then, as if impelled by the mind and iron nerve of one man, and that man their commander, they charged with a terrible shout, and in a moment were inside the works, and victorious over a defeated and flying foe. I well remember seeing Gen. Draper in that critical moment, when our line wavered and seemed about to fall back and abandon the attempt to carry the rebel works at the point of the bayonet, he was standing upon a slight eminence, sword in hand, every vestige of color had left his face, but he was cognizant of everything going on about him, and fully realized the gravity of the situation. He was always cool and collected, and in my opinion was a stranger to fear under every and all circumstances. After taking their works we hurried on towards Richmond, and bivouacked for the night near Fort Harrison, participating the next day in the capture of that work.

"I have knowledge of but one raid from Point Lookout. June 11, 1864, Gen. Draper embarked on steamboats with the 36th Regt., U. S. troops, and about fifty regular cavalry; we steamed up the James River, and landed on Sunday morning at a place called Nomani Cliffs, on the south bank of the river. Some delay in landing was caused by having to lower the horses over the side of the boats and swim them ashore, which enabled the people near the shore to send mounted messengers through the country lying between the James and Rappahannock Rivers to warn the inhabitants of our coming. Gunboats were sent up, horses, cattle and farming implements, with which to stock a contraband farm then just established in St. Mary's Co., Md. After landing and getting in order to move, Gen. Draper divided the forces, which had been augmented by the addition of fifty armed sailors from the gunboats, and turning over one-half of the command to me, with orders to pass up the river road to a certain point, then to cross over the country in a southerly direction, and report to him at Warsaw Court House at 7 o'clock on the following evening. We moved down the river road, and thence across to Warsaw. We both arrived at Warsaw on Monday evening, each with a long train of wagons and carts, filled with farming tools and drawn by horses, mules and oxen, sequestrated en route. Subsequently we operated together until we reached the Rappahannock, when we embarked with our plunder, and returned to Point Lookout after being absent eleven days. On June 17 we had a lively skirmish with a portion of the 9th Virginia Infantry, then at home, as we were informed, on a furlough. This force had been hovering in our rear for several days, occasionally capturing a straggler from our ranks, and at once shooting him on the spot. We found one man lying by the roadside, as we were returning over the road for the purpose of engaging with this force, as stated above, with bullet holes through both feet. Exaggerated reports, not official, of this raid were sent to the War Department at Washington, and an investigation was ordered by the Secretary of War, on the grounds that Gen. Draper had undertaken it without any authority, or that, if he had any orders, he had greatly exceeded his authority. But nothing came of it that I could ever learn.

"These were the only occasions that I saw Gen. Draper under fire, except at the siege of Petersburg, when we were continually under fire night and day for several weeks."

After the close of active hostilities, Gen. Draper reached home. May 13, on a thirty days' furlough. In the meantime there were certain mysterious movements of troops under Sheridan towards Texas, the object of which was guessed at by many, but known to but few. Before Gen. Draper's furlough had expired, while amid the affection of his family, the congratulations of his friends, and the general joy of the public, he was ordered to join his command, and was sent to Brazos, Santiago, Texas. He sailed for Texas about the 1st of June, 1865, with the 25th Corps under Major Gen. Neitzel, a part of which he commanded till within a few days of his death. A short time before receiving the fatal wound, he was relieved of his duties at Brazos and appointed to the command of a post at Indianola. He was mortally wounded in the back, Aug. 30, by a stray musket ball, carelessly fired by some unknown hand. At the time he was riding out attended only by an orderly, and was observed to suddenly fall from his horse. As no sound of a musket was heard, and as the ball lodged in the spine and did not penetrate the body further, the only explanation is that he was hit by a stray ball coming from a great distance. Men were continually firing off their muskets over all the island. He died the 3d of September. On being told by the surgeons that there was not much hope of recovery, his reply was: "Gentlemen, I am not afraid to die." On the day of his death his men flocked to his headquarters, and one who was present states that he never heard such expressions of heart-felt grief.

Upon hearing that he was wounded, his wife and mother started for Texas that day that they might be with him and minister to his sufferings. They proceeded as far as New Orleans; but learning at that point that he was dead, they returned with sad hearts to their homes, never again in this life to look upon his face. His remains were brought home by Capt. Richard F. Andrews, his brother-in-law, appointed by Gen. Sheridan to that sad duty, accompanied also by the General's brother, a Captain in the same regiment.

The following extract from the "Lynn Weekly Reporter," of Sep. 30, 1865, relates to Gen. Draper's funeral: —

"As soon as the melancholy fact of the death of Brevet Brig.-Gen. Draper was known in this city, his Honor the Mayor called a special meeting of the two branches of the City Council, which was held on Friday evening of last week. At that meeting a committee was appointed, consisting of his Honor the Mayor and Aldermen Patch and Lewis, and the President and Messrs. Medbury, Davis and Aborn, of the Council, with authority to make all proper arrangements for the funeral services, and also to prepare a series of' resolutions expressive of the feelings of the citizens and the authorities on this melancholy occasion. These resolutions, so prepared, were reported and unanimously adopted at meetings of the two branches held on Tuesday evening.

"Wednesday afternoon last was assigned as the time for the obsequies, and by 2 o'clock the Common Street M. E. Church— the use of which had been kindly tendered for the occasion — was filled with the friends of the deceased and sympathizing citizens. The body of the house was principally occupied by the mourners, the members of the City Government and Veteran Association. The remains, which had been temporarily placed in the receiving tomb at the Eastern Burial Ground, were taken in charge by the Eleventh

Unattached Company, Capt. Bacheller, and escorted to the church, where they remained outside upon the funeral car prepared for the occasion. The city authorities were escorted from the City Hall to the church by Company D, Capt. Merritt. The pall bearers were Gen. E. W. Hinks, Gen. W. F. Tilton, Gen. Wm. Cogswell, Col. A. F. Devereux, Col. Godfrey Boyd, Col. B. F. Peach, Col. Wm. Palmer and Col. A. P. Caraher. The services in the church were conducted by Rev. C. W. Biddle, pastor of the First Universalist Church. The discourse was long and most eloquent, and closed with a feeling allusion to the relations that existed between the deceased and the weeping mourners. A procession was then formed in front of the church, under direction of Capt. E. A. Chandler as chief marshal, assisted by Capts. E. Parsons, Jr., J. E. Smith, J. T. Whittier and E. Carp. First came the funeral car bearing the remains; next the pall bearers and family and relatives of the deceased in carriages; next the members of the City Government and several past Mayors, preceded by the Boston Brigade Band, and closing the procession a large delegation from the Lynn Veteran Association, bearing a silk flag draped m mourning. The whole was preceded by a military escort, consisting of Companies D and F, and the Eleventh Unattached, the whole under the command of Capt. Stone, of Company F, and marching left in front, with arms reversed, and followed by Gilmore's Band — which was generously sent by the State authorities for this occasion — playing a mournful dirge. It was a solemn but impressive sight as the cortege slowly wended its way toward Pine Grove Cemetery, where the remains were temporarily deposited. The car which bore the remains consisted of a raised platform, covered with black cloth, as were also the wheels, and festooned with red, white and blue silk, fastened with black and white rosettes. At the four corners were silk flags looped with black crape. On each side the car were the initials "A. G. D." in silver. On the car was placed the coffin, which enclosed a leaden casket, and was covered with black cloth, studded with silver stars, and having three handles of the same material on each side, and one on either end. An American flag covered the coffin lid and was looped around the sides. On the coffin rested the hat, sword, sash and belt of the deceased, and also a profusion of beautiful flowers. The whole was drawn by two black horses, with black and white plumes in their heads, led by two of our colored citizens. The flags upon the City Hall, the Common and all the private flag-staffs in the city were flying at half-mast during the day, in token of respect for the memory of the deceased.

"The name of Gen. Draper will occupy a prominent place among those who served their country faithfully and well, and by their death bore testimony to their fidelity to the cause of human liberty and a free and united country."

CHILDREN, ALL .B. LYNN, MASS.:

170. I. Adelaid Andrews, b. Mar. 12, 1857.
171. II. Richard Francis, b. Aug. 29, 1858. d. Lynn, Oct. 14, 1861.
172. III. Sarah Lilian, b. Feb. 18, 1861. d. Lynn, Feb. 1, 1862.

173. IV. Gustavus Alonzo & 174. V. Endora Elizabeth, (Twins), b. Nov. 25, 1862. Endora d. Lynn, Mar. 24, 1872.

175. VI. Minnie Granville, b. Dec. 18, 1864. d. Lynn, Mar. 9, 1872.

165. Algernon. (131. Alonzo, 12. Benjamin, 3. Boston, 2. Samuel, 1. Thomas.) 4th child, 2d s, of Alonzo Draper and Hannah Vose Cram. m. Boston, Mass., July 29, 1869, Clarissa A., dau. of Horatio Ferrin and Mary Ann Emerson, of S. Boston. She was b. Boston, Aug. 20, 1850; and, on her husband's death, m. 2dly: Frank, s. of Thomas and Ellen Hill, June 16, 1881.

Algernon Draper received a Franklin medal when he graduated from the grammar school. He was a member of the English High School, and was 17 years old when he enlisted as drummer in the 1st Mass. Heavy Artillery Regt., July 21, 1862. He was mustered in as 2d Lieut, of the 36th U. S. Colored Troops, Mar. 21, 1864; as 1st Lieut., Apr. 27, 1864; as Capt., the same regiment, Feb. 28, 1865, and was mustered out as Capt. with company, Oct. 28, 1866, in Texas. He served in the trenches before Petersburg, and was afterwards on detached duty with his company at Dutch Gap, Va.

The following is an extract from the "Boston Globe": "There is mourning for Capt. Algernon Draper, late of the 36th U. S. C. I., not only in the bosom of his bereaved family and among many brother officers and friends, but far away among the freedmen whom he led on to victory. When Gen. Alonzo Draper fell many hearts were bleeding among the poor sons of Africa, and now the death of Capt. Algernon Draper, the only brother of the General, will open the wound afresh. Long will brother officers and men, friends and neighbors, remember, love and honor him. When the war opened, Capt. Draper, being but a youth of 17 or 18, enlisted in the 1st Mass. Heavy Artillery. From this regiment he was promoted to a Lieutenancy in the 36th U. S. C. I., and before he was 20 years of age he received the commission of a Captain. He sacrificed ease and home, and put his life in peril again and again to defend his country. He was a man not only of singular sagacity, but of strong and quick passions, full of the chivalry of the military profession. He was indeed beloved by officers and men, and all who formed his acquaintance. When under a heavy fire of the enemy, sometimes for days at a time, he was always cool and deliberate, encouraging his men, and with a watchful eye looking out for their comfort and safety. He was a faithful officer, true to the cause for which he battled and suffered, true to his men and true to his manhood.

"One prominent element of his character was to stand firm for justice and truth. If he believed and felt a measure to be right, whether popular or unpopular, he would stand by it without regard to personal consequences. And on the same principle, if he believed and knew an act to be wrong, he would oppose it to the last. On one occasion, when an unscrupulous officer in command of the regiment requested of him what he had no right to do, Capt. Draper replied, 'Sir, I respect your shoulder straps, but your manhood I do not respect.' And the words that he uttered when he breathed his last — 'I have tried to do my duty, I have tried to do right' — were true to the letter.

"After the fall of Richmond he followed the fortunes of the regiment over the burning plains of Texas, and after his return home to Boston, he engaged in business, refusing a good position in the Boston Custom House offered to him about this time. For the last two years or more he has been in the firm of Camille Ried & Co. He was an honest, energetic business man, beloved and respected by all his customers, and an honor to the firm he represented. He died on Saturday evening, at 9 o'clock. Mar. 14, at the age of 28 years, 8 months. He looked beautiful in death, covered with the floral offerings of loved and mourning friends."

CHILDREN, B. BOSTON:

176. I. Algernon Henry, b. Apr. 29, 1870.

177. II. Horace Ferrin, b. Feb. 7, 1872. d. Boston, Nov. 17, 1875.

137. Benjamin Franklin. (12. Benjamin, 3. Boston, 2. Samuel, 1. Thomas.) 7th child, 3d s. of Benjamin Draper and Amy Mead. m. 1st: his cousin, Tryphena Worster. She was b. W. Swanzey, N. H., May 5, 1815. He m. 2dly: Salem, Mass., Jan. 14, 1863, Maria Fitzgerald, b. Co. Kerry, Ireland, Feb. 14, 1845. He was a skilled mechanic.

CHILDREN, BY 1ST MARRIAGE:

178. I. Delphia, b. Swanzey, Nov. 8, 1836. m. 1st: 1855, Jeremiah Pelkey. He d. Joliet, Ill., 1869, and she m. 2dly: Brattleboro, Vt., Mar. 26, 1870, Homer Thayer. She obtained a divorce from him in Middlesex County, Mass., Dec. 8, 1884, and m. sdly: Orleans S. Eaton, in Swanzey, N. H., Jan. 12, 1887. He was b. Winchester, N. H., Dec. 17. 1833. She d. Aug. 23, 1888. Children, by 1st marriage (no issue by 2d and 3d marriages):- I. Frank A., 184. b. Vernon, Vt., 1856. m. and lives in Seward, Neb. H. Alberto, 185. b. Swanzey, N. H., 1857.

179. II. Jason, b. Brooklyn, N. Y., May 5, 1837. d. Feb. 13, 1885, in Hubbard City, Hill Co., Tex. m. Nov. 16, 1862, Mary Ette Ray. She was b. Dec. 8, 1846. Children:— I. Rhoda, 186. b. Aug. 27, 1863. m. Dec. 22, 1880, to Henry Griswold. (Child: — Frederick Benjamin, 190. b. Jan. 5, 1882. She d. Nov. 27, 1884.) H. Jane, 187. b. Jan. 4, 1865. d. Apr. 17, 1871. ni. Benjamin Edward, 188. b. Jan. 27, 1867. d. Dec. 29, 1884. IV. Clara, 189. b. Oct. 11, 1869. m. Sep. 6, 1886, George F. Murray. He was b. Mar. 13, 1865.

180. III. Clara Melissa, b. Boxboro. d. Dakota, 1890.

181. IV. George, b. Boxboro. d. Brooklyn, N. Y., 1863.

CHILDREN, BY 2D WIFE:

182. V. Laura Maria, b. Chicago, Nov. 5, 1863. d. there July 6, 1871.

183. VI. George Franklin, b. Wonowoc, Wis., Aug. 26, 1866. m. Danvers, Mass., May 24, 1886, Jessie E. Abbot. She was b. there May 7, 1867. Child:— May, 191. b. July 15, 1891.

138. Simon Whitney. (12. Benjamin, 3. Boston, 2. Samuel, 1. Thomas.) 8th child, 4th s. of Benjamin Draper and Amy Mead. m. 1st: Salem, Mass., Aug. 27, 1842, Nancy Shillaher Hailey. She was b. Tuftenborough, N. H., Nov. 18, 1825.

d. Roxbury, Mass., July 16, 1869. Hem. 2dly: 1870, at Belfast, Me., Bridget Pitcher. She was b. Waldoboro, Me., 1820. d. Northport, Me., July, 1882.

Mr. Draper was a man who was greatly beloved. He was a pianomaker, and invented a harp attachment for pianos. He also, in connection with his brother Reuben, 140, invented a patent mill picking machine, by which they gained considerable property.

CHILDREN, BY 1st MARRIAGE (NO ISSUE BY 2D):

192. I. Nancy Emma, b, Boxboro, Sep. 17, 1844. d. there Jan. 10, 1847.

193. II. Benjamin Whitney, b. Boxboro, June 25, 1846. d. Roxbury, Mar. 13, 1862.

194. III. Nancy Emma 2d, b. Boxboro, Nov. 4, 1848. d. Roxbury, Sep. 3, 1867.

195. IV. Simon Eugene, b. Boxboro, Nov. 1, 1849.

196. V. John Robert, b. Boxboro, Dec. 31, 1851.

197. VI. Willie Hailey, b. Dedham, Mar. 14, 1854. d. there Dec. 31, 1854.

198. VII. Mary Eliza, b. Roxbury, Dec. 5, 1855. d. there Mar. 23, 1856.

199. VIII. Mary Eliza 2d, b. Roxbury, Sep. 23, 1857. d. there Sep. 5, 1867.

200. IX. Louis Shillaher, b. Salem, Mass., Sep. 11, 1862. d. there Feb. 24, 1863.

196. John Robert. (138. Simon Whitney, 12. Benjamin, 3. Boston, 2. Samuel, I, Thomas.) 5th child, 3d s. of Simon Whitney Draper and Nancy S. Hailey. m. Boston, Aug. 25, 1875, Lilian M. Geri. She was b. Boston, July 12, 1857.

CHILDREN, B. BOSTON:

201. I. Ferdinando John, b. Jan. 3, 1877.

202. II. A son, b. May, 1880.

203. III. Emma Adeline, b. May 28, 1882.

204. IV. Lilian Magdalene, b. Sep. 4, 1884.

205. V. Charles Alonzo, b. Dec. 13, 1886.

206. VI. Mabel Elizabeth, b. Dec. 25, 1890.

139. Granville W. (12. Benjamin, 3. Boston, 2. Samuel, 1. Thomas.) 9th child, 5th s. of Benjamin Draper and Amy Mead. He m. 1st: Elizabeth, 97, dau. of Boz Brown Draper, 9. He m. 2dly: Ellen Nelligan. She was b. 1820.

CHILD, BY 2D WIFE:

207. I. Charles Granville, b. Plymouth, Mass., Nov. 21, 1853. m. Sep. 28, 1890, Mary R. Fairbanks. She was b. Lowell, Mass., Aug. 3, 1869.

140. Reuben Mead. (12. Benjamin, 3. Boston, 2. Samuel, 1. Thomas.) 10th child, 6th s. of Benjamin Draper and Amy Mead. m. Apr. 30, 1845, Hannah Maria, dau. of James Stevens and Martha Varnum Barrow. She was b. Chelmsford, Mass., Nov. 1, 1820.

Mr. Draper was held in high esteem by his fellow citizens. He was one of the good men of the times whose memory will ever remain in the hearts of his friends.

CHILDREN, B. BOXBORO, MASS.:

208. I. Helen Maria, b. July 28, 1846. m. Boxboro, Aug. 15, 1874, Edward F., s. of Edward and Jane A. Kelleran, of Thomastown, Me. He d. Feb, 10, 1885. Children: — I. Helen Frances, 3x6, b. Ayer, Mass., Dec. 24, 1878. II. Edward Mead, 217. b. Ayer, Mass., June 25, 1881. d. Aug. 25, 1881. III. Isora M., 218. b. Wollaston, Mass., Oct. 13, 1882.

209. II. Emma Isora, b. Oct. 25, 1847. m. Dec. 3, 1871, at Groton, Mass., Charles E., s. of David F. and Hannah B. Woods, of Amherst, N. H. Children: — I. Reuben Edward, 219. b. Ayer, Mass., Sep. 4, 1872. II. Charles E., 220. d. Clinton, Mass., Nov. 26, 1873.

210. III. Charles Edwin, b. Jan. 5, 1850. d. Ayer, Mass., Oct. 17, 1880.

211. IV. Anna Eliza, b. May 2, 1851. d. Worcester, Mass., Sep. 21, 1880. m. July 19, 1872, at Lancaster, Mass., Herbert W., s. of Charles L. and Susannah C. Whitney of Lancaster. Children: — I. Herbert Gordon, 221. b. Ayer, Mass., Aug. 28, 1874. d. Jan. 31, 1891.

212. V. Martha Louisa, b, Dec. 10, 1853. m. Clinton, Mass., June 20, 1874, Hiram K., s. of Hiram and Arvilla A. Stewart, of Fairfax, Vt. He d. Mentone, Cal., Jan. 25, 1887. Children: — I. Charles Hiram, 222. b. Richford, Vt., Mar. 9, 1878. II. Ethel Maria, 223. b. Richford, Vt., July 31, 1879. III. Harold Draper, 224. b. Troy, Vt. Mrs. Stewart m. 2dly: Feb. 28, 1888, Edwin J. Roberts, of San Bernardino, Cal. Children: — I. Mabel Louisa, 225. b. Mentone, Cal., Dec. 11, 1880. II. Myrtle Isora, 226. b. Crafton, Cal., July 18, 1888.

213. VI. James Stevens, b. May 1, 1855. m. Lancaster, Dec. 13, 1881, Endora S., dau. of Charles L. and Susannah C. Whitney. Child: — I. Harry Read, 227. b. Ayer, Mass., July 18, 1884.

214. VII. Maria Mead, b. May 17, 1860, m. Groton, Mass., Dec. 7, 1878, Raymond G., s. of Edward and Jane A. Kelleran, of Thomastown, Me. Children: — I. Lois Marion, b. Ayer, Mass., ""Aug. 30, 1879. II. Helen Leslie, 228. b. Ayer, Oct. 13, 1881. III. Lena Maud, 229. b. Ayer, Nov. 8, 1882. IV. Beatrice Romeyne, 230. b. Ayer, Apr. 23, 1891.

215. VIII. Reuben Lewis, b. June 16, 1862. d. Worcester, Sep. 29, 1880.

He was a member of the class of 1879 which graduated at the High School, Ayer, Mass., and was loved and respected by his classmates.

Drapers of Virginia - Descendants of Thomas Draper

This branch of the Drapers it is impossible to locate correctly, except that it is known that 2. Thomas Draper, who is supposed to have been a son of i. Peter and Hannah Draper, was of Virginia. Whether Thomas emigrated from England to Virginia, or his father was the emigrant, it is impossible to state. We know, however, that Thomas married Lucy Coleman, and that they moved from Virginia to South Carolina about 1760. Lucy Coleman had a sister whose name was Frances. She married Zachariah Gibbs, who was a Colonel in the English Army. By this marriage there were two children, Susan and Martha, who, during the prevalence of smallpox in the City of Charleston, S. C, about 1781, were sent to the country to escape it. Their mother, however (Frances), died in Charleston of the disease. The Revolutionary War having closed, her husband. Col. Gibbs, went to England, his property having been confiscated by the Continental Congress. His two lonely little daughters waited long for their father, who never returned, nor did they ever receive a word from him during their lives. They grew up and were married. Susan married Daniel Draper (10), son of the above Thomas Draper, and her own cousin. In later years it was ascertained that Col. Gibbs received a pension from the English Government and a grant of a thousand acres of land in Canada. He went to Canada, took possession of this land, and finally sold it, and departed for South Carolina to claim his children. The vessel in which he sailed was lost at sea.

2. Thomas, (1. Peter.?) s. of Peter and Hannah Draper, m. Lucy Coleman about 175-.

CHILDREN:

I. Sarah, b. Va., Oct. 6, 1758.

II. William, b. S. C, Apr. 6, 1761. d. in infancy.

III. Anna, b. S. C, Aug. 26, 1763.

IV. James, b. S. C, Feb. 5, 1766.

V. Thomas, b. S. C, Sep. 15, 1768.

VI. Philip, b, S. C, June 14, 1771. 9. VII. Catherine, b. S. C, Jan. 27, 1774.

10. VIII. Daniel, b. S. C, Apr. 1, 1776. d. June 22, 1856.

11. IX. Travis, b. S. C, Sep. 16, 1778.

12. X. William 2d, b. S. C, June 28, 1781. d. Jersey Co., Ill., Feb., 1841. He went from S. C. to Randolph Co., N. C; from thence to Tenn., and then to Ill.

13. XI. Joshua, b. S. C, June 11, 1784.

10. Daniel. (2. Thomas, i. Peter.) 8th child, 5th s. of Thomas Draper and Lucy Coleman, m. Feb. 13, 1798, Susan, dau. of Col. Zachariah Gibbs and Frances Coleman. They were first cousins and were probably m. in S. C. She was b. Mar. 3, 1775. d. Oct. 23, 1832.

They removed prior to 1811 to Smith Co., Tenn., and from thence to Lincoln Co., Md., in 1816, where he died.

CHILDREN:

14. I. Zachariah Gibbs, b. Dec. 2, 1798. d. July 2, 1856.

15. II. Lucy, b. Dec. 27, 1800. d. May 27, 1873. m. Oct. 10, 1819, in Auburn, Mo., Philip Orr. He d. Mar. 12, 1844. Children: — I. Susannah, 23. b. 1822. d. in infancy. II. Elizabeth, 24. b. Dec. 24, 1824. d. Aug. 30, 1891. m. Dr. H. K. Jones. III. Thomas, 25. b. 1826. d. Mar. 14, 1844. IV. Martha Jane, 26. b. June 25, 1828. m. Kellogg. V. William Draper, 27. b. Mar. 2, 1831. d. Mar. 13, 1884. (m. and had:— I. Lucy K., 31. II. Charles L., 32. III. Rose E., 33. IV. Maud S., 34. V. Mary E., 35. VI. Daniel D., 36.) VI. Mary Gibbs, 28. b. Mar. 19, 1834. m.

South. VII. Lucy Draper, 29. b. Aug., 1836. d. 1866. VIII. Daniel Edwin, 30. b, Aug. 8, 1842. d. May 13, 1873.

16. III. Henry Clinton, b. Smith Co., Tenn., Dec. 18, 1802. d. Mar. 5, 1844.

17. IV. Martha, b. Apr. 12, 1805. d. Apr. 23, 1884. m. Jan. 19, 1826, Auburn, Mo., William Kerr. Children: — I. Susan, 37. m. Hyman E. Block. II. Mary Clark, 38. m. William H., s. of John Purse and Susan De Grove Purse. He was b. Sep. 6, 1824, New York City. They had three (44, 45, 46,) children, all deceased. III. Elizabeth, 39. m. Samuel M. Martin. IV. John, 40. m. Susan F. Purse. V. William, 41. d. 1870, single. VI. Thomas, 42. d. single. VII. Martha, 43. d. single.

18. V. Edwin, b. July 16, 1808. d. Aug. 8, 1887.

19. VI. James, b. June 24, 1809. d. July 23, 1830. (Unmarried. Drowned, St. Louis, Mo.)

20. VII. Philander, b. Aug. 26, 1811. d, Louisiana, Mo,, Feb. 18, 1883.

21. VIII. Daniel, b. Nov. 21, 1815. d. Oct. 13, 1875.

22. IX. John Campbell Harbison, b. May 5, 1817. d. in infancy.

14. Zachariah Gibbs. (10. Daniel, 2. Thomas, i. Peter.) Eldest s. and child of Daniel Draper and Susan Gibbs. m. Rolls Co., Mo., Oct. 13, 1823, Elinor M. Briggs. She d. 1875.

CHILDREN:

47. I. Henry von Phal, b. 1823.

48. II. Julia Ann, b. 1829. m. ____ Simmons, d. 1856, leaving one child (52).

49. III. Maria, b. 1833. m. Mr. Jones.

50. IV. Susannah, b. 1835. d. 1845.

51. V. Charles, b. 1850. d. 1881.

16. Henry Clinton. (10. Daniel, 2. Thomas, 1. Peter.) 3d child, 2d s. of Daniel Draper and Susan Gibbs. m. Pike Co., Mo., Nov. 11, 1832, Mary Kerr, dau. of Richard and Margaret Jones. She was b. Mercer Co., Ky., Aug. 1, 1808.

CHILDREN:

53. I. Susan, b. Pike Co., Mo., Nov. 8, 1833.

54. II. Margaret, b. Lincoln Co., Mo., Feb. 23, 1835. d. Feb. 12, 1849.

55. III. James Kerr, b. Pike Co., Mo., Jan. 31, 1837. d. Indianola, Tex., Nov. 20, 1852.

56. IV. Henry Clay, b. Pike Co., Mo., Apr. 2, 1840.

57. V. John Brown, b. Pike Co., Mo., Oct. 28, 1842.

58. VI. Mary Clinton, b. Pike Co., Mo., June 11, 1844.

56. Henry Clay. (16. Henry Clinton, 10. Daniel, 2. Thomas, i. Peter.) 4th child, 2d s. of Henry Clinton Draper and Mary Kerr Jones, m. Franklin Co., Mo., Apr. 29, 1875, Anne E. Murdoch.

Henry Clay Draper served in Co. E, 3d Regt. Cavalry, Mo. S. M., U. S. A.

CHILDREN:

59. I. John Murdoch, b. Apr. 29, 1876.

60. II. Eliza, b. Sep. 3, 1878. d. in infancy.

61. III. Julia, b. July 23, 1879.

62. IV. Adah, b. June 23, 1884.

57. John Brown. (16. Henry Clinton, 10. Daniel, 2. Thomas, 1. Peter.) 5th child, 3d s. of Henry Clinton Draper and Mary Kerr Jones, m. 1st: Louisiana, Mo., June 30, 1870, E. Augdina Murdoch. She d. Oswego, Kansas, Mar. 28, 1874. He m. 2dly: June 21, Lucy Pheins.

Dr. John B. Draper served during the Civil War as Lieut. of Co. C, 33 Mo. V. L

CHILDREN, BY 1st WIFE:

63. I. Arthur Clinton, b. Apr. 1, 1872.

64. II. John Murdoch, b. Mar. 19, 1874. d. same day.

CHILDREN, BY 2D WIFE, B. OSWEGO, KANSAS:

65. III. Henry Fenton, b. July 17, 1879.

66. IV. Albert & 67. V. Florence (Twins), b. Jan. 4, 1882.

68. VI. James B., b. Nov. 21, 1886.

69. VII. Elinor, b. Jan. 30, 1889.

18. Edwin. (10. Daniel, 2. Thomas, 1. Peter.) 5th child, 3d s. of Daniel Draper and Susan Gibbs. m. Pike Co., Mo., June 14, 1839, Urania L. Rouse. She d. Jacksonville, Ill., Aug., 1887.

CHILDREN:

70. I. Charles Levi, b. Louisiana, Mo., May 21, 1840. m. May 23, 1866, St. Charles, Mo., Mary Peyton, dau. of Robert A. Wolton and Emily C. Bates. Children: — Edith Wolton, 75. b. 1871. d. in infancy. Alice Leonore, 76. b. Louisiana, Mo., July 29, 1872.

71. II. Martha Lucy, d. in infancy.

72. III. Urania, d. in infancy.

73. IV. Ada Marvin, d. in infancy.

74. V. Susan Augusta, b. Louisiana, Mo., 1850. (Unmarried.)

20. Philander, (10. Daniel, 2. Thomas, 1. Peter.) 7th child, 5th s. of Daniel Draper and Susan Gibbs. m. 1st: Feb. 18, 1835, Eliza A. Clarke. She d. Auburn, Mo., June 29, 1838. m. 2dly: Sarah, dau. of Richard Fenton and Ann Hassall. She was b. Manchester, Eng., Mar. 10, 1816.

CHILDREN, BY 2D WIFE:

77. I. Daniel Marshall, b. Montgomery, Mo., 1837, m. Julia Stewart.

A lawyer by profession. At the age of 25 he enlisted, Feb. 21, 1862, at Danville, Mo., and was mustered into service as a Captain in Company C, 9th Regt. of Cavalry, Missouri S. M., for three years. He was commissioned a Captain, Feb. 28, 1862, with rank from Feb. 21; promoted Major, May 3, 1862, with rank from May 3; promoted Lieut.-Col., July 13, 1863, with rank from July i; resigned April, 1865. Commissioned Brigadier-Gen. of the 4th Military, 1st Division, Missouri S. M., Feb. 20, 1865. Vacated Apr. 8, 1865.

78. II. Eliza Clarke, m. ____ Zook.

79. III. Ann H.

80. IV. Charles Clinton, m. Fanny McClug. He served in Co. C, 3d Regt. Cavalry, Mo. S. M., U. S.

81. V. Ed. F. m. 1st: Lizzie Templeton. m. 2dly: ____ Grubb.

82. VI. Laura. (Single.)

83. VII. Fannie. (Single.)

84. VIII. Arthur Gibbs.

21. Daniel. (10. Daniel, 2. Thomas, 1. Peter.) 8th child, 6th s. of Daniel Draper and Susan Gibbs. m. Lincoln Co., Mo., Apr. 13, 1840, Julia A. Riggs.

CHILDREN:

85. I. William, b, Jan. 7, 1841. d. July 26, 1842.

86. II. Mary E., b. Apr. 2, 1842. d. Jan. 19, 1845.

87. III. Henry Clinton, b. Feb. 3, 1845.

88. IV. Frank R., b. Mar. 13, 1849. m. Barry, Ill., Dec. 13, 1875, Katie Drumrey. Child:— De Witt, 90. b. Farber, Mo., Mar. 7, 1877.

89. V. Bertha, b. Nov. 23, 1862. d. Oct. 11, 1863.

87. Henry Clinton. (21. Daniel, 10. Daniel, 2. Thomas, i. Peter.) 3d child, 2d s. of Daniel Draper and Julia A. Riggs. m. Ashley, Mo., Nov. 8, 1871, Ellen E. Strother.

CHILDREN:

91. I. Bertha M., b. Louisiana, Mo., Aug. 9, 1872.

92. II. Daniel C, b. Louisiana, Mo., Aug. 5, 1879.

93. III. Harry L., b. Louisiana, Mo., July 5, 188r.

94. IV. Robert S., b. Chicago, Ill., Aug. 5, 1883.

95. V. Julia A., b. Chicago, Ill., Aug. 7, 1888. d. Aug. 8, 1888.

13. Joshua. (2. Thomas, 1. Peter.) 8th s., youngest child of Thomas Draper and Lucy Coleman, m. Feb. 8, 1803, Nancy Wilkin.

CHILDREN:

96. I. Polly, b. Dec, 4, 1804.

97. II. Sarah, b. Mar. 6, 1806.

98. III. Lucinda, b. May 1, 1808.

99. IV. Diana, b. Apr. 4, 1810.

100. V. Elizabeth, b. Apr. 22, 1812.

101. VI. James Terrell, b. Apr. 18, 1814.

102. VII. Catherine, b. Jan. 4, 1816.

103. VIII. Daniel Davis, b. Dec. 14, 1817. d. Apr. 30, li

104. IX. Robert Wilkin, b. Apr. 27, 1820.

105. X. Joshua, b. Jan. 26, 1824.

106. XI. Millie Gondalock, b. June 6, 1827.

103. Daniel Davis. (13. Joshua, 2. Thomas, 1. Peter.) 8th child, 2d s. of Joshua Draper and Nancy Wilkin, m. Caroline M. Wood, Jan. 2, 1840.

CHILDREN:

107. I. William Wood, b. Mar. 21, 1841. m. Dec. 21, 1871, Emma E. Moore.

108. II. Nancy Elizabeth, b. July 10, 1843. m. Feb. 18, 1862, S. E. Green.
109. III. Joshua, b. Aug. 26, 1845. m. Dec. 21, 1882, Donnise Nichols.
110. IV. James Robert, b. Apr. 23, 1848. m. Oct. 19, 1882, Florence K. Stockley.
111. V. Mattie C, b. Feb. 13, 1851. m. Oct. 24, 1872, W. D. Smyth.
112. VI. Sallie L., b. Dec. 5, 1853. m. Oct. 30, 1877, Wm. G. Ledbetter.
113. VII. Millie C., b. Mar. 14, 1856. m. June 29, 1874, A. N. Wood.
114. VIII. Ida Emma, b. Sep. 13, 1858.
115. IX. Davis Coleman, b. Nov. 16, 1860. d. Feb. 8, 1862.
116. X. Susan Fannie, b, Oct. 6, 1862. d. July 16, 1863.

The Drapers of Drapersville, VA.

For a fuller account of this branch of the Drapers in America the reader is respectfully referred to two memoirs by Prof. George F. Barker, in memoriam of Dr. John William Draper and his son, Dr. Henry Draper. These memoirs are very extensive, and are but just tributes to the memory of two members of the Draper family, whose illustrious lives and achievements have, for all time to come, brought out the name prominently and brilliantly before the world, and cast a lustre upon it, such as no others who have borne it have so far succeeded in doing.

The achievements of these two men in the natural sciences and in literature have been very great, and the two other sons of Dr. John William Draper — namely, the late John Christopher Draper and the present Dr. Daniel Draper — have served to increase the respect and admiration of the world for a branch of the Draper family wherein all the men were illustrious and all the women distinguished.

The list of achievements of this little branch, so soon to become extinct, are too highly written on the annals of scientific research for the author to attempt to even give a synopsis of the same within the narrow limits of a work of this description. He would have been glad to have embodied Prof. Barker's two papers within its pages had that been possible.

John William Draper was born in the Parish of St. Helens, Liverpool, England, May 5, 1811. His father was the Rev. John C. Draper, a Wesleyan clergyman, who died in 1829. Before the Revolutionary War certain of Dr. John W. Draper's ancestors, on his mother's side, had come to America, and settled in Virginia, founding there a small Wesleyan community. Subsequently others of the family crossed the ocean and joined the little colony. Urged by these relatives, and accompanied by his mother and one of his sisters, John William Draper came to America in 1832, and settled with his relatives at Christianville, Mecklenburgh Co., Va. The post-office at that point was named Drapersville, after Dr. Draper, and it is a little place quite well known in that section, as the author is able to testify, having constructed a railroad within 15 miles of the same. Young Draper's mother and sisters taught school in the neighborhood, and he himself graduated as an M.D. at the University of Pennsylvania, and in 1836 he became Professor of Chemistry and Natural Philosophy at Hampton Sidney, Prince Edward Co., Va. In 1837 he accepted the Professorship of Chemistry in the University of the City of New York, and thereafter he and his sons were identified with New York, its universities and colleges, and its scientific researches, to the present day.

Dr. Draper, whilst a student at the University of London, Eng., in the year 1830, boarded with a friend of his father's — Mrs. Barker by name — and there met her niece. Miss Antonia Coetania Gardner. She was the only daughter of Dr. Gardner, of Rio Janeiro, the attending physician of the Emperor Dom Pedro of Brazil. Dr. Gardner's wife was the daughter of Senor de Piva Pereira, of Portugal, whose great-grandfather was captain of Vasco de Gama's ship when he circumnavigated Africa in 1498. Within a few months they became engaged, and in 1831, not long after the death of Dr. Gardner in Brazil, they were married. Six children were born to them, one of whom died in infancy. The eldest son, John Christopher, born in Virginia in 1835, died in New York in 1885, and left no children. He, after his father's death, became his successor as Professor of Chemistry in the Medical Department of the University of New York.

The second son, Henry, born in Virginia in 1837, became Professor of Physiology and Sub-Professor of Analytical Chemistry in the University of New York. He early turned his attention in the direction of physical research, especially in its relation to astronomy, and was elected a member of the National Academy in 1877. His early death, in 1882, alone prevented his rising to an equal eminence as an investigator with that obtained by his distinguished father. He married, in 1867, Mary Anna, daughter of Courtland Palmer, of New York, who survives him, but left no issue.

The third son, Dr. Daniel Draper, is at present the Director of the Meteorological Observatory in Central Park, New York. He has two daughters, but no son.

Dr. John William Draper's daughters were Virginia, afterwards Mrs. Maury, named for the State in which she was born, who died in 1885; and Antonia, at present Mrs. Edward H. Dixon.

No record of this branch of the family which did not mention Dr. John William Draper's elder sister, Dorothy Catherine, would be quite complete. She accompanied the newly married couple from England to Virginia. Having shared her brother's taste for scientific pursuits, she became his assistant in research, and rendered him most valuable aid. Her portrait was the first ever taken from the life by the daguerreotype process, and the colored plates which illustrate his memoir were the work of her pencil. She was a constant inmate of his family, and during the many years of his wife's ill health, she was as a mother to the children. She has outlived her brother, and resides at the family mansion at Hastings-on-the-Hudson.

2. John Christopher, s. of 1. John and Elizabeth Draper, b. Nov. 8, 1777, in London, England, d. Feb. 3, 1829, at Sheerness, Kent, Eng. m. a dau. of William and Dorothy Ripley. She d. Boydton, Va., Feb. 2, 1834.

CHILDREN:

3. I. Dorothy Catherine, b. Newcastle-on-Tyne, Northumberland, Eng., Aug. 6, 1807.

4. II. Elizabeth Johnson, b. Penrith, Cumberland, Eng., Apr. 13, 1809. d. Oct. 8, 1880, at Waterbury, Conn. m. Mr. North.

5. III. John William, b. St. Helens, Lancashire, Eng., May 5, 1811. d. Jan. 4, 1882, at Hastings-on-the-Hudson, N. Y.

6. IV. Sarah Ripley, b. Lincoln, Eng., June 24. 1813. d. New York City, Nov., 1864. m. Daniel Pereira Gardner. (Had seven children.)

5. John William. (2. John Christopher, i. John.) 3d child, only s. of John Christopher Draper and Miss Ripley, m. 1831, Antonia Coetania de Piva Pereira, only dau. of Dr. Gardner, of Rio Janeiro and Coetania de Piva Pereira, of Portugal. She d. July 31, 1870, at Hastings-on-the-Hudson, N. Y.

CHILDREN:

7. I. John Christopher, b. Va., Mar. 31, 1835. d. New York City, Dec. 20, 1885. m. in New York City, but had no issue.

8. II. Henry, b. Va., Mar. 7, 1837. d. New York City, Nov. 20, 1882. m. Nov. 11, 1867, in New York City, Mary Anna, dau. of Courtland Palmer. (No issue.)

9. III. Virginia, b. Va., Dec. 26, 1839. d. Oct. 26, 1885, at Hastings-on-the-Hudson, N. Y. m. May 22, 1865, at Hastings-on-the-Hudson, N. Y., Rev. Mylton Maury. Children: — I. Antonia Coetania de Piva Pereira, 13. 11. Sarah, 14. III. Carlotta Joanquina, 15. IV. John William Draper, 16.

10. IV. Daniel, b. New York City, Apr. 2, 1841. m. Apr. 28, 1887, Ann, dau. of F. M. Ludlow, at St. Louis, Mo. She is a great-niece of Lieut. M. F. Maury. Children:— I. Dorothy Catherine, 17. II. Harriet Maury, 18.

11. V. William, b. New York City, Nov., 1845. d. Hastings-on-the-Hudson, N. Y., Sep. 21, 1853.

12. VI. Antonia Coetania de Piva Pereira, b. New York City, Nov. 15, 1849. m. July 16, 1879, at Hastings-on-the-Hudson, N. Y., Edward H., s. of Senator Nathan F. Dixon, of Westly, R. I. Had one s., 19, who d. in infancy.

Drapers of Pulaski County, VA.

Draper's Valley, Va., was named after John Draper, Sr., the first white man who settled in that section of the country, about 1765-6. He was b. within the limits of Philadelphia, and was the son of George Draper and Ellen Harden, who came from Ireland. George Draper moved from there to Pattonsburgh on the James River, Va. He went from there to survey some lands in Western

Virginia, and was never heard from again; he was thought to have been killed by the Indians. His wife and two children then moved to a place in Montgomery County, Va., called Draper's Meadows.

CHILDREN:

John. Moved on his father's death to Draper's Valley, Va.

Mary. m. Col. Ingles, and settled at Ingles Ferry, 20 miles east of Draper's Valley.

An account of the thrilling adventures of this family with the Indians may be read in a work by Dr. J. P. Hale, of Charleston, Kanawha Co., W. Va., called "Trans-Alleghany Pioneers." Dr. Hale was a descendant of Mary Draper.

The Drapers of Ireland in America

The Drapers of Ireland sprang from two brothers, commissioned officers in the English Army in the reign of King Charles II., and Englishmen by birth, who went over to Ireland in the year 1676 to the relief of Derry. Draperstown, a town in the north of Ireland, is called after them.

This Irish branch of the Draper family now in America owe their immediate origin to Richard Draper (1) (or Dreaper, as it is frequently spelt in Ireland), who at one time lived in County Kilkenny, but from whence he removed to Gurteen, Moneygall, Kings Co., probably towards the close of last century. He married a Miss Sheppard, and had the following

CHILDREN:

2. I. Richard.
3. II. William.
4. III. John.
5. IV. James.
6. V. Joseph, m. Elizabeth Hewsorperary, Ireland.
7. VI. Robert. 8. VII. Benjamin.
9. VIII. Sally, m. William Wall.

2. Richard, (1. Richard.) Eldest s. and child of Richard Draper and Miss Sheppard. m. Emily Searson, of Killea, Templemore, County Tipperary.

They moved to Balynakill, County Tipperary, and had the following

CHILDREN:

10. I. John, b. County Tipperary, about 1816. d. Brooklyn, N. Y., July 16, 1891.

11. II. Benjamin. Resides in County Tipperary, Ireland.

12. III. Eliza, d. Brooklyn, N. Y. (Unmarried.)

13. IV. Richard. (Married.) Several children. One dau. Lizzie, 44. m. John Myers, of Oneida, N. Y.

14. V. William, d. Galway, Ireland. (Married.) Children: — I. Emily, 45. m. Mr. Ogle. (Child:— William, 46.) Mr. Ogle d. in Ireland. Mother and son reside at Orange, N. J. II. James, 47. III. John, 48. IV. Richard, 49.

15. VI. Frederick, d. Canada. (Unmarried.)

16. VII. James. (Married.) He and his wife dead and buried in Ireland. Children: — I. Emily, 50. II. Lizzie, 51. III. Maria, 52. All married and living in New York State.

17. VIII. Charles. Lives in Kansas City, Mo. (Unmarried.)

18. IX. Arthur, d. Toronto, Can. (Married.)

10. John. (2, Richard, i. Richard.) Eldest s. and child of Richard Draper and Emily Searson. m. Frances, dau. of Richard Dagg and Margaret Mooney, of Knockincrea, County Tipperary, Ireland. She d. Brooklyn, N. Y., Dec, 1862, and is buried in Greenwood Cemetery, Brooklyn.

The following obituary was published in the Brooklyn "Eagle," July 26, 1891: — "Among the old residents of South Brooklyn, the late John Draper was a familiar figure. He had lived among them for years, and as a business man, citizen and head of a family, was esteemed by all who knew him. Last Sunday his remains were interred in Greenwood Cemetery. Death was caused by paralysis, and the deceased was confined to his bed several weeks before he died. While his mind was still clear he said to his faithful children, 'I don't want any display at my funeral. No flowers. Put a plain headstone over my grave.' These instructions were characteristic of the man. In business he was unostentatious, although at times engaged in large transactions. He was a man of quiet, modest ways, yet had an iron will. His children, Richard, Thomas, William and Margaret, idolized him and he them. Day and night his daughter attended to his wants during his illness, and Thomas secured for him the attendance of two of the most eminent specialists in the medical fraternity of New York. He lacked for nothing that love or money could do for him."

A cotton merchant of this city, who knew Mr. Draper when he was engaged in the same business, said to an "Eagle" representative: — "Permit me to correct some errors concerning John Draper which crept into print. He and his son William were, for a long time, in the cotton business. His word was so well thought of that he could buy cotton by simply putting up his finger. His word was all that was required, where others would have to make a deposit on purchases. William stood as well. Here was a favorite saying of the deceased: — 'Make but few promises, make no bad promises, and never break a promise.' John Draper was born in the County Tipperary, Ireland, and so were his daughter Margaret and sons Thomas, Richard and William. Richard is still living in Ireland, and in prosperous circumstances. He visited his father last December. In 1848 the deceased, with his wife, daughter, William and Thomas, came to Brooklyn, and took a residence in the Second Ward. He subsequently removed to the Twelfth Ward, and finally to the Sixth Ward, where he died in the 75th year of his age, in his home, 16 Butler Street. Thomas and William will be remembered by South Brooklyn firemen as popular members of Hope Hose No. 90. Their mother died in Brooklyn in 1862. John Draper lived a quiet, model life. He did not mix up in politics, and was warden of the Church bf Our Saviour for several years. At his funeral a chorus from Gorman's choir of the Church of Christ sang several hymns, and Rev. Dr. Jewett of the New York Theological Society officiated. The deceased had many friends in church circles. He died as he lived— an upright and modest, yet courageous, citizen and an affectionate father. Thomas Draper is a stalwart, nervy man, yet he cried like a child by the side of the casket that contained the remains of the best friend he ever had on earth, with the exception of his mother. Thomas did all in his power to prolong his father's life and to make easy his dying hours. The son's tears did credit to his heart."

CHILDREN:

19. I. Margaret, b. County Tipperary, Ireland, m. Brooklyn, N. Y., Florence Herzberg. Children:— I. Frederick, 53. (Single.) II. William, 54. (Single.) III. Emma, 55. d. 1863, and buried in Greenwood Cemetery, Brooklyn. IV. Frances, 56. m. Hewlett Duryea.

20. II. William, b. County Tipperary, Ireland. Lives in New York City.

21. III. Thomas, b. County Tipperary, Ireland, m. Jane, dau. of John Mooney and Margaret Morris, of Manchester, Eng. Lives in New York City.

22. IV. Richard, b. Ciamhatcha, Newport, County Tipperary, Ireland.

22. Richard. (10. John, 2. Richard, 1. Richard.) Youngest child, 3d s. of John Draper and Frances Dagg. m. June 10, 1880, at Templederry Protestant Church, County Tipperary, Ireland, by Rev. F. H. Archbold, Eleanor, dau. of James Dagg and Mary Ellen Holland, of Gurteen, County Tipperary, and granddaughter of Anthony and Mary Holland, of Knockbrook, Whitegate, County Galway. Lives in Ireland.

CHILDREN:

23. I. George, b. July 17, 1881.

24. II. Mary Ellen, b. Mar. 12, 1884.

25. III. Frances, b. Feb. 27, 1885. d. Mar. 13, 1885.

26. IV. Frances Margaret, b. Sep. 23, 1885. d, Mar. 9, 1891.

27. V. Matilda Eleanor, b. Oct. 19, 1887.

28. VI. Elizabeth Emily, b. Mar. 25, 1889.

29. VII, Thomas John, b, Sep. 30, 1890.

3. William, (1. Richard.) 2d child, 2d s. of Richard Draper and Miss Sheppard. m. Miss Wall, dau. of William Wall, of Corrigan, Tipperary, Ireland.

CHILDREN:

30. I. Benjamin, of Killea, Tipperary. Now lives in Galveston, Texas, m. Margaret Eadds, of Dunmore East, County Waterford, Ireland. Children: — I. William Henry, 57. Lives in England. II. Martha Ann, 58. Lives in Belfast. III. John Thomas, 59. Lives in Brooklyn, m. Eliza Brown, of Cheshire, Eng. (Child: — John Benjamin, 60. b. Brooklyn.) IV. Joseph, 61. Lives in Galveston, Texas. V. Margaret, 62. Lives in Nantucket, Mass. VI. Benjamin, 63. Lives at Queenstown, Ireland. VII. Charles, 64. (Deceased.) VIII. Helen Rosa, 65. Lives in England.

31. II. John, Lives in Dublin.

32. III. William. Lives in Ireland.

33. IV. Sarah, m. Joseph Smith, of Cloughjordan, County Tipperary, Ireland.

34. V. Thomas. Lives in Canada.

35. VI. Joseph. (Deceased.)

Joseph Draper, a first cousin of John Draper, 10, lives in Canada, and is a conductor on the Gd. Trunk R. R. m. Miss Sheppard, of Birr, King's County, Ireland.

CHILDREN:

36. I. Mary Jane. m. Rody Morgan, of Roscrea, County Tipperary, Ireland.

37. II. Elizabeth, m. Allen Giles, of Derrymore, Ireland.

38. III. John. m. Sarah Willis, of Cloughjordan, County Tipperary. Ireland.

39. IV. Joseph, m. Rebecca Rea, from the North of Ireland. Child: — James, 66. Lives at Clonakenny, County Tipperary, Ireland, m. by Rev. James W. Smith, at Bournea Church, Oct. 12, 1877, Maria Pratt. (Children:— I. Sarah Jane, 67. II. Elizabeth, 68. III. Annie, 69. IV. John Joseph, 70.)

40. V. Sarah, m. Joseph Hayes, of Cloughjordan, County Tipperary, Ireland.

41. VI. Fanny, m. Benjamin Atkinson, of Roscrea, County Tipperary, Ireland.

42. VII. Margaret, m., in America, Jolin Hardy.

43. VIII. Jane. m. Richard Orange, of Clonmore, Roscrea. County Tipperary, Ireland.

The Dagg Family

A daughter of this family married John Draper (10), of Brooklyn, N. Y., and is the mother of the present Drapers of this branch.

Richard Dagg, of Knockincrea, Parish of Templederry, County Tipperary, Ireland, m. Margaret Mooney, of Knockincrea. They had 16 children. Eight d. when young. The eight that lived were:

I. James. Went from Ireland to Illinois over 40 years ago. (Married.) Had two children:— Richard and Margaret, who live in Bluford, Ill. James Dagg d. several years ago.

II. Thomas, m. Mary Dagg, of Lissen Hall, County Tipperary.

III. Richard. (Unmarried.) d. aged 20.

IV. John. (Unmarried.) d. aged 50.

V. Frances, m. John Draper, 10. d. Brooklyn, N. Y., Dec, 1862.

VI. Elizabeth, m. William Knaggs, of Turtulla, Thurles, County Tipperary, Ireland, d. Buried in Greenwood Cemetery, Brooklyn, N. Y.

VII. Ellen, m. George Powell, of Templederry, County Tipperary. d. and buried at Templederry.

VIII. Margaret, m. Ambrose Kyte, of Turtulla, Silvermines, County Tipperary. Both are dead.

EXTRACT from a letter from Roscrea, County Tipperary, Ireland.

James Draper, of Tenderry, killed by a fall from his horse, in 1890. m. Miss Llewellan, of Rathdowney.

"A good Churchman, a consistent Christian, a successful farmer."

CHILDREN:

I. Benjamin, b. about 1873. II. Ellen. III. Fanny.
IV. Mary Ann. V. Abigail. VI. Lizzie.

EXTRACT from Mrs. Draper's letter from Pinstero House, Kilkenny, Ireland.

Richard Draper came from Munster to County Kilkenny about 1790. m. Eliza Houghton.

CHILDREN:

I. James.

II. John. m. Miss Whitehead. Lives in Ireland. Has a descendant named Somerville, who m. 1st: Miss Edge, and 2dly: Miss Bloomfield. Has a large family.

III. Richard, m. Ann Kenny.

He went to America and settled at Kingston, Canada.

The Drapers of County Cork, Ireland

This branch of the Drapers of Irish extraction, now in America, are the children of a Draper of Bandon, County Cork, who was the only son of his father. He married, and apparently had five children, i. James Draper, b. 1781, was the oldest son, and heir to a vast estate, but, owing to some technicality, it did not come to him, but reverted to the Crown, and all the family emigrated to New Brunswick. A myth has been handed down from one generation to another that a stranger called on an ancestor of the present descendants, and pronounced a curse on him and his heirs forever, mysteriously disappearing immediately after. This is recalled as the reason so many choice opportunities have been lost, and so many of the family never attain great fortunes, though one and all are industrious, thrifty and noted for their intelligence, good moral character and great sense of honor in business transactions.

It is impossible to give any further data of the earlier ancestors of the Bandon Drapers. Mrs. Dr. Eunice Draper Kinney (13) has endeavored to trace her branch of the family, but, up to the time of going to press, nothing more than what follows has been ascertained.

It is presumable that all the Irish branches of the Draper family are descendants of the two English officers of the name, who went to the relief of Derry in 1676, and after whom Draperstown in the north of Ireland is named. The War Office in London has been requested to furnish the names of these two officers, but, although payment for a search among their records has been offered, they decline to institute such a search. The Drapers of this branch who came to America were:

1. I. James, b. May 22, 1781, in Bandon, County Cork, Ireland.
2. II. Nathanial. Emigrated to Massachusetts.
3. III. Isaac.
4. IV. Mary, b. 1790. d. 1874.
5. V. Jane, b. 1802. d. 1874.

1. James, m. Oct. 22, 1814, by Rev. W. Newman, in County Cork, Ireland, Elizabeth Homan. She was b. May, 1789. d. Feb. 5, 1872, in York County, N. B.

CHILDREN:

6. I. Isaac, b. Aug. 11, 1815. He went to Europe in 1856, and has not been heard of since.

7. II. Humphrey Homan, b. Sep. 1, 1817. d. Feb. 27, 1818.

8. III. James, b. Fredericksburg, Va., Sep. 6, 1819. d. Brook Station, Safford County, Va.

9. IV. John Homan, b. Dec. 26, 1822.

10. V. Elizabeth, b. July 16, 1825. m. Jesse Baker, Apr. 15, 1866. (No issue.)

11. VI. George, b. Jan. 7, 1829.

12. VII. Mary Jane, b. Mar. 21, 1833, in New Brunswick, d. Jan. 27, 1841.

8. James, (1. James.) 3d child, 3d s. of James Draper, 1, and Elizabeth Homan. m. 1st: Catherine, dau. of Abraham and Eunice Hillman Schriver, Nov. 13, 1851, in York County, N. B. She d. Dec. 13, 1867. He m. 2dly: Oct. 20, 1869, Sarah Jane, dau. of Peter and Rebecca Gartley.

Mr. Draper had considerable inventive talent. At the "Centennial," he exhibited a vessel he had built entirely by himself. The house in which he died at Brook Station, Safford County, Va., is said to have been the one in which Mrs. Southworth wrote "The Hidden Hand."

CHILDREN, BY 1ST WIFE, B. SOUTHAMPTON, YORK COUNTY, N. B.:

13. I. Eunice, b. Sep. 29, 1852. m. Aug. 6, 1884, at Boston, Mass., John Mozart, s. of Lewis and Eliza Carr Kinney, of Wareham, Mass.

14. II. James Humphrey, b. Nov. 11, 1854. (Unmarried.) Now living in Texas.

CHILDREN, BY 2D WIFE, B. SOUTHAMPTON, YORK COUNTY, N. B.:

15. III. Peter, b. Dec. 26, 1870.

16. IV. George, b. July 21, 1872.

17. V. Samuel, b. Apr. 7, 1875.

9. John Homan. (1. James.) 4th child, 4th s. of James Draper, 1, and Elizabeth Homan. m. Aug. 29, 1857, in York County, N. B., Mary Jane, dau. of Emanuel and Naomi Ingraham.

Mr. Draper was a great traveler, having journeyed to China, India, Africa, Australia, Europe, etc. He was preparing an account of his travels at the time of his death.

CHILDREN:

18. I. Horace, b. Nov. 4, 1858. m. Alice Chapman, Nov. 8, 1887. (No issue.)

19. II. Annie, b. Feb. 27, 1860, m. July 22, 1890, Levi McElvain. Child:—Frederick, 43. b. May 10, 1891.

20. III. Jane, b. July 23, 1861. m. Almon Chapman, Apr. 27, 18S7. (No issue.)

21. IV. Mary, b. Feb. 3, 1863. m. Aug. 9, 1878, Claude McDonald. Children:—I. Edgar, 44. b. Mar. 14, 1880. II. Errol, 45. b. Jan. 14, 1882. III. Annie, 46. b. June 8, 1883. IV. Jessie, 47. b. Mar. 25, 1885. V. Arthur, 48. b. July 12, 1886. VI. Walter, 49. b. Sep. 8, 1888. VII. Norris, 50. b. Nov. 2, 1890.

22. V. Elizabeth, b. Nov. 22, 1864. m. Aug. 12, 1884, Robertson Bartlett. (No issue.)

23. VI. John, b. Nov. 16, 1866. Lives in Boston, Mass.

24. VII. George, b. Feb. 26, 1869. Lives in Boston, Mass.

25. VIII. Isaac, b. July 3, 1872.

11. George, (1. James.) 6th child, 5th s. of James Draper, 1, and Elizabeth Homan. m. Aug. 29, 1857, in York County, N. B., Joanna Schriver, sister of Catherine Schriver, who m. his brother James, 8, and dau. of Abraham and Eunice Hillman Schriver.

CHILDREN:

26. I. George Warren, b. July 12, 1858. d. July 29, 1867.

27. II. Gilbert Andrew, b. Nov. 20, 1859. m. Alice Price, July, 1882. Children: — 51. George Warren, b. June 25, 1883. 52. Eunice, b. Nov. 5, 1884. 53. Lillian, b. June 2, 1886. 54. Stanley, b. Mar. 8, 1888. 55. Alda. b. Aug. 21, 1889. 56. John. b. Feb. 12, 1891.

28. III. Ansley N., b. Sep. 25, 1871.

29. IV. Joanna, b. Nov. 1, 1873.

3. Isaac. He emigrated with his brother, James, 1, to America, but no record has been furnished as to who he married.

CHILDREN:

30. I. Hetty. (Deceased.)

31. II. Ann.

32. III. William, m. Susan Johnson. Children: — I. Mary, 57. II. William, 58. III. Melville, 59. IV. George, 60. V. Bessie, 61.

33. IV. Nelson, m. Kate Vickery. Children: — I. Willie, 62. II. Hess, 63. III. Edith, 64.

4. Mary. Sister to James Draper, 1. m. John Vickery.

CHILDREN:

34. I. Bessie, m. Paul Daly. Children: — I. James Michael, 65. II. Jane, 66. III. Hester, 67. m. Robert Brown. IV. Henry, 68.

35. II. Mary. m. John Willie. Children: — I. Bessie, 69. m. William Davidson. (Children:— I. William. II. Mary. III. Gertrude. IV. Alice. V. John.) II. Charles, 70. m. Louisa Baird. (Children: — I. Louisa, II. Helen.) III. John, 71.

36. III. Kate. m. her cousin, Nelson Draper, 33.

5. Jane. Sister to James Draper, 1. m. John Howe.

CHILDREN:

37. I. Mary. (Deceased.)

38. II. Jonas, m. Jane Parker in 1878.

39. III. John D. m. Ada Bustin in 1885. Children: — I. Jonas, 41. b. Apr. 4, 1886. II. Isabel B., 42. b. July, 1888.

40. IV. Jane.

The Canton Drapers

The various families of Drapers located at Canton, Mass., or originating therefrom, are of ancestry more recently transplanted in America than most of the lines herein recorded, and form, in a measure, an independent colony. They are the offspring of Thomas and James, who emigrated from Melbourne, Derbyshire, England, and settled in Canton in 1851.

Without doubt this branch belongs to the parent tree of Yorkshire, Eng., for, as in ancient days, all roads led to Rome, so Yorkshire would seem to be the Mecca of our race, and as the counties of Yorkshire and Derbyshire border upon each other and are closely allied, it is but natural to suppose that this Melbourne branch is descended from our common ancestry of Yorkshire.

The name of Draper appears on the parish records of Melbourne for many years in the past, the earliest noted being that of William Draper, who was wedded to Mary Hall in the old Norman church in 1692. Names of the descendants of William and Mary are found on the same church records for the succeeding generations with frequency, but there is perhaps no way of making accurate accounts of the various lines, as the Registration Act in England did not come in force until 1837, and prior to that year only the names of members of the Church of England appear, all dissenters' names being usually omitted. The old registers give only the baptismal, marriage and burial dates, which further complicate the making of connected lists of families, and prevents satisfactory researches in the ancestral tree.

The Canton Drapers are true to the name and traditions of our earliest progenitors, as they are manufacturers of woolen cloth and deal in various lines of fancy knitted fabrics and draperies.

Melbourne, England.

Melbourne is a picturesque and quaint old English town, located in the southeastern part of the County of Derbyshire and lies in the charming valley of the Trent. It is eight miles from Derby and six from Ashby-de-la-Zouch, the tournament scene of "Ivanhoe." Melbourne also includes the hamlet of King's Newton, the ancestral home of the gallant Gen. Hardinge, who was Gov.-General of India and who succeeded Wellington as Commander-in-Chief.

Melbourne is of very ancient origin, and Roman coins, bearing date of 327 A. D., have been found there. Roman pottery has also been obtained in its neighborhood. It had a castle, supposed to have been demolished by Cromwell, the foundations or keep of which are thought to have been built before the Norman invasion.

Melbourne Church is famous for its beauty and antiquity, being regarded by students in archaeology as one of the finest and best preserved Norman structures in England.

The noted Hall and Gardens are near the old church, and are perhaps the chief attraction to the visitor. In the Hall many distinguished men have resided, and it was here that Baxter wrote his "Saint's Rest." It contains many valuable paintings by old masters.

The Gardens are a curious relic of the old style of horticulture, being modelled from those of Holland in the time of William III., and are strikingly peculiar in character. They cover nearly twenty acres of ground and contain the largest "wisteria" in the world.

Melbourne has been famed for its lace trade, especially in lace gloves, mittens, silk, spun silk, Lisle, cotton, woolen and woolen-cloth gloves. Market gardening is also carried on to some extent. It has a population of less than five thousand souls and is a delightfully quiet, pretty and retired little town.

1. William Draper, m. Mary Hall, July 24, 1692, in the ancient stone church at Melbourne, Derbyshire, Eng.

2. John. From the old church records supposed to be a son of William Draper and Mary Hall. m. Ruth ____. She was buried June 13, 1763, at Melbourne, Derbyshire, Eng.

CHILDREN, ALL B. AT MELBOURNE:

3. I. William, bap. Jan. 14, 1753.

4. II. Thomas, bap. July 18, 1756.

5. III. Mary, buried Aug. 22, 1758.

6. IV. Joseph, bap. Aug. 11, 1759.

3. William. (2. John, 1. William.) 1st child of 2. John and Ruth. m. April 4, 1774, at Melbourne, Mary Pass (her name was probably Morton, the name Pass being given by adoption). She died at Melbourne Sep. 30, 1827, "being then 75 years of age." He was buried July 23. 1836.

He was a gardener and was employed in the Melbourne Hall Gardens, of which mention has been made elsewhere. Although well advanced in years, the direct cause of his death was from accidental burning.

CHILDREN, BOTH B. AT MELBOURNE:

7. I. William, bap. July 27, 1774.

8. II. Sarah, m. William Warren, a blacksmith. May 19. 1822, at Melbourne. She was buried July 9, 1827 (aged 26), at Melbourne.

7. William. (3. William, 2. John, 1. William.) 1st child of William Draper and Mary Pass (or Morton), m. May 26, 1806, at Melbourne, Martha Bailey. She died at Melbourne and was buried there in the Baptist churchyard.

CHILDREN ALL B. AT MELBOURNE:

I. William, b. 1807. d. 1827, Melbourne.

II. Thomas, b. Oct. 20, 1809. d. May 29, 1856, Canton, Mass.

III. Mary, b. Dec. 21, 1810. d. Jan. 19, 1889, Coalville, Eng.

IV. James, b. Sept. 17, 1813. d. May 23, 1873, Canton, Mass.

V. Hannah, b. May 11, 1815. d. May 10, 1840, Melbourne.

VI. Ann, died young.

VII. Edwin, died young.

VIII. Samuel, died young.

IX. Edwin, b. Nov. 19, 182-. d. Dec. 27, 1885, Wolverhampton. Eng.

10. Thomas. (7. William, 3. William, 2. John, 1. William.) 2d child of William Draper and Martha Bailey, m. Mar. 22, 1829, at Melbourne, Mary, dau. of Thomas and Ann Chetwynd. She was b. at Melbourne, and d. there Feb. 1, 1839, aged 31 years.

The loss of his mother, and consequent separation of the family, threw Thomas early upon his own resources, and forced him to earn his livelihood. His boyhood, being a struggle, must have developed in him that quality of character which begets perseverance and self-reliance. He was brought up in the lace industry of Melbourne, and became familiar with the machines used in its manufacture. The knowledge thus acquired he was afterwards able to successfully apply in the production, from the same frames, of other lines of goods, for which he found a demand. In 1846 he sailed for America and landed at Boston. He first located at Chelsea, Mass., where he engaged in the manufacture of knit woolen goods. In 1851 he moved his machinery to Canton, Mass., and continued his business there, enlarging his plant. Hand power only was employed, but in time the demand for his goods increased so rapidly that the mill was operated day and night. Thomas died suddenly in his 48th year. He was a man of enterprise and ability, of exceedingly fine presence, kind, gentlemanly and warm hearted. He was the pioneer of the woolen knitting industry in Canton.

CHILDREN, B. AT MELBOURNE:

18. I. Fanny, b. Oct. 11, 1830.

19. II. Charles, b. Dec. 7, 1832.

11. Mary. (7. William, 3. William, 2. John, i. William.) 3d child of William Draper and Martha Bailey, m. James Hood, in 1837, at Melbourne. He was b. Aug. 11, 1802, at Melbourne, and d. there Apr. 9, 1876.

CHILDREN, B. AT MELBOURNE:

20. 1, Hannah, b. May 19, 1838. m. Alfred Andrews, May 16, 1864, at Derby.

21. II. Fanny, b. Nov. 12, 1841. m. 1st: William Hulse, Nov. 20, 1865. He d. May 20, 1869. m. 2dly: Edmund Jackson, Dec. 30, 1880.

22. III. Martha, b. July, 1844.

12. James. (7. William, 3. William, 2. John, 1. William.) 4th child of William Draper and Martha Bailey, m. 1st: Feb. 29, 1836, at Melbourne, Mira, dau. of

James and Bessie (Hemsley) Hollingworth. She was b. Nov. 18, 1814, at Melbourne, and d. there Mar. 3, 1841. m. 2dly: Oct. 22, 1842, at Melbourne, Ann, dau. of William and Elizabeth (Lucas) Bailey. She was b. Dec. 6, 1809, at Brighton, Eng., and d. June 30, 1877, at Canton, Mass.

In the "History of Norfolk County, Mass.," published in 1884, the following biographical sketch appears: —

James Draper

"Among those who were foremost in introducing and establishing the woolen industry in Canton, the name of James Draper stands prominent. He was a man of great energy, untiring industry and superior business capacity. With a thorough knowledge of his trade, great practical sagacity, and an indomitable perseverance, he did much to promote the growth and prosperity of the town during the past thirty years.

"Being early thrown upon his own resources, his mechanical turn of mind led him to adopt the knitting trade as an occupation, and his ingenuity and skill were developed in the general lace manufacturing interest, but especially in lace gloves, for which Melbourne was famous.

"He came to Canton with his family in April, 1851. The sailing vessel in which he arrived dropped anchor in Boston harbor on the morning following the memorable storm which destroyed the ill-fated Minot's Ledge lighthouse. An elder brother, named Thomas, had preceded him to the States, who had purchased in Canton the old Dr. Stone estate, at the corner of Washington and Pleasant Streets, and at the time of the arrival of James was engaged in fitting up a shop to receive knitting machinery. Here for several years he assisted Thomas in organizing and developing the woolen business. This was the pioneer introduction of the knitting industry into Canton.

"In the Spring of 1856, after the death of his brother Thomas, we find James in business for himself, in the building at the Centre known as the Everett house. Here a great variety of fancy knitted goods were produced, and the business rapidly increased.

"In 1861 a partnership was formed with Mr. George Frederic Sumner, and the business continued under the name of Draper & Sumner.

"In February, 1865, the firm purchased the Morse machine-shops and water-privilege at South Canton. They made the necessary alterations to adapt the property to the requirements of their business; built a dye-house, put in three sets of woolen-cards, with their complement of spinning machinery, and a full line of knitting frames. Here a thriving business was transacted until June, 1870, when the buildings and contents were destroyed by fire.

"In April, 1869, the firm had bought the property of the Canton Woolen Mills, and at the time of the fire were running three factories— the Everett Mill and the Canton Woolen Mills at the Centre, and the Morse Mill at South Canton.

"It was deemed inexpedient to rebuild at South Canton, and the foundations were immediately started for a spinning mill at the Centre, making a valuable addition to the Canton Woolen Mills.

"The new mill was completed before Winter, and was equipped with seven sets of woolen cards, with a basement occupied by shuttle-looms and knitting machinery. At the time of Mr. Draper's death, three years later, the firm was doing a large and prosperous business.

"Any sketch of James Draper would be imperfect that gave no hint of the sturdy individuality of his nature, and the generous impulses, which knew no limit but his means. His heart was pure gold. It was alive with tenderness to the wants of the young, the aged, the poor and the unfortunate. To lift another's burden seemed to lighten his own. His cardinal doctrine was, 'Flee pleasure and it will pursue you. Strive for the happiness of others and your own will abound.' The light of his life was to serve, cheer, encourage and minister to the comfort of those who came within his sphere. The only value he put on money was its blessing power. His happiest moments were when he was giving. He was liberal to all appeals, but he most loved to dispense benefactions with his own hand, and be his own judge of deserving merit.

"Whatever he achieved in life was due to his own efforts; he was self-made in the full meaning of the word. In the England of his boyhood, education was not the fostered child it is to-day. But in almost every town could be found a morning and evening school, where, for a small sum, a determined spirit could acquire the rudiments of knowledge. The only education he had was obtained at these schools, by a brief hour snatched from the forelock of the day's labor, or added at its close, to satisfy the craving for intellectual advancement.

"In his business, and in everything he did, thoroughness was his motto. 'Whatever was worth doing at all was worth doing well.' The maxims of industry, economy and sound common sense, which all human experience indorses and commends, he inculcated wherever he found idleness, extravagance or folly.

"Mr. Draper was plain in manners, determined in opinions, and inflexible in principle. He was a genuine hater of shams and pretense, and would rebuke with almost merciless severity a would-be spirit or a mean act. The love of justice was the dominant principle of his nature, and at his grave an appreciative friend remarked that the most fitting inscription that could be placed upon his tombstone would be —

'He was too noble to do a wrong act.'"

He keenly appreciated the value of an unbroken home and earnestly strove to keep his own children from being divided and scattered, as his mother's had been.

For this end he planned and labored, and to-day all his descendants are clustered together within the limits of a half mile, eight families being represented.

His widow, Ann (Bailey), the partner of thirty-two years of his wedded life, survived him but four years. She was a good wife, a faithful and affectionate mother.

After the death of James, his five sons, viz.: Robert, Alfred, Thomas, James, Charles, and his only daughter, Mira (represented by her husband, William John Williams), continued the woolen knitting business, organizing under the firm name of "Draper Brothers," and had an increased and successful trade in the manufacture of men's and women's knit wear, and fleeced linings for rubber boots, shoes and leather gloves. After the death of Robert, in 1886, the business was incorporated under the title of "Draper Brothers Company," and at the present time is one of the successful industries of the substantial town of Canton.

CHILDREN:

23. I. Robert, b. Nov. 21, 1836, Melbourne, Eng. d. Mar. 16, 1886, Canton, Mass.

24. II. Alfred, b. Dec. 10, 1838, Melbourne, Eng.

25. III. Mira Elizabeth, b. May 26, 1843, Melbourne, Eng.

26. IV. Thomas Bailey, b. Oct. 31, 1844, Melbourne, Eng.

27. V. George Lucas, b. Aug. 31, 1846, Melbourne, Eng. d. Feb. 19, 1849.

28. VI. James Lucas, b. June 30, 1849, Melbourne, Eng.

29. VII. Charles Norris, b. June 6, 1851, Canton, Mass.

30. VIII. Washington, b. May 26, 1853, Canton, Mass. d. May 28, 1853.

17. Edwin. (7. William, 3. William, 2. John, 1. William.) 9th child of William Draper and Martha Bailey, m. Oct. 1, 1859, to Mary Haywood.

"Was a tailor by trade and a great rover."

CHILDREN:

31. I. Annie, b. Oct., 1860.

32. II. Charles, b. May 6, 1865.

18. Fanny. (10. Thomas, 7. William, 3. William, 2. John, 1. William.) 1st child of Thomas Draper and Mary Chetwynd. m. Nov. 27, 1867, Thomas Blanchard, at Brockton, Mass. He was born at Boston, Eng., April 19, 1842. Resides at Stoughton, Mass.

CHILDREN, B. AT CANTON, MASS.:

33. 1, Mabel Pauline, b. Mar. 10, 1870.

34. II. Bertha Fanny, b. June 26, 1872. d. Aug. 18, 1872.

19. Charles. (10. Thomas, 7. William, 3. William, 2. John, 1. William.) 2d child of Thomas Draper and Mary Chetwynd. m. Jan. 1, 1857, at Boston,

Mass., Fanny, dau. of Henry and Eliza (Bailey) Ward. She was b. Dec. 6, 1838, at Melbourne, Derbyshire, England.

Charles came to America with his father in 1846, and was identified with the woolen industries of Canton, Mass., for many years, covering the period from 1851 to 1886. As before noted, his father (Thomas) brought the first wool knitting machinery into Canton. At his father's death Charles continued the business until 1860, when new arrangements were made. The family of Charles consists of seven sons. A singularity in connection with the Drapers of Canton and Dedham, Mass., who bear the name of Charles, is in their children all being *sons.* A *daughter* has yet to be born to a Draper of this name in this section. Resides at Falmouth Heights, Mass.

CHILDREN, ALL B. CANTON, MASS.

35. I. Frank Thomas, b. Sep. 25, 1859.
36. II. Charles Albert, b. Oct. 24, 1861.
37. III. Henry Arthur, b. Nov. 6, 1862.
38. IV. Nelson Chetwynd, b. Dec. 18, 1864.
39. V. Frederic Ward, b. Dec. 23, 1869.
40. VI. Alexis Lumb, b. Nov. 19, 1871.
41. VII. Webster Lucas, b. Feb. 14, 1874.

23. Robert. (12. James, 7. William, 3. William, 2. John, 1. William.) 1st child of James Draper and Mira Hollingworth. m. July 5, 1857, at Franklin, N. H., Mary Adaline, dau. of Robert and Emeline (Herbert) Colby. She was born Aug. 20, 1835, at Franklin, N. H.

Robert left Melbourne for America in May, 1849, and landed at New York on June 23. He first proceeded to Wisconsin, where some pioneer relatives had located, but in 1853 he joined his father at Canton, Mass. He subsequently spent several years at Franklin, N. H., but finally returned to Canton, and assisted his father in the woolen business.

In 1868 he engaged for his own account in the manufacture of cotton stockinet, etc., but in June, 1870, his building, machinery and stock were a total loss by fire. Characteristic energy developed a new start, which proved successful, and in 1880 a large four-story brick factory supplanted smaller buildings of wood which had become inadequate for an increased business. To this new factory an extensive addition was made a few years later. Robert was also a member of the firm of Draper Brothers and at the time of his death was salesman and treasurer for the company. His sudden and unexpected decease was a great shock to his many friends, who recognized and appreciated his interest, energy and enthusiasm in all good works; he had created an industry of benefit to his adopted town; he was an active worker in many matters relating to town, parish and the community. For a number of years he was Superintendent of the First Parish (Unitarian) Sunday-school. He was gifted with great social qualities, being fond of music and singing; for many years he was a member of the choir of his church; on several occasions he taught singing schools in Canton.

In public meetings he could speak forcibly and to the point. Being impulsive by nature, he was quick to give utterance to his convictions. He was a sympathizing and trusty friend, and a man to be depended on in times of trial and affliction. He loved his home and fireside, and was a self-sacrificing and indulgent father.

His youth had afforded him but limited means for acquiring an education, but persevering study at home gave him what stern necessity had denied. He had good literary ability, and in 1883 he published, for private distribution, a volume of poems entitled "Early Aspirations," most of the pieces having been written in his youthful days. He was taken in the prime of manhood and in the meridian of his usefulness. At his funeral his pastor said of him, "He loved the good, hated the wrong and scorned oppression."

CHILDREN:

42. I. William Herbert, b. July 14, 1858, at Canton, Mass.

43. II. Mira Emma, b. Apr. 16, 186r, at Lake Village, N. H. d. Aug. 19, 1862, at Franklin, N. H.

44. III. Gertrude Hollingworth, b. Canton, Mass., Feb. 16, 1867. m. by Rev. Henry T. Jenks, at Canton, Mass., Feb. 16, 1892, George Benjamin Neal, s. of Jackson Flanders and Catherine Porter White (a descendant of the "Mayflower" Whites).

45. IV. Robert Lincoln, b. Mar. 18, 1870, Canton, Mass.

24. Alfred. (12. James, 7. William, 3. William, 2. John, 1. William.) 2d child of James Draper and Mira Hollingworth. m. Sep. 10, 1865, at Milton, Mass., by Rev. Thos. B. Fox, to Sarah, dau. of Charles and Mary (Rotheric) Hartley. She was b. at Halifax, Yorkshire, Eng., Oct. 24, 1843.

CHILDREN, ALL B. AT CANTON, MASS.:

46. I. Bessie Hollingworth, b. Sep. 1, 1872.

47. II. Mary Elizabeth, b. Oct. 22, 1876.

48. III. Charlotte Hartley, b. Sep. 23, 1887.

25. Mira Elizabeth. (12. James, 7. William, 3. William, 2. John, 1. William.) 1st child of James Draper and Ann Bailey, m. June 11, 1865, at Dedham, Mass., by Rev. Wm. H. Mills, William John, s. of William and Isabella (Pringle) Williams. He was b. Aug. 3, 1839, at London, Eng.

CHILDREN, all B. AT CANTON, MASS.:

49. I. Annie Draper, b. Mar. 9, 1866.

50. II. Helen Rachel, b. Aug. 6, 1871,

51. III. Roger James, b. Jan. 3, 1874.

26. Thomas Bailey. (12. James, 7. William, 3. William, 2. John, i. William.) 2d child of James Draper and Ann Bailey, m. Dec. 6, 1863, at Milton, Mass., by Rev. John H. Morrison, D. D., Sarah Draper (No. 151 5 of descendants of James and Miriam Draper), dau. of James Turner and Sarah Everett Gerald. She was b. Nov. 11, 1844, at Canton, Mass.

CHILDREN, ALL B. AT CANTON, MASS.:

52. I. Mira Theresa, b. Apr. 27, 1864. d. Dec. 16, 1867.
53. II. Nancy Turner, b. Oct. 7, 1866.
54. III. James Sumner, b. Oct. 3, 1868.
55. IV. Alfred Ernest, b. Jan. 10, 1871.
56. V. George Thomas, b. Sep. 12, 1873.
57. VI. Edward Bailey, b. Mar. 27, 1876.
58. VII. Ruth Mabel, b. Apr. 17, 1882.

28. James Lucas. (12. James, 7. William, 3. William, 2. John, 1. William.) 4th child of James Draper and Ann Bailey, m. Dec. 3, 1868, at Dorchester, Mass., by Rev. Thomas J. Mumford, Catherine Warren, dau. of Charles and Priscilla (Warren) Stretton. She was b. Sep. 20, 1845, at Leicester, Eng.

CHILDREN, ALL B. AT CANTON, MASS.:

59. I. Arthur Warren, b. June 22, 1869. d. Aug. 14, 1870.
60. II. Walter Scott, b. Oct. 13, 1871.
61. III. Amy Louise, b. June 17, 1873.
62. IV. Elsie Warren, b. Nov. 24, 1875.
63. V. Percy Lucas, b. Mar. 12, 1885.

29. Charles Norris. (12. James, 7. William, 3. William, 2. John, 1. William.) 5th child of James Draper and Ann Bailey, m. Sep. 29, 1872, at Milton, Mass., by Rev. John H. Morrison, D. D., Martha Howard, dau. of Augustus and Hannah Porter (Drake) Gill. She was b. Aug. 25, 1851, at Canton, Mass.

CHILDREN, ALL B. AT CANTON, MASS.:

64. I. Benjamin Gill, b. Apr. 19, 1876. d. Feb. 27, 1882.
65. II. Joseph Porter, b. Jan. 16, 1879.
66. III. John Howard, b. Feb. 5, 1883.
67. IV. Paul Augustus, b. Aug. 31, 1886.
68. V. James Battles, b. Nov. 7. 1888.
69. VI. Charles Norris, Jr., b. Mar. 8, 1892.

35. Frank Thomas. (19. Charles, 10. Thomas, 7. William, 3. William, 2. John, 1. William.) 1st child of Charles Draper and Fanny Ward. m. Dec. 25, 1882, at Canton, Rose Ella, dau. of Bernard and Bridget (Conroy) Curran. She was b. at Canton, Nov. 13, 1857. Resides at Campello, Mass.

38. Nelson Chetwynd. (19. Charles, 10. Thomas, 7. William, 3. William, 2. John, I. William.) 4th child of Charles Draper and Fanny Ward. m. Nov. 11, 1889, at Ottumwa, Iowa, by Judge D. W. Stuart, Elizabeth Roletta, dau. of Martin Luther and Mary Francis (Dunleary) Powers. She was b. at Sheffield, Ill., Oct. 28, 1866.

42. William Herbert. (23. Robert, 12. James, 7. William, 3. William, 2. John, I. William.) 1st child of Robert Draper and Mary Adaline Colby, m. Sep. 22, 1881, at Canton, by Rev. Wm. H. Savary, Ella Sarah, dau. of Azel Kinsley and Sarah Ann (Peterson) Billings. She was b. Sep. 3, 1859, at Canton, Mass.

CHILD:

69. Herbert Kinsley, b. Canton, Mar. 16, 1882.

45. Robert Lincoln. (23. Robert, 12. James, 7. William, 3. William, 2. John, i. William.) 4th child of Robert Draper and Mary Adaline Colby, m. Feb. 7, 1890, at Boston, by Rev. Albert S. Stafford, Jessie Violet Pamelia, dau. of Robert and Margaret (Muttart) Mobbs. She was b. Feb. 4, 1870, at Willimantic, Conn.

CHILD:

70. Madeline Herbert, b. Canton, Aug. 3, 1890.

Descendants of David Draper

1. David Draper, m. Cynthia Clark, of Scotland.

CHILDREN:

2. I. Lyman, b. May 12, 1800. d. Aug. 23, 1870. m. Mary Holman, of Dorset or Topsham, Vt. Children: — I. Andrew, 5. b. Mar. 12, 1825. m. Statira Dow, of Granby, Canada. (Children: — I. Myron, 11. d. young. II. Gardner D., 12. b. Apr. 7, 1852. m. Clara Barton. Children:— I. George, 18, and II. Fred, 19. III. Ella L., 13. b. Aug. 13, 1854. m. Peter Shangrean. Two children, 20 and 21. IV. [*] Almon M., 14. b. Jan. 9, 1857. m. Florence W. Brooks, of Lynn, Mass. (No issue.) V. Paulina, 15. b. Feb. 9, 1860, m. Cyrus Harvey, of Waterloo, Canada. Two children, 22 and 23. VI. George, 16. d. young. VII. Frank E., 17. b. Oct. 26, 1865.) II. Stephen E., 6. b. Aug. 24, 1831. d. Nov. 29, 1877. III. William C. E., 7. b. Mar. 24, 1834. m. Luchia ____. (Children: — 1. Frank, 24. m. Miss Sweet. Two children, 26 and 27, II. Jane, 25. m. Two children, 28 and 29.) IV, Mary M., 8. b. May 17, 1840. m. Mr. Humphries. Lives in Fairmont, Minn. V. Dorwin I., 9. b. May 3, 1844. m. Jane Wilcox, of Danville, Canada. VI. Sarah J., 10, b. June 16, 1846. m. Mr. Hyatt, of Minnesota.

3. II. John, Children: — I. John, 30. 11, Dorwin, 31, III, A dau., 32. m. Frank Williams, of Sweetsburg, Canada. IV, A dau., 33. m. Joseph Westover, of Sutton, Canada. V. Alva, 34. m, Rachel, adopted dau. of his father, John, 3.

4. Ill, Stephen, d. without issue.

[*] Almon Draper (s. of Andrew, 5, and grandson of Lyman Draper, 2) thinks his father is second cousin to an Alonzo Draper. This branch of the family is very musical, and supposed to come from the line of a David and George, two brothers who emigrated from England.

Drapers of Delaware

Thomas Draper, said to be one of three brothers who came to this country from Wales. Eng., settled in Dover, Delaware. His brothers settled, one in New York, the other in Pennsylvania. Thomas Draper had one s., Thomas, now living at Dover, Delaware, who states he is connected with the Fisher family, and that a Benjamin Draper, living near Harrington, Kent Co., is a connection.

1. Benjamin Draper, m. Ruth Fisher, of Philadelphia, and resided at Dover, Delaware. Both d. about 1809-10.

CHILD:

2. James Fisher, b. Dover, Delaware, Dec. 31, 1802 or 1804. d. Liverpool, Ill., Nov., 1884. m. 1st: 1836, Sarah Jane, dau. of Dr. Samuel and Margaret McAdams, of Madison County, Ill. She was b. Huntsville, Ala., 1816. d. St. Louis, Mo., July 5, 1844. He m. 2dly: 1845, Maria Bickstead.

James Fisher Draper was adopted, on his parents' death, by his mother's sister, Mrs. Lydia McClasky, of Philadelphia. While with her he was given a musical education, and was noted as an instructor in vocal and instrumental music. Was also a composer, and one of his productions, the "St. Louis Grand March," was dedicated to the St. Louis Greys. In 1821 he went to the West Indies and joined the U. S. Navy, remaining some ten years in the service as purser's clerk. About 1830 he went to St. Louis, Mo., where he married. In 1852 he went to Liverpool, Ill., where he engaged in the grocery business. He was for a number of years connected with the firm of Balmer & Weber, dealers in music and musical instruments, in St. Louis.

CHILDREN, BY 1st WIFE:

3. I. Josephine Lydia, b. Dec. 13, 1836. m. Mr. Sebastian.

4. II. James Henry, b. Nov. 23, 1839. m. St. Louis, Mo., Oct. 22, 1866, Rosalie, dau. of William A. and Caroline Thomas. Child: — Cara Alice, 11. b. Duquain, Ill., 1868.

Mr. Draper attended school in St. Louis and a public school in Illinois. When about fourteen he left home, and took a position in a country store at Maples Mills, Fulton Co., Ill. Later he was employed with a grocery firm in Canton, Ill. In 1861 he volunteered as a member of the 55th Illinois Regimental Band, and served three months. Was afterwards with the Union Army as a civilian until Aug., 1863, when he returned to St. Louis, and became bookkeeper with the E. St. Louis ___ Co. Later was secretary to the Union Dock Co. until 1875, when he became a stockholder and director in the St. Louis Sectional Dock Co., and in 1876 was placed in charge of the company's office and business at the Carondelet Marine Railway. In Oct., 1885, he sold out his interest in the concern, and removed to Florida, where he had, in 1875, purchased an orange grove.

CHILDREN, BY 2D WIFE:

5. III. Margaret.
6. IV. Anna.
7. V. Alta.
8. VI. Rosalie.
9. VII. Charlotte.
10. VIII. Charles, b. Oct. or Nov., 1863.

Leicestershire, England, Drapers in America

1. John Draper. Only child of John Draper. Lived in Loughborough, Leicestershire. Moved to Derby. Derbyshire. Had four daus., now all deceased:— Ann, 2. Sarah, 3. Elizabeth, 4. Grace, 5. Also four sons:— John H., 6. Henry, 7. Thomas. 8. William L., 9.

John H. (6) lives in Healdsburg, Sonoma Co., Cal. Has one son, Joseph F. A daughter, Carrie (10), who died a few years ago.

Henry (7) and Thomas (8) were killed in battle.

William L. (9) came to Lowell, Mass., when 17 years old. Worked there, then went to Virgenis, Vt., and learnt the carriage trade. Later in N. Chelmsford, Mass., Jan., 1866, In July, 1861, married Jane E. Nornborun. One child:— Elizabeth J., 11.

Descendants of Dyer Burdick Draper

1. Dyer Burdick Draper, b. Mar. 3, 1790, in Massachusetts. He was an only s. Had one sister, Olive, 2, who m. Reuben Bedell, of Geneva, N. Y. She and her husband are dead. Dyer Draper m. Hannah Clemons, at Geneva, N. Y., 1818.

He was high up in Masonry; was lecturer and degree master for a number of years. During the anti-Masonic times in New York, when most of the lodges were abandoned on account of the Morgan difficulty, he was custodian of the books and records of Geneva Lodge. He was a volunteer in the War of 1812.

CHILDREN:

3. I. Jeanette. Lives in Canandaigua, N. Y. b. about 1822.

4. II. Lavinia. Lives in Canandaigua, N. Y. b. about 1827.

5. III. Adaline. d. aged eleven.

6. IV. Volney V. He removed to Phelps, N. Y., in 1846. m. May 29, 1849, Elizabeth Shirrell, of Phelps, N. Y.

He was a merchant tailor. In 1864 he moved to Marshalltown, Iowa, where he continued until 1887, when he moved to Mandan, N. D., where he is engaged in the mercantile business.

CHILDREN:

7. I. Allan David, b. Mar. 18, 1850, at Phelps, N. Y. m. Dec. 29, 1881, Bertha F. Stontenburgh, of Phelps, N. Y. Child:— I. Robert Allan, 10. b. July 29, 1883.

Mr. Draper graduated in classical department of the Iowa State University in the Class of 1876. Also graduated in the Union Theological Seminary of New York City Class of 1879. Was ordained in Red Creek, N. Y., by the Presbytery of Lynn, Sep. 24, 1879. Was pastor of the Presbyterian Church in Red Creek nearly five years; was pastor in Bergen, N. Y., four years; of the First Presbyterian Church, Batavia, N. Y., nearly four years; and is at present pastor of the Fourth Presbyterian Church, Syracuse, N. Y.

8. II. Mary Olivia, b. Sep. 9, 1851. m. E. C. Rice, attorney, and lives in Mandan, N. D.

9. III. Charles E. V., b. Oct. 18, 1855. m. Oct. 1, 1878, Hattie A. Loundsberry, of Bismarck, N. D. Child: — I. Olivia Medora, 11. b. Mar. 29, 1890.

Charles Draper is an electrician by profession, and also interested in the furniture business at Mandan, N. D. He graduated at the Iowa State University Law School, and was admitted to the bar in 1881.

Utah Drapers

These Drapers are presumed to have descended from, 1. Thomas Draper and Lydia Rogers, who had a s. 2. William, who married Lydia Lothrop. She was born in Pennsylvania. They had a son 3. William, born Apr. 24, 1807, in Medland Co., Canada; died Spring of 1886. The family claim a Puritan ancestry. William Draper (3) became a convert to the Church of Latter Day Saints, and was a thorough and consistent believer in its tenets and practises.

3. William. (2. William, 1. Thomas.) s. of William Draper (2) and Lydia Lothrop. m. 1st: Elizabeth Staker. b. Canada, d. 1886. He m. 2dly: Martha W. b. in Pa. He m. 3dly: Mary Ann Manhard. b. Johnstown, Canada, Aug. 15, 1827. He m. 4thly: Nephi. b. Utah, 1849. He m. 5thly: Mary H. He m. 6thly: Fanny Newton, Dec, 1857. She was b. Mar. 1, 1834, at Hunslett, Yorkshire, Eng. He m. 7thly: Ruth Hannah Newton, Apr., 1854. She was b. Hunslett, Yorkshire, Eng., 1839.

CHILDREN, BY 1st WIFE:

4. I. Henry, b. Canada, Feb. 16, 1826.
5. II. Julianna, b. Canada, July 1, 1828.
6. III. Roxana, b. Sep. 30, 1830.
7. IV. Moses, b. Canada, July 9, 1832.
8. V. Harriet, b. Ohio, Dec. 1, 1834.
9. VI. Miles, b. Ohio, Feb. 2, 1837.
10. VII. William L., b. Ohio, Mar. 5, 1838.
11. VIII. Albert E., b. Illinois, Dec. 13, 1840.
12. IX. Parley P., b. Illinois, Mar. 30, 1843.
13. X. Isaac G., b. Illinois, Oct. 6, 1845.
14. XI. Amanda M., b. Iowa, July 3, 1848.

CHILD, BY 2D WIFE:

15. XII. Almon B., b. Kansville, Iowa, 1847.

CHILDREN, BY 3D WIFE:

16. XIII. Mary Ann, b. Iowa, Feb. 21, 1849.
17. XIV. Corroline, b. Utah, Oct. 2, 1850.
18. XV. David P., b. Utah, May 6, 1852.
19. XVI. Eliza Jane, b. Utah, Feb. 13, 1854.
20. XVII. Brigham M., b. Utah, Oct. 11, 1855.

21. XVIII. Artimossy, b. Utah, Aug. 20, 1857.
22. XIX. Franklin, b. Utah, Apr. 19, 1859.
23. XX. Malony, b. Utah, Dec. 13, 1860.
24. XXI. Olzena, b. Utah, Feb. 2, 1862.
25. XXII. Oren, b. Utah, May 26, 1864.
26. XXIII. Sarah Melissa, b. Utah, Oct. 21, 1867.
27. XXIV. Amy, b. Utah, Oct. 7, 1869.
28. XXV. Ordense, b. Utah, Aug. 9, 1871.

CHILDREN, BY 5TH WIFE (NO ISSUE BY 4TH):

29. XXVI. George H., b. Utah, Jan. 4, 1855.
30. XXVII. Luna A., b. Utah, Apr. 8, 1857.
31. XXVIII. James, b. Utah, Mar. 19, 1859.
32. XXIX. Irene, b. Utah, Mar. 8, 1861.
33. XXX. John, b. Utah, July 9, 1863.
34. XXXI. Orille, b. Utah, Apr. 8, 1865.
35. XXXII. Alfred, b. Utah, Feb. 6, 1869.
36. XXXIII. Thomas C, b. Utah, Sep. 2, 1871.

CHILDREN, BY 6TH WIFE:

37. XXXIV. Emeline, b. Utah, Jan. 8, 1855.
38. XXXV. Riley N., b. Utah, May 7, 1857.
39. XXXVI. Martha J., b. Utah, Feb. 6, 1859.
40. XXXVII. Louis, b. Utah, May 8, 1862.
41. XXXVIII. Althero, b. Utah, July 29, 1864.
42. XXXIX. Marvin C, b. Utah, Feb. 5, 1867.
43. XL. Fanny L., b. Utah, July 14, 1869.

CHILDREN, BY 7TH WIFE:

44. XLI. Almira, b. Utah, Sep. 22, 1855.
45. XLII. Kembaflf, b. Utah, July 21, 1857.
46. XLIII. Barnabas, b. Utah, Sep. 4. 1859
47. XLIV. Joseph O., b. Utah, Mar. 19, 1861.
48. XLV. Amos, b. Utah, Mar. 4, 1863.
49. XLVI. Tranquilla, b. Utah, May 16, 1865.
50. XLVII. Sunny Olive, b. Utah, Nov. 29, 1868.
51. XLVIII. Ruth Hannah, b. Utah, Nov. 22, 1869.
52. XLIX. Charles, b. Utah, Sep. 22, 1873.
53. L. Myram E., b. Utah, Sep. 22, 1875.

Addenda - Items Received Too Late For Insertion in the Body of the History

Department of the Interior, Bureau of Pensions.

Washington, D. C., Feb. 18, 1892.

"Simeon Draper (339) enlisted January 12, 1781, at the town of Spencer, Mass., as a private in Captain Drew's Co., Col. Wm. Shepard's Massachusetts Regt. February, 1782, appointed Corporal in Capt. Clapp's Co., Col. Jackson's Regt. June, 1783, appointed Sergt. in the same Co. and Regt., and was honorably discharged as such at West Point in the month of November, following. No mention is made of any engagements in which he participated.

"He applied for pension from Brookfield, Mass., Aug. 14, 1832, aged 61 years. Both he and his widow, Catherine C, were pensioners. The soldier states in his application, that he resided in Spencer, Mass., until 1795, when he removed to Brookfield. He died Dec. 28, 1848."

(Signed,) GREEN B. RAUM.

Treasury Department, j. m. m.
Office of the Third Auditor,

Washington, D. C, April 18, 1892.

T. Waln-Morgan Draper, Esq.,
45 Broadway, New York City.

Sir: — Referring to the enclosed letter relative to the service of Simeon Draper in the War of 1812, you are informed that the name of Simeon Draper is borne as a private on the rolls of Capt. B. Straight's Company, of Lt.-Col. E. Filield's Regiment, Vt. Mil., from Oct. 25 to Nov. 30, 1812.

The name of Benjamin Bemis is borne as a private upon the rolls of Captain John B. Walback's Company, of Col. Burbeck's 1st Regt., U. S. Art'y, from enlistment, Mar. 16, 1808, to Dec. 31, 1815.

This soldier resided at Westminster, Mass., and enlisted Mar. 16, 1808, for five years, and was discharged Mar. 16, 1813, by reason of expiration of term of service, and re-enlisted Mar. 16, 1813, for five years, and appears upon the rolls of the Company, commanded by the above named Captain, to Dec. 31, 1815, and was stationed at Ft. Constitution, Portsmouth Harbor, N. H.

The subsequent rolls of the Company are supposed to be on file in the office of the Adjutant General of the Army.

The above named Benjamin Bemis is the only soldier by that name appearing in the records of payments made by paymasters who paid the troops which participated in the War of 1812.

Respectfully yours,

W. H. HART, *Auditor.*

Nathanial Draper. Served 36 months, from Concord. Col. commanding Co., 6th Regt.

William Draper. 13th Regiment. Served 4 months, 13 days, from Bridgewater. Dead. Capt. Allen's Co.

Richard Draper. 15th Regiment. Served 4 months, 29 days. Enlisted for 3 years. Dead. From Worcester. Capt. Pierce's Co.

Capt. Ebenezer Mason's Co. of Spencer, Col, Jonathan Warner's Regiment, 19th of April, 1775.

Drummer James Draper (141). Served 14 days. Private John Draper (140). Served 14 days. Private Joshua Draper, Jr. (334). Served 14 days. They marched 116 miles.

Abijah Draper (137) from Suffolk Co. Major 1st Regt. (Senior Major). Entered Army as 2d Major, 1st Regt., Feb. 14, 1776.

Stephen Draper, 2d Lieut., 5th Regt. of Worcester, 11th Company. Henry Clark, Capt. Danl. Falkner, 1st Lieut.

Transferred to 14th Company, 11th Regt. Isaac Stacey, Capt. Danl. Falkner, 1st Lieut.

Paul Draper, 1st Lieut., 5th Company, 1st Suffolk Militia. Thomas Mayo, Jr., Capt. Noah Davis, 2d Lieut.

John Draper, Private. Time engaged, Apr. 1, 1778. Bounty, 2. per month. Service, 3 months, 2 days. Discharged July 2, 1778. Total Bounty, 628.

Muster Roll, 1st Company of Militia, Dedham. Capt. Joseph Lewis. Col. Wm. McIntyh.

Marched into camp, Dorchester, Mass., Mar. 4, 1776. William Draper, Private.

Marched 11 miles. Two-pence per mile. 4 days' service. Pay Roll of Capt. Nathan Thayer's Company, in Col. Ebenezer Thayer's Regiment of new levies from the County of Suffolk, Mass., mustered July 14. 1780. Daniel

Draper, Private, Served 3 months, 6 days. In Pay Roll of a Company of Militia that marched from Watertown, by order of Gen. Washington, to reinforce the army in taking possession of Dorchester Heights,

Mar. 17, 1776, Private John Draper. Signed by Capt. Phineas Starns. In Pay Roll of Capt. Joshua Woodbridge's Company, Col. Nathan Tyler's Regiment of new levies from Massachusetts for service in Rhode Island, for the months of June, July, August, September, October and November, 1779. Samuel Draper,

Private, enlisted July 25. Served 5 months, 6 days.

Harriet G., dau. of Nathanial Draper. Plymouth, N. H., and widow of Mr. Hadley. m. Rufus Kendrick, a merchant in Nashua, afterwards in Boston and Manchester whose 1st wife was a dau. of the Hon. Thomas and Susannah Chandler (From Chandler Family History.) Sarah Draper, m. Thomas Christie, May 10, 1792Both of Boston. {Genealogies and Estates of Charlestown, Mass)

Elizabeth Draper, bap. July 22, 1693.

Lydia Draper, dau. of Nathanial Draper and Elizabeth Draper, b. July 21, 1699.

John, of Stephen and Mercy Draper, b. Aug. 25, 1700.

John, of John and Joanna Draper, b. May 24, 1709.

Frederick, s. of Whiting and Delia H. Draper, b. Dedham, Aug. 20, 1856.

Mary Ann, of Edmond and Margaret Draper, b. July 30, 1857.

____ Draper, b. 93 Brighton St., Boston, Oct. 20, 1863. s. of Jeremiah (a machinist), b. Winchen, and Mary, b. N. H.

James Draper, b. Aug. 25, 1869, Wilberforce Place, Boston, s. of John (a laborer), b. Richmond, Va., and Mary, b. Va.

Annie Raymond Draper, b. Feb. 23, 1878, at Chelsea, Boston, dau. of Charles H., b. Dedham, and Annie, b. Nova Scotia.

Florence Abbie Draper, b. Mar. 15, 1880, at 108 E. Canton St., Boston, dau. of George E., b. Cambridge, and Georgiana H., b. Boston.

George Henry Smith Draper, b. Oct. 23, 1881, at 165 Shawmut Ave., Boston, s. of George E., b. Cambridge, and Georgiana H,, b. Boston.

___ Draper, b. Aug. 11, 1883, at 24 McLean St., Boston, s. of George, and Mary, b. Manchester, N. H.

Intentions of Marriage — Boston Records.

Hannah Draper and Jonathan Eaton, Dec. 29, 1802.

Rachel Draper, of Boston, and Wm. Preeson, of Gt. Britain, Jan. 14, 171 1.

Nathan Draper and Theodora Pomroy, Aug. 21, 1733. Both of Boston.

John Draper and Elizabeth Avery, Oct. 27, 1737. Both of Boston.

William Draper, of Roxbury, and Elizabeth Whiting, of Boston, Dec. 30, 1757. (m. at Trinity Church, Jan. 28, 1758.)

Mrs. Elizabeth Draper, of Boston, and Wm. Wetter, of Preston, Conn., Aug. 6, 1767.

Sarah Draper and Joseph Sweetser, Aug. 28, 1767. Both of Boston.

Anthony Draper and Dorothy Hartshorne, May 29, 1781. Both of Boston.

William Draper and Hannah Harris, Oct. 8, 1791. Both of Boston, (m. in Kings Chapel.)

Elijah H. Draper and Eliza Winchester, July 5, 1828.

Mary Draper and Cornelius Harrington, Aug. 27, 1839.

Lucella Draper and John R. Haslem, Dec. 2, 1844.

Ezra J. Draper and Frances E. Butler, Nov. 10, 1847.

Julia A. Draper and Stephen W. Corey, Sep. 14, 1848.

Boston Church Records.

Marie Louise Draper and George Blakely Davis, m. Aug, 28, 1851, at New Jerusalem Church. Settled in Boston.

Dr. Edgar L. Draper, Probationer of First Christian Church, Feb. 2, 1869. Lived in Marble Place, Boston.

Elijah H. Draper and Eliza Winchester, m. Dec. 31, 1828, in 1st Universalist Church.

Amelia Frances Draper, dau. of Alonzo and Sarah E., b. July 29, 1832. (1st Church, Dorchester.)

Lavinia C. Draper, removed with certificate, July 17, 1853, from Broomfield St. Church.

Richard Draper, dismissed, acct. of death, from Old South Church, July 30, 1686.

Hannah R. Draper, confirmed at St. Matthew's Church, S. Boston, Mar. 16, 1864, by Bishop Manton Eastburn. Removed away Mar. 16, 1864.

Clara A. Draper, confirmed at St. Matthew's P. E. Church, S. Boston, Jan. 20, 1878, by Bishop B. H. Paddock.

Sarah Draper, m. Nathl. Whiting, Jr., at Trinity Church, Boston, Sep. 23, 1767. Both of Roxbury.

Elizabeth Draper, m. Benaiah Whiting, Apr. 29, 1776, at Trinity Church, Boston.

Joanna Draper, bap. Sep. 1, 1700. (A currier's dau.)

Brattle St. Church

Elizabeth Draper, of Boston, and William Wetter, of Preston, Conn., m. Sep. 9, 1767.

South Congregational Church

Laura Elvira Draper, buried Aug. 3, 1854. Residence, Pleasant Street.

Purchase St. Church

Daniel Draper, 20 years, buried May 2, 1849.

New North Church

Sarah L. (Mrs.) Draper, buried Aug. 20, 1822, aged 67.

West Church

Margaret Draper, dau. of Richard Collier, about 6 or 7 years old, bap. Under the care of Richard Draper.

First Church

John Draper, admitted July 16, 1693. Rachel Draper, admitted Mar. 28, 1697. Samuel Draper, admitted Jan. 30, 1763.

ROXBURY RECORDS in City Register's Office, Boston

Mary Draper, of Benjamin and Mary, b. July 19, 1739.

Mary Draper, dau. of Aaron and Mary, b. Jan. 21, 1761.

Roxbury Marriages

William Draper and Rachel Aldis, May 2, 1716.

William Draper and Kezia Whiting, Sep. 24, 1767.

John Draper and Elizabeth Lyon, Feb. 29, 1768.

Aaron Draper and Martha G. Prescott, Nov. 27, 1850.

Olive Draper Gay and Joel Scavenus, Jan. 20, 1811.

Kesia Draper and Oliver Vose, Feb. 5, 1778, by Rev. Thomas Abbott.

Joseph Draper, of Dedham, and Abigail Richardson, of Sherborne, May 12, 1760, by Rev. Saml. Lock, at Sherborne.

Free Love Draper and John Swain, Jan. 16, 1757.

Mary Draper and Wm. Foster, June 11, 1778, by Rev. Thomas Abbott.

Nathan Draper and Anna Jones, July 3, 1780.

Mrs. Sarah Draper and Simon Pratt, Feb. 5, 1795.

Mary Draper and Samuel Burridge, Oct. 31, 1754.

Abigail Draper and Jeremiah Dean, Jr., Dec. 17, 1762. s. of Jeremiah Dean and Mrs. Mary Fisher, b, Oct. 24, 1743. By Rev. Thomas Balch.

Mary Draper and Joshua Weld, Dec. 14, 1756.

Mary Draper and Joseph Tyler, Sep. 26, 1756.

Elizabeth Draper and Jacob Robinson, Jan. 21, 1764, by Rev. Mr. Walter.

William Draper and Lydia Smith, Dec. 19, 1785.

Miriam Draper and Nathanial Lewis, Jan. 16, 1729. He d. before his wife. She d. Nov. 15. 1757.

Nathanial Draper and Experience Hartshorne, Jan. 29, 1754. (Both of Dedham.)

Miriam Draper (b. Jan. 26, 1744,) and Joseph Ellis, Apr. 24, 1766. (Both of Dedham.)

Mrs. Anna Draper and Hezekiah Fuller (both of Dedham), by Rev. Jason Haven, Dec. 28, 1760. (He d. Feb. 3, 1776.) Children: — Anna, b. Oct. 11, 1761. m. Joseph Onion, Apr. 15, 1779. Catherine, b. July 12, 1764. m. Rev. Thomas Thacher, Nov. 26, 1783. (Both of Dedham.)

Hannah Draper, of Dedham, and Samuel Burridge, of Newton, Dec. 14, 1780, by John Woodward, J. P.

James Draper, of Southboro, and Lucy D. Doud, of Dedham, May 9, 1822, by Jabez Chickering, J. P.

Deaths.

Charles H. Draper, May 30, 1847, 1½.

Wm. E. Draper, Oct. 4, 1848, aged 2 mo. 7 days.

Mary Draper, dau. of Aaron and Mary, Jan. 25, 1761. Bap.

Mary Draper, dau. of Benjamin and Mary, July 10, 1739. Bap.

Anna Draper, dau. of Ebenezer and Sarah, June 18, 1766. Bap.

Betsy and Sally Draper, daus. of David Draper, Apr. 24, 1814. Bap.

George Briggs Draper, s. of Wm. and Catherine, b. Dec. 27, 1820.

Nathanial Draper, b. Sep. 18, 1732.

Miriam Draper, b. Mar. 7, 1730.

Rebecca Draper, b. Oct. 16, 1734.

EXTRACTS from Providence, R. I., Register.

Frank Smith, s. of Alpha and Lydia H. Draper. A farmer of Lincoln, R. L, 25 years of age. b. in N. Providence, m. July 6, 1873, Lois Jenks, dau. of Crawford J. and Esther B. Manton. She was b. Smithfield, 1855.

James Pickering, aged 44. b. New York, s. of Isaac and Eliza P. Draper, m. Oct. 12, 1871, Marion Dennis Palmer, of New York, aged 27. b. Roxbury,

Mass., and dau. of William and Elizabeth V. Phipps. This is the 2d marriage of both.

Hiram Draper, 25 years old. b. in Shutsburg, Mass. s. of Stephen and Sarah Draper, m. June 16, 1867, Annie M., dau. of William and Mary Corkoran, of Ireland. He d. Jan. 5, 1879. She d. Dec. 4, 1887, aged 39.

Mary E., b. Aug. 6, 1872. d. Feb. 2, 1874.

Agnes A., b. Jan. 16, 1876. d. Oct. 27, 1877.

Marriages

Albert H. Draper and Nancy E. Read, Mar. 20, 1837.

David W. Draper and Bethuna Acorn, Oct. 9, 1849.

Hannah Draper and Benjamin Jeyscar, Nov. 5, 1815.

Mary Draper and Pliny Pray, Apr. 10, 1850.

William Draper and Alice B. Brown, July 25, 1814.

Edward George Draper and Charlotte Selina. dau. of the late Rev. Robert French, of New Brunswick, m. by Rev. R. S. MacArthur, D.D., assisted by Rev. F. R. Morse, D.D., at Calvary Baptist Church, New York, Tuesday, Nov. 3, 1891. Mr. Draper was late of the 8th Hussars.

Births

Pearl E., dau. of James H. and Georgiana A. Draper, Nov. 27, 1887.

A son, Mar. 4, 1886.

A daughter, of Edwin and Amelia Draper, Feb. 11, 1871. John N., s. of William and Hannah H. Draper, July 9, 1858. Joseph Draper, Sep. 14, 1873.

621½. Lewis Charles Chandler, b. Germantown, Pa., Dec. 28, 1891. s. of Frank Draper Lewis (615) and Mary H. Chandler.

Deaths

James, s. of James Draper, Aug. 23, 1854, aged 14 months.

Marvin R., s. of James N. Draper, Apr. 22, 1851, aged 5 years.

Jonathan G., s. of Aaron and Mildred Draper, Dec. 27, 1887, aged 87 years.
1969. Dr. Joseph Draper, d. Brattleboro, Vt., Mar. 17, 1892.

Mrs. Anne C. (Ballard) Draper, widow of George Gardiner Draper (491), d. Montclair, N. J., Mar. 21, 1892.

Rev. Lorenzo Draper (492), d. Feb., 1892, at Claremont, N. H. His 2d wife, Matilda Fay, d. within a few hours of him.

1104. Lorenzo Draper, d. Mar., 1892, at N. Attleboro, Mass.

Notes from Mrs. E. Draper Corrie, of Gloversville, N. Y.

Mary Harper, d. Dec. 16, 1840, aged 27.

Betsy Kennedy, d. Nov. 9, 1840, aged 33.

Ara. N. Draper, d. Aug. 18, 1846, aged 37.

Simeon Draper, d. ___.

William Draper, d. Mar. 1, 1844, aged 38.

John Niles Draper, d. Jan. 3, 1853, aged 49.

www.ingramcontent.com/pod-product-compliance
Lightning Source LLC
LaVergne TN
LVHW091047080826
845145LV00002B/660